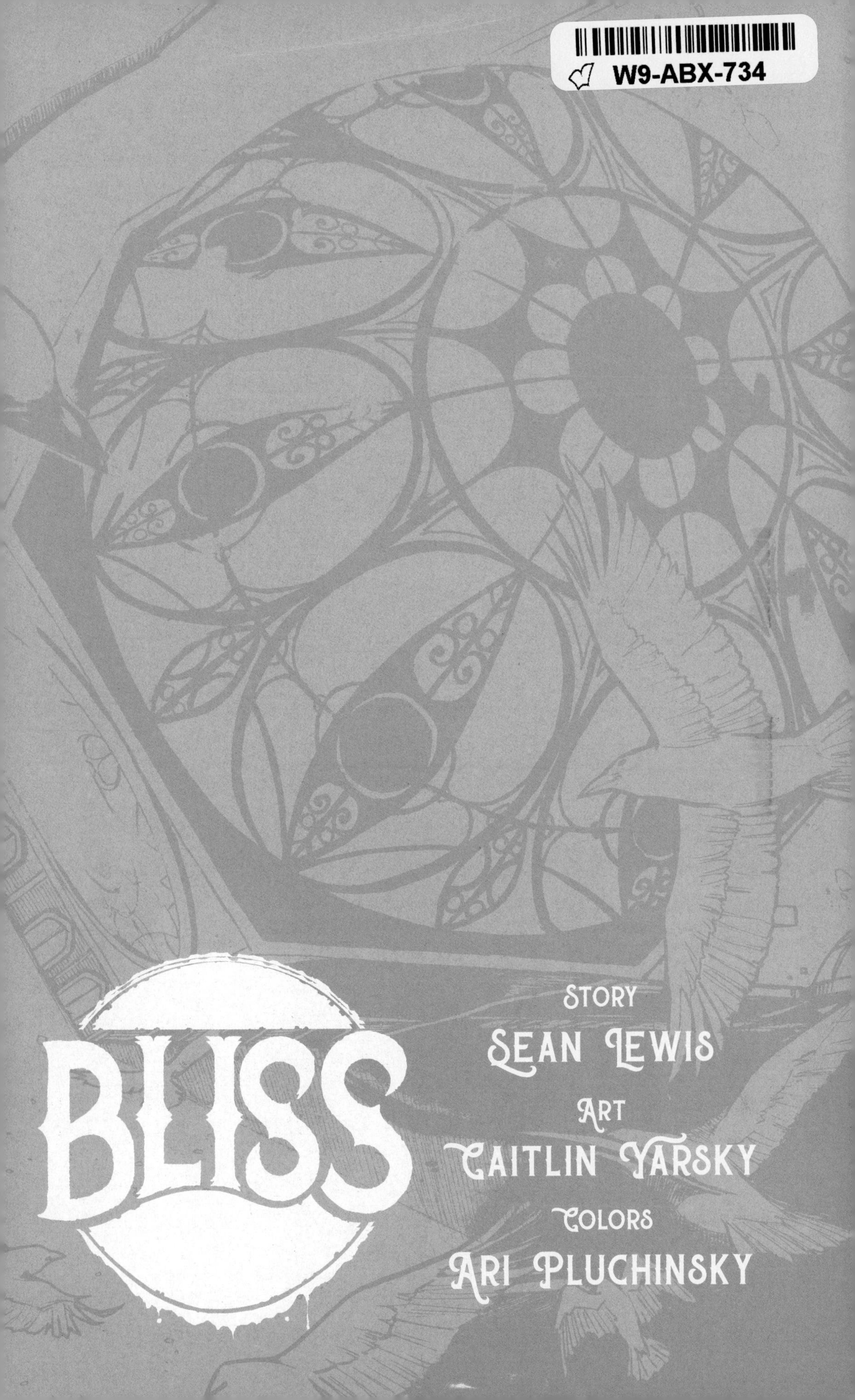

BLISS

STORY
SEAN LEWIS
ART
CAITLIN YARSKY
COLORS
ARI PLUCHINSKY

1

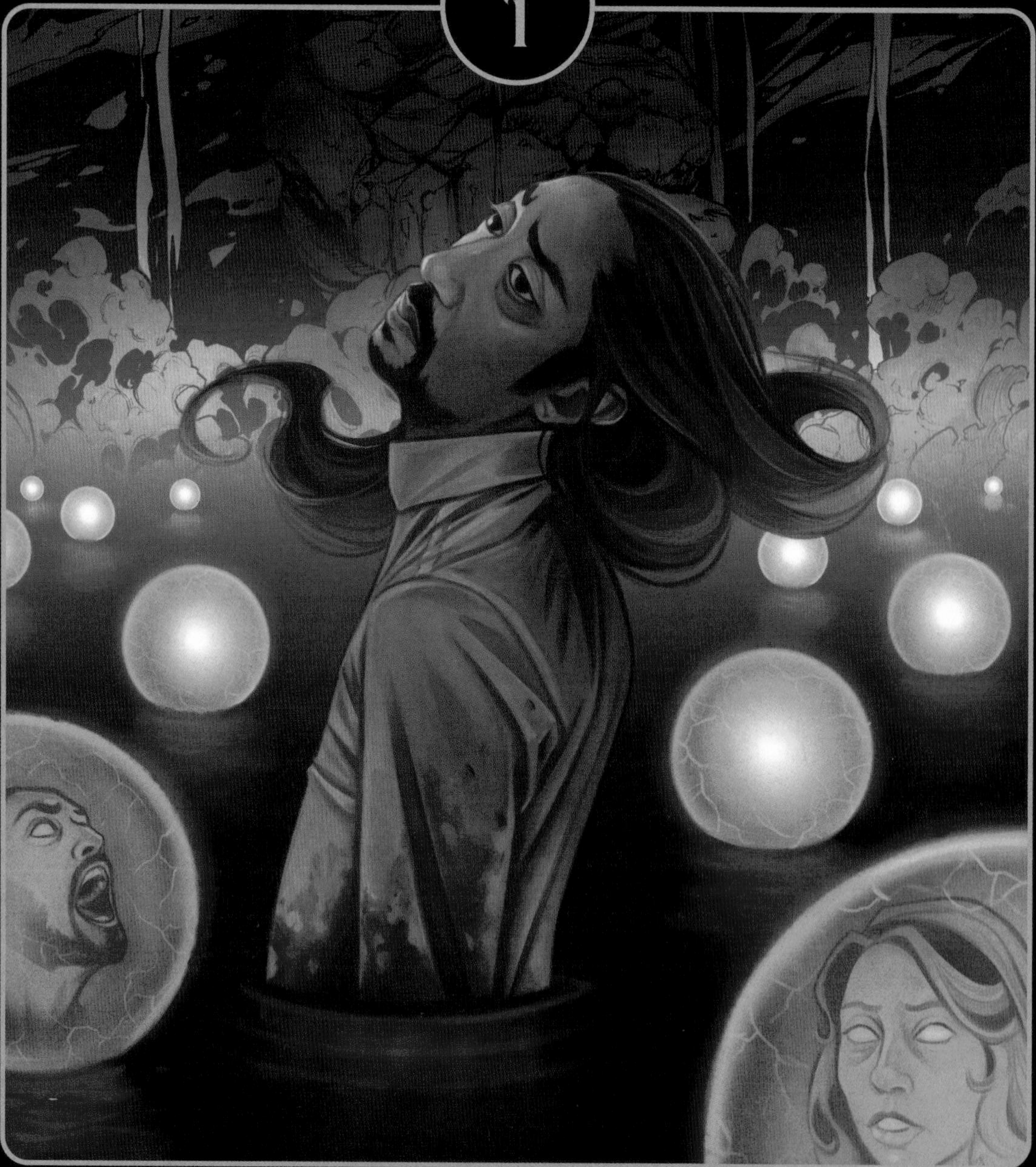

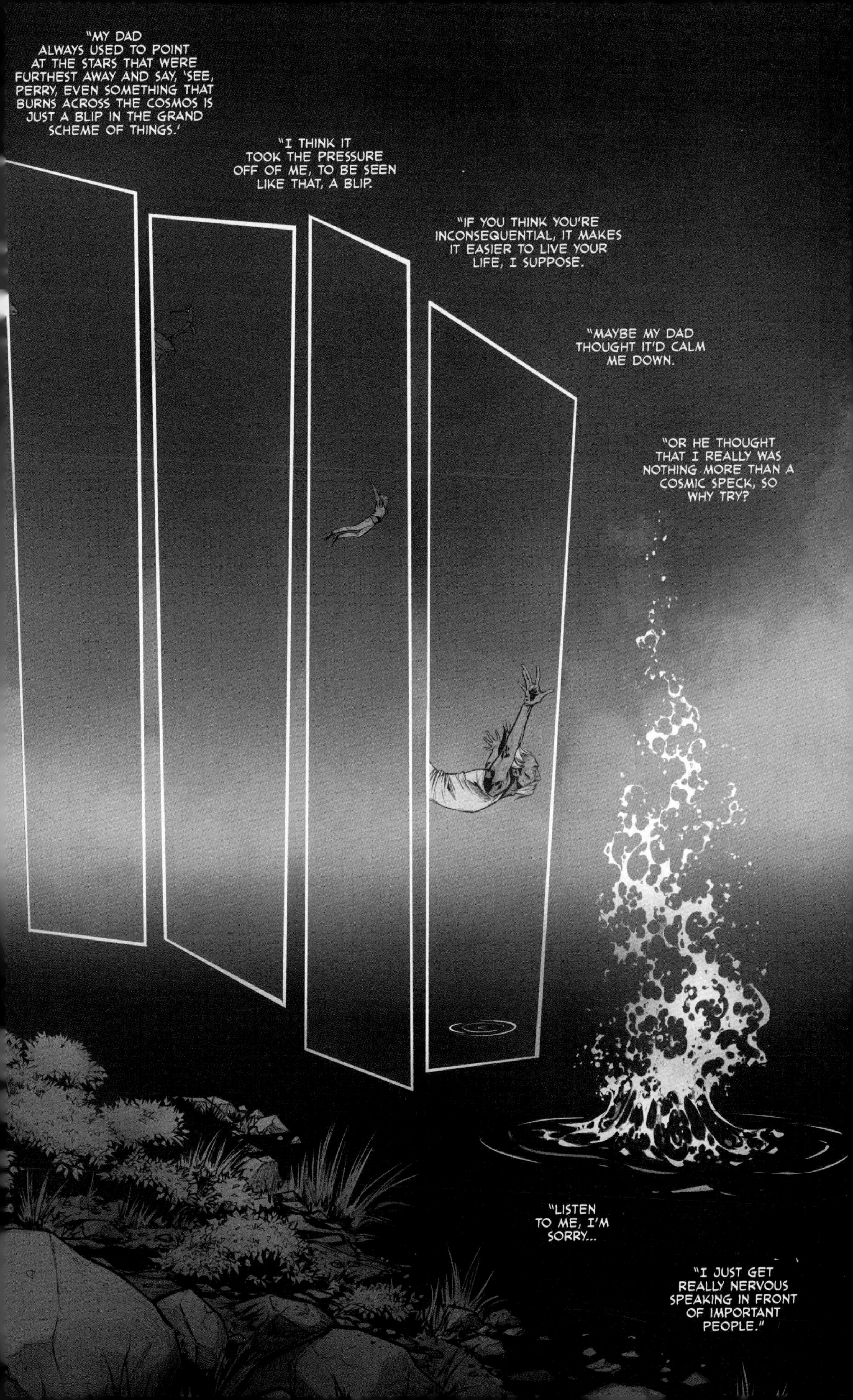
"MY DAD ALWAYS USED TO POINT AT THE STARS THAT WERE FURTHEST AWAY AND SAY, 'SEE, PERRY, EVEN SOMETHING THAT BURNS ACROSS THE COSMOS IS JUST A BLIP IN THE GRAND SCHEME OF THINGS.'
"I THINK IT TOOK THE PRESSURE OFF OF ME, TO BE SEEN LIKE THAT, A BLIP.
"IF YOU THINK YOU'RE INCONSEQUENTIAL, IT MAKES IT EASIER TO LIVE YOUR LIFE, I SUPPOSE.
"MAYBE MY DAD THOUGHT IT'D CALM ME DOWN.
"OR HE THOUGHT THAT I REALLY WAS NOTHING MORE THAN A COSMIC SPECK, SO WHY TRY?
"LISTEN TO ME, I'M SORRY...
"I JUST GET REALLY NERVOUS SPEAKING IN FRONT OF IMPORTANT PEOPLE."

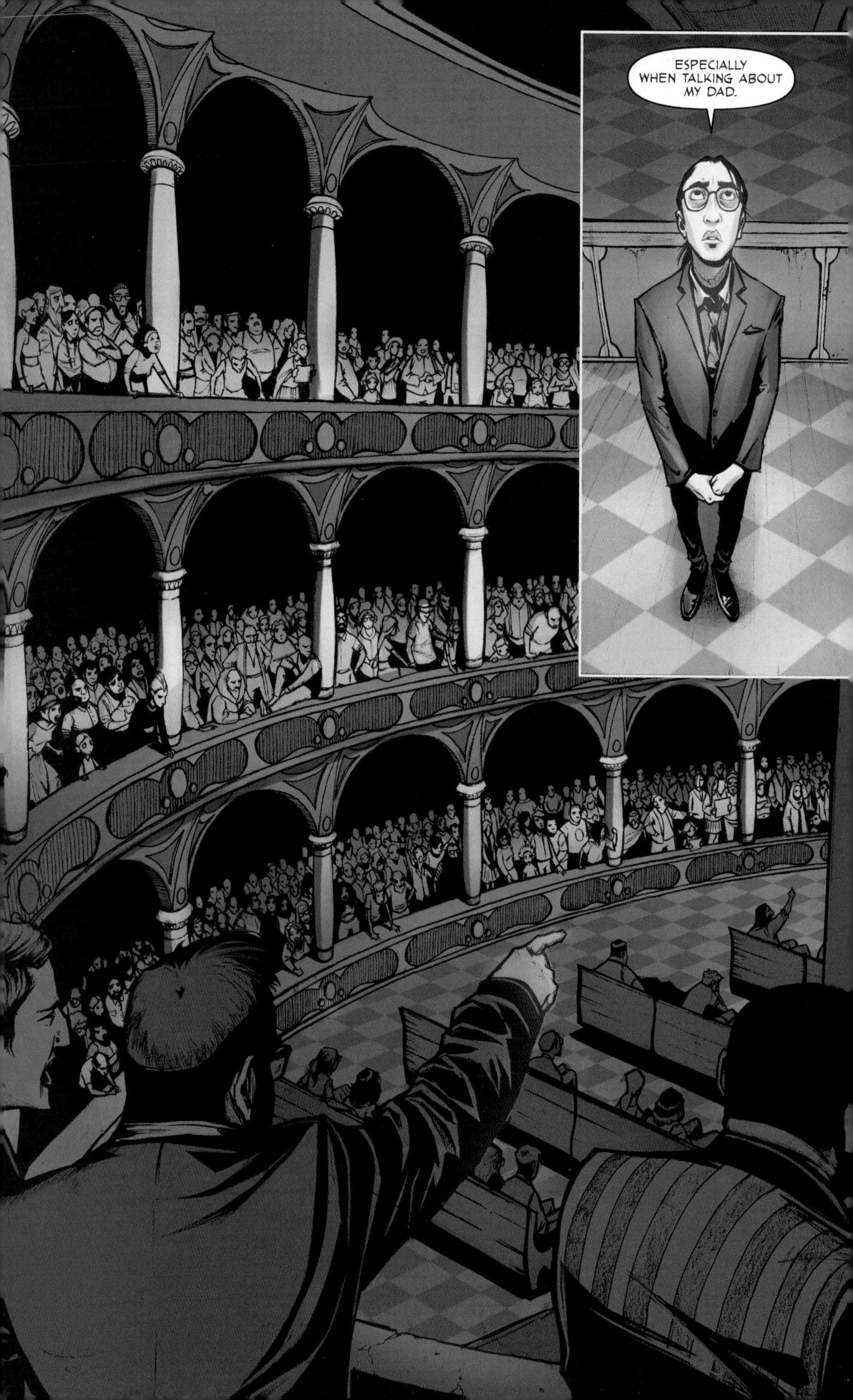
ESPECIALLY WHEN TALKING ABOUT MY DAD.

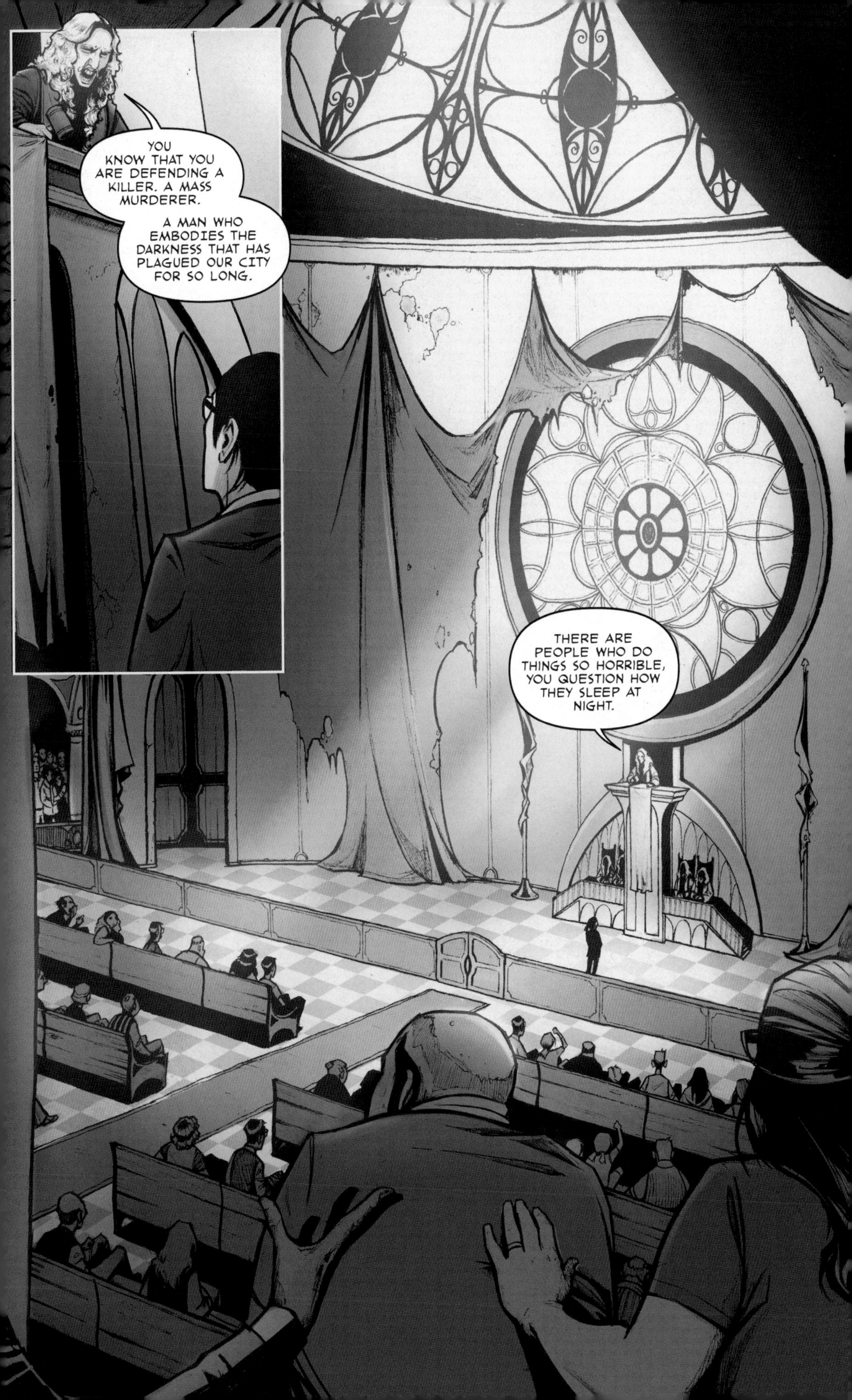
YOU KNOW THAT YOU ARE DEFENDING A KILLER. A MASS MURDERER.
A MAN WHO EMBODIES THE DARKNESS THAT HAS PLAGUED OUR CITY FOR SO LONG.
THERE ARE PEOPLE WHO DO THINGS SO HORRIBLE, YOU QUESTION HOW THEY SLEEP AT NIGHT.

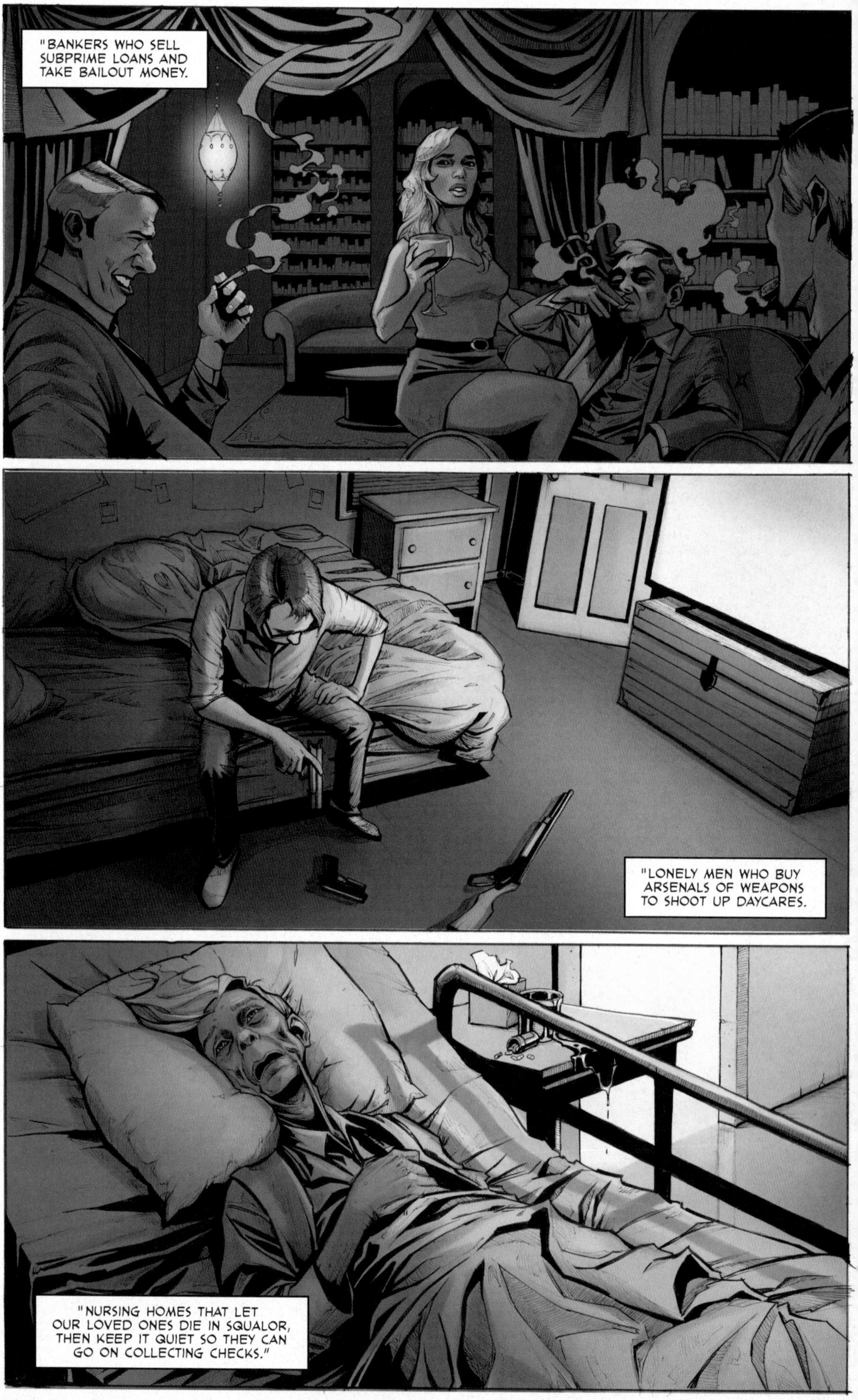
"BANKERS WHO SELL SUBPRIME LOANS AND TAKE BAILOUT MONEY.
"LONELY MEN WHO BUY ARSENALS OF WEAPONS TO SHOOT UP DAYCARES.
"NURSING HOMES THAT LET OUR LOVED ONES DIE IN SQUALOR, THEN KEEP IT QUIET SO THEY CAN GO ON COLLECTING CHECKS."

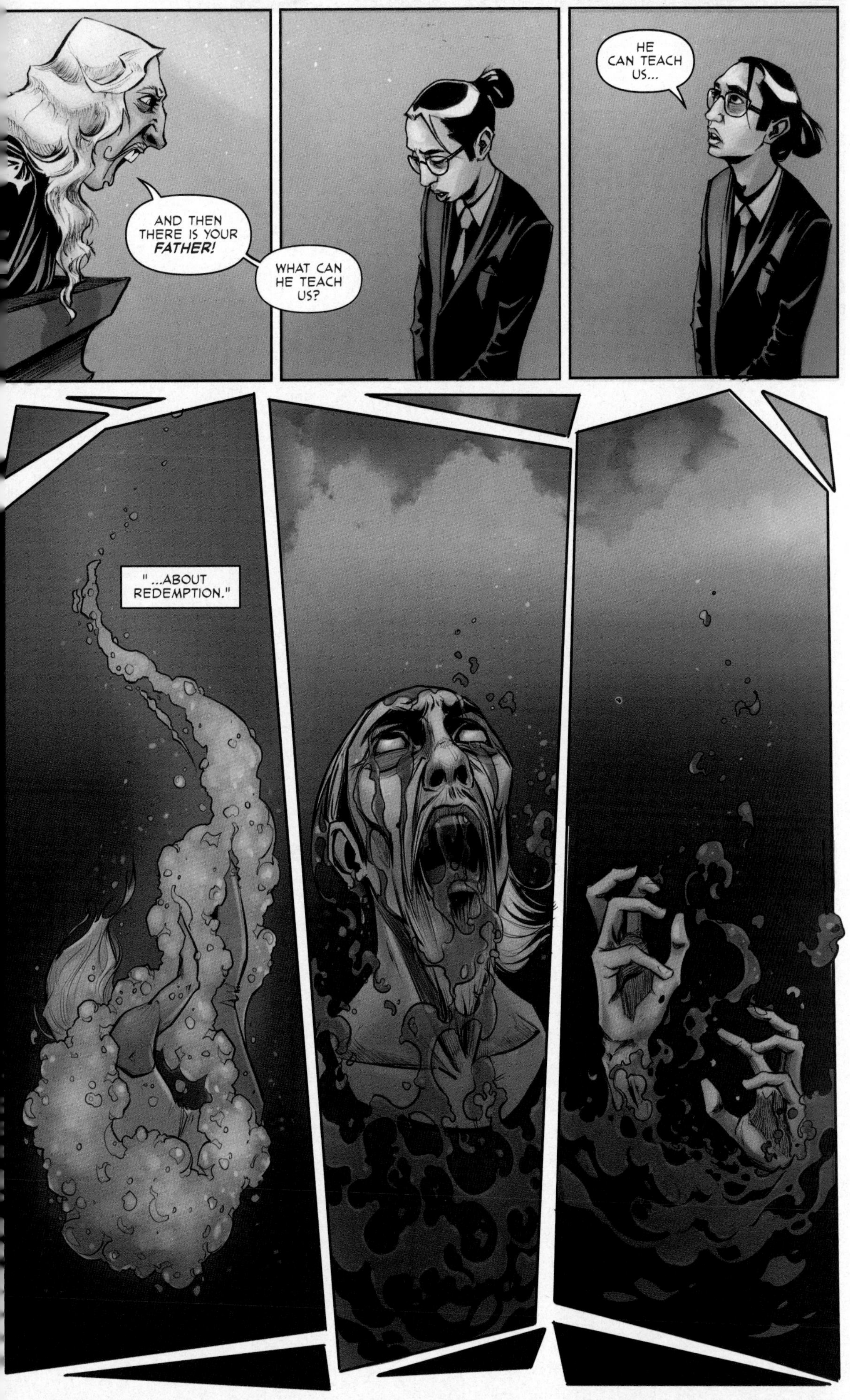
AND THEN THERE IS YOUR FATHER!
WHAT CAN HE TEACH US?
HE CAN TEACH US...
"...ABOUT REDEMPTION."

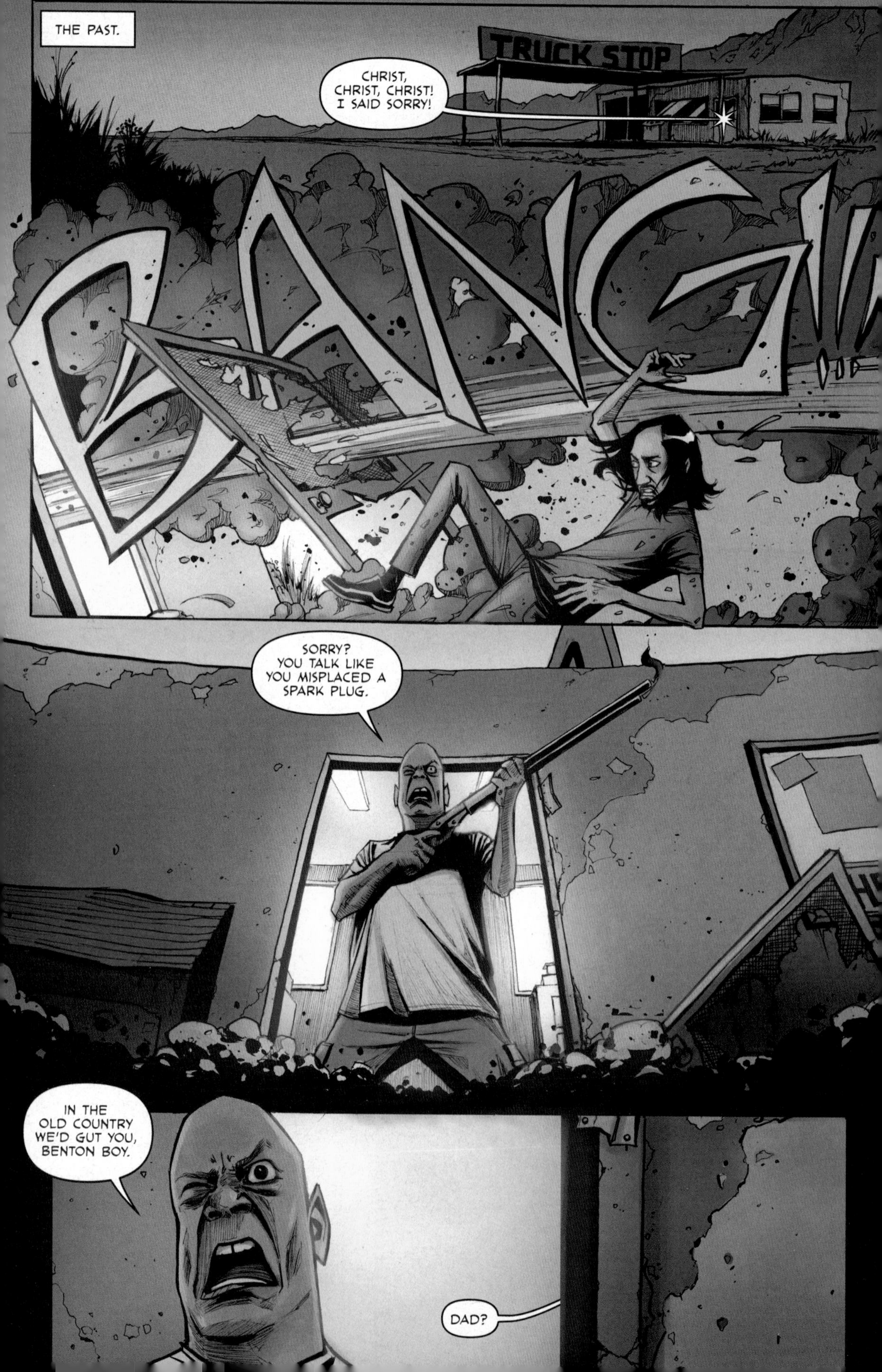
THE PAST.
TRUCK STOP
CHRIST, CHRIST, CHRIST! I SAID SORRY!
BANG!!
SORRY? YOU TALK LIKE YOU MISPLACED A SPARK PLUG.
IN THE OLD COUNTRY WE'D GUT YOU, BENTON BOY.
DAD?

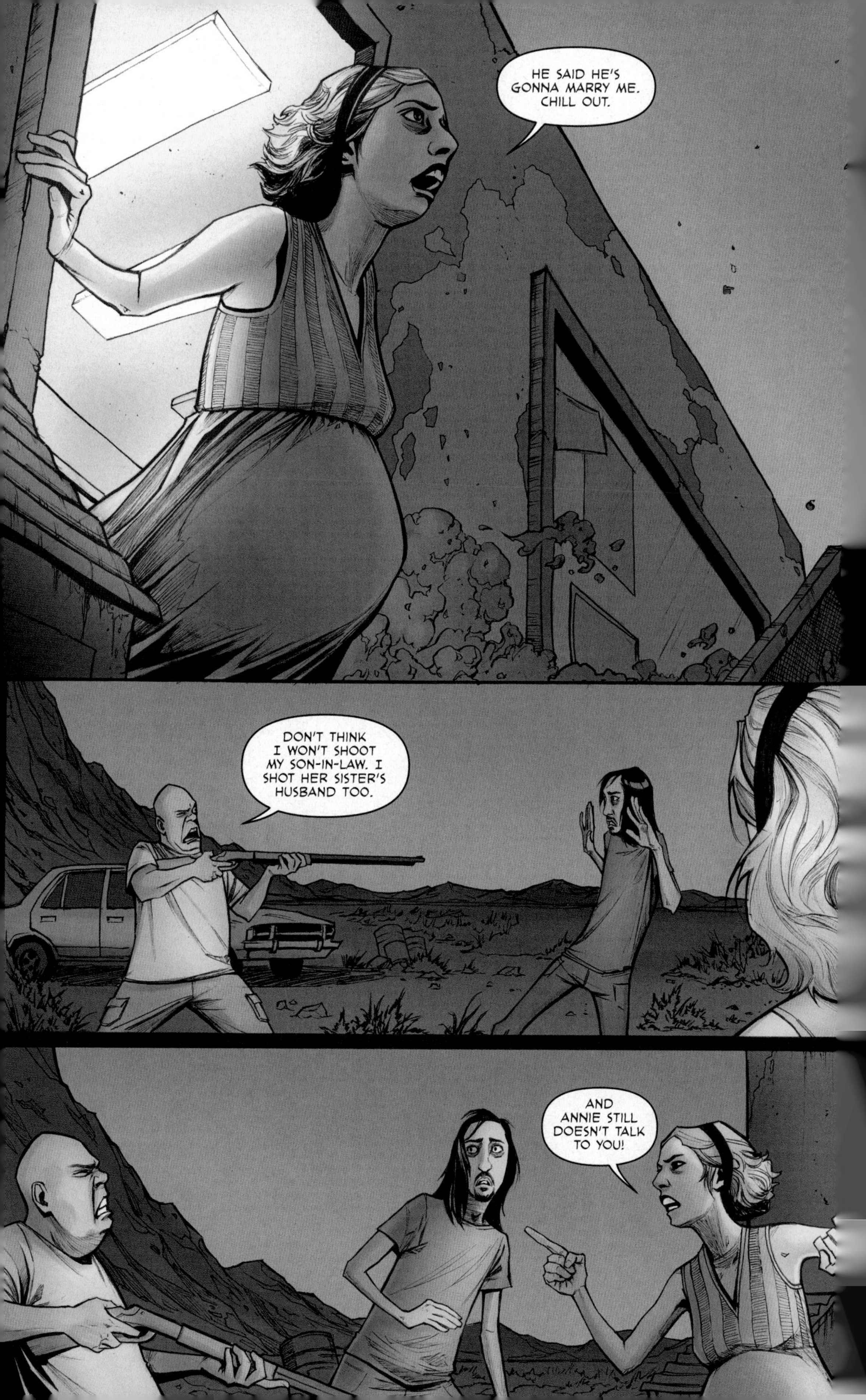
HE SAID HE'S GONNA MARRY ME. CHILL OUT.
DON'T THINK I WON'T SHOOT MY SON-IN-LAW. I SHOT HER SISTER'S HUSBAND TOO.
AND ANNIE STILL DOESN'T TALK TO YOU!

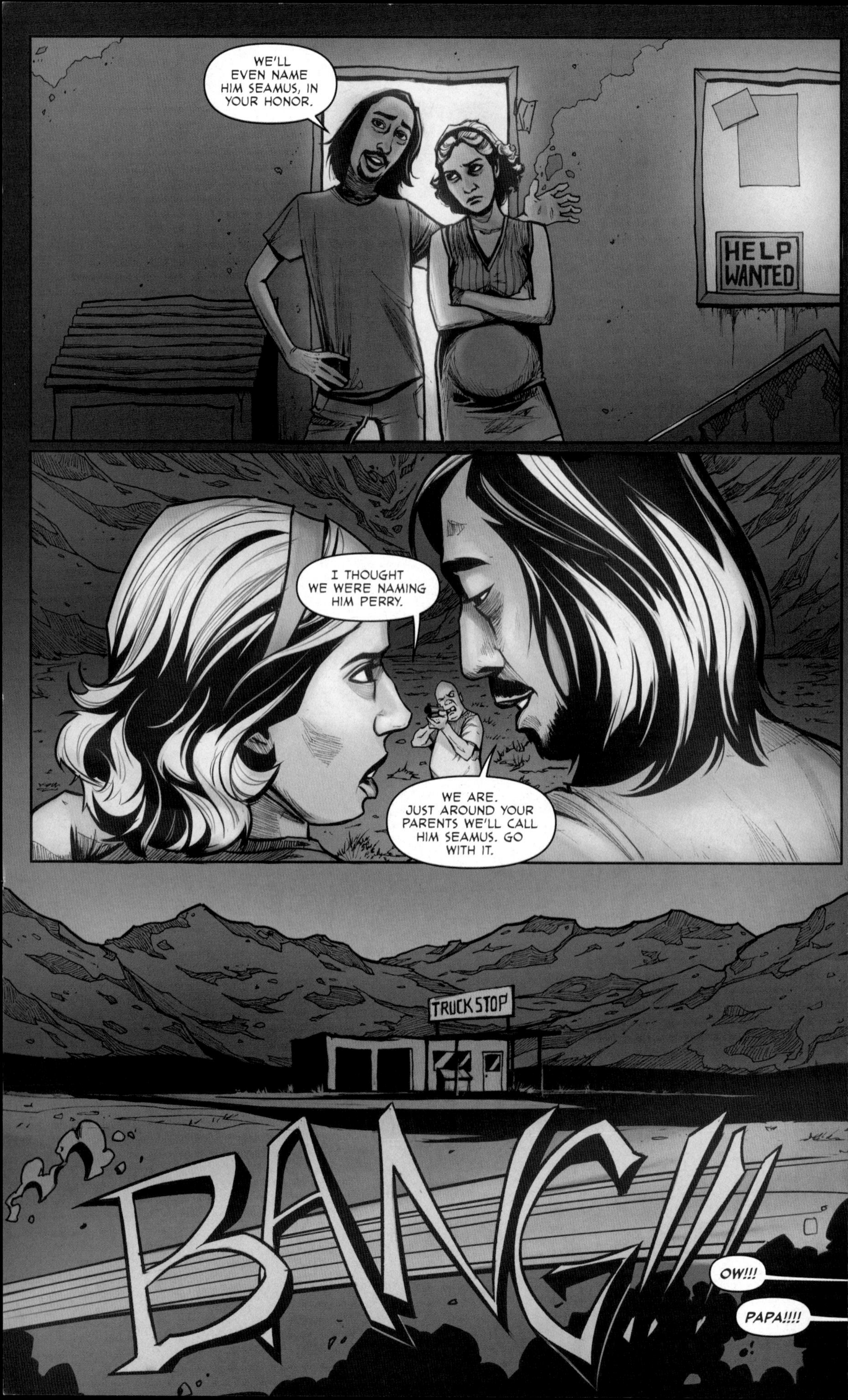
WE'LL EVEN NAME HIM SEAMUS, IN YOUR HONOR.
HELP WANTED
I THOUGHT WE WERE NAMING HIM PERRY.
WE ARE. JUST AROUND YOUR PARENTS WE'LL CALL HIM SEAMUS. GO WITH IT.
TRUCK STOP
BANG!!
OW!!!
PAPA!!!!

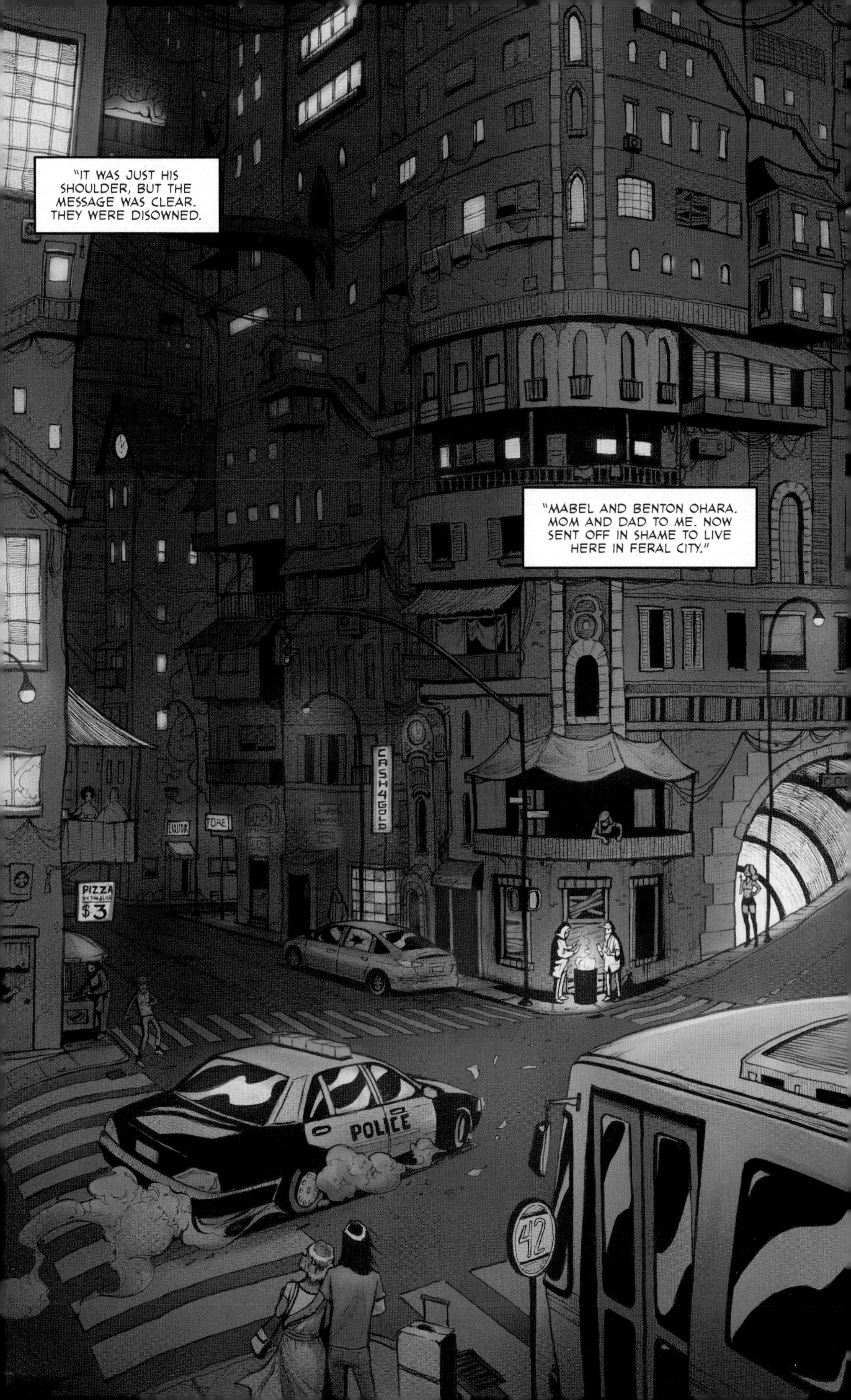
"IT WAS JUST HIS SHOULDER, BUT THE MESSAGE WAS CLEAR. THEY WERE DISOWNED.
"MABEL AND BENTON OHARA. MOM AND DAD TO ME. NOW SENT OFF IN SHAME TO LIVE HERE IN FERAL CITY."
CASH4GOLD
LIQUOR
GIRLS
PIZZA
$3
POLICE
42

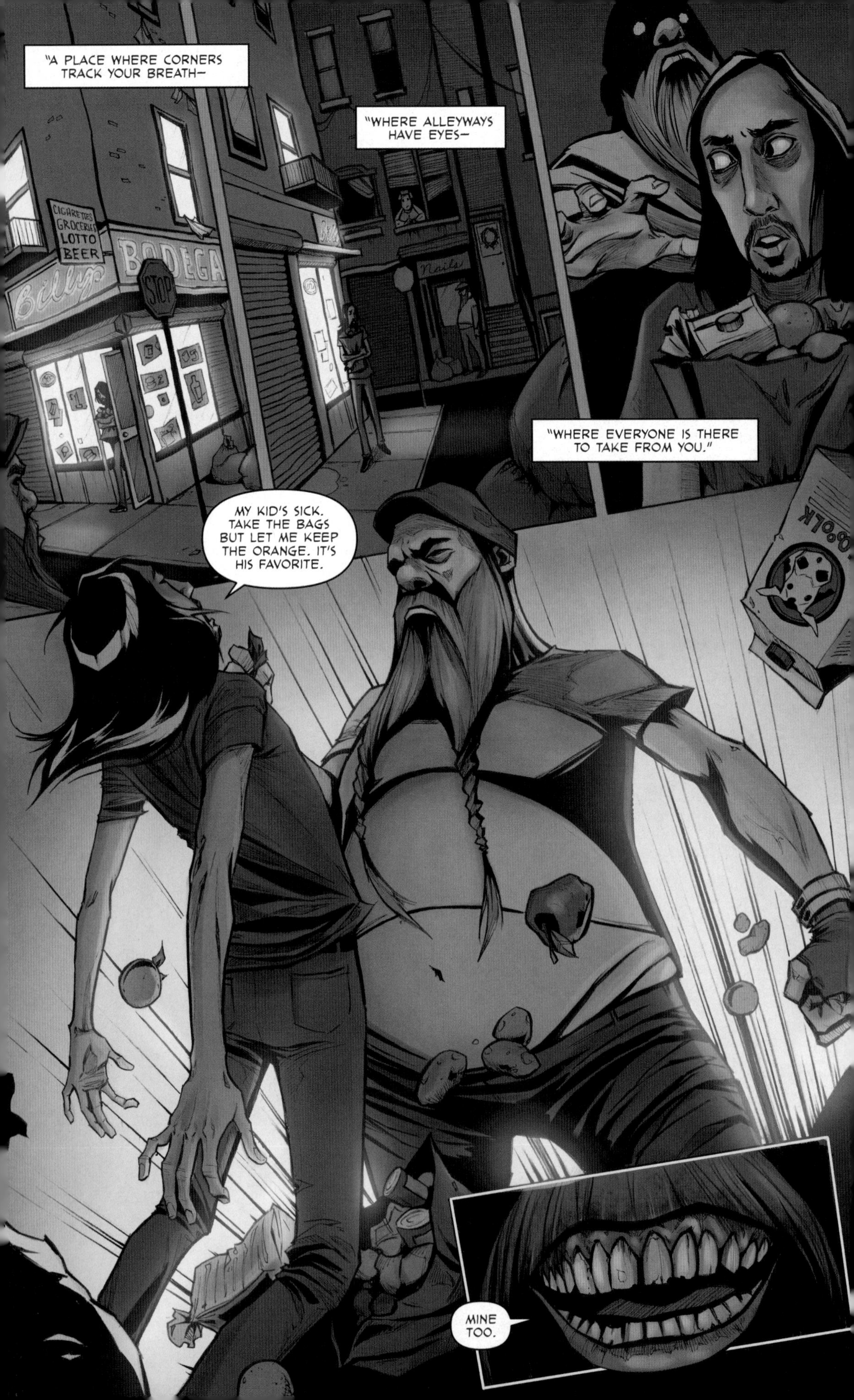
"A PLACE WHERE CORNERS TRACK YOUR BREATH—
CIGARETTES GROCERIES LOTTO BEER
BODEGA
STOP
"WHERE ALLEYWAYS HAVE EYES—
"WHERE EVERYONE IS THERE TO TAKE FROM YOU."
MY KID'S SICK. TAKE THE BAGS BUT LET ME KEEP THE ORANGE. IT'S HIS FAVORITE.
MINE TOO.

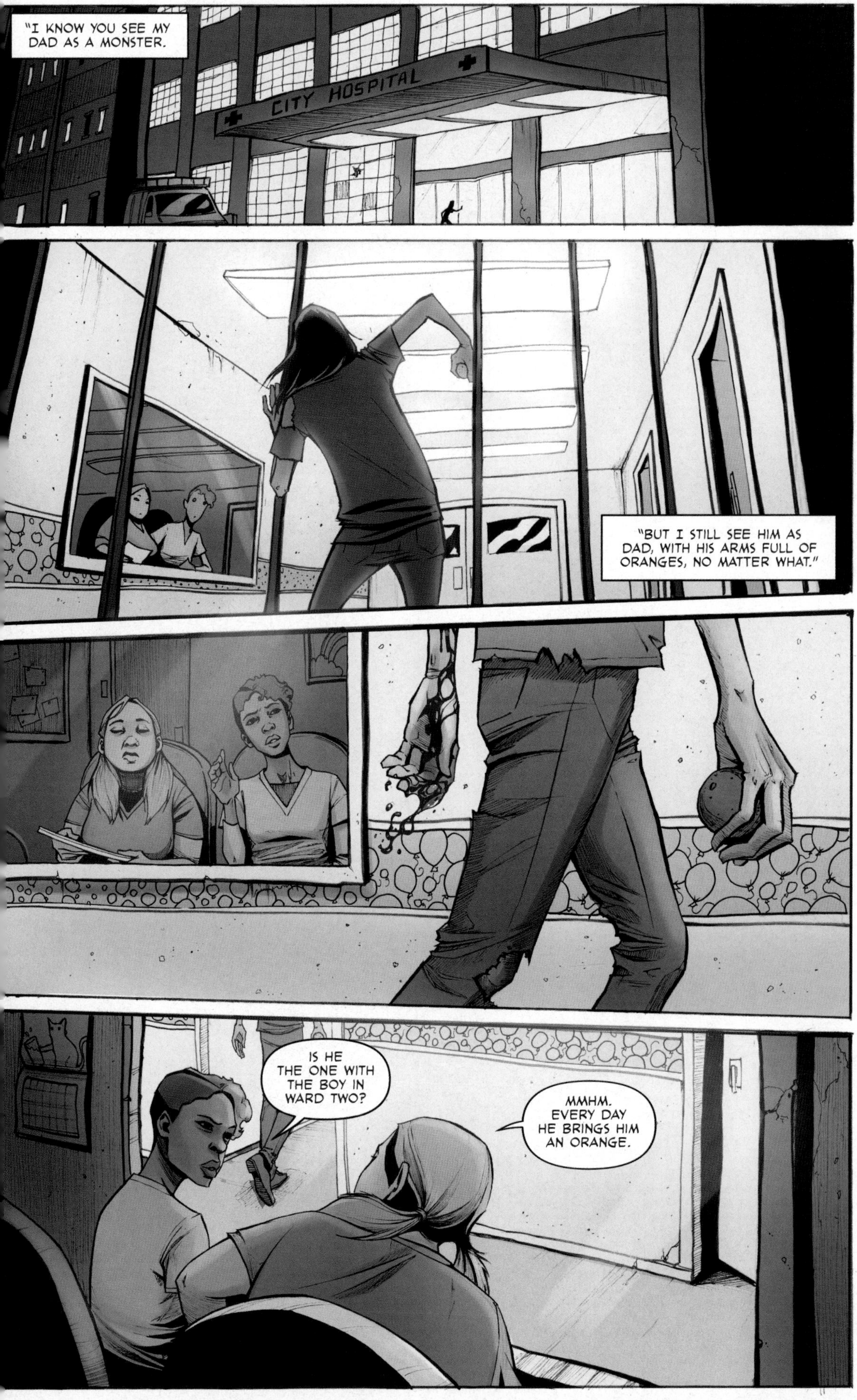
"I KNOW YOU SEE MY DAD AS A MONSTER.
CITY HOSPITAL
"BUT I STILL SEE HIM AS DAD, WITH HIS ARMS FULL OF ORANGES, NO MATTER WHAT."
IS HE THE ONE WITH THE BOY IN WARD TWO?
MMHM. EVERY DAY HE BRINGS HIM AN ORANGE.

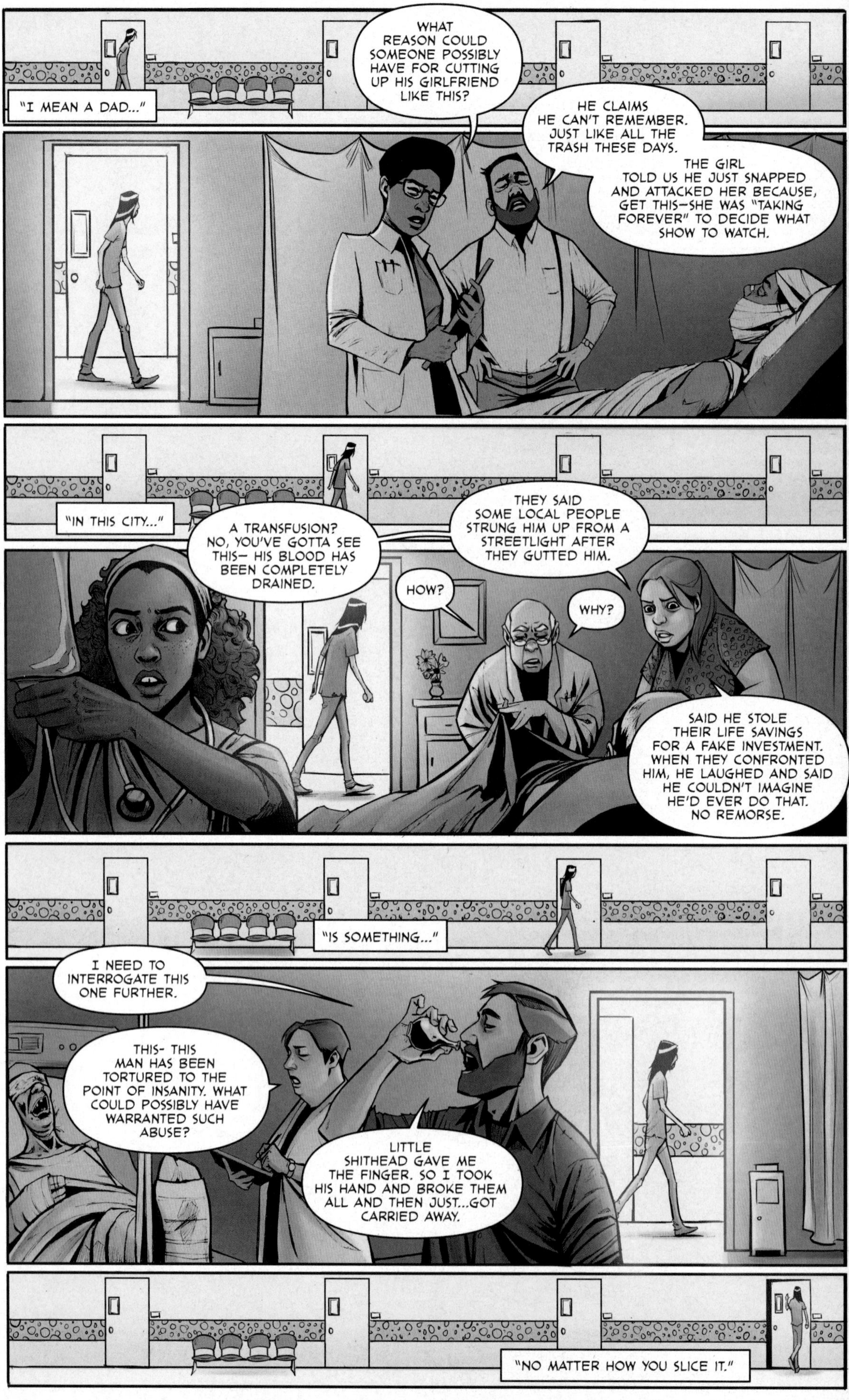
"I MEAN A DAD..."
WHAT REASON COULD SOMEONE POSSIBLY HAVE FOR CUTTING UP HIS GIRLFRIEND LIKE THIS?
HE CLAIMS HE CAN'T REMEMBER. JUST LIKE ALL THE TRASH THESE DAYS.
THE GIRL TOLD US HE JUST SNAPPED AND ATTACKED HER BECAUSE, GET THIS—SHE WAS "TAKING FOREVER" TO DECIDE WHAT SHOW TO WATCH.
"IN THIS CITY..."
A TRANSFUSION? NO, YOU'VE GOTTA SEE THIS— HIS BLOOD HAS BEEN COMPLETELY DRAINED.
THEY SAID SOME LOCAL PEOPLE STRUNG HIM UP FROM A STREETLIGHT AFTER THEY GUTTED HIM.
HOW?
WHY?
SAID HE STOLE THEIR LIFE SAVINGS FOR A FAKE INVESTMENT. WHEN THEY CONFRONTED HIM, HE LAUGHED AND SAID HE COULDN'T IMAGINE HE'D EVER DO THAT. NO REMORSE.
"IS SOMETHING..."
I NEED TO INTERROGATE THIS ONE FURTHER.
THIS- THIS MAN HAS BEEN TORTURED TO THE POINT OF INSANITY. WHAT COULD POSSIBLY HAVE WARRANTED SUCH ABUSE?
LITTLE SHITHEAD GAVE ME THE FINGER. SO I TOOK HIS HAND AND BROKE THEM ALL AND THEN JUST...GOT CARRIED AWAY.
"NO MATTER HOW YOU SLICE IT."

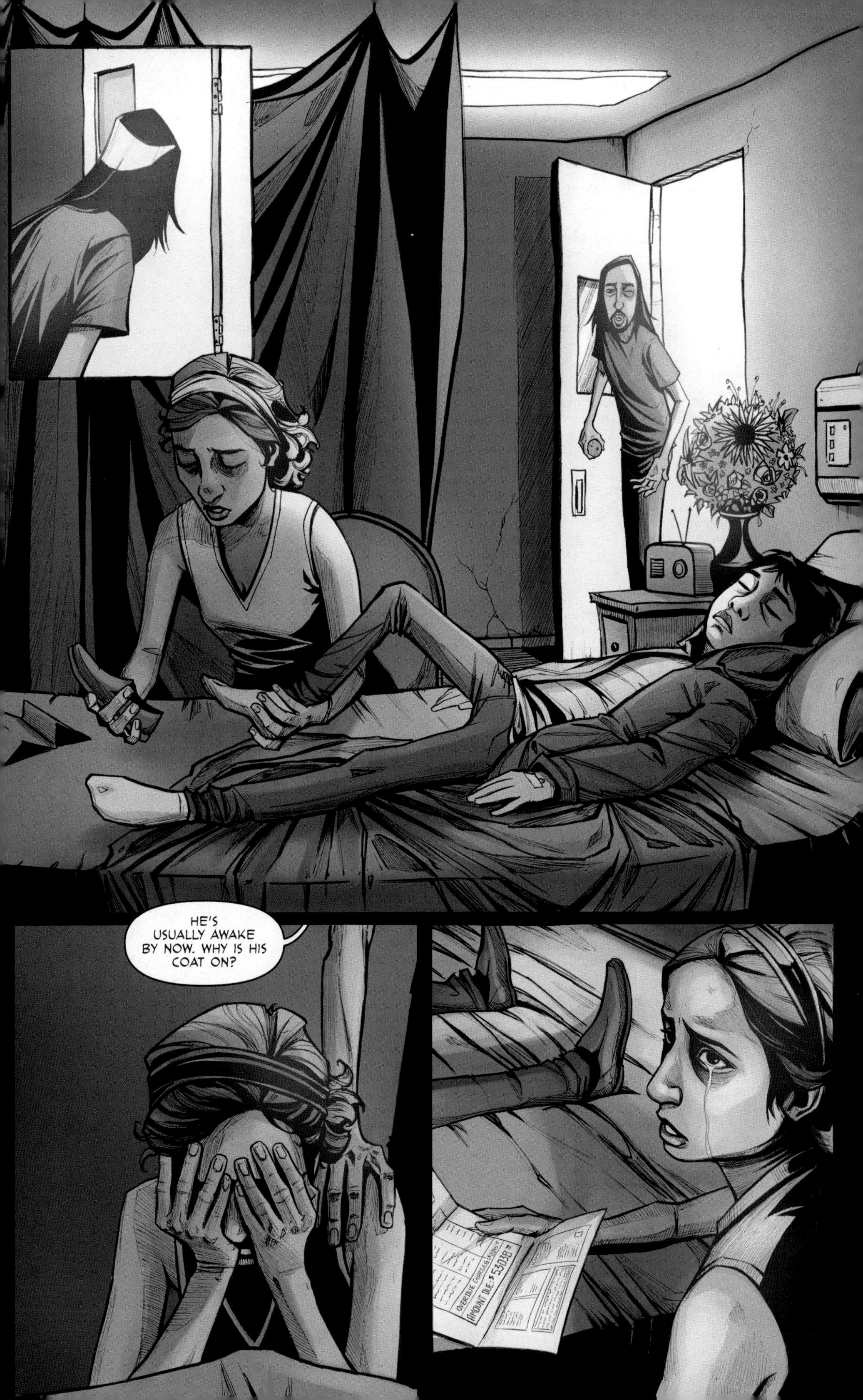
HE'S USUALLY AWAKE BY NOW. WHY IS HIS COAT ON?
OVERDUE CHARGES
AMOUNT DUE:$53038

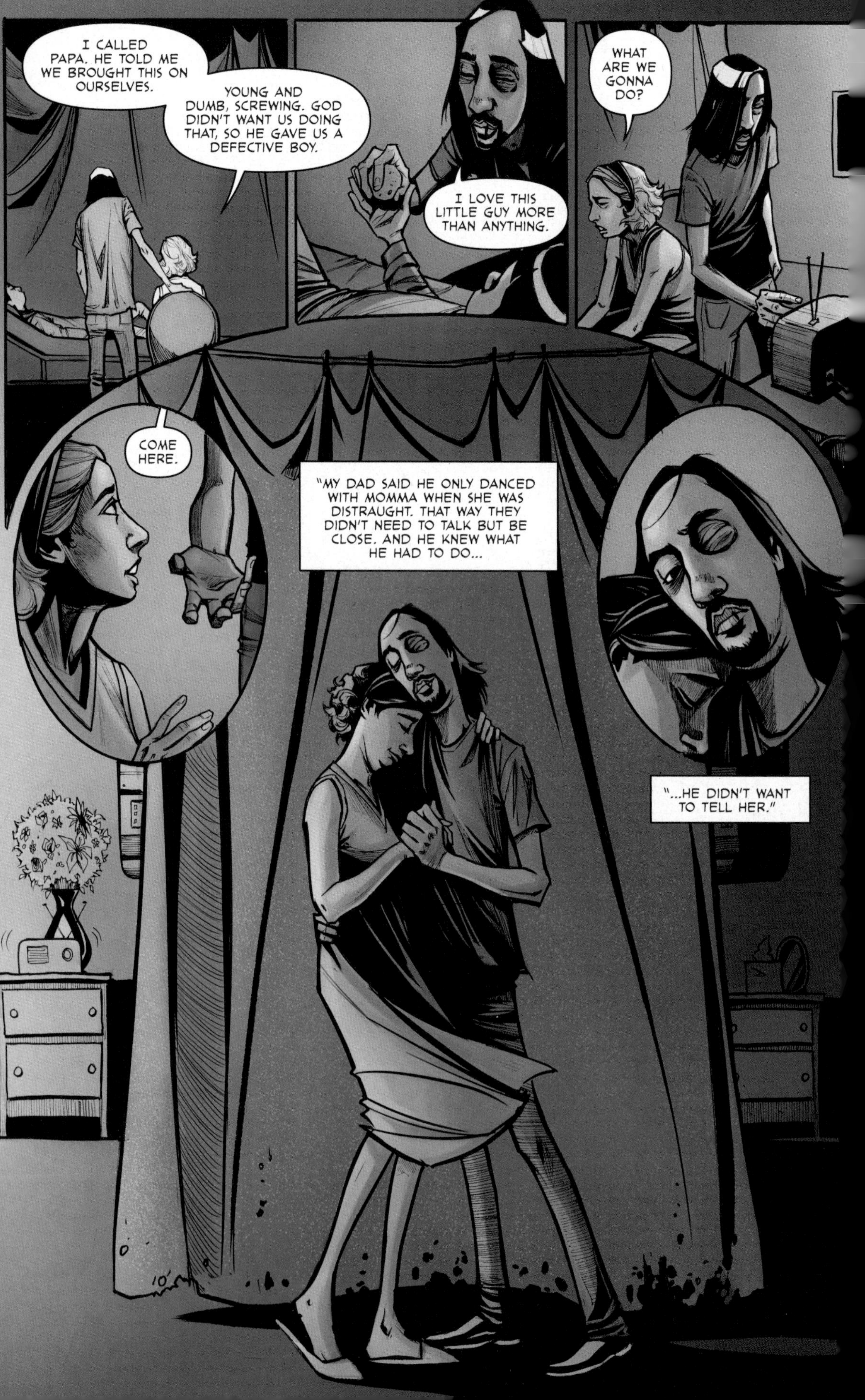
I CALLED PAPA. HE TOLD ME WE BROUGHT THIS ON OURSELVES.
YOUNG AND DUMB, SCREWING. GOD DIDN'T WANT US DOING THAT, SO HE GAVE US A DEFECTIVE BOY.
I LOVE THIS LITTLE GUY MORE THAN ANYTHING.
WHAT ARE WE GONNA DO?
COME HERE.
"MY DAD SAID HE ONLY DANCED WITH MOMMA WHEN SHE WAS DISTRAUGHT. THAT WAY THEY DIDN'T NEED TO TALK BUT BE CLOSE. AND HE KNEW WHAT HE HAD TO DO...
"...HE DIDN'T WANT TO TELL HER."

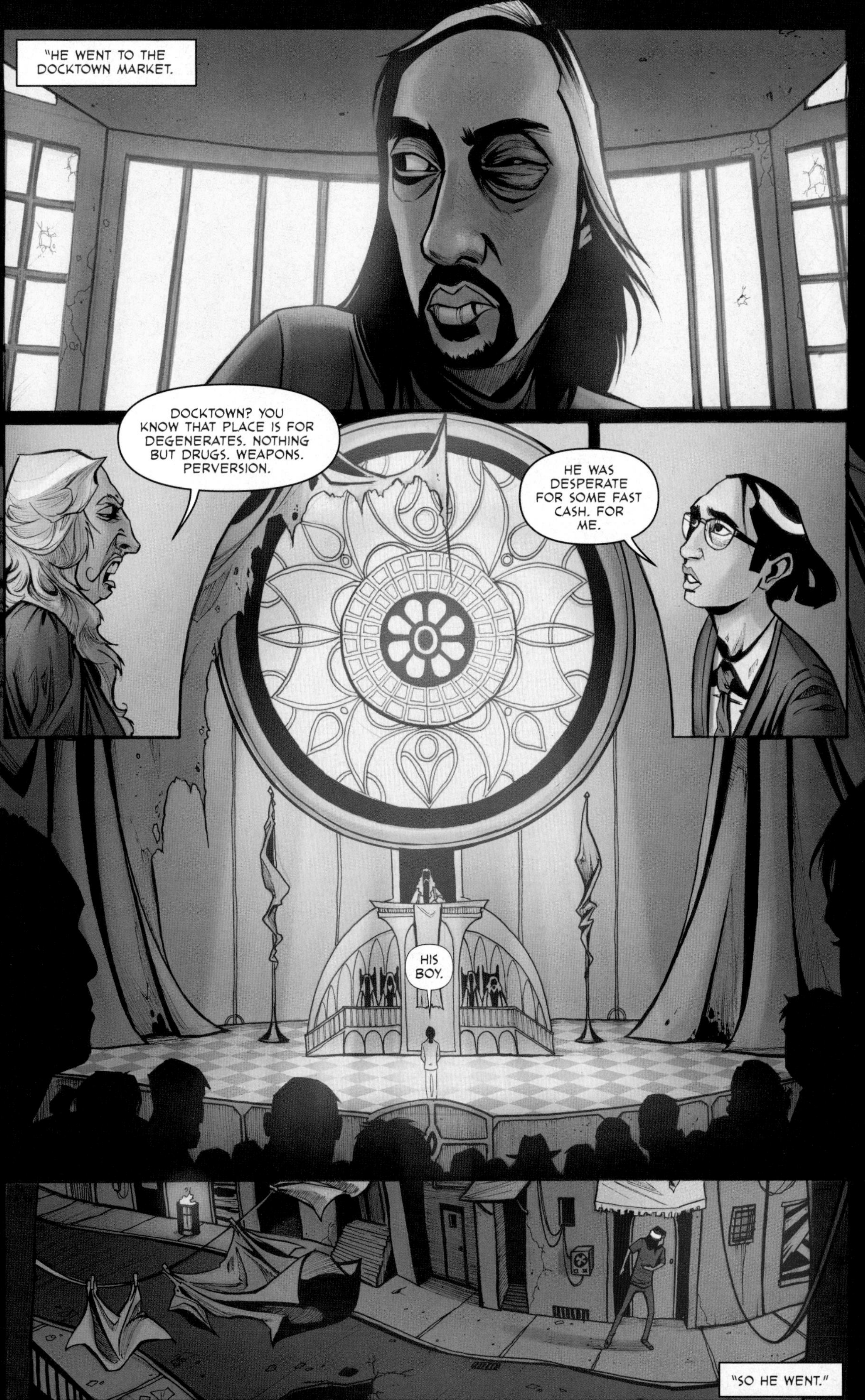
"HE WENT TO THE DOCKTOWN MARKET.
DOCKTOWN? YOU KNOW THAT PLACE IS FOR DEGENERATES. NOTHING BUT DRUGS. WEAPONS. PERVERSION.
HE WAS DESPERATE FOR SOME FAST CASH. FOR ME.
HIS BOY.
"SO HE WENT."

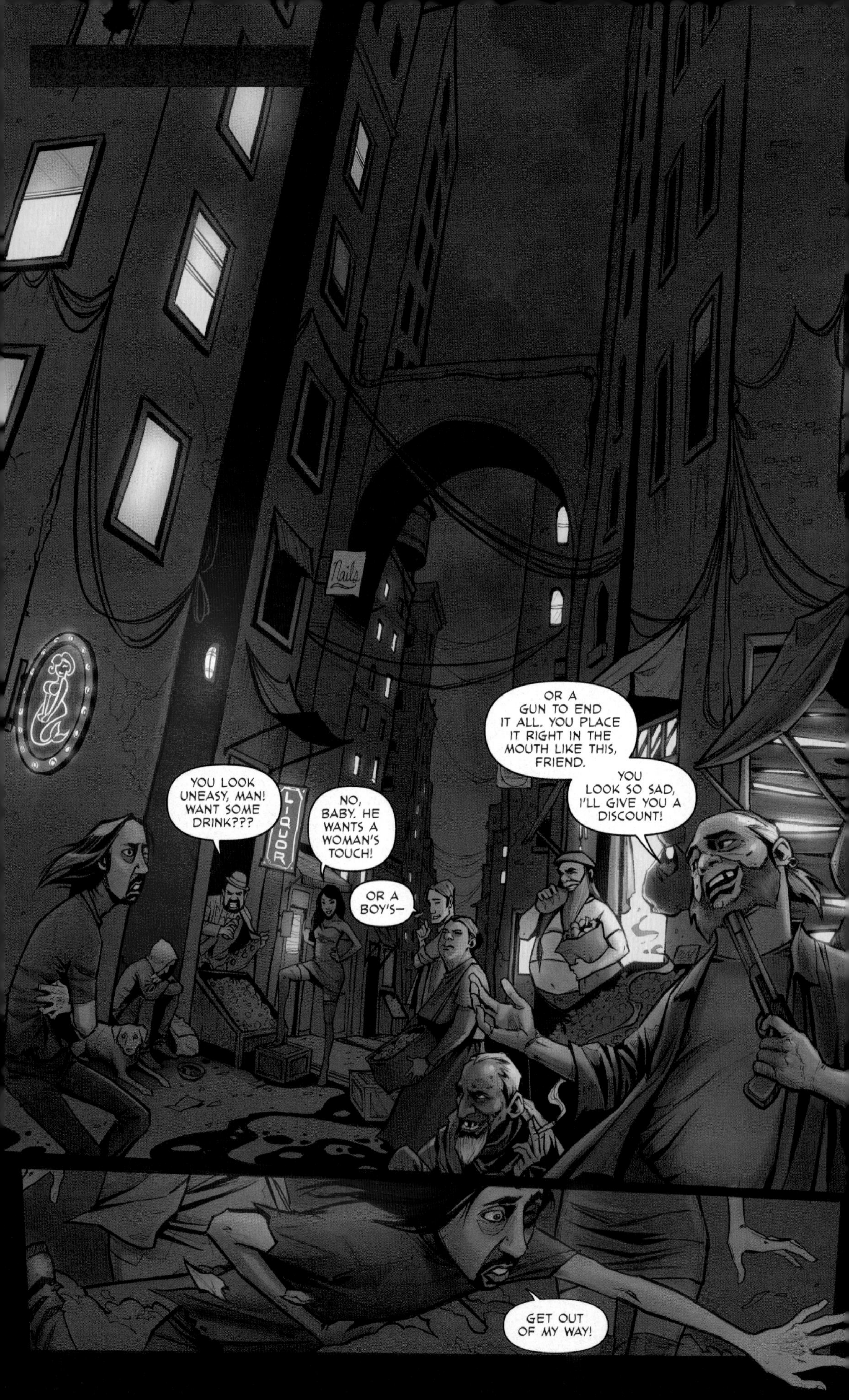
YOU LOOK UNEASY, MAN! WANT SOME DRINK???
LIQUOR
Nails
NO, BABY. HE WANTS A WOMAN'S TOUCH!
OR A BOY'S—
OR A GUN TO END IT ALL. YOU PLACE IT RIGHT IN THE MOUTH LIKE THIS, FRIEND.
YOU LOOK SO SAD, I'LL GIVE YOU A DISCOUNT!
GET OUT OF MY WAY!

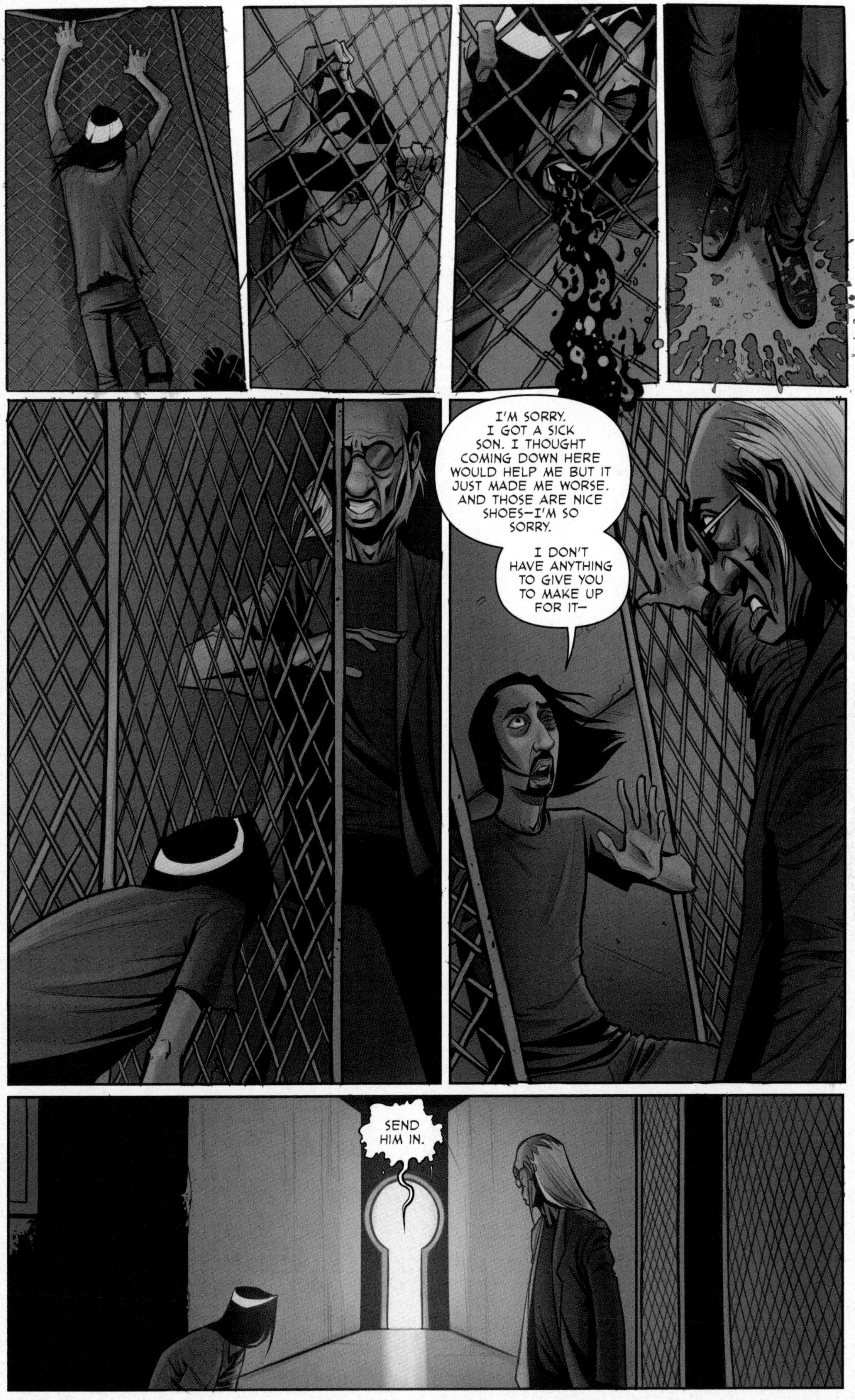
I'M SORRY. I GOT A SICK SON. I THOUGHT COMING DOWN HERE WOULD HELP ME BUT IT JUST MADE ME WORSE. AND THOSE ARE NICE SHOES—I'M SO SORRY.
I DON'T HAVE ANYTHING TO GIVE YOU TO MAKE UP FOR IT—
SEND HIM IN.

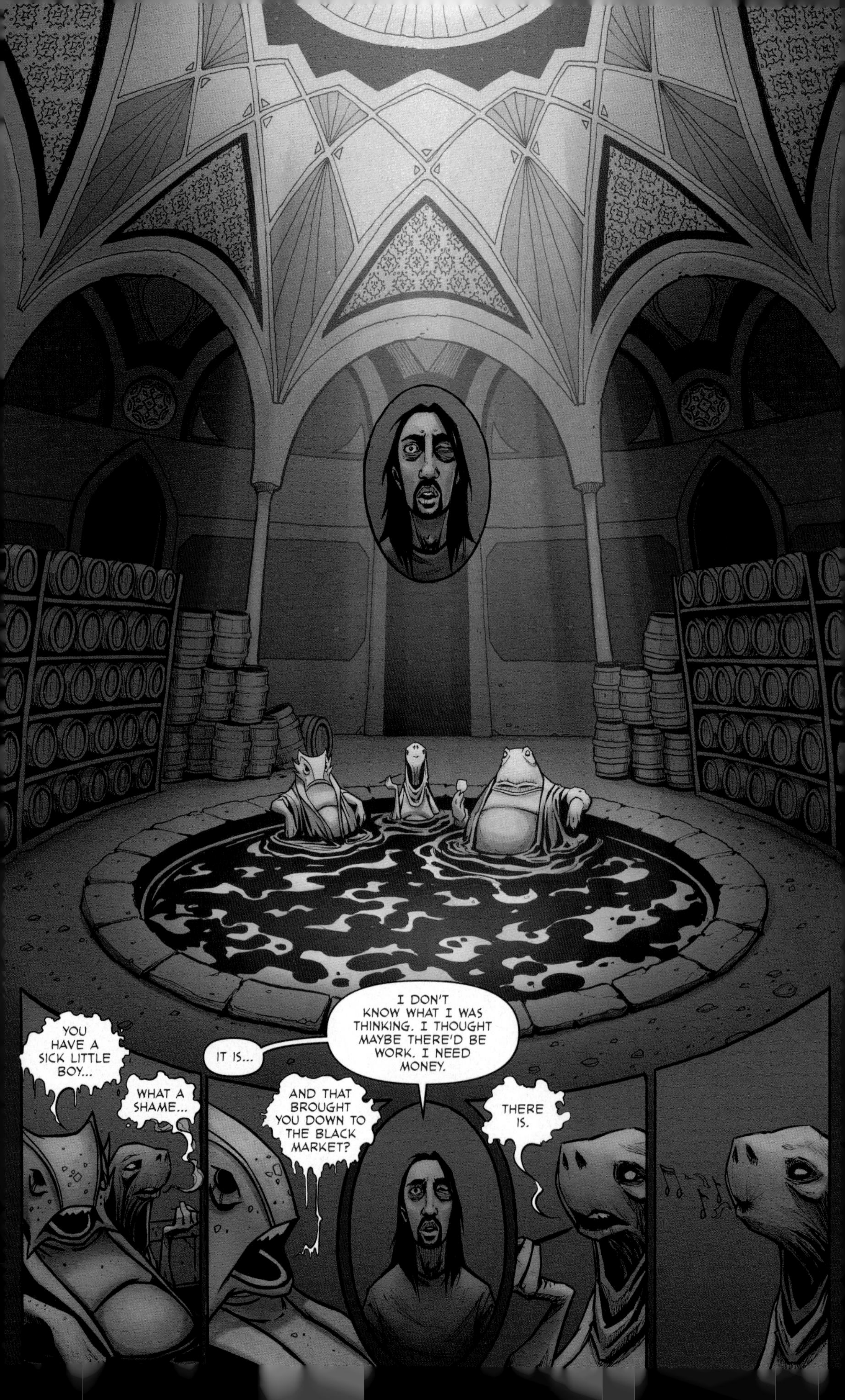
YOU HAVE A SICK LITTLE BOY...
WHAT A SHAME...
IT IS...
I DON'T KNOW WHAT I WAS THINKING. I THOUGHT MAYBE THERE'D BE WORK. I NEED MONEY.
AND THAT BROUGHT YOU DOWN TO THE BLACK MARKET?
THERE IS.

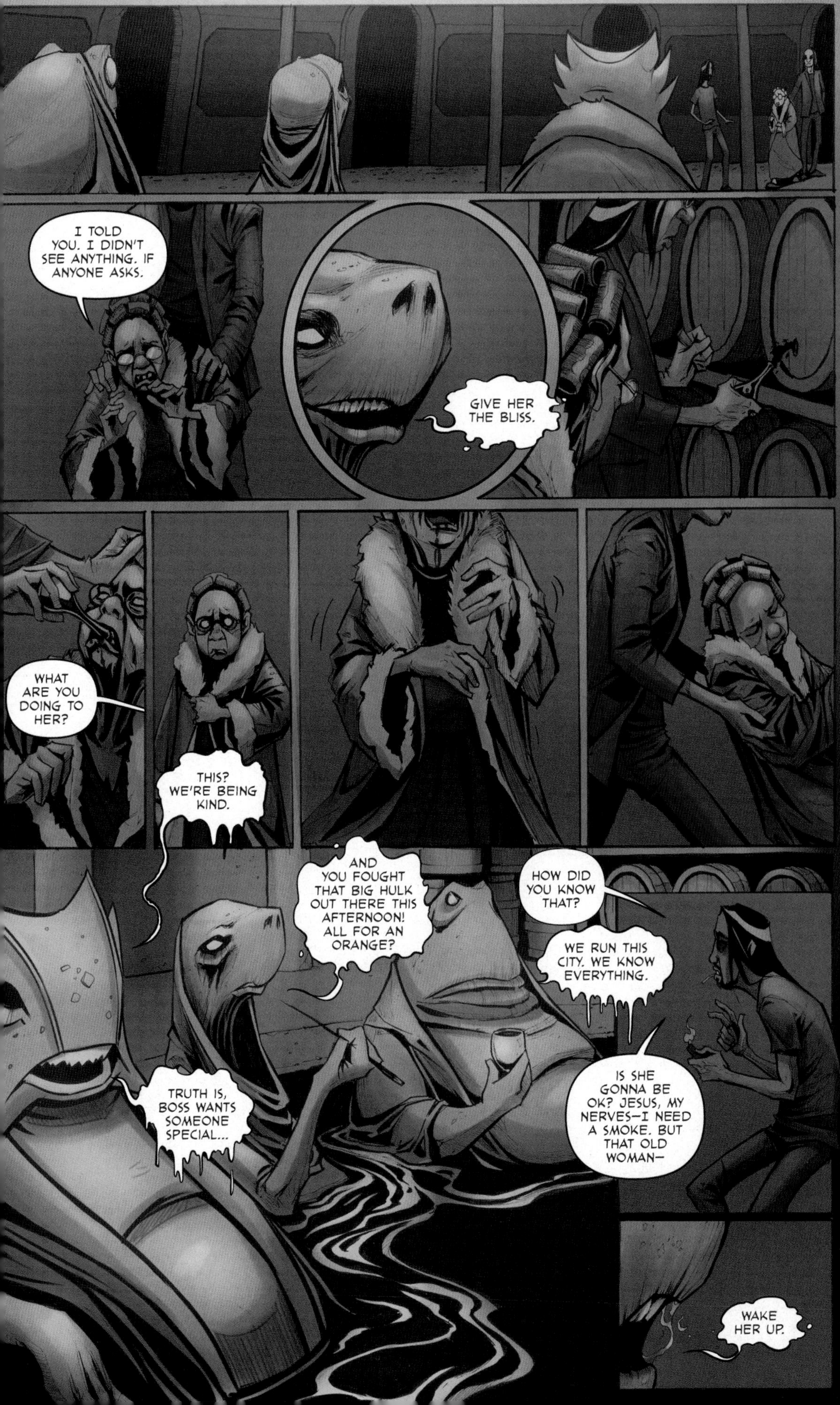
I TOLD YOU. I DIDN'T SEE ANYTHING. IF ANYONE ASKS.
GIVE HER THE BLISS.
WHAT ARE YOU DOING TO HER?
THIS? WE'RE BEING KIND.
AND YOU FOUGHT THAT BIG HULK OUT THERE THIS AFTERNOON! ALL FOR AN ORANGE?
HOW DID YOU KNOW THAT?
WE RUN THIS CITY. WE KNOW EVERYTHING.
TRUTH IS, BOSS WANTS SOMEONE SPECIAL...
IS SHE GONNA BE OK? JESUS, MY NERVES—I NEED A SMOKE. BUT THAT OLD WOMAN—
WAKE HER UP.

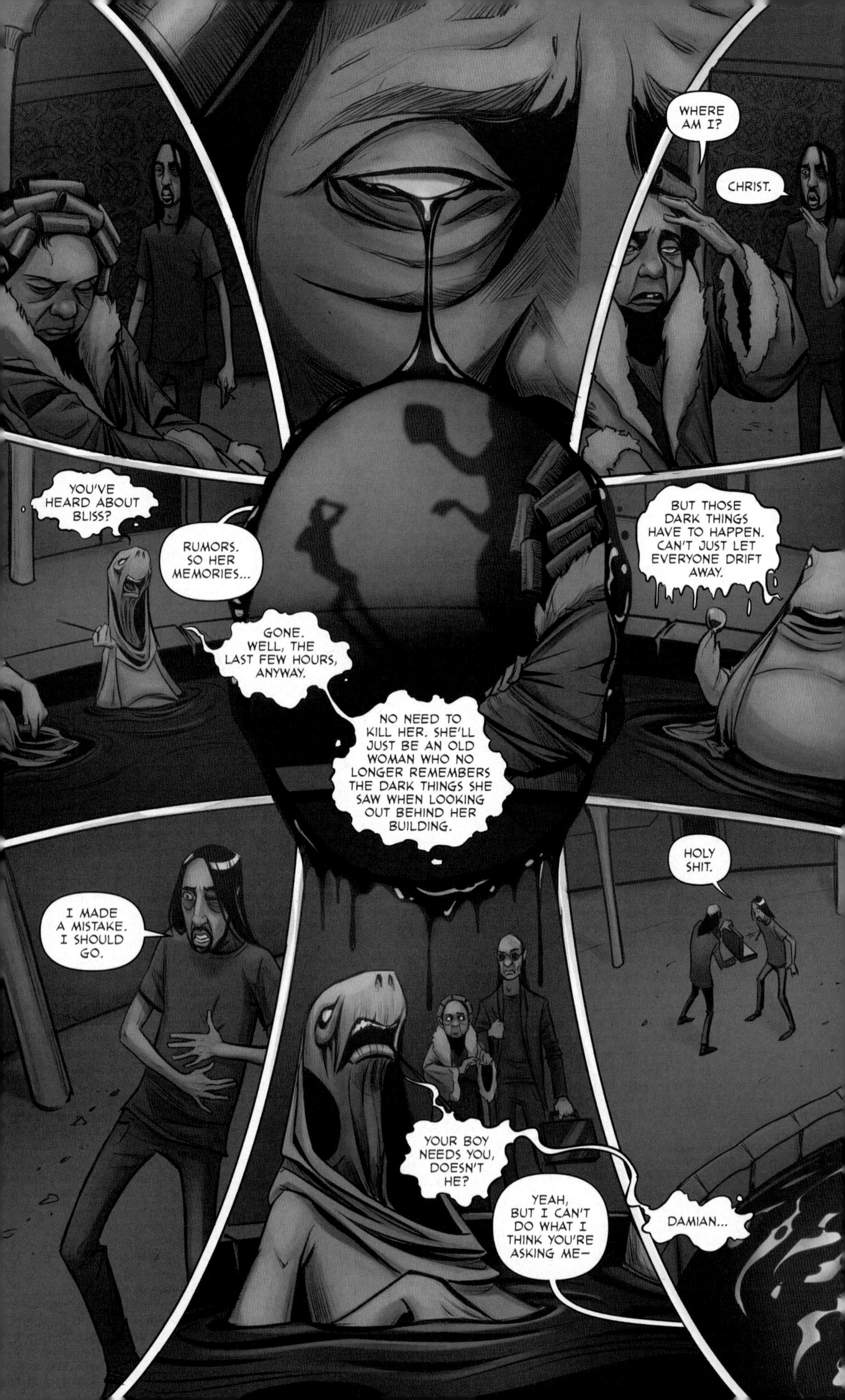
WHERE AM I?
CHRIST.
YOU'VE HEARD ABOUT BLISS?
RUMORS. SO HER MEMORIES...
GONE. WELL, THE LAST FEW HOURS, ANYWAY.
NO NEED TO KILL HER. SHE'LL JUST BE AN OLD WOMAN WHO NO LONGER REMEMBERS THE DARK THINGS SHE SAW WHEN LOOKING OUT BEHIND HER BUILDING.
BUT THOSE DARK THINGS HAVE TO HAPPEN. CAN'T JUST LET EVERYONE DRIFT AWAY.
I MADE A MISTAKE. I SHOULD GO.
YOUR BOY NEEDS YOU, DOESN'T HE?
YEAH, BUT I CAN'T DO WHAT I THINK YOU'RE ASKING ME—
HOLY SHIT.
DAMIAN...

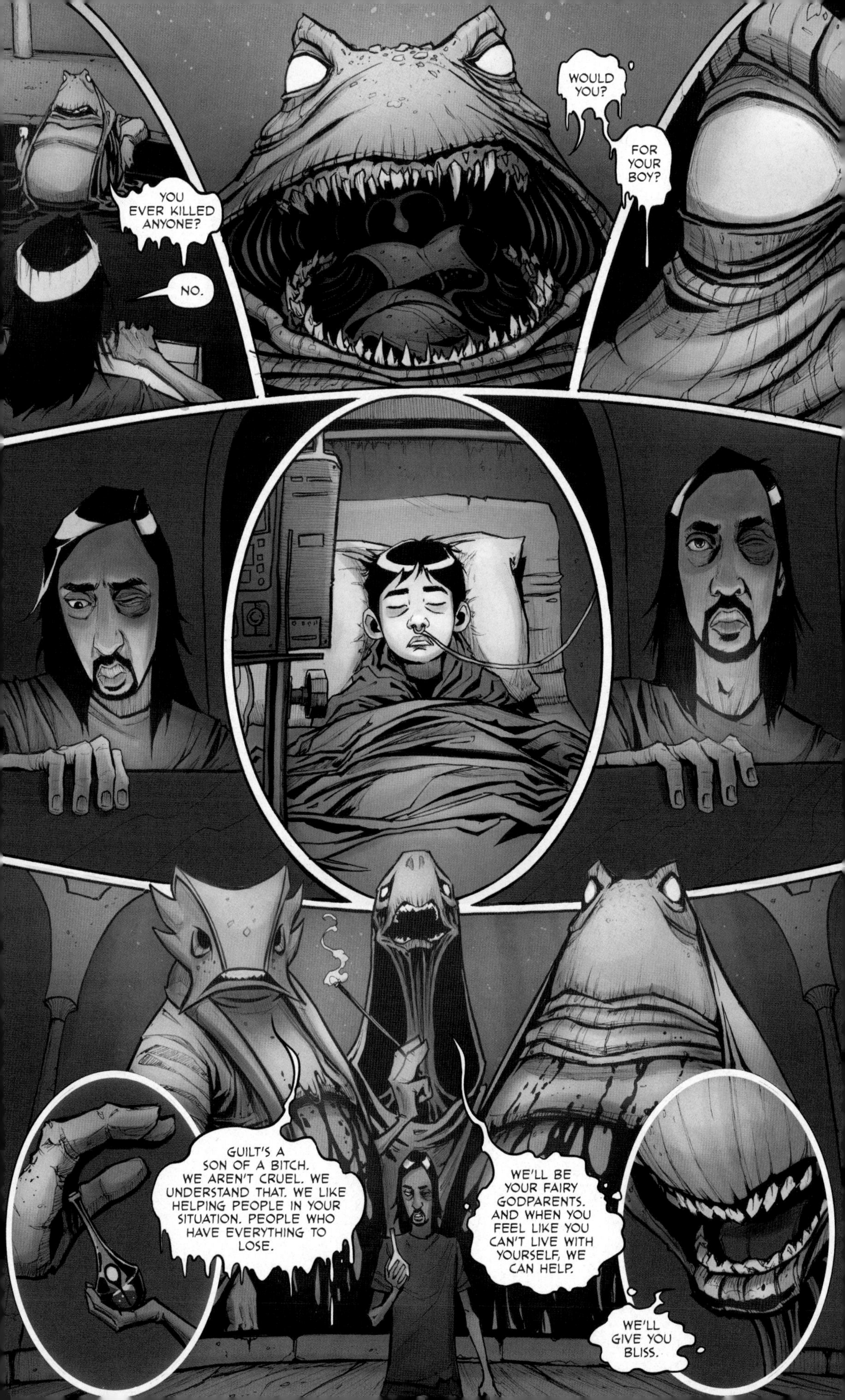
YOU EVER KILLED ANYONE?
NO.
WOULD YOU?
FOR YOUR BOY?
GUILT'S A SON OF A BITCH. WE AREN'T CRUEL. WE UNDERSTAND THAT. WE LIKE HELPING PEOPLE IN YOUR SITUATION. PEOPLE WHO HAVE EVERYTHING TO LOSE.
WE'LL BE YOUR FAIRY GODPARENTS. AND WHEN YOU FEEL LIKE YOU CAN'T LIVE WITH YOURSELF, WE CAN HELP.
WE'LL GIVE YOU BLISS.

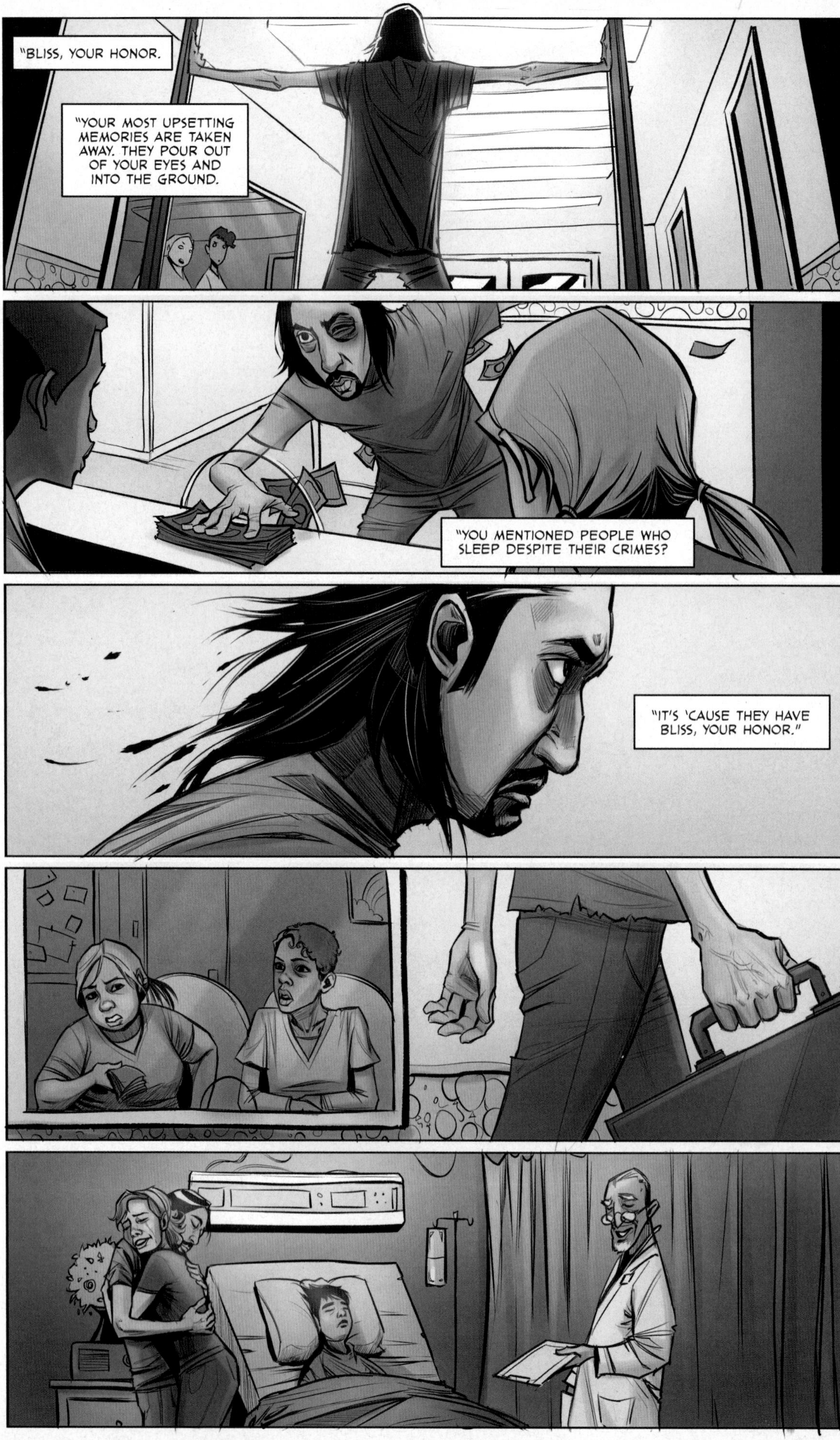
"BLISS, YOUR HONOR.
"YOUR MOST UPSETTING MEMORIES ARE TAKEN AWAY. THEY POUR OUT OF YOUR EYES AND INTO THE GROUND.
"YOU MENTIONED PEOPLE WHO SLEEP DESPITE THEIR CRIMES?
"IT'S 'CAUSE THEY HAVE BLISS, YOUR HONOR."

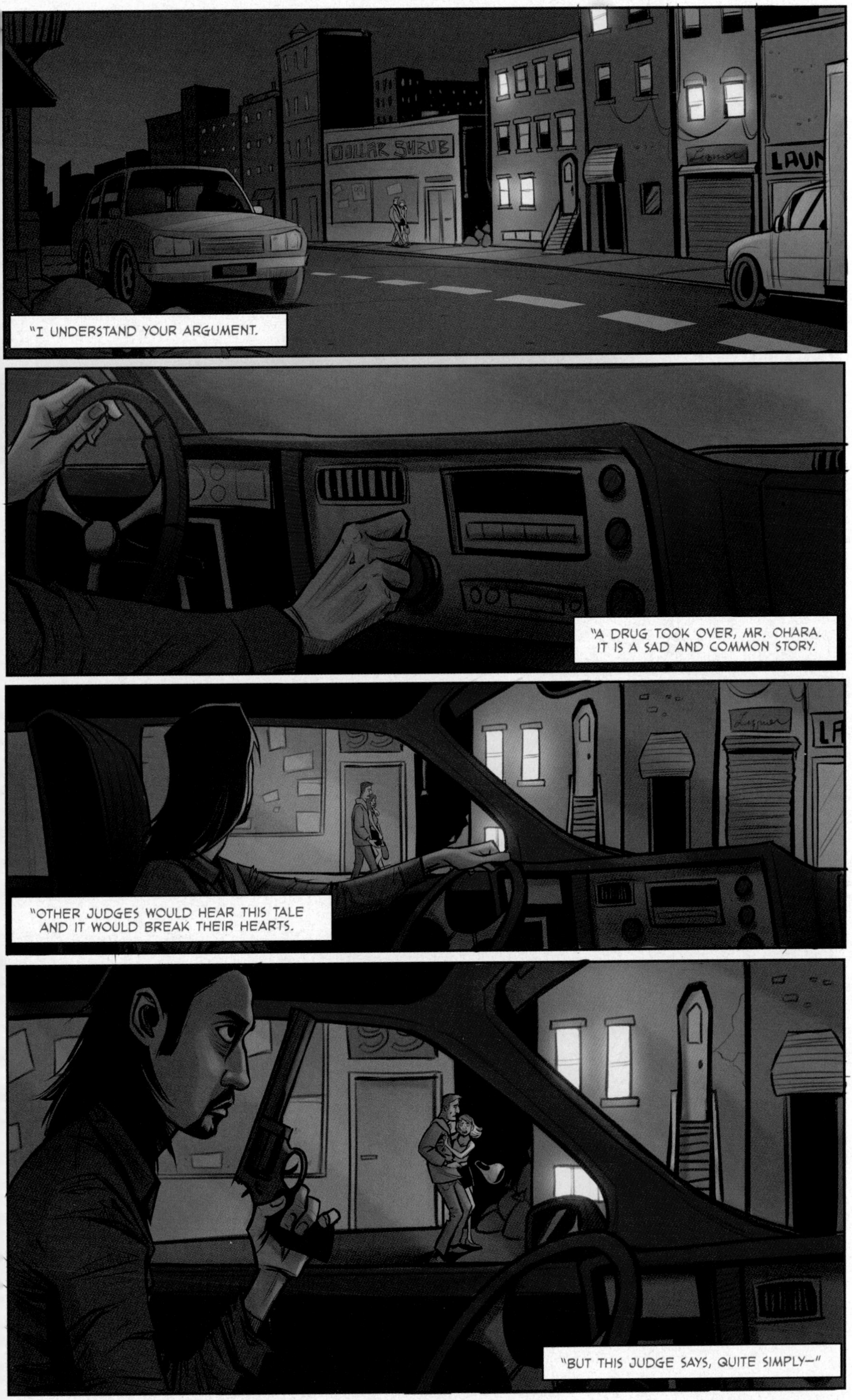
"I UNDERSTAND YOUR ARGUMENT.
"A DRUG TOOK OVER, MR. OHARA. IT IS A SAD AND COMMON STORY.
"OTHER JUDGES WOULD HEAR THIS TALE AND IT WOULD BREAK THEIR HEARTS.
"BUT THIS JUDGE SAYS, QUITE SIMPLY—"

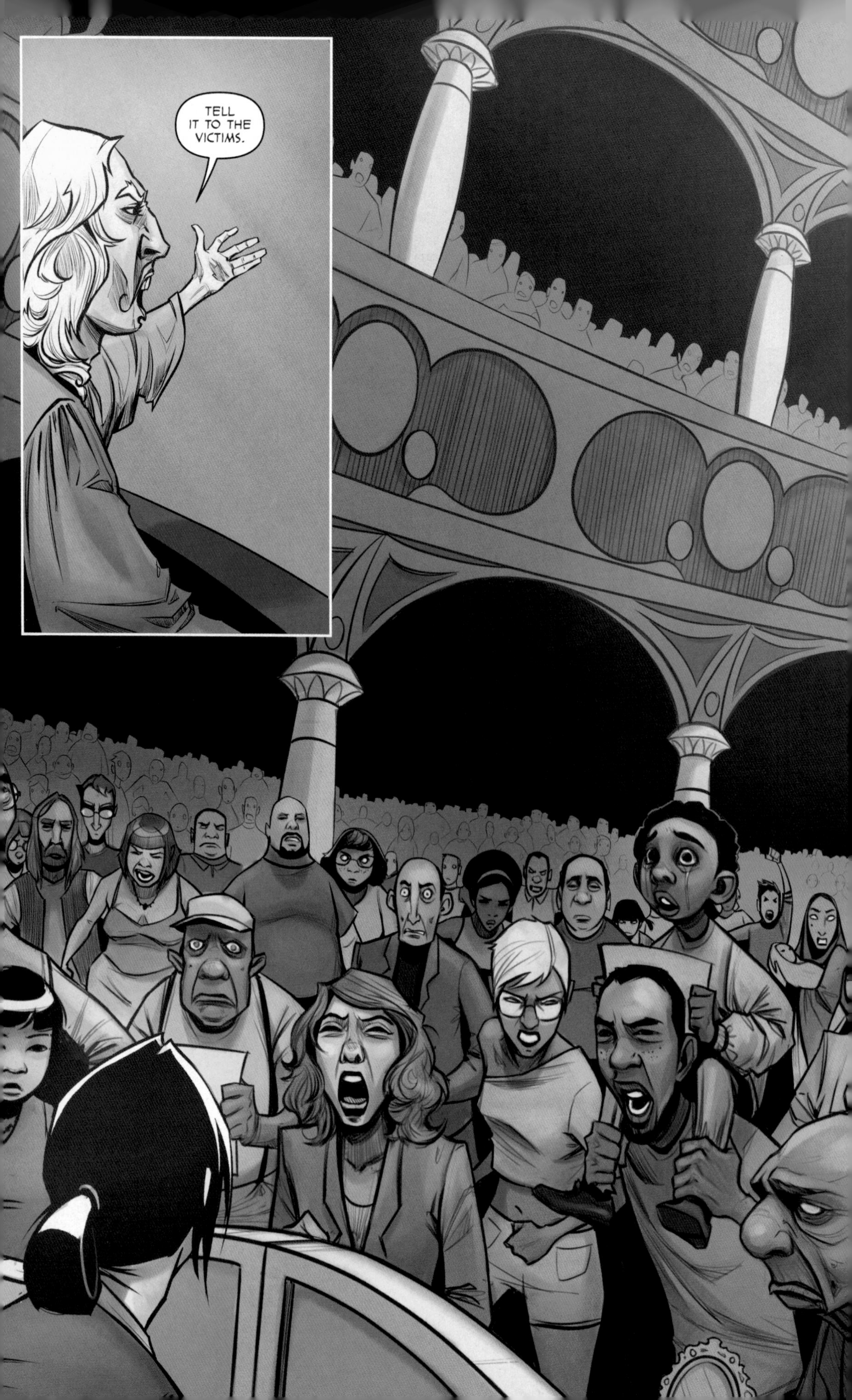
TELL IT TO THE VICTIMS.

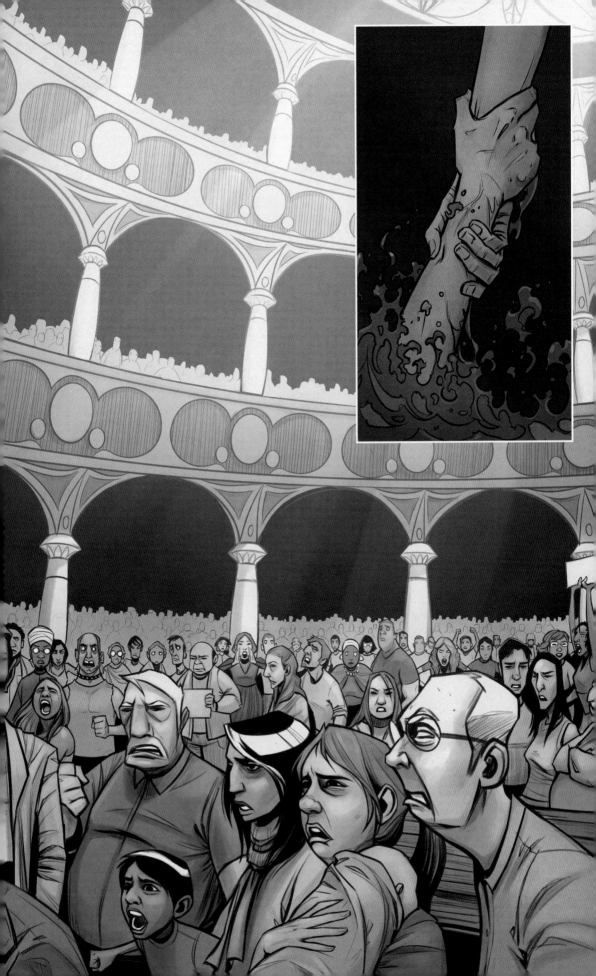

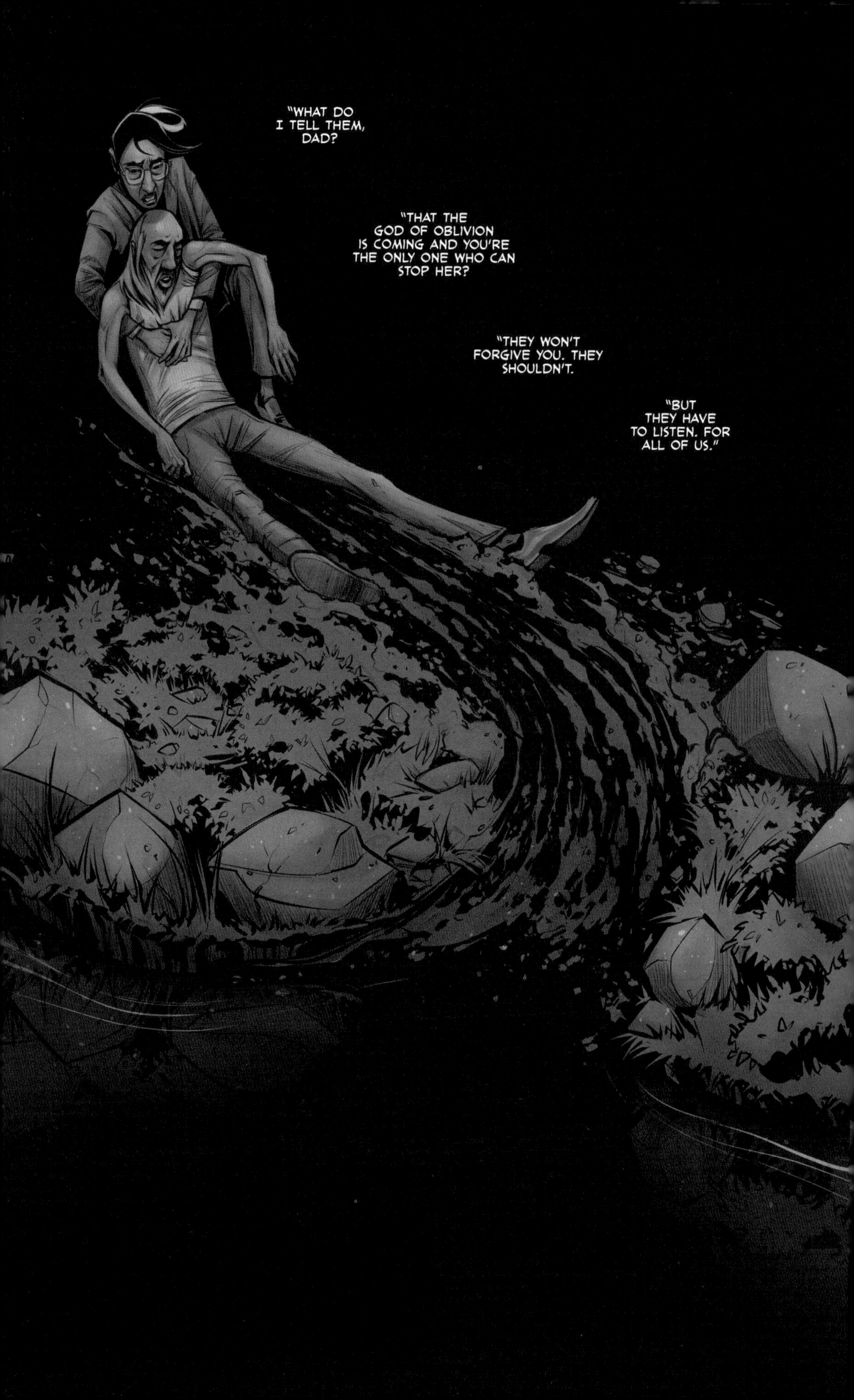
"WHAT DO I TELL THEM, DAD?
"THAT THE GOD OF OBLIVION IS COMING AND YOU'RE THE ONLY ONE WHO CAN STOP HER?
"THEY WON'T FORGIVE YOU. THEY SHOULDN'T.
"BUT THEY HAVE TO LISTEN. FOR ALL OF US."

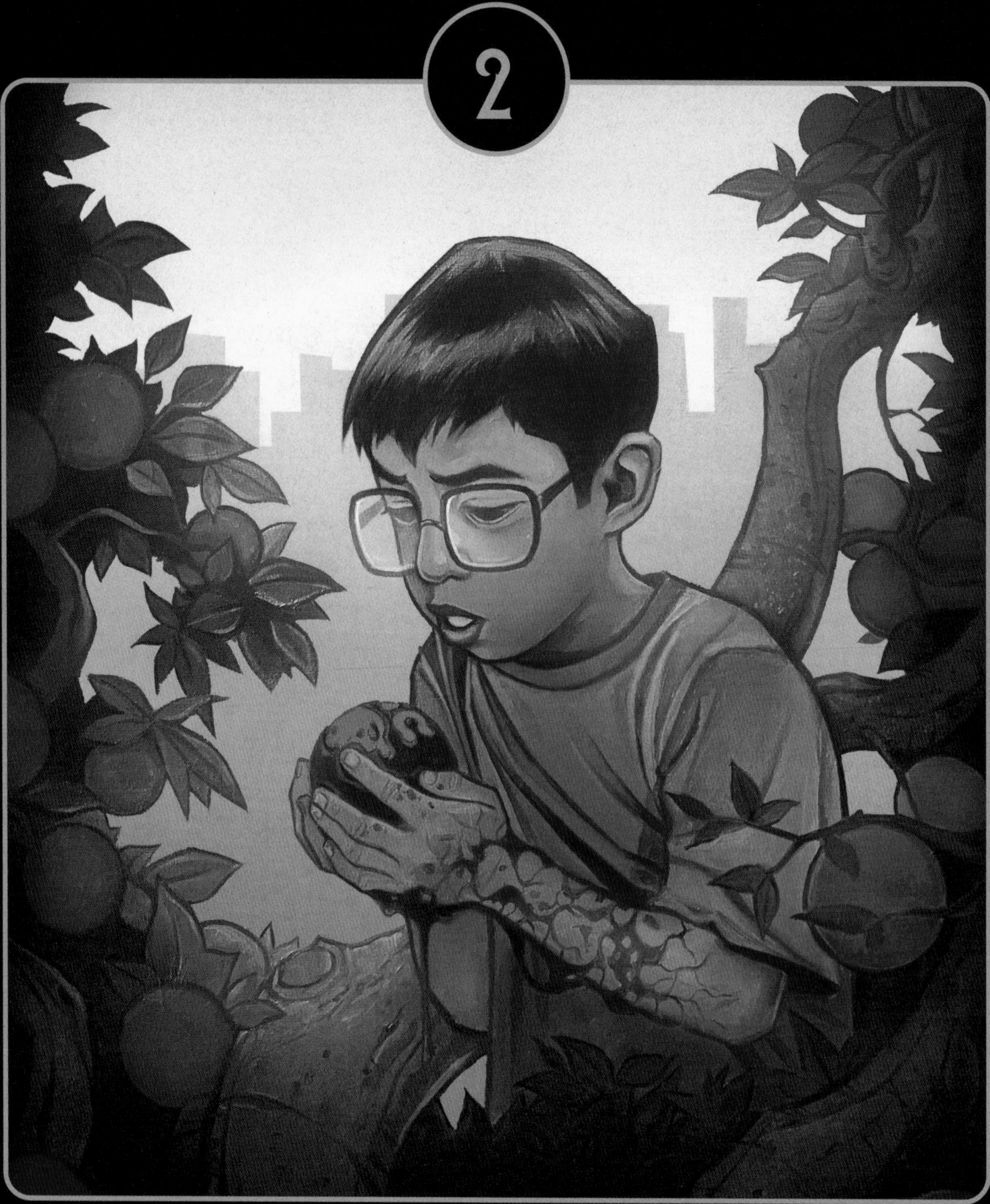
2

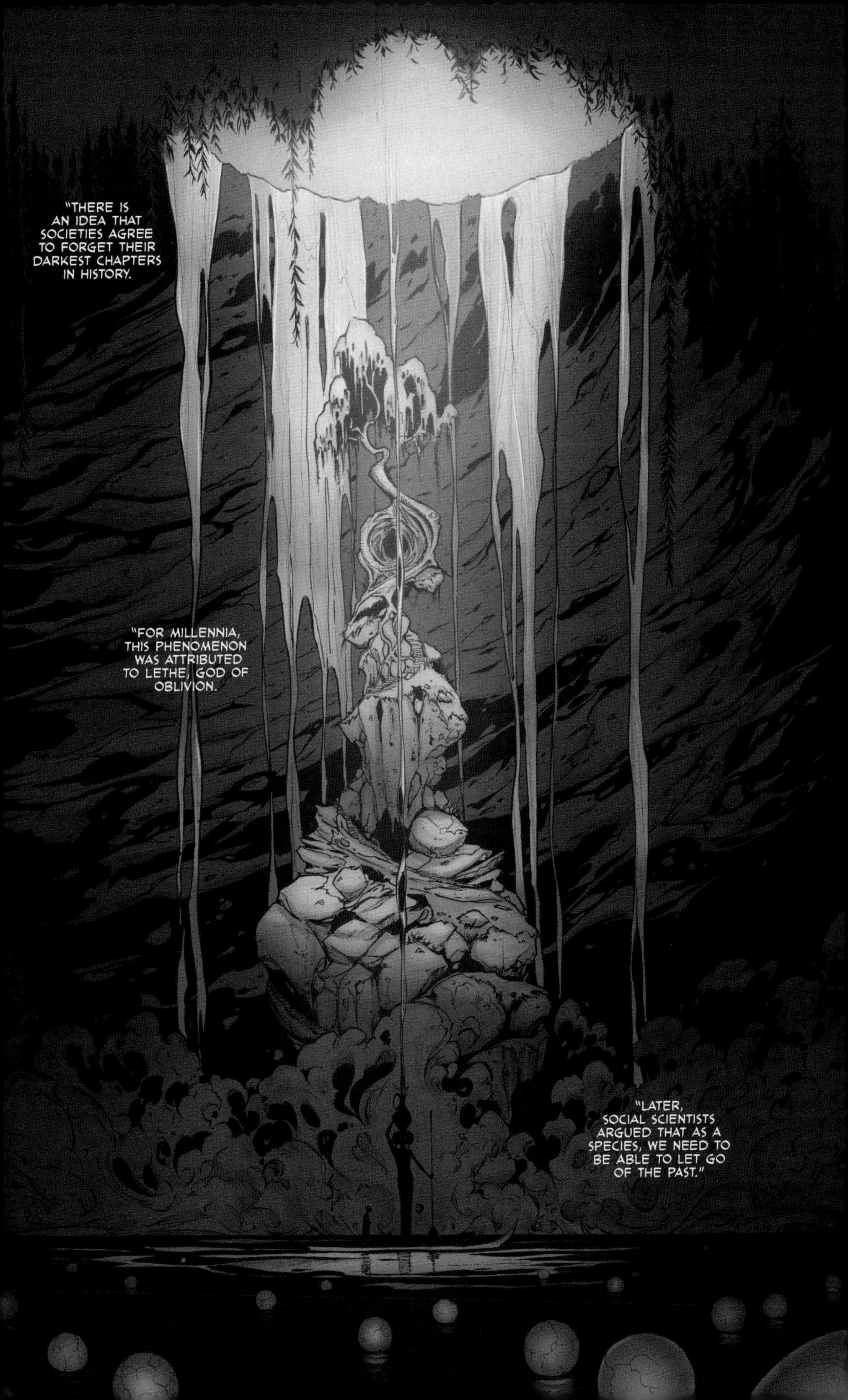
"THERE IS AN IDEA THAT SOCIETIES AGREE TO FORGET THEIR DARKEST CHAPTERS IN HISTORY.
"FOR MILLENNIA, THIS PHENOMENON WAS ATTRIBUTED TO LETHE, GOD OF OBLIVION.
"LATER, SOCIAL SCIENTISTS ARGUED THAT AS A SPECIES, WE NEED TO BE ABLE TO LET GO OF THE PAST."

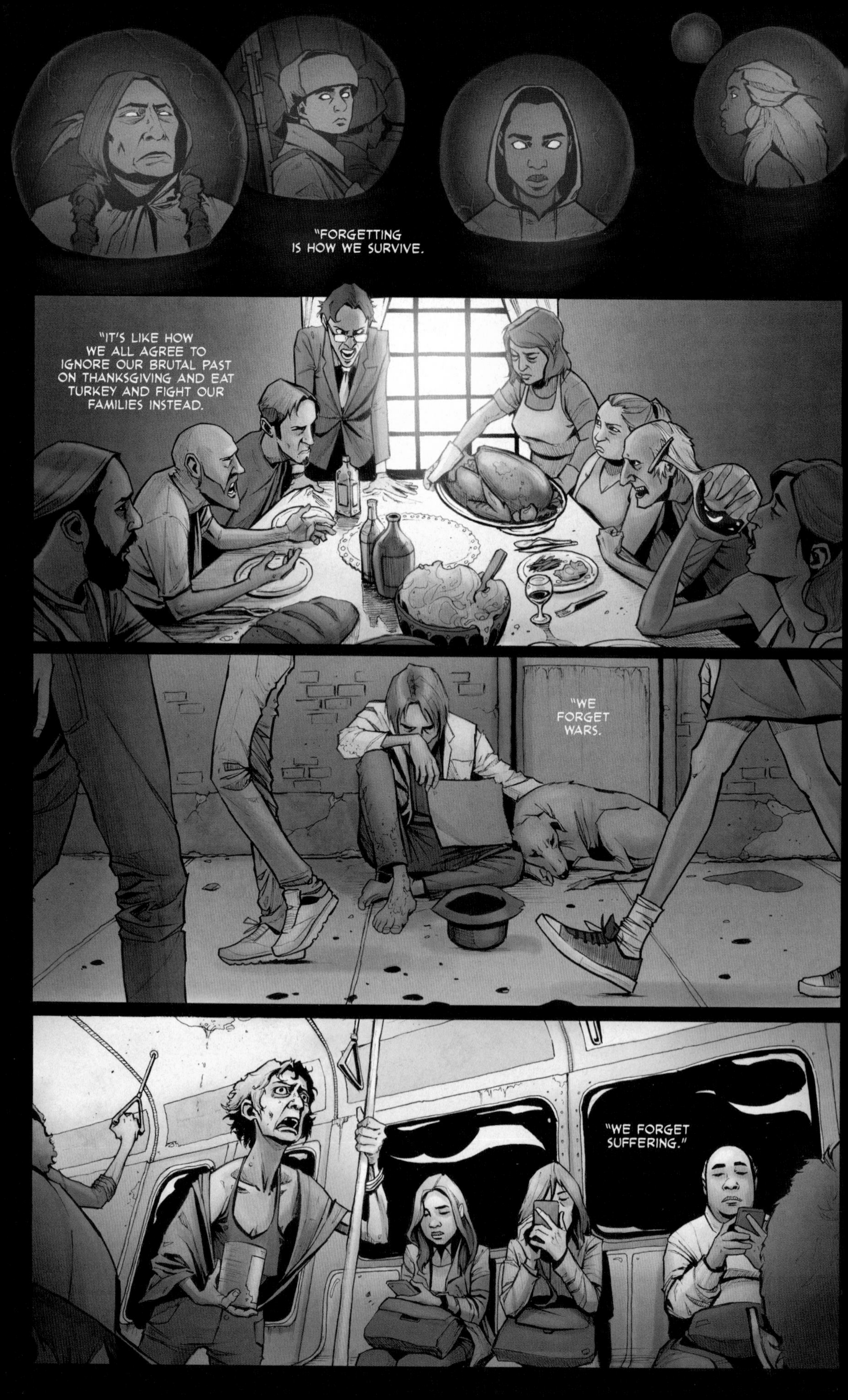
"FORGETTING
IS HOW WE SURVIVE.
"IT'S LIKE HOW WE ALL AGREE TO IGNORE OUR BRUTAL PAST ON THANKSGIVING AND EAT TURKEY AND FIGHT OUR FAMILIES INSTEAD.
"WE FORGET WARS.
"WE FORGET SUFFERING."

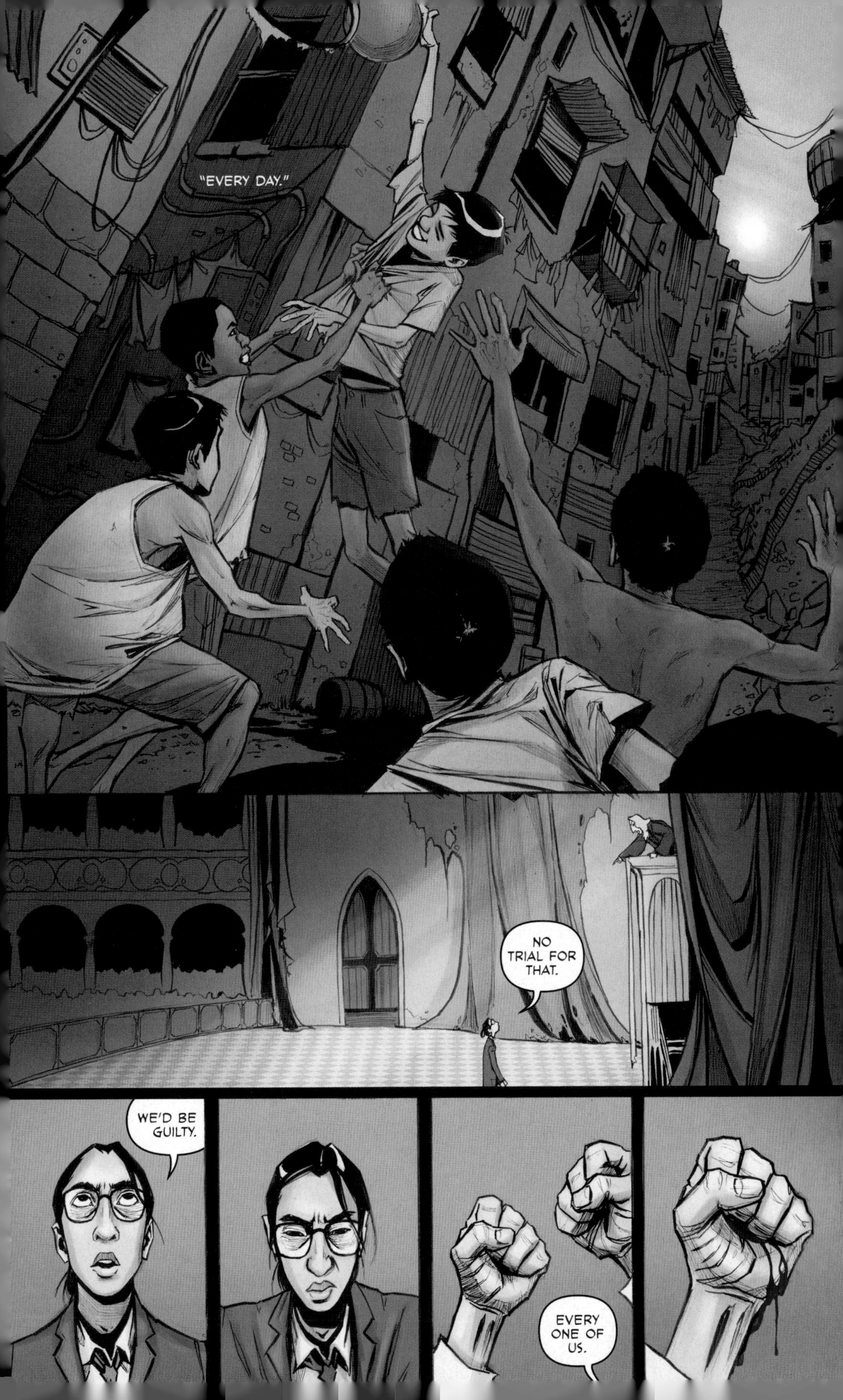
"EVERY DAY."
NO TRIAL FOR THAT.
WE'D BE GUILTY.
EVERY ONE OF US.

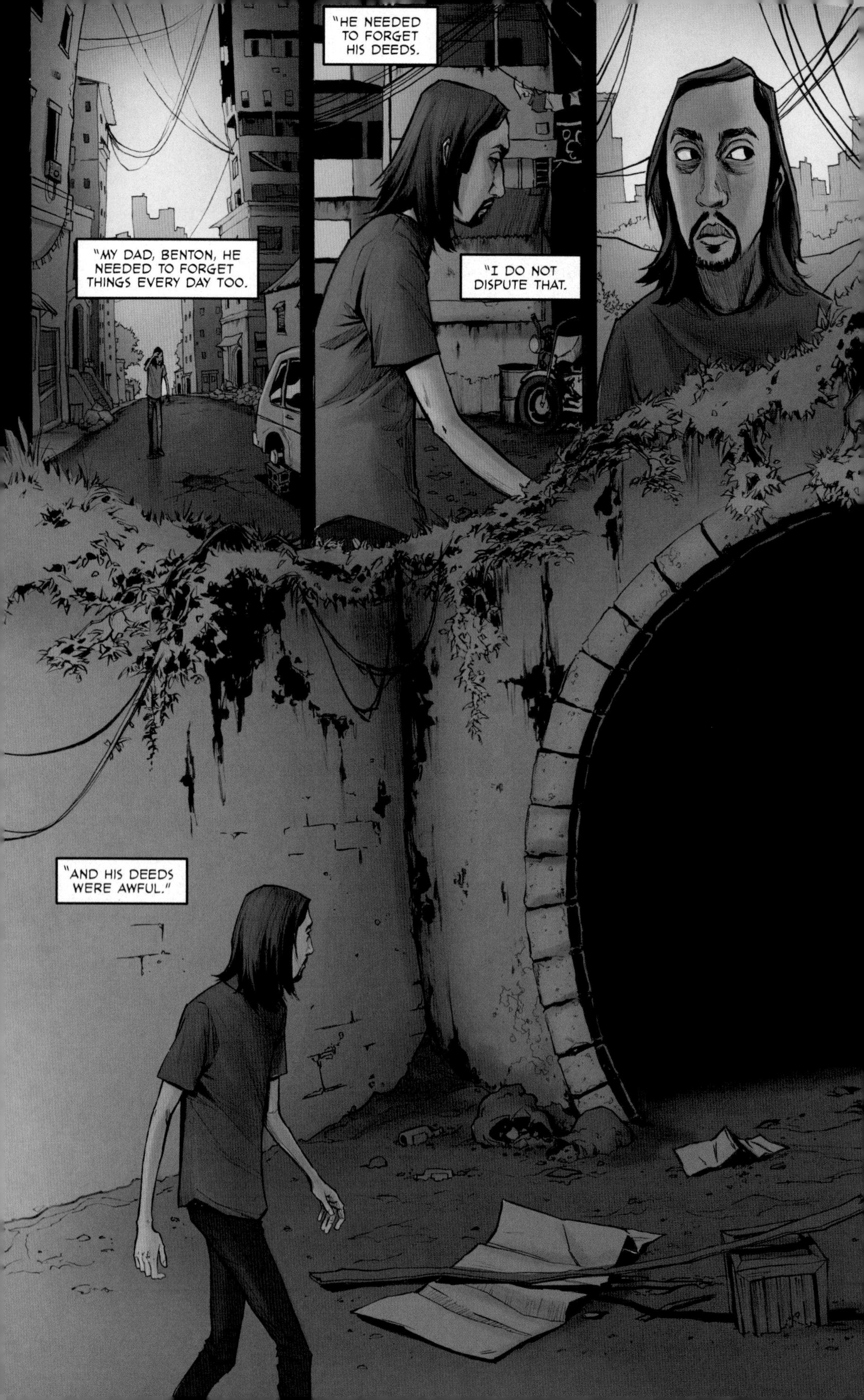
"MY DAD, BENTON, HE NEEDED TO FORGET THINGS EVERY DAY TOO.
"HE NEEDED TO FORGET HIS DEEDS.
"I DO NOT DISPUTE THAT.
"AND HIS DEEDS WERE AWFUL."

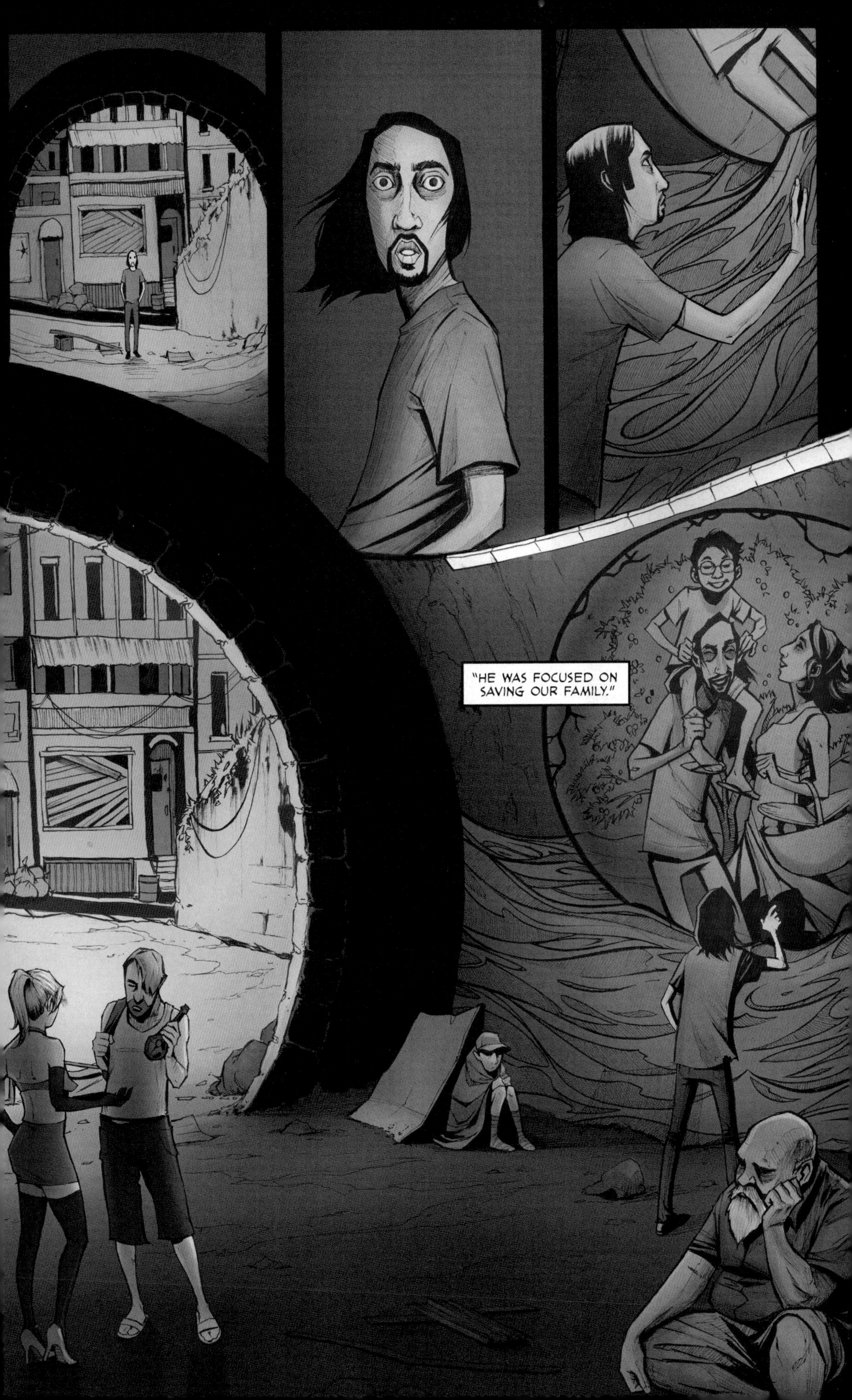
"HE WAS FOCUSED ON SAVING OUR FAMILY."

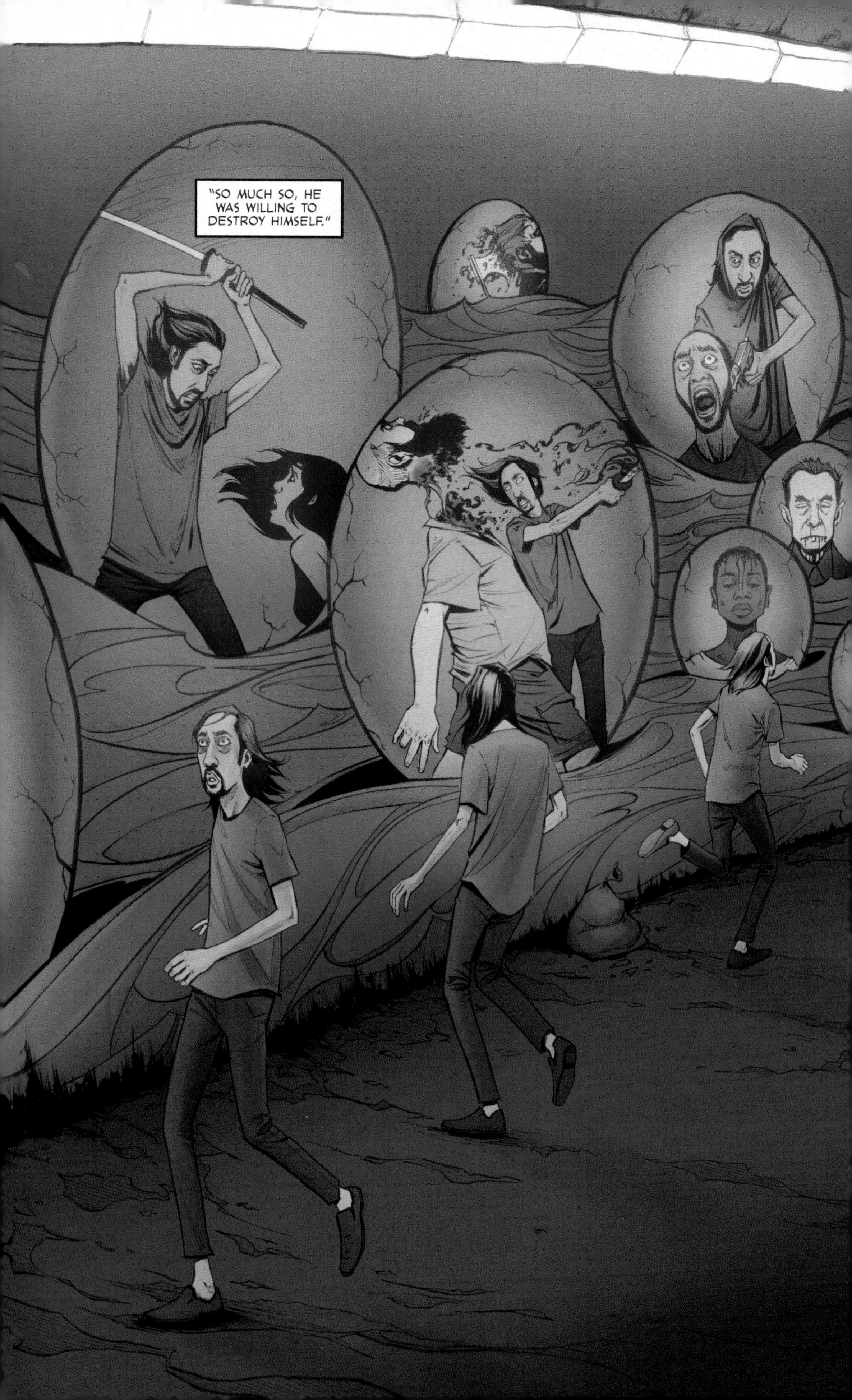
"SO MUCH SO, HE WAS WILLING TO DESTROY HIMSELF."

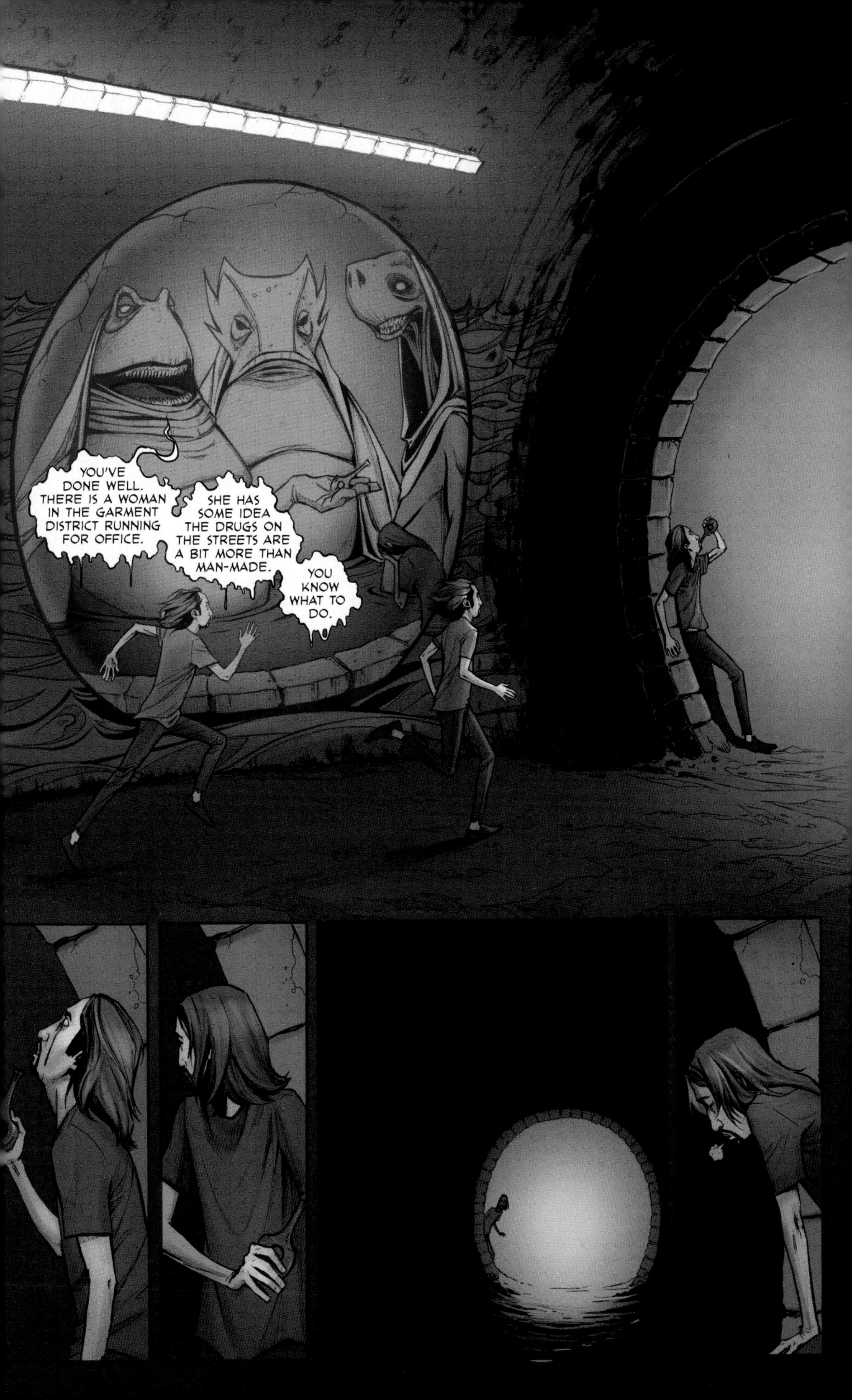
YOU'VE DONE WELL. THERE IS A WOMAN IN THE GARMENT DISTRICT RUNNING FOR OFFICE.
SHE HAS SOME IDEA THE DRUGS ON THE STREETS ARE A BIT MORE THAN MAN-MADE.
YOU KNOW WHAT TO DO.

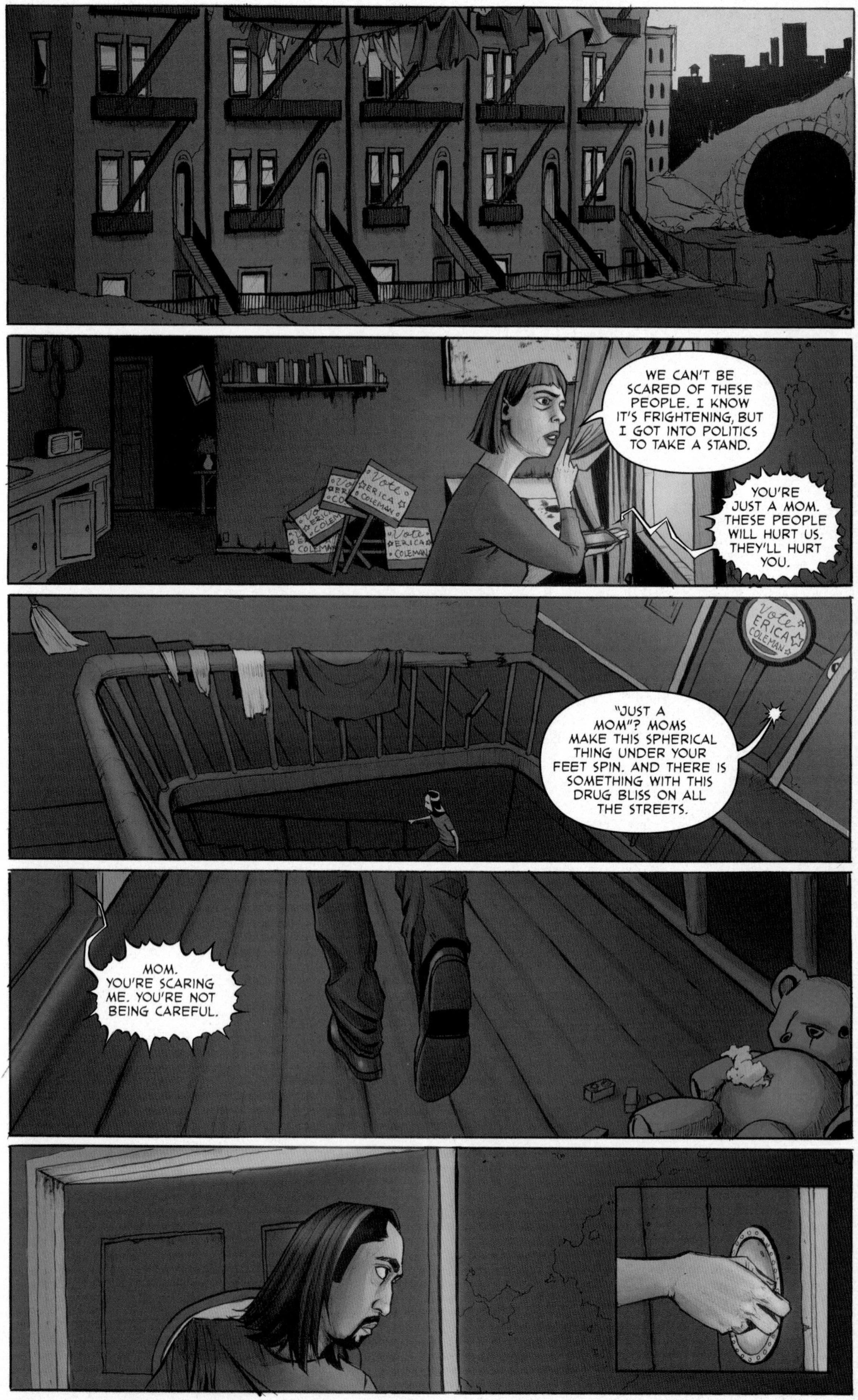
WE CAN'T BE SCARED OF THESE PEOPLE. I KNOW IT'S FRIGHTENING, BUT I GOT INTO POLITICS TO TAKE A STAND.
Vote ERICA COLEMAN
YOU'RE JUST A MOM. THESE PEOPLE WILL HURT US. THEY'LL HURT YOU.
Vote ERICA COLEMAN
"JUST A MOM"? MOMS MAKE THIS SPHERICAL THING UNDER YOUR FEET SPIN. AND THERE IS SOMETHING WITH THIS DRUG BLISS ON ALL THE STREETS.
MOM. YOU'RE SCARING ME. YOU'RE NOT BEING CAREFUL.

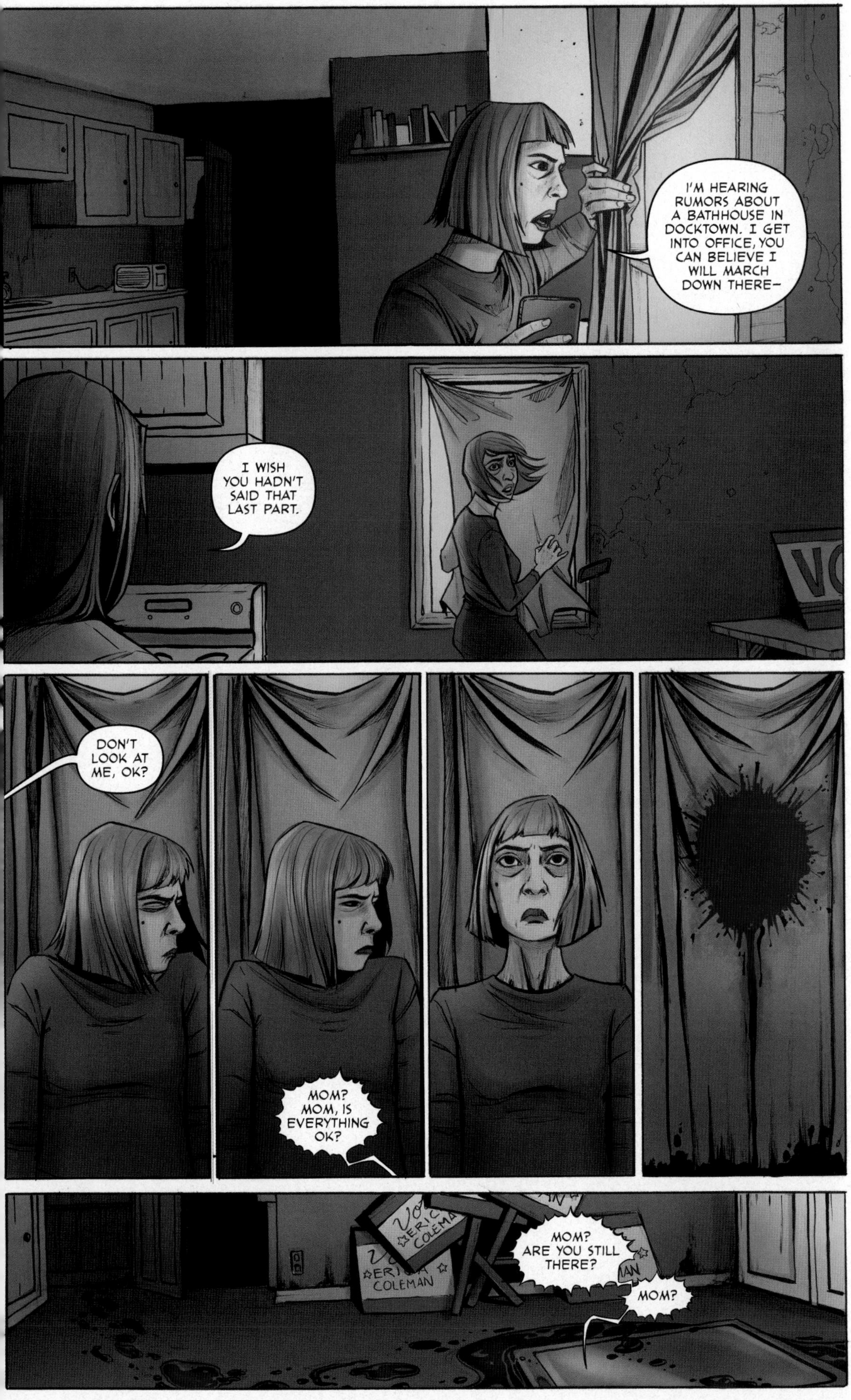
I'M HEARING RUMORS ABOUT A BATHHOUSE IN DOCKTOWN. I GET INTO OFFICE, YOU CAN BELIEVE I WILL MARCH DOWN THERE–
I WISH YOU HADN'T SAID THAT LAST PART.
VO
DON'T LOOK AT ME, OK?
MOM? MOM, IS EVERYTHING OK?
VOTE ERICA COLEMAN
VOTE ERICA COLEMAN
MOM? ARE YOU STILL THERE?
MOM?

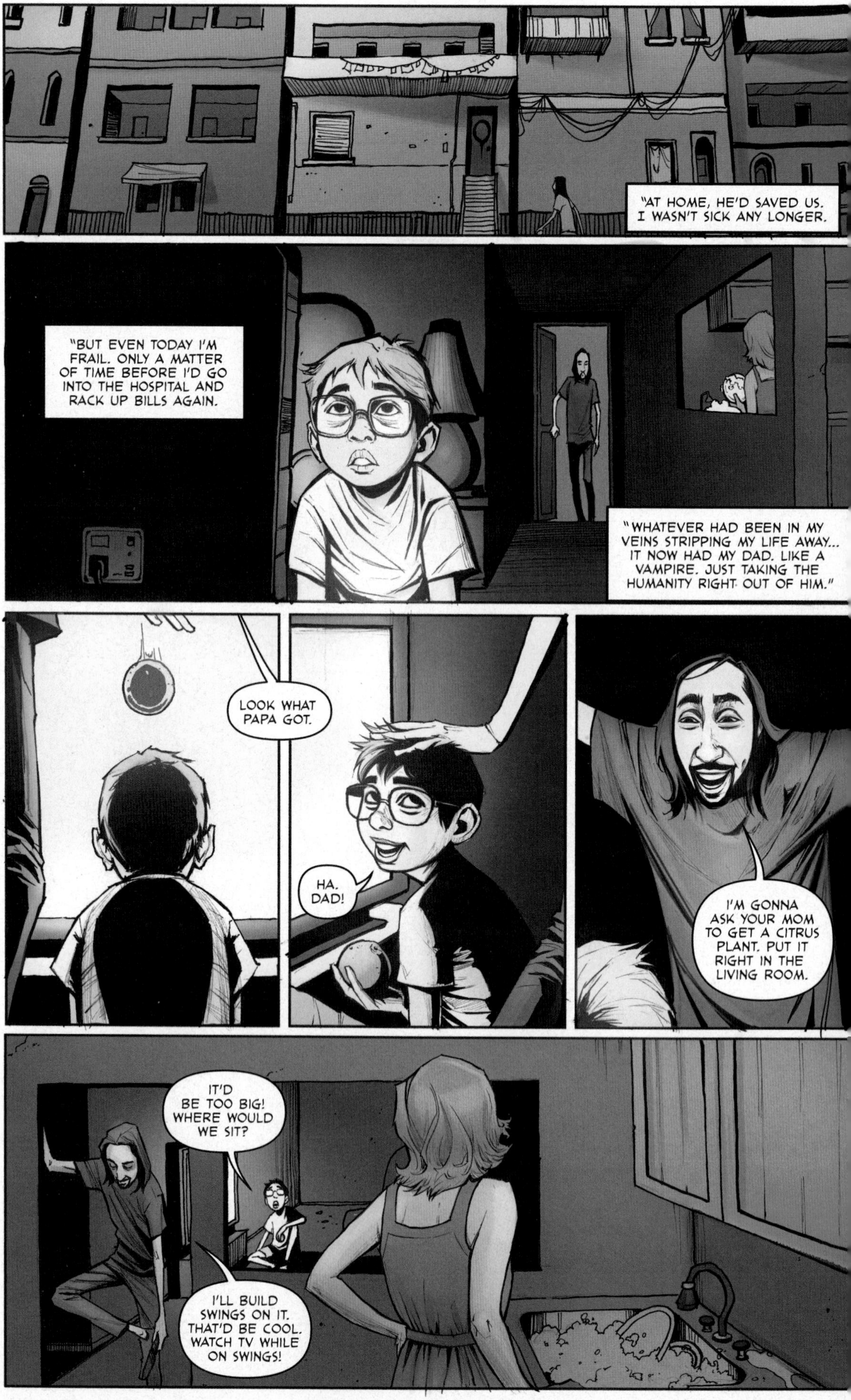
"AT HOME, HE'D SAVED US. I WASN'T SICK ANY LONGER.
"BUT EVEN TODAY I'M FRAIL. ONLY A MATTER OF TIME BEFORE I'D GO INTO THE HOSPITAL AND RACK UP BILLS AGAIN.
"WHATEVER HAD BEEN IN MY VEINS STRIPPING MY LIFE AWAY... IT NOW HAD MY DAD. LIKE A VAMPIRE. JUST TAKING THE HUMANITY RIGHT OUT OF HIM."
LOOK WHAT PAPA GOT.
HA. DAD!
I'M GONNA ASK YOUR MOM TO GET A CITRUS PLANT. PUT IT RIGHT IN THE LIVING ROOM.
IT'D BE TOO BIG! WHERE WOULD WE SIT?
I'LL BUILD SWINGS ON IT. THAT'D BE COOL. WATCH TV WHILE ON SWINGS!

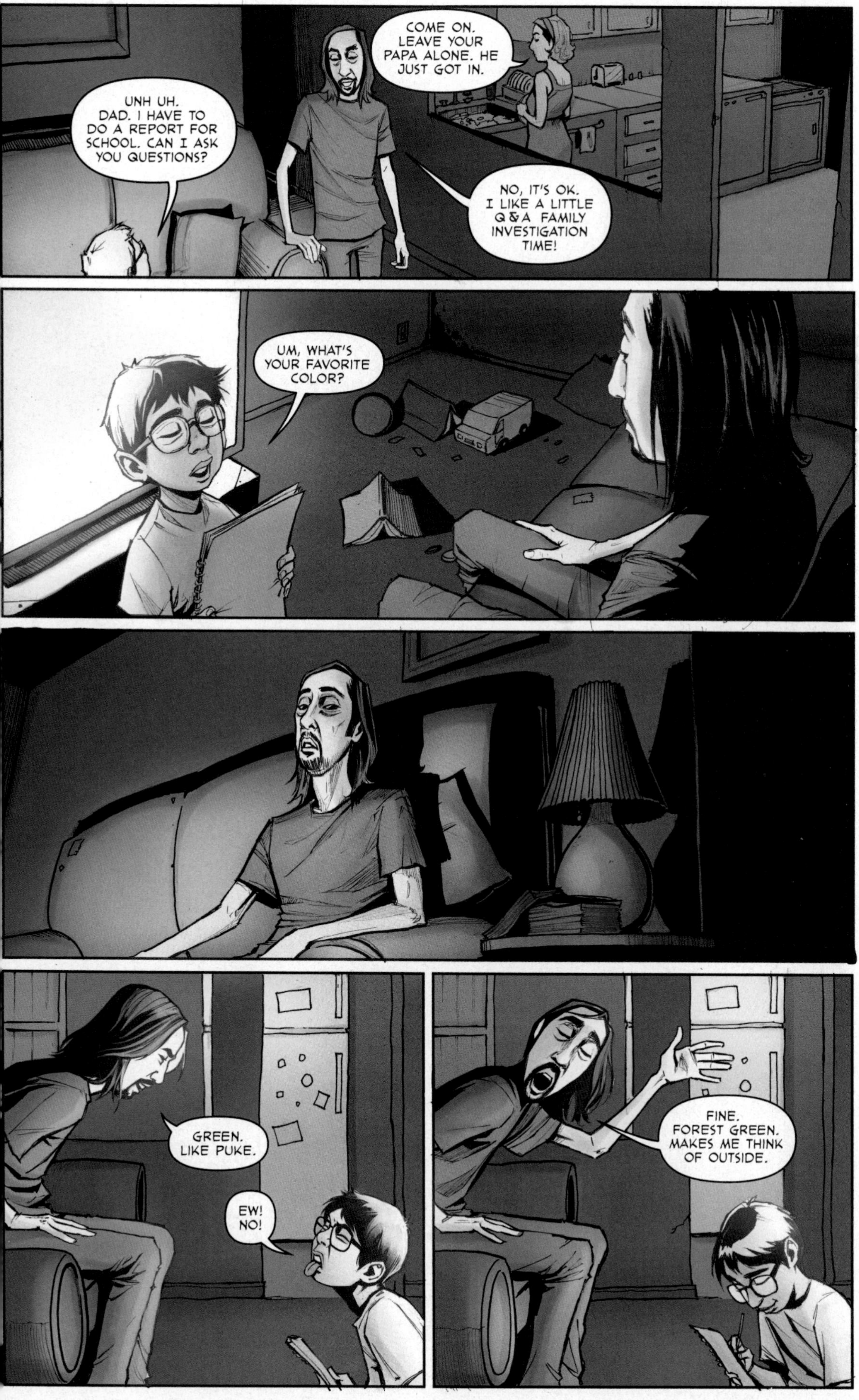
UNH UH.
DAD. I HAVE TO DO A REPORT FOR SCHOOL. CAN I ASK YOU QUESTIONS?
COME ON. LEAVE YOUR PAPA ALONE. HE JUST GOT IN.
NO, IT'S OK. I LIKE A LITTLE Q&A FAMILY INVESTIGATION TIME!
UM, WHAT'S YOUR FAVORITE COLOR?
GREEN. LIKE PUKE.
EW! NO!
FINE. FOREST GREEN. MAKES ME THINK OF OUTSIDE.

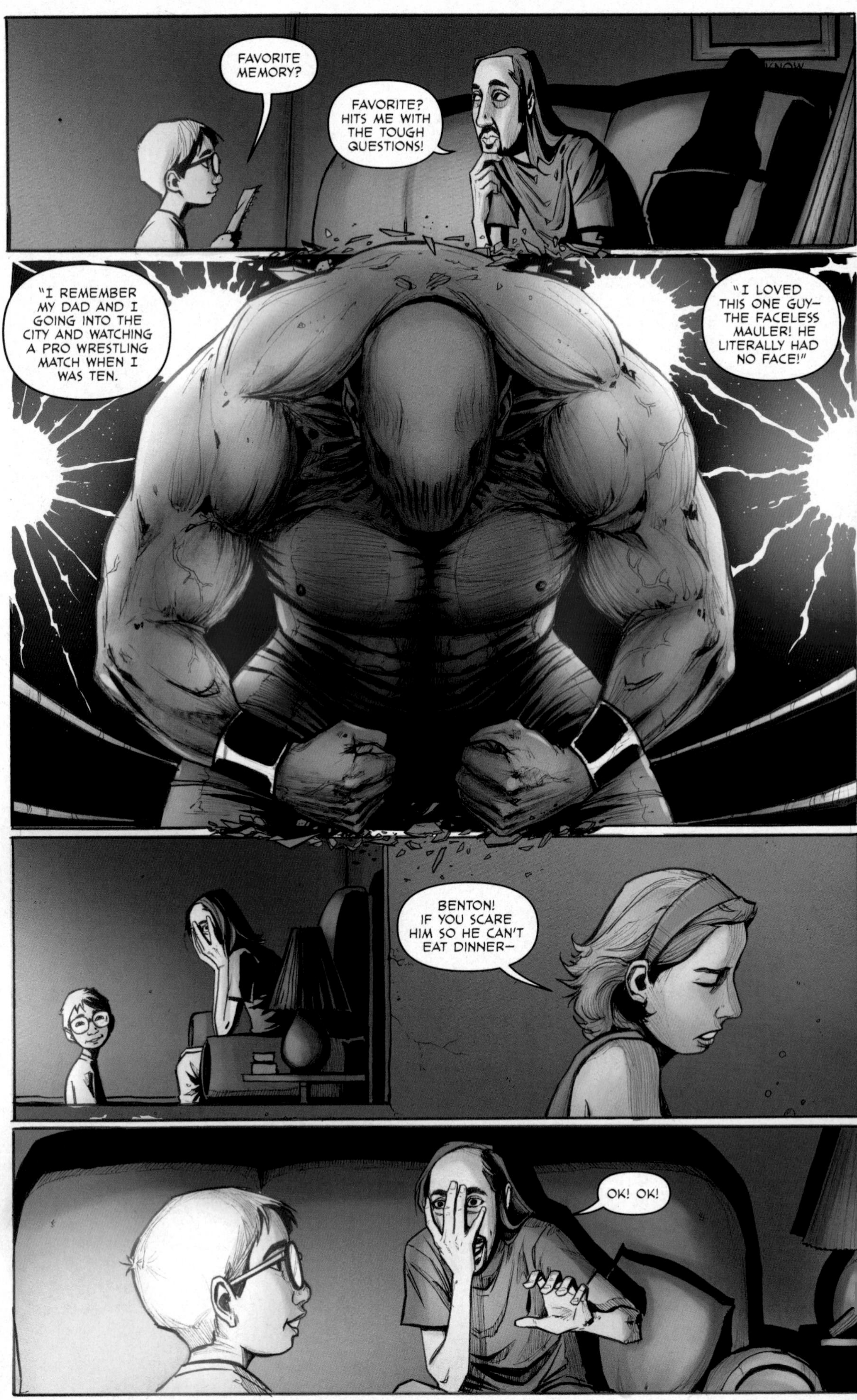
FAVORITE MEMORY?
FAVORITE? HITS ME WITH THE TOUGH QUESTIONS!
"I REMEMBER MY DAD AND I GOING INTO THE CITY AND WATCHING A PRO WRESTLING MATCH WHEN I WAS TEN.
"I LOVED THIS ONE GUY— THE FACELESS MAULER! HE LITERALLY HAD NO FACE!"
BENTON! IF YOU SCARE HIM SO HE CAN'T EAT DINNER—
OK! OK!

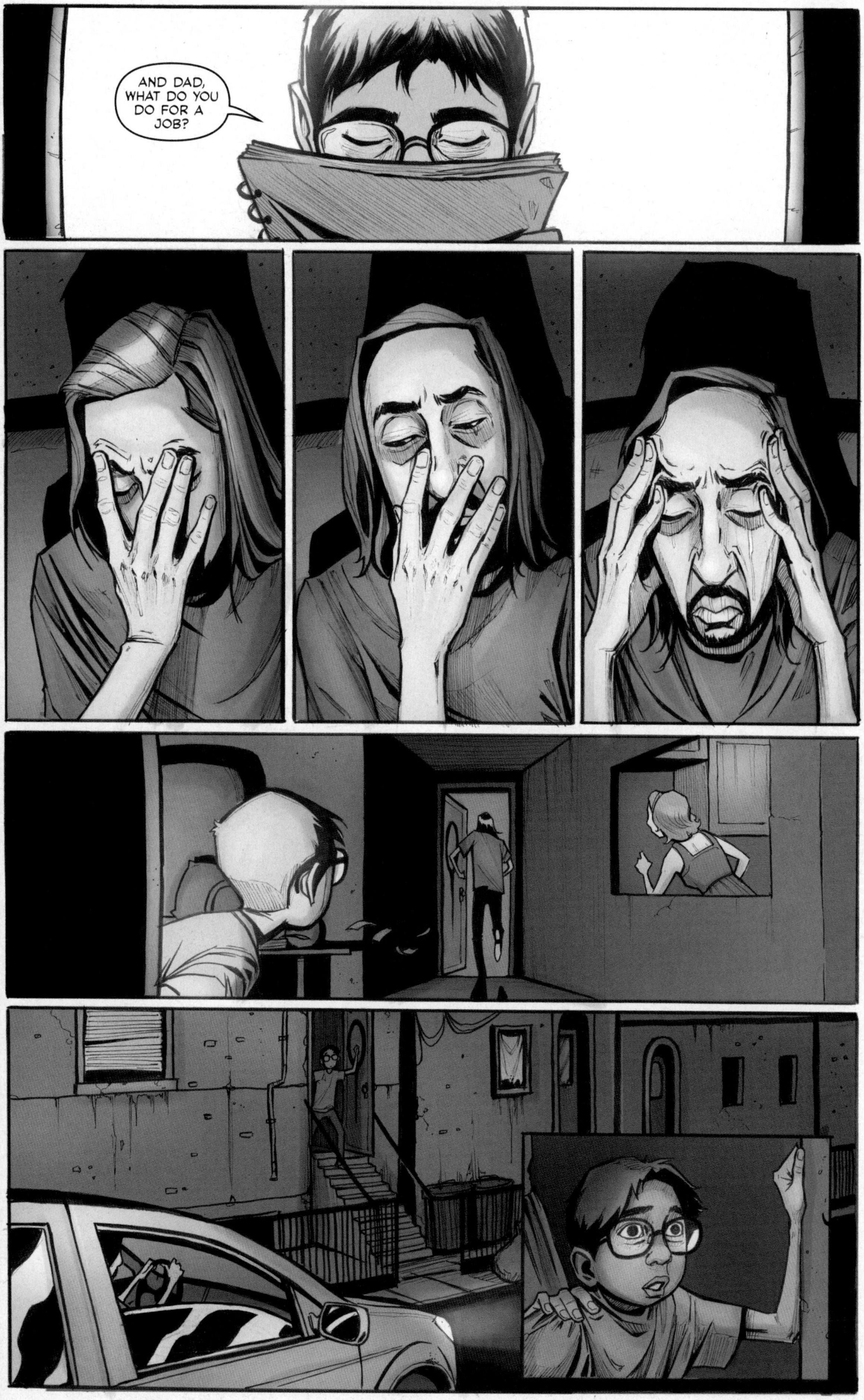
AND DAD, WHAT DO YOU DO FOR A JOB?

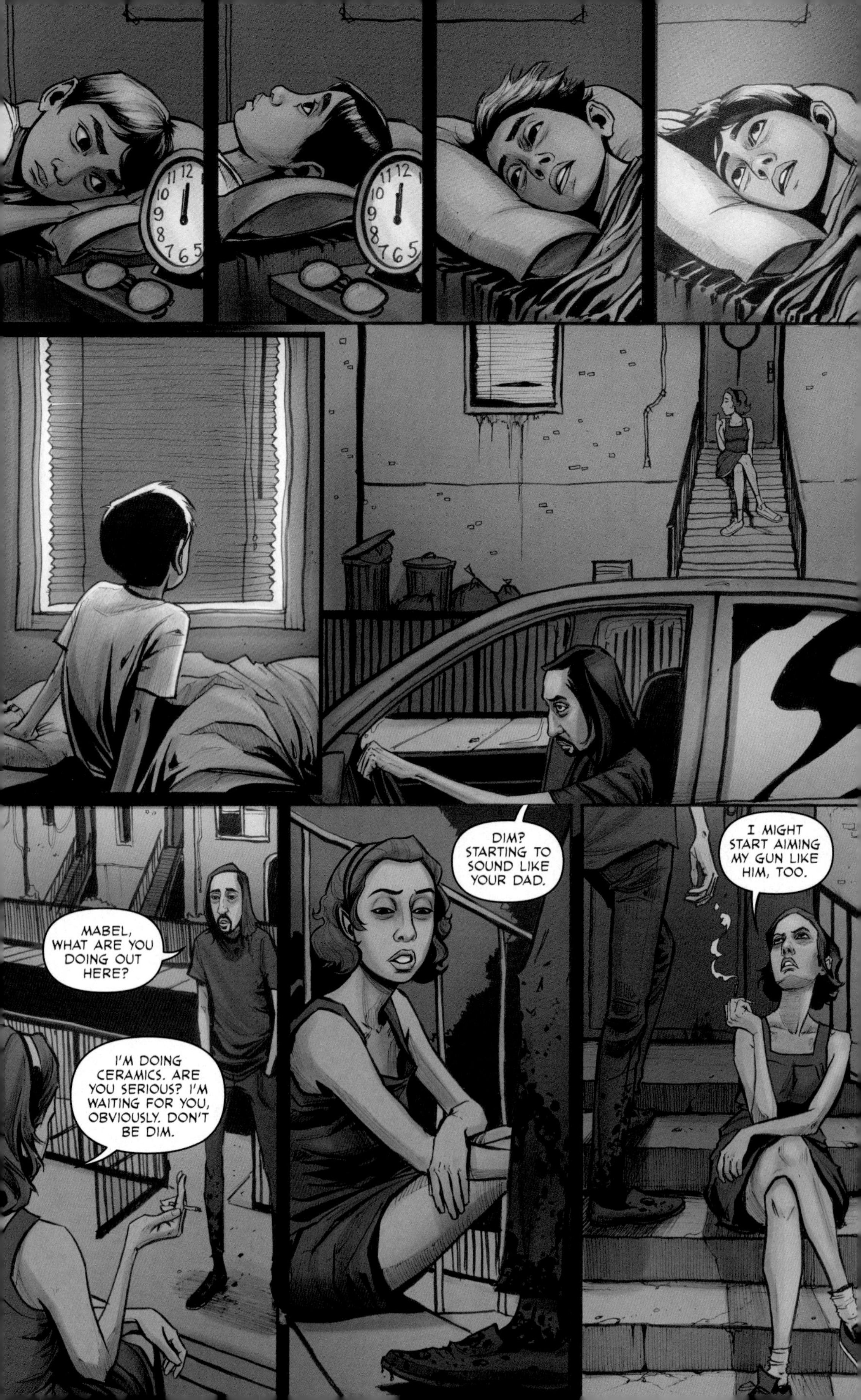
MABEL, WHAT ARE YOU DOING OUT HERE?
I'M DOING CERAMICS. ARE YOU SERIOUS? I'M WAITING FOR YOU, OBVIOUSLY. DON'T BE DIM.
DIM? STARTING TO SOUND LIKE YOUR DAD.
I MIGHT START AIMING MY GUN LIKE HIM, TOO.

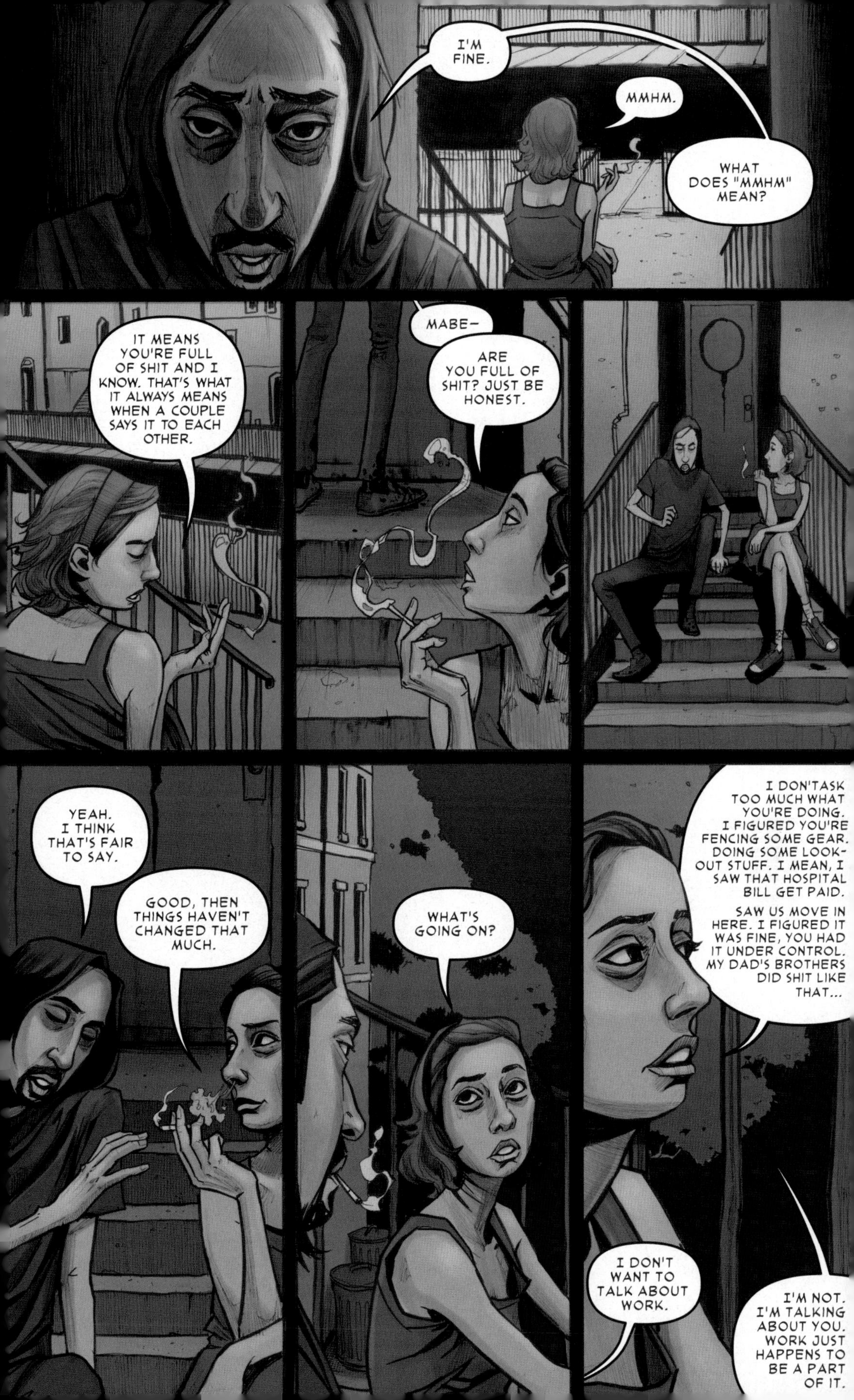
I'M FINE.
MMHM.
WHAT DOES "MMHM" MEAN?
IT MEANS YOU'RE FULL OF SHIT AND I KNOW. THAT'S WHAT IT ALWAYS MEANS WHEN A COUPLE SAYS IT TO EACH OTHER.
MABE—
ARE YOU FULL OF SHIT? JUST BE HONEST.
YEAH. I THINK THAT'S FAIR TO SAY.
GOOD, THEN THINGS HAVEN'T CHANGED THAT MUCH.
WHAT'S GOING ON?
I DON'TASK TOO MUCH WHAT YOU'RE DOING. I FIGURED YOU'RE FENCING SOME GEAR. DOING SOME LOOK-OUT STUFF. I MEAN, I SAW THAT HOSPITAL BILL GET PAID.
SAW US MOVE IN HERE. I FIGURED IT WAS FINE, YOU HAD IT UNDER CONTROL. MY DAD'S BROTHERS DID SHIT LIKE THAT...
I DON'T WANT TO TALK ABOUT WORK.
I'M NOT. I'M TALKING ABOUT YOU. WORK JUST HAPPENS TO BE A PART OF IT.

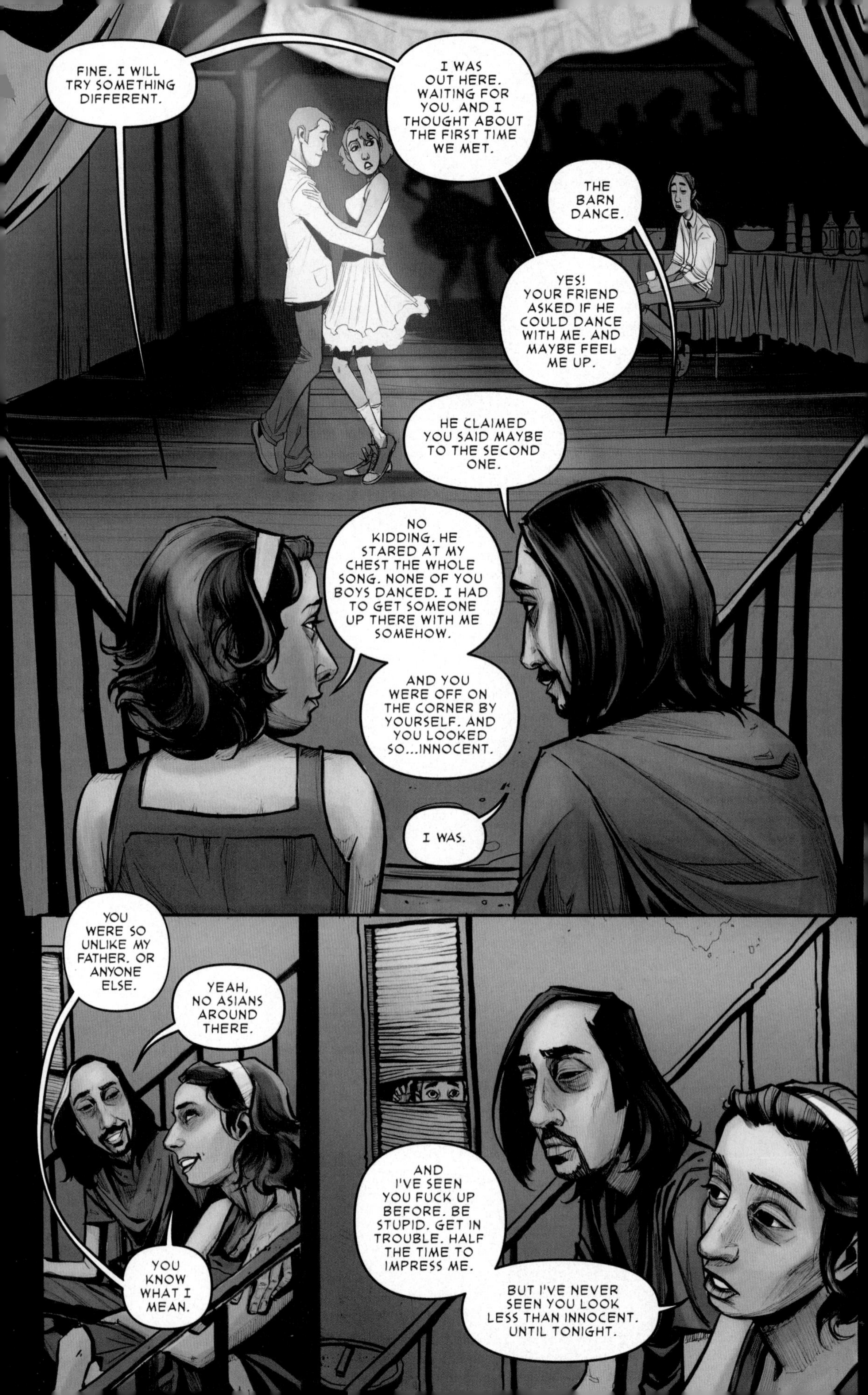
FINE. I WILL TRY SOMETHING DIFFERENT.
I WAS OUT HERE. WAITING FOR YOU. AND I THOUGHT ABOUT THE FIRST TIME WE MET.
THE BARN DANCE.
YES! YOUR FRIEND ASKED IF HE COULD DANCE WITH ME. AND MAYBE FEEL ME UP.
HE CLAIMED YOU SAID MAYBE TO THE SECOND ONE.
NO KIDDING. HE STARED AT MY CHEST THE WHOLE SONG. NONE OF YOU BOYS DANCED. I HAD TO GET SOMEONE UP THERE WITH ME SOMEHOW.
AND YOU WERE OFF ON THE CORNER BY YOURSELF. AND YOU LOOKED SO...INNOCENT.
I WAS.
YOU WERE SO UNLIKE MY FATHER. OR ANYONE ELSE.
YEAH, NO ASIANS AROUND THERE.
YOU KNOW WHAT I MEAN.
AND I'VE SEEN YOU FUCK UP BEFORE. BE STUPID. GET IN TROUBLE. HALF THE TIME TO IMPRESS ME.
BUT I'VE NEVER SEEN YOU LOOK LESS THAN INNOCENT. UNTIL TONIGHT.

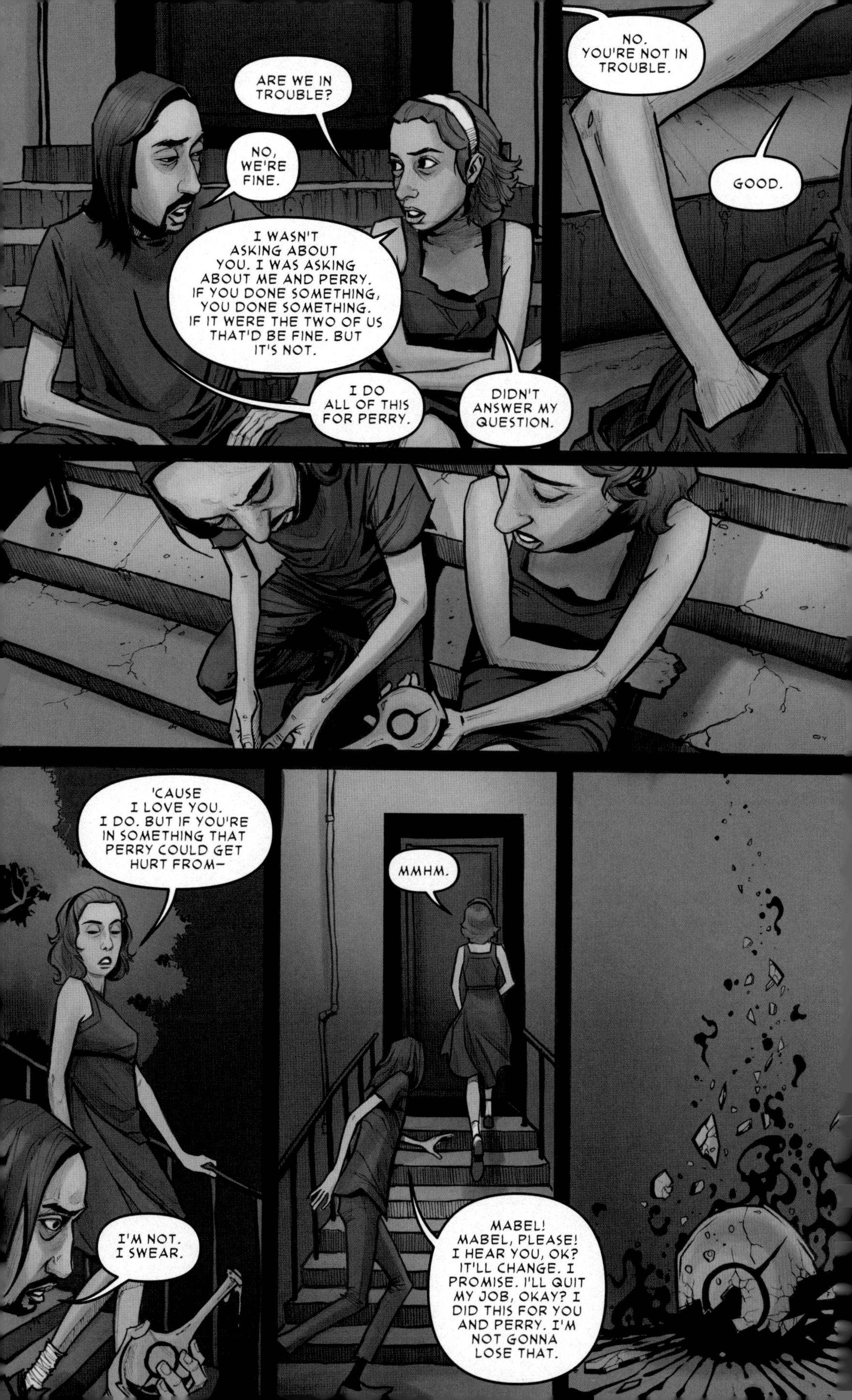
ARE WE IN TROUBLE?
NO, WE'RE FINE.
I WASN'T ASKING ABOUT YOU. I WAS ASKING ABOUT ME AND PERRY. IF YOU DONE SOMETHING, YOU DONE SOMETHING. IF IT WERE THE TWO OF US THAT'D BE FINE. BUT IT'S NOT.
I DO ALL OF THIS FOR PERRY.
DIDN'T ANSWER MY QUESTION.
NO. YOU'RE NOT IN TROUBLE.
GOOD.
'CAUSE I LOVE YOU. I DO. BUT IF YOU'RE IN SOMETHING THAT PERRY COULD GET HURT FROM—
I'M NOT. I SWEAR.
MMHM.
MABEL! MABEL, PLEASE! I HEAR YOU, OK? IT'LL CHANGE. I PROMISE. I'LL QUIT MY JOB, OKAY? I DID THIS FOR YOU AND PERRY. I'M NOT GONNA LOSE THAT.

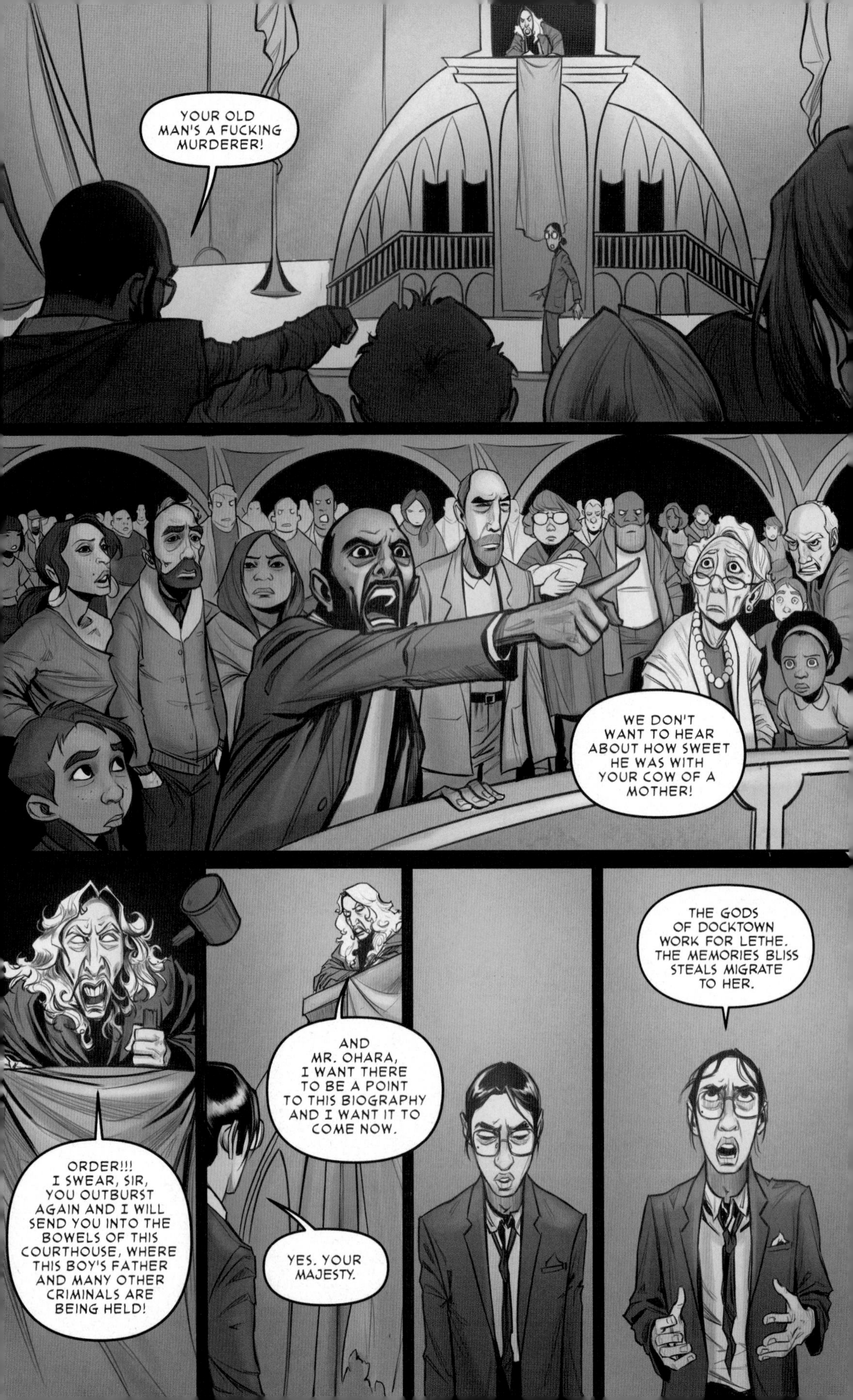
YOUR OLD MAN'S A FUCKING MURDERER!
WE DON'T WANT TO HEAR ABOUT HOW SWEET HE WAS WITH YOUR COW OF A MOTHER!
ORDER!!! I SWEAR, SIR, YOU OUTBURST AGAIN AND I WILL SEND YOU INTO THE BOWELS OF THIS COURTHOUSE, WHERE THIS BOY'S FATHER AND MANY OTHER CRIMINALS ARE BEING HELD!
AND MR. OHARA, I WANT THERE TO BE A POINT TO THIS BIOGRAPHY AND I WANT IT TO COME NOW.
YES. YOUR MAJESTY.
THE GODS OF DOCKTOWN WORK FOR LETHE. THE MEMORIES BLISS STEALS MIGRATE TO HER.

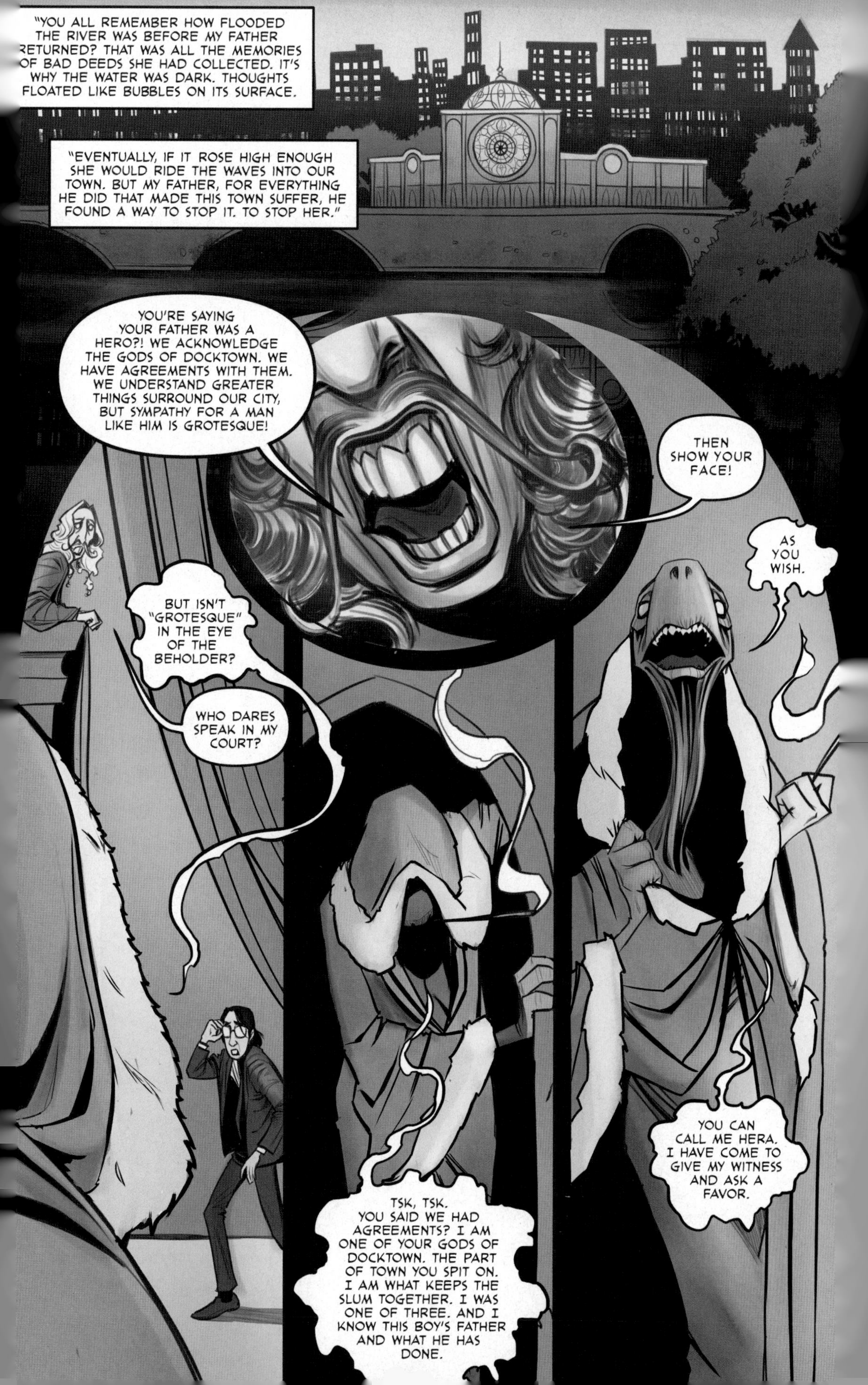
"YOU ALL REMEMBER HOW FLOODED THE RIVER WAS BEFORE MY FATHER RETURNED? THAT WAS ALL THE MEMORIES OF BAD DEEDS SHE HAD COLLECTED. IT'S WHY THE WATER WAS DARK. THOUGHTS FLOATED LIKE BUBBLES ON ITS SURFACE.
"EVENTUALLY, IF IT ROSE HIGH ENOUGH SHE WOULD RIDE THE WAVES INTO OUR TOWN. BUT MY FATHER, FOR EVERYTHING HE DID THAT MADE THIS TOWN SUFFER, HE FOUND A WAY TO STOP IT. TO STOP HER."
YOU'RE SAYING YOUR FATHER WAS A HERO?! WE ACKNOWLEDGE THE GODS OF DOCKTOWN. WE HAVE AGREEMENTS WITH THEM. WE UNDERSTAND GREATER THINGS SURROUND OUR CITY, BUT SYMPATHY FOR A MAN LIKE HIM IS GROTESQUE!
BUT ISN'T "GROTESQUE" IN THE EYE OF THE BEHOLDER?
WHO DARES SPEAK IN MY COURT?
THEN SHOW YOUR FACE!
AS YOU WISH.
TSK, TSK. YOU SAID WE HAD AGREEMENTS? I AM ONE OF YOUR GODS OF DOCKTOWN. THE PART OF TOWN YOU SPIT ON. I AM WHAT KEEPS THE SLUM TOGETHER. I WAS ONE OF THREE. AND I KNOW THIS BOY'S FATHER AND WHAT HE HAS DONE.
YOU CAN CALL ME HERA. I HAVE COME TO GIVE MY WITNESS AND ASK A FAVOR.

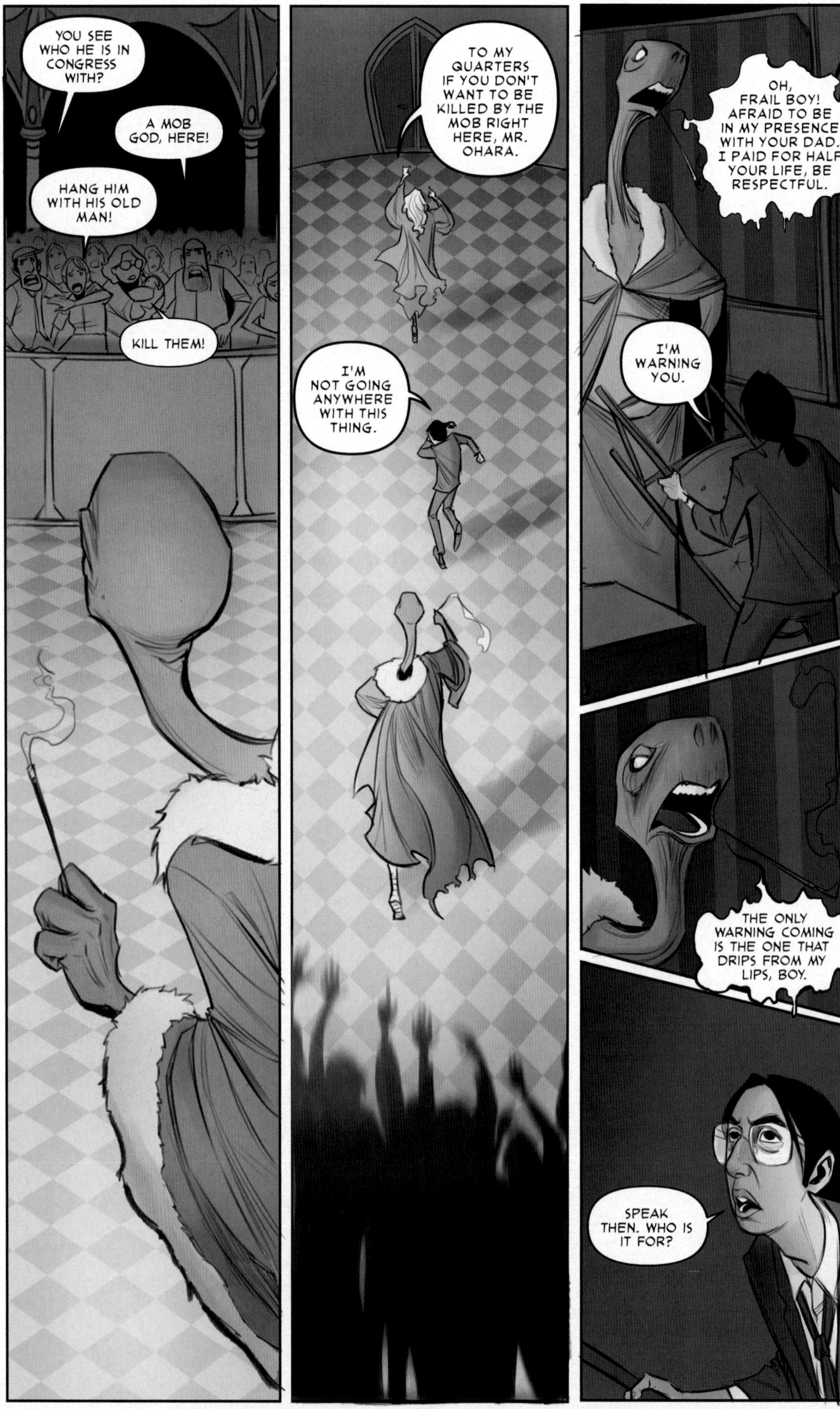
YOU SEE WHO HE IS IN CONGRESS WITH?
A MOB GOD, HERE!
HANG HIM WITH HIS OLD MAN!
KILL THEM!
TO MY QUARTERS IF YOU DON'T WANT TO BE KILLED BY THE MOB RIGHT HERE, MR. OHARA.
I'M NOT GOING ANYWHERE WITH THIS THING.
OH, FRAIL BOY! AFRAID TO BE IN MY PRESENCE WITH YOUR DAD. I PAID FOR HALF YOUR LIFE, BE RESPECTFUL.
I'M WARNING YOU.
THE ONLY WARNING COMING IS THE ONE THAT DRIPS FROM MY LIPS, BOY.
SPEAK THEN. WHO IS IT FOR?

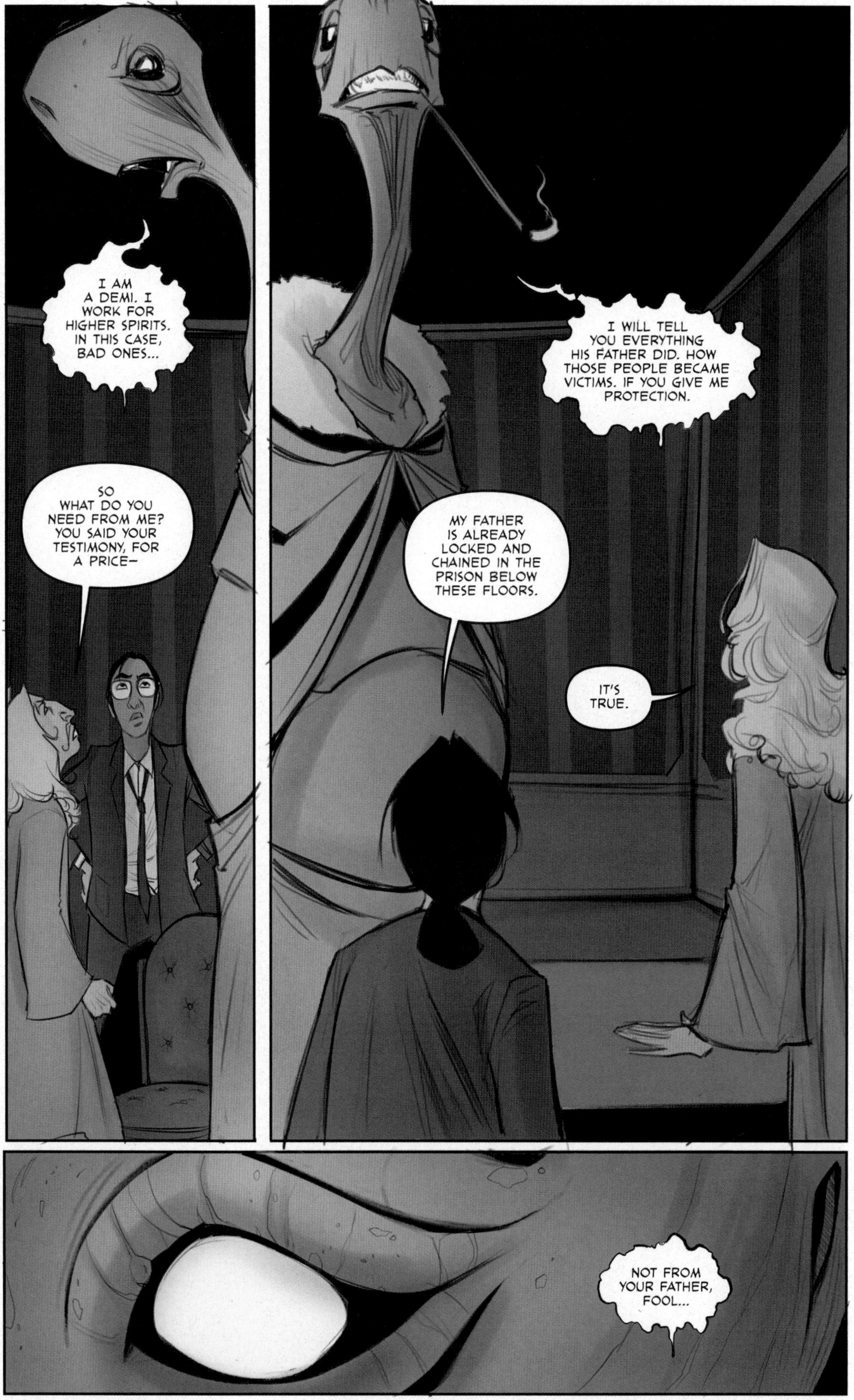
I AM A DEMI. I WORK FOR HIGHER SPIRITS. IN THIS CASE, BAD ONES...
I WILL TELL YOU EVERYTHING HIS FATHER DID. HOW THOSE PEOPLE BECAME VICTIMS. IF YOU GIVE ME PROTECTION.
SO WHAT DO YOU NEED FROM ME? YOU SAID YOUR TESTIMONY, FOR A PRICE–
MY FATHER IS ALREADY LOCKED AND CHAINED IN THE PRISON BELOW THESE FLOORS.
IT'S TRUE.
NOT FROM YOUR FATHER, FOOL...

"FROM LETHE.
GOD OF OBLIVION.
AND MY FORMER
MASTER."

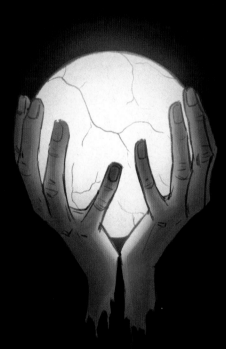

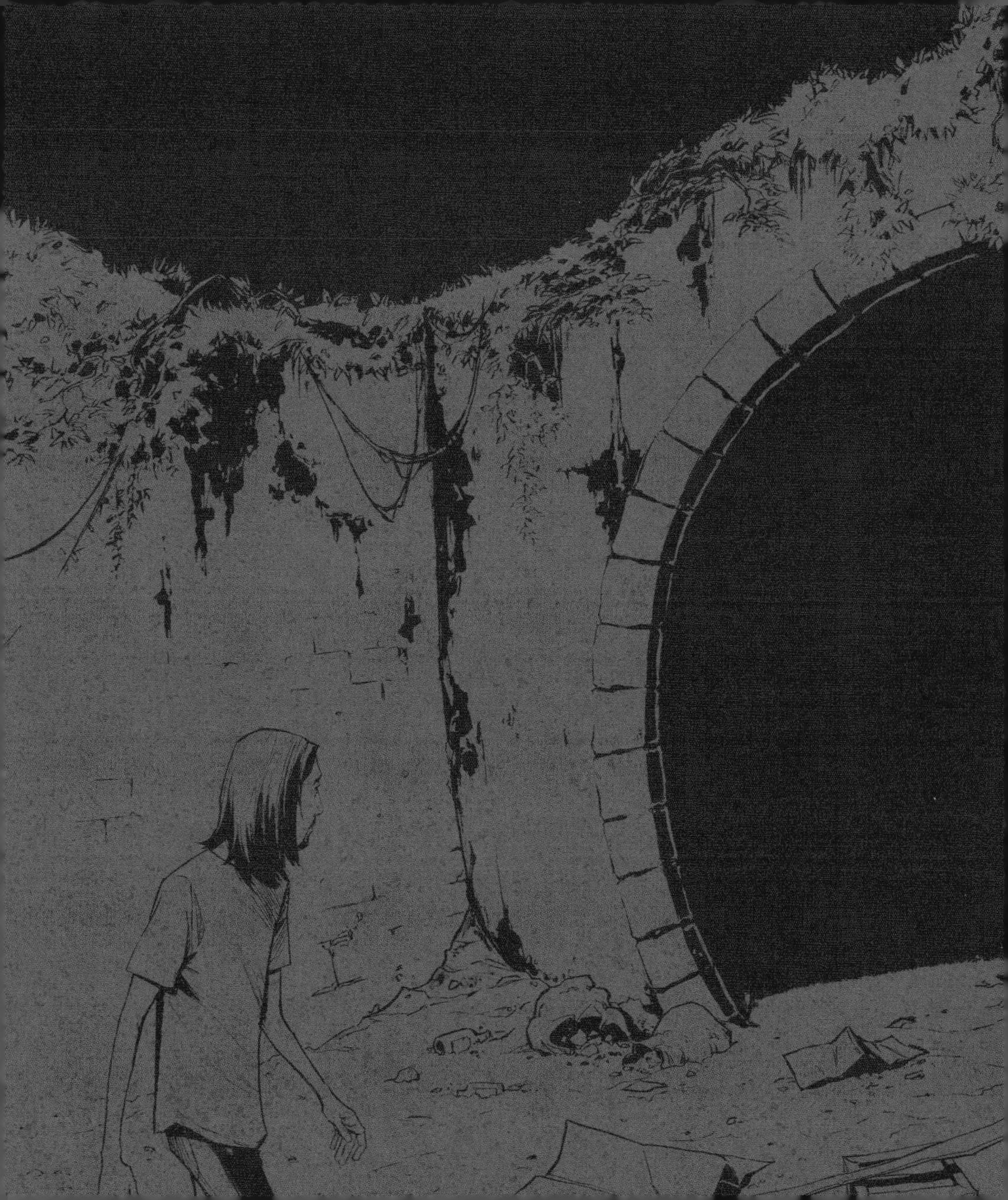

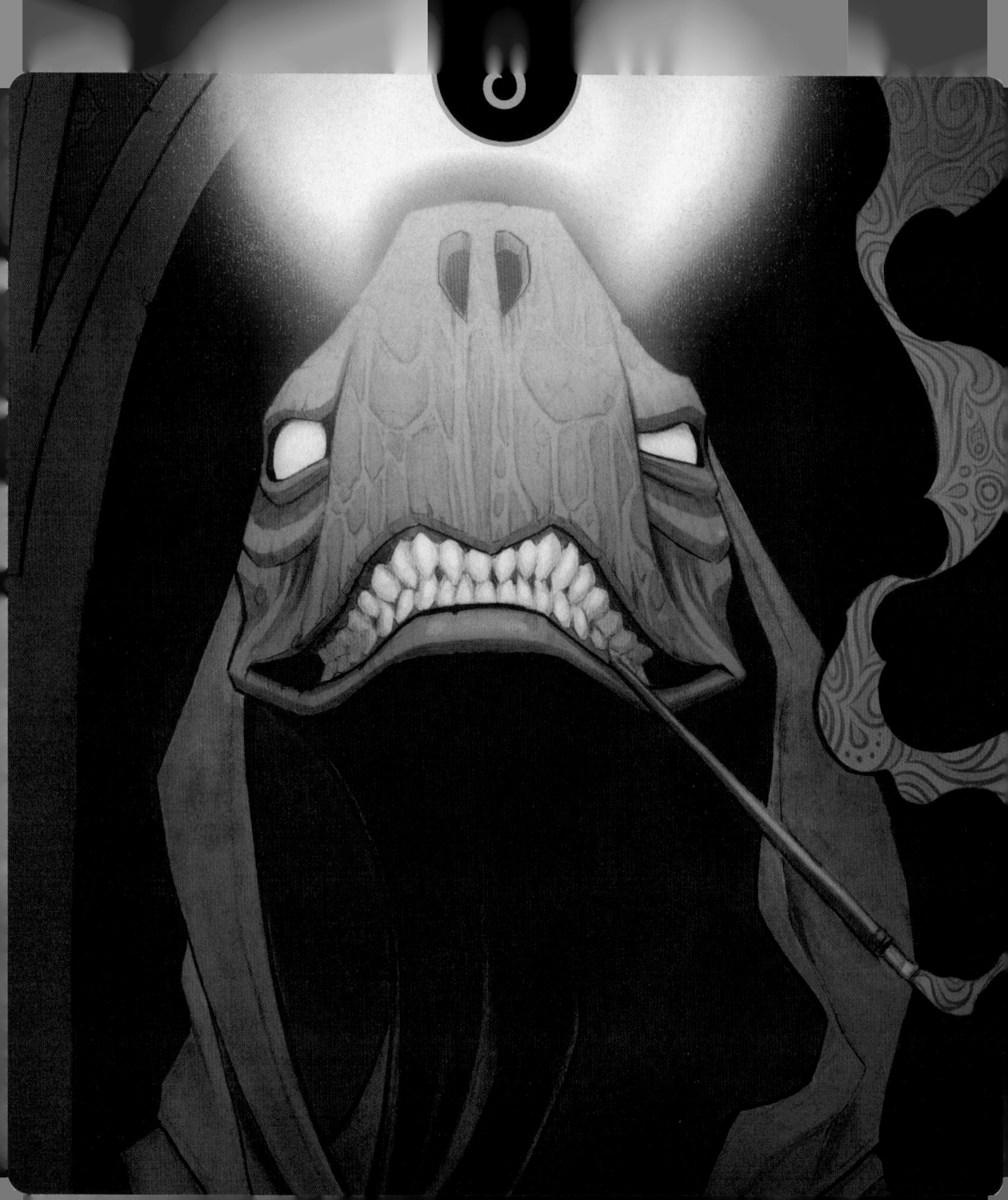

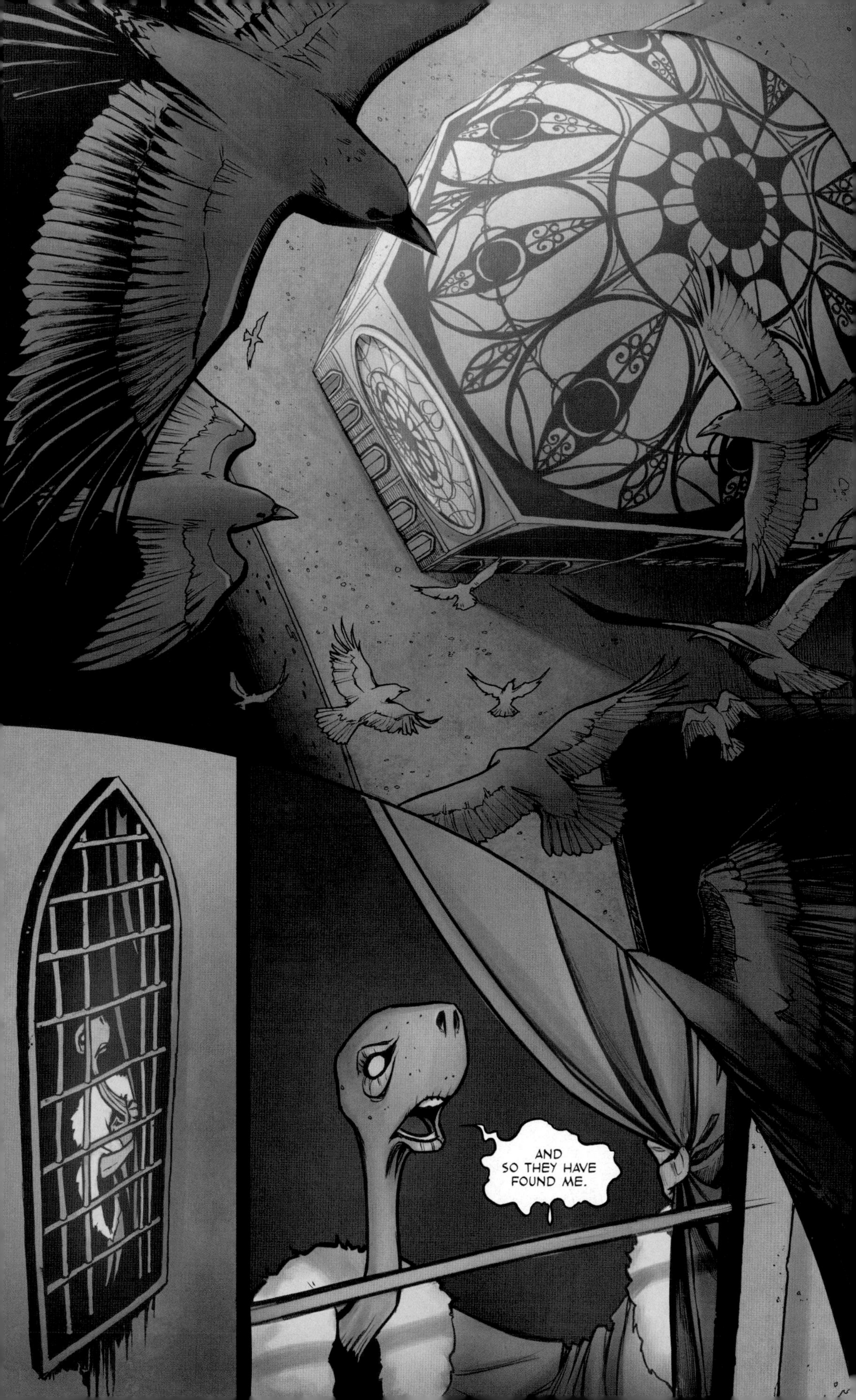
AND SO THEY HAVE FOUND ME.

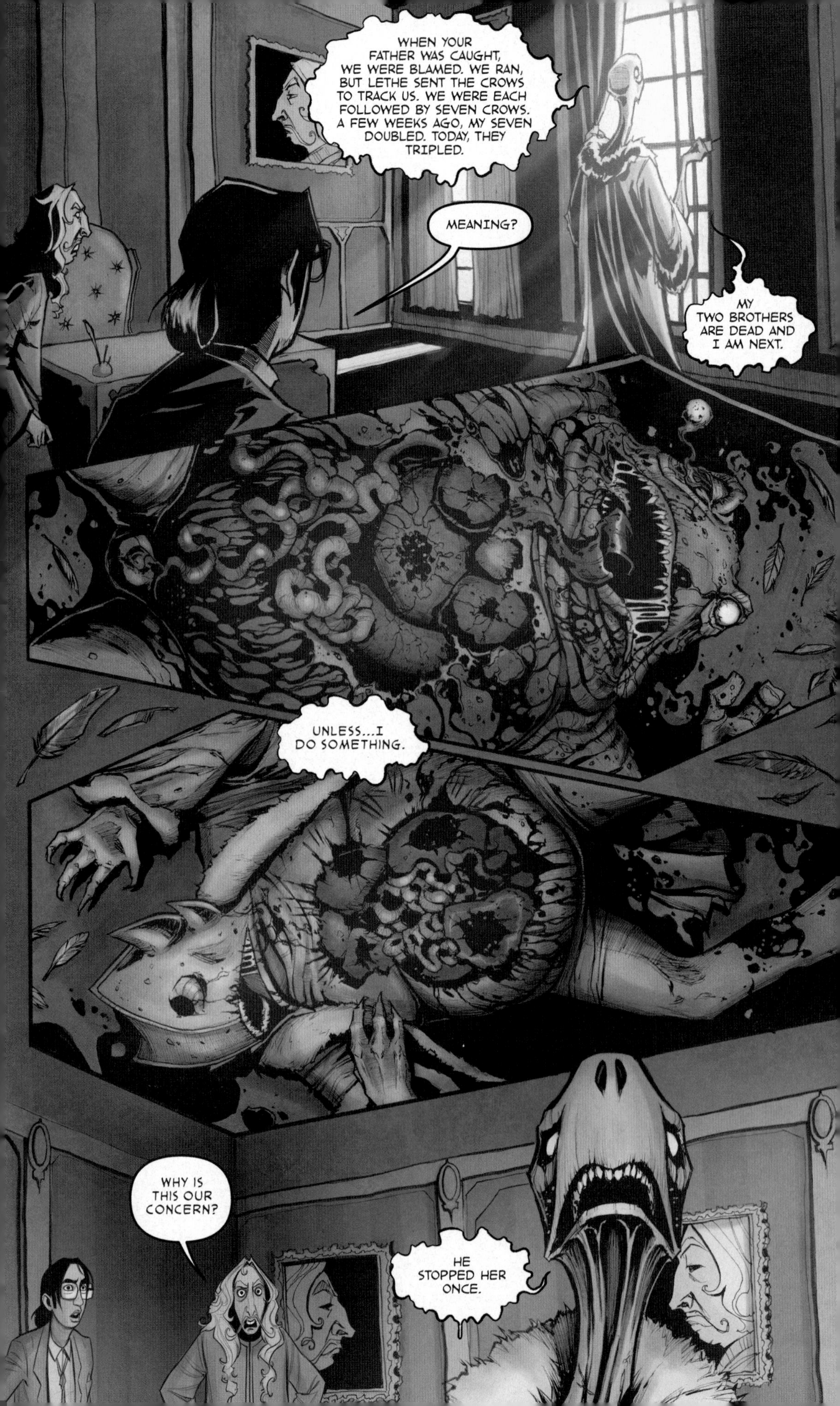
WHEN YOUR FATHER WAS CAUGHT, WE WERE BLAMED. WE RAN, BUT LETHE SENT THE CROWS TO TRACK US. WE WERE EACH FOLLOWED BY SEVEN CROWS. A FEW WEEKS AGO, MY SEVEN DOUBLED. TODAY, THEY TRIPLED.
MEANING?
MY TWO BROTHERS ARE DEAD AND I AM NEXT.
UNLESS...I DO SOMETHING.
WHY IS THIS OUR CONCERN?
HE STOPPED HER ONCE.

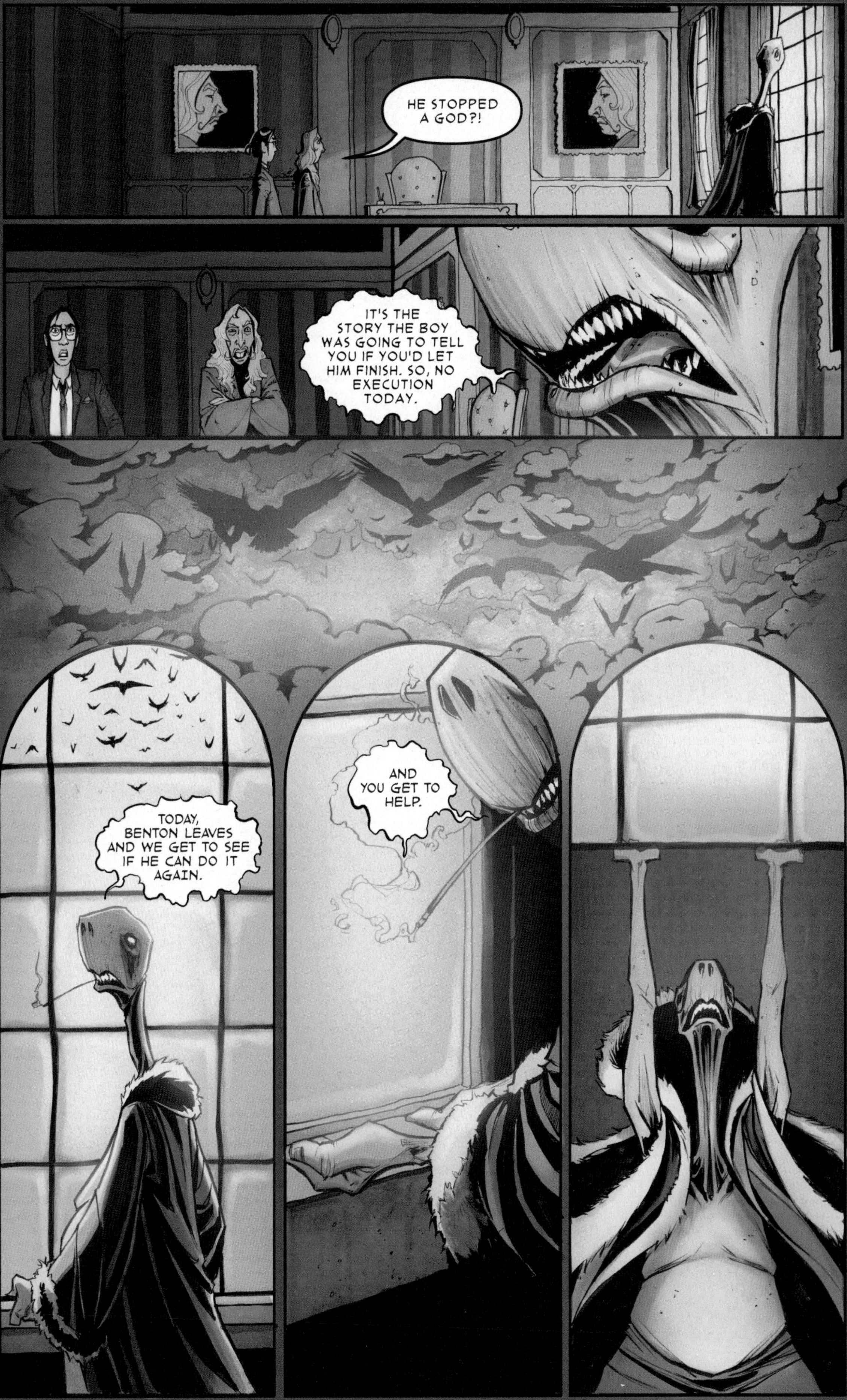
HE STOPPED A GOD?!
IT'S THE STORY THE BOY WAS GOING TO TELL YOU IF YOU'D LET HIM FINISH. SO, NO EXECUTION TODAY.
TODAY, BENTON LEAVES AND WE GET TO SEE IF HE CAN DO IT AGAIN.
AND YOU GET TO HELP.

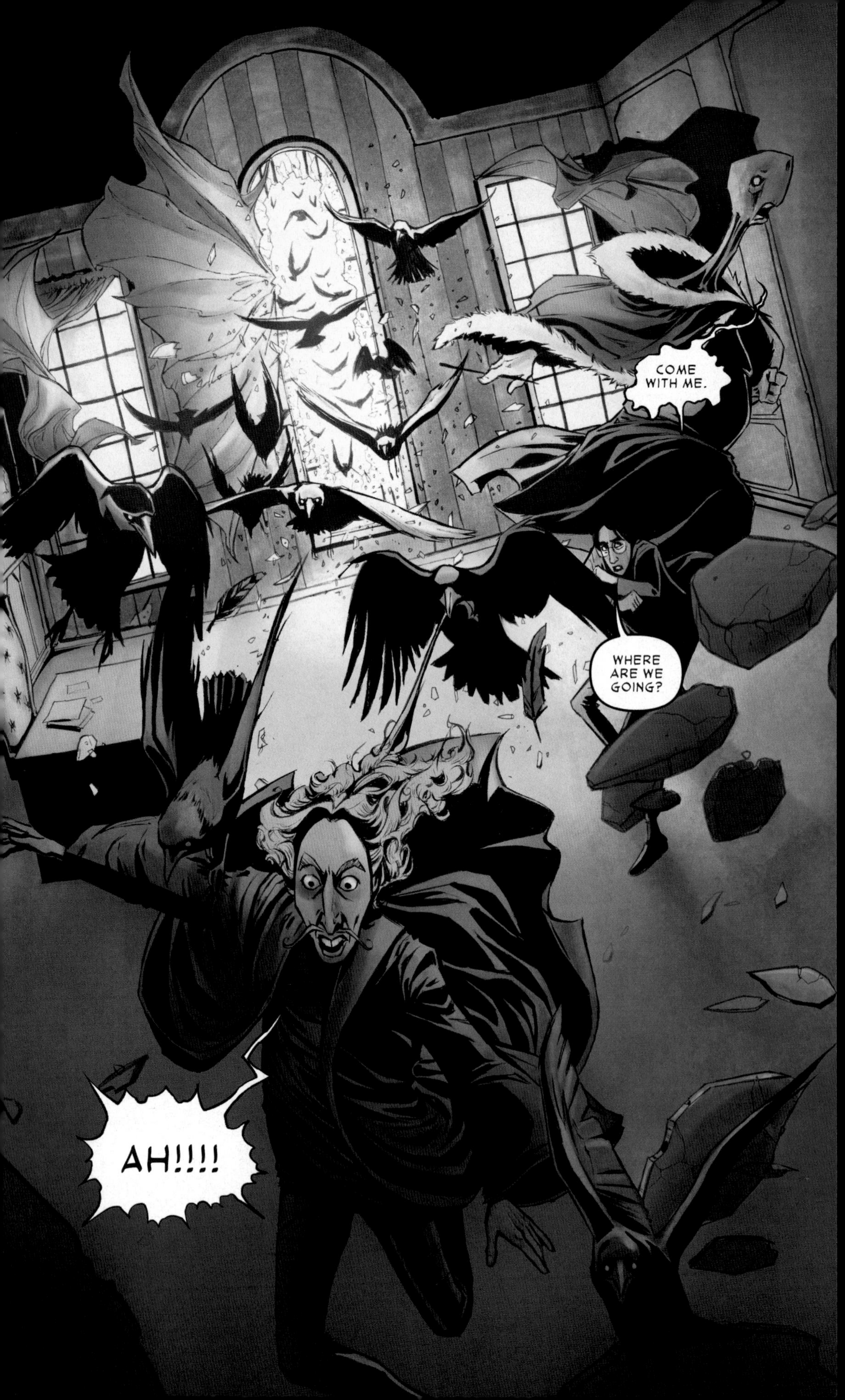
COME WITH ME.
WHERE ARE WE GOING?
AH!!!!

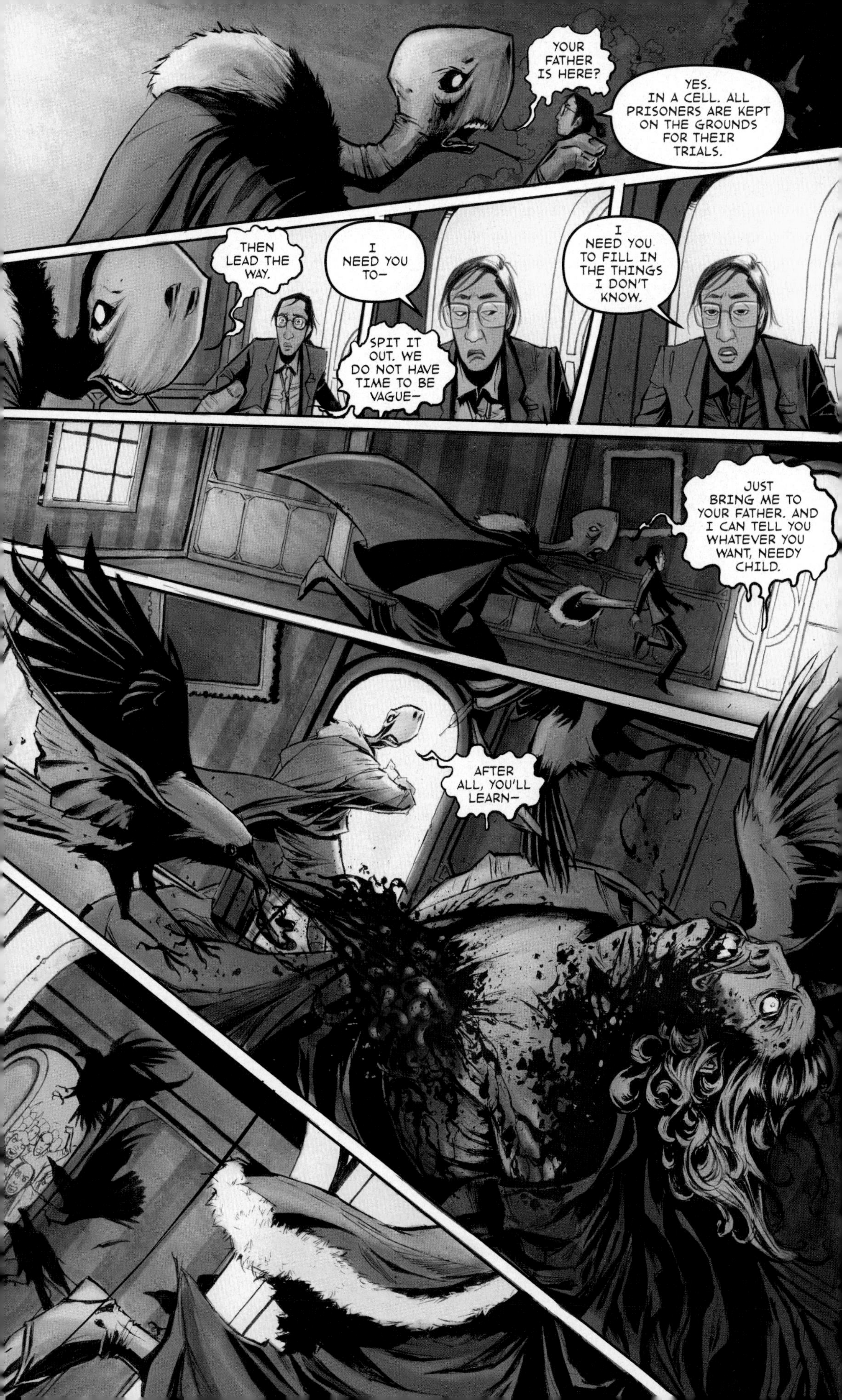

YOUR FATHER IS HERE?
YES. IN A CELL. ALL PRISONERS ARE KEPT ON THE GROUNDS FOR THEIR TRIALS.
THEN LEAD THE WAY.
I NEED YOU TO—
SPIT IT OUT. WE DO NOT HAVE TIME TO BE VAGUE—
I NEED YOU TO FILL IN THE THINGS I DON'T KNOW.
JUST BRING ME TO YOUR FATHER. AND I CAN TELL YOU WHATEVER YOU WANT, NEEDY CHILD.
AFTER ALL, YOU'LL LEARN—

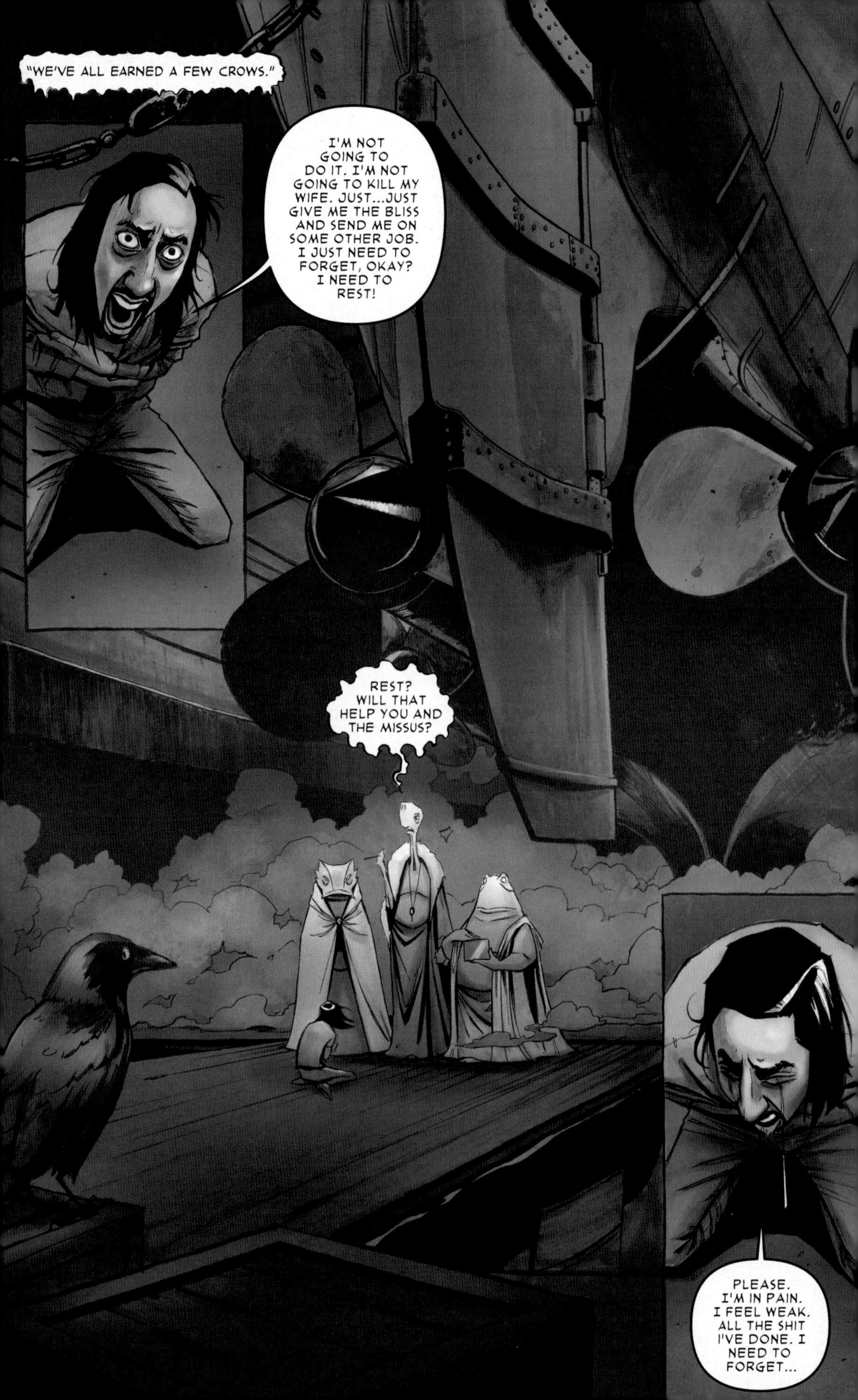
"WE'VE ALL EARNED A FEW CROWS."
I'M NOT GOING TO DO IT. I'M NOT GOING TO KILL MY WIFE. JUST...JUST GIVE ME THE BLISS AND SEND ME ON SOME OTHER JOB. I JUST NEED TO FORGET, OKAY? I NEED TO REST!
REST? WILL THAT HELP YOU AND THE MISSUS?
PLEASE. I'M IN PAIN. I FEEL WEAK. ALL THE SHIT I'VE DONE. I NEED TO FORGET...

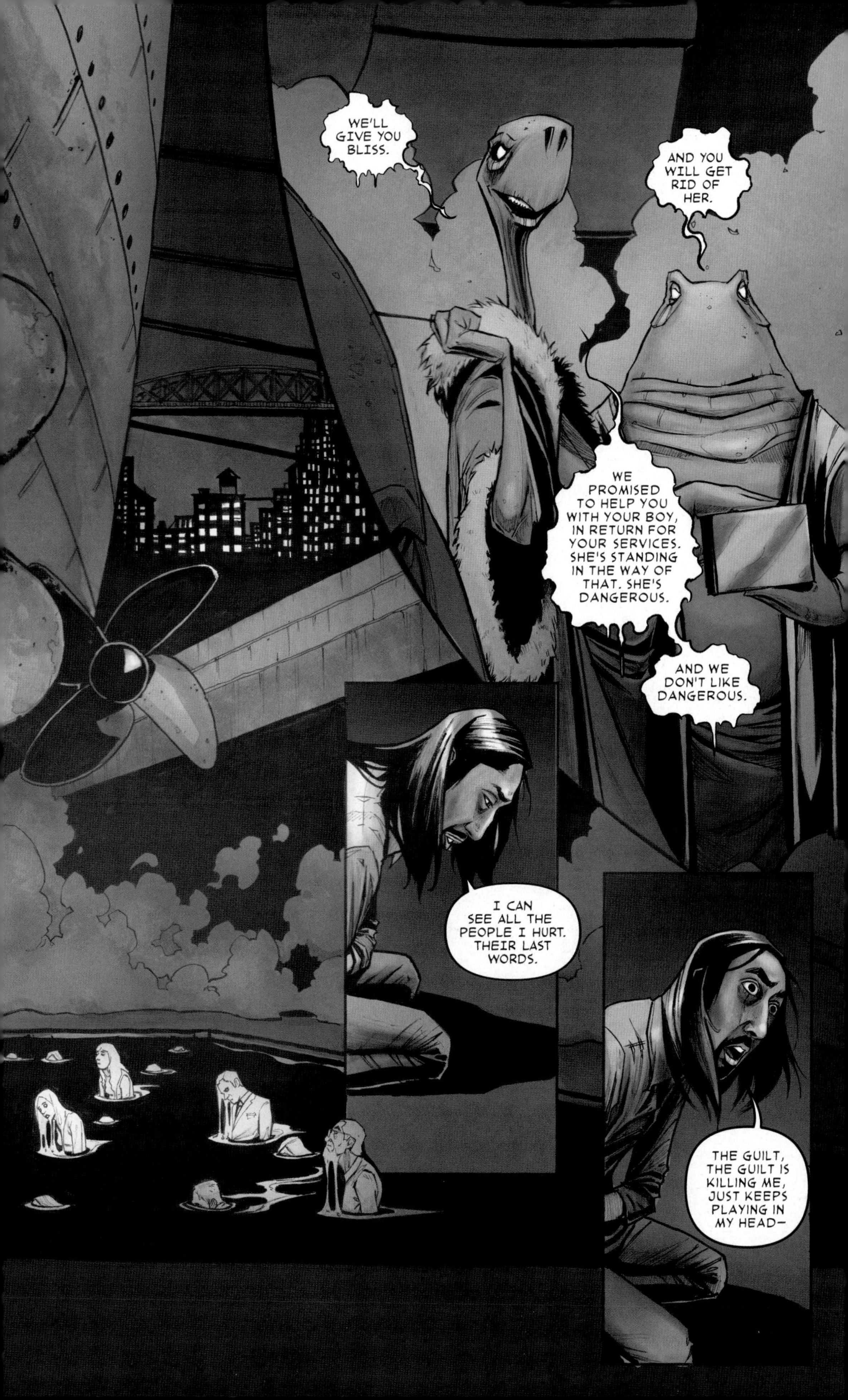
WE'LL GIVE YOU BLISS.
AND YOU WILL GET RID OF HER.
WE PROMISED TO HELP YOU WITH YOUR BOY, IN RETURN FOR YOUR SERVICES. SHE'S STANDING IN THE WAY OF THAT. SHE'S DANGEROUS.
AND WE DON'T LIKE DANGEROUS.
I CAN SEE ALL THE PEOPLE I HURT. THEIR LAST WORDS.
THE GUILT, THE GUILT IS KILLING ME, JUST KEEPS PLAYING IN MY HEAD—

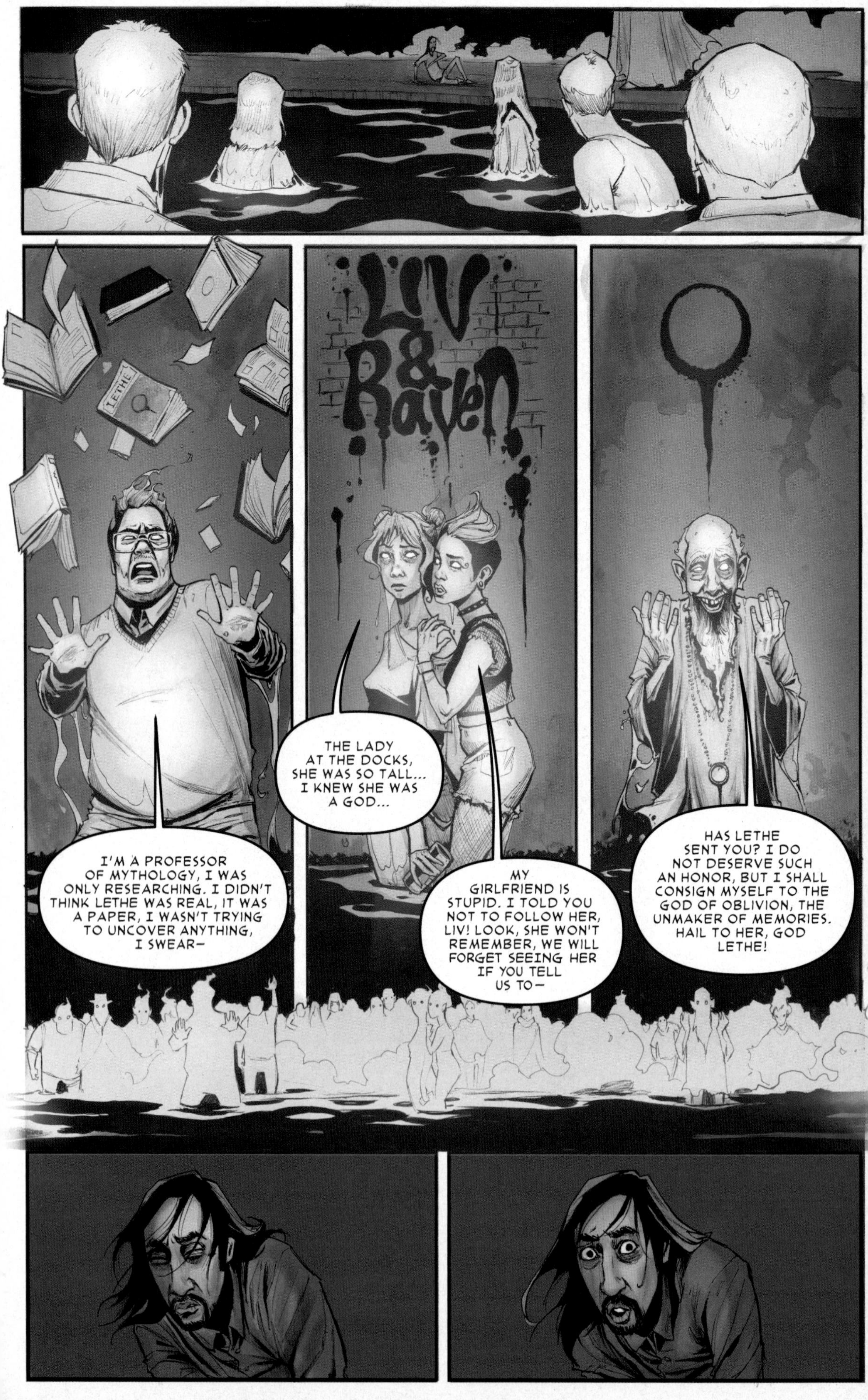
LETHE
LIV & RAVEN
I'M A PROFESSOR OF MYTHOLOGY, I WAS ONLY RESEARCHING. I DIDN'T THINK LETHE WAS REAL, IT WAS A PAPER, I WASN'T TRYING TO UNCOVER ANYTHING, I SWEAR–
THE LADY AT THE DOCKS, SHE WAS SO TALL... I KNEW SHE WAS A GOD...
MY GIRLFRIEND IS STUPID. I TOLD YOU NOT TO FOLLOW HER, LIV! LOOK, SHE WON'T REMEMBER, WE WILL FORGET SEEING HER IF YOU TELL US TO–
HAS LETHE SENT YOU? I DO NOT DESERVE SUCH AN HONOR, BUT I SHALL CONSIGN MYSELF TO THE GOD OF OBLIVION, THE UNMAKER OF MEMORIES. HAIL TO HER, GOD LETHE!

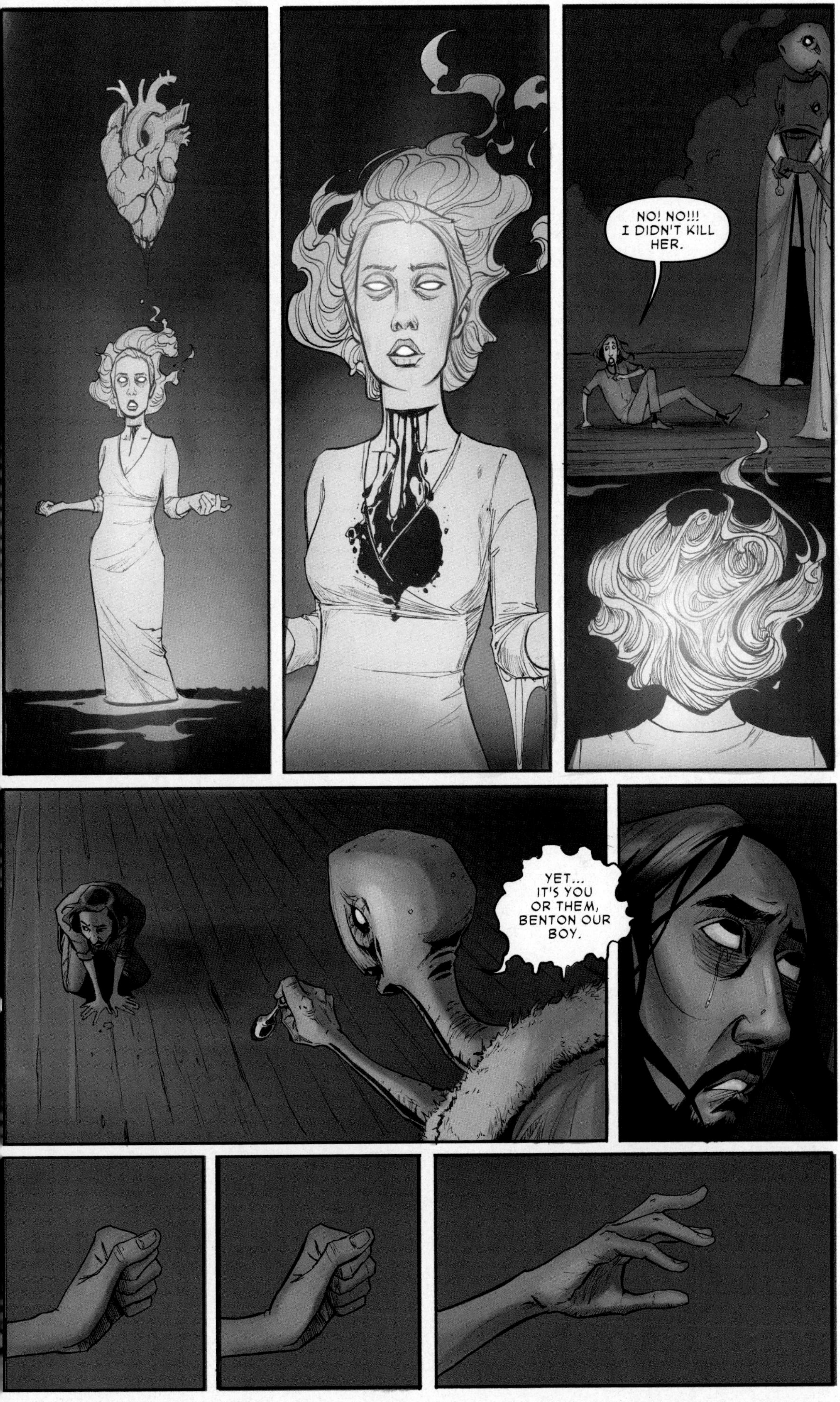
NO! NO!!! I DIDN'T KILL HER.
YET... IT'S YOU OR THEM, BENTON OUR BOY.

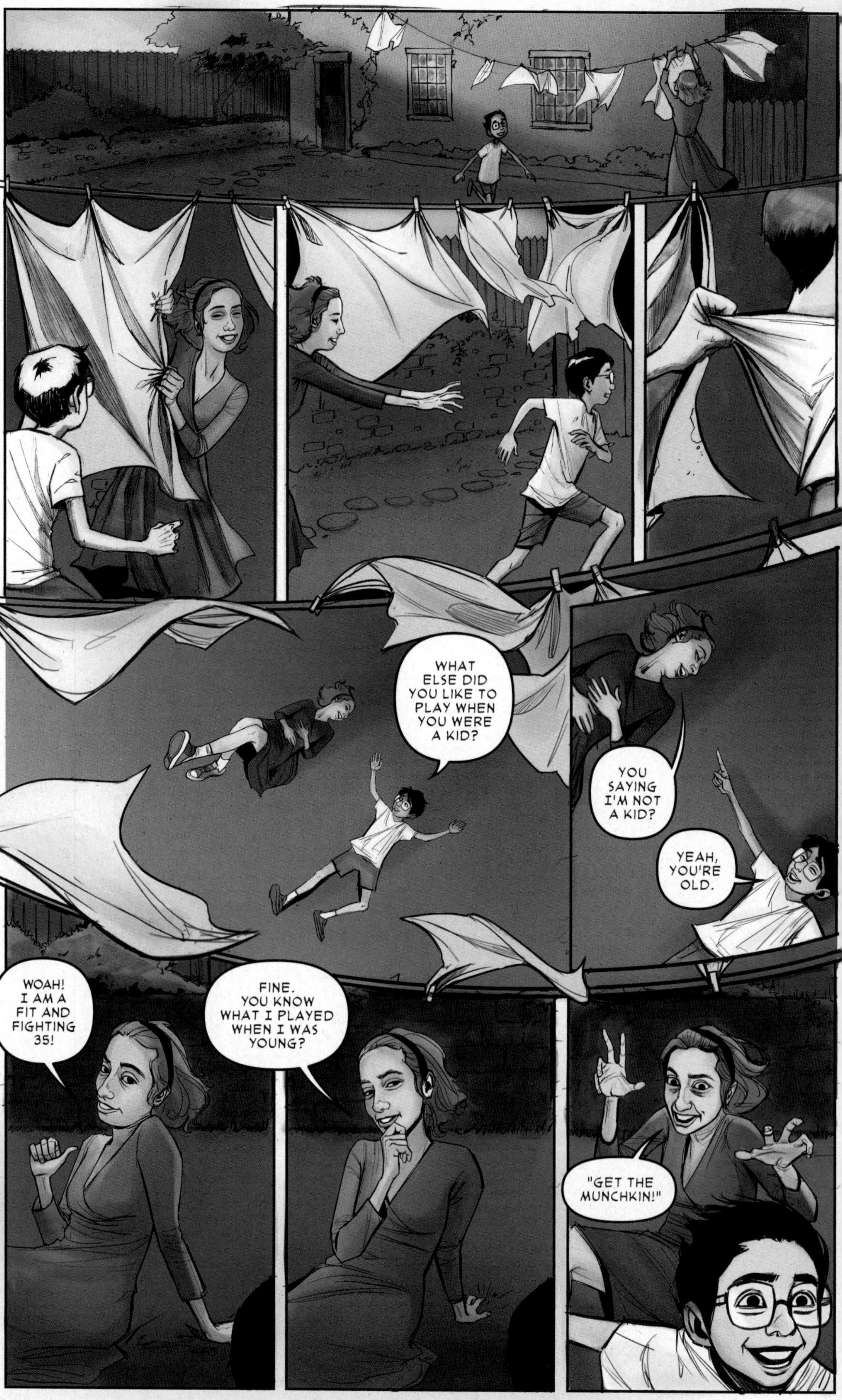
WHAT ELSE DID YOU LIKE TO PLAY WHEN YOU WERE A KID?
YOU SAYING I'M NOT A KID?
YEAH, YOU'RE OLD.
WOAH! I AM A FIT AND FIGHTING 35!
FINE. YOU KNOW WHAT I PLAYED WHEN I WAS YOUNG?
"GET THE MUNCHKIN!"

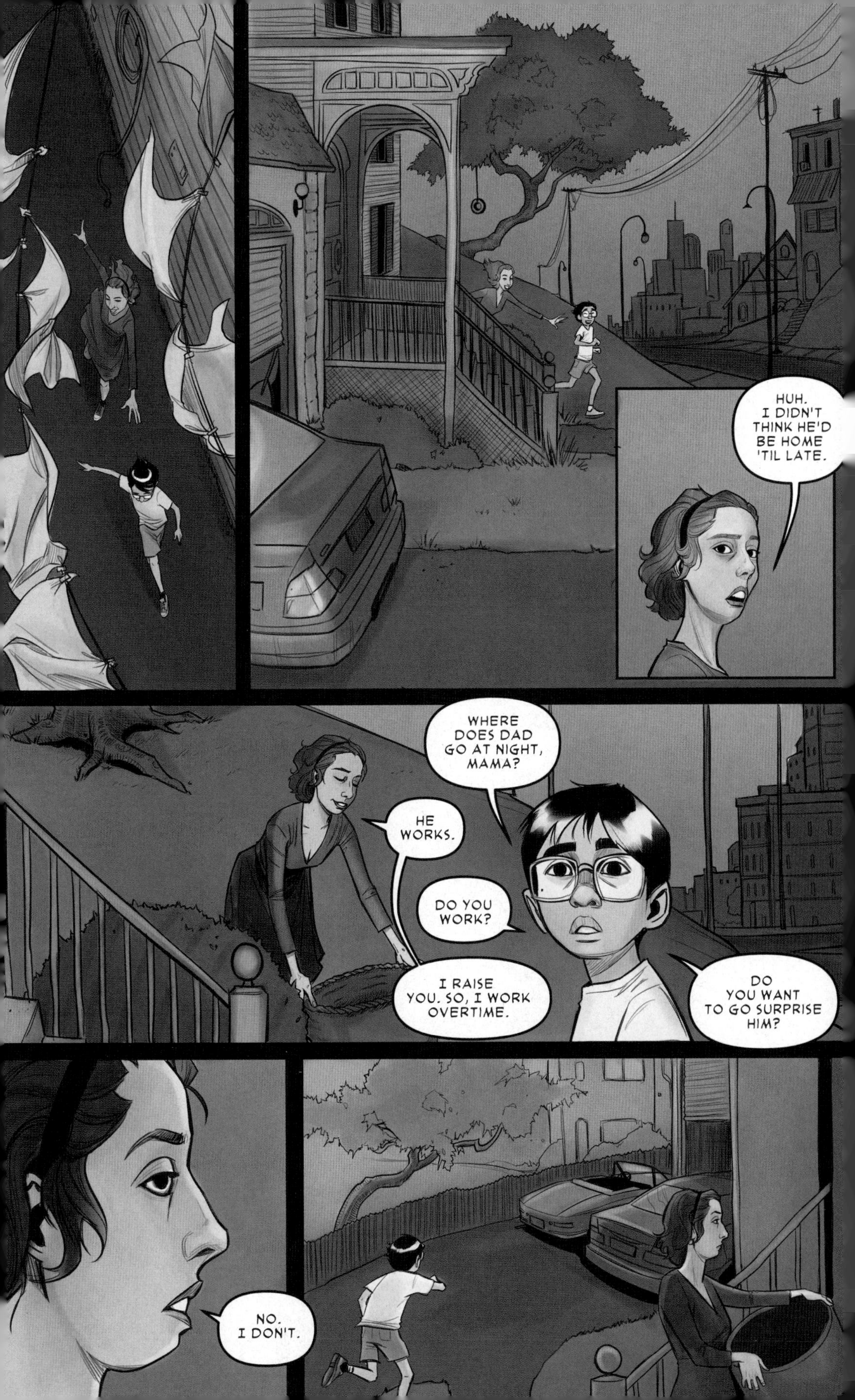
HUH. I DIDN'T THINK HE'D BE HOME 'TIL LATE.
WHERE DOES DAD GO AT NIGHT, MAMA?
HE WORKS.
DO YOU WORK?
I RAISE YOU. SO, I WORK OVERTIME.
DO YOU WANT TO GO SURPRISE HIM?
NO. I DON'T.

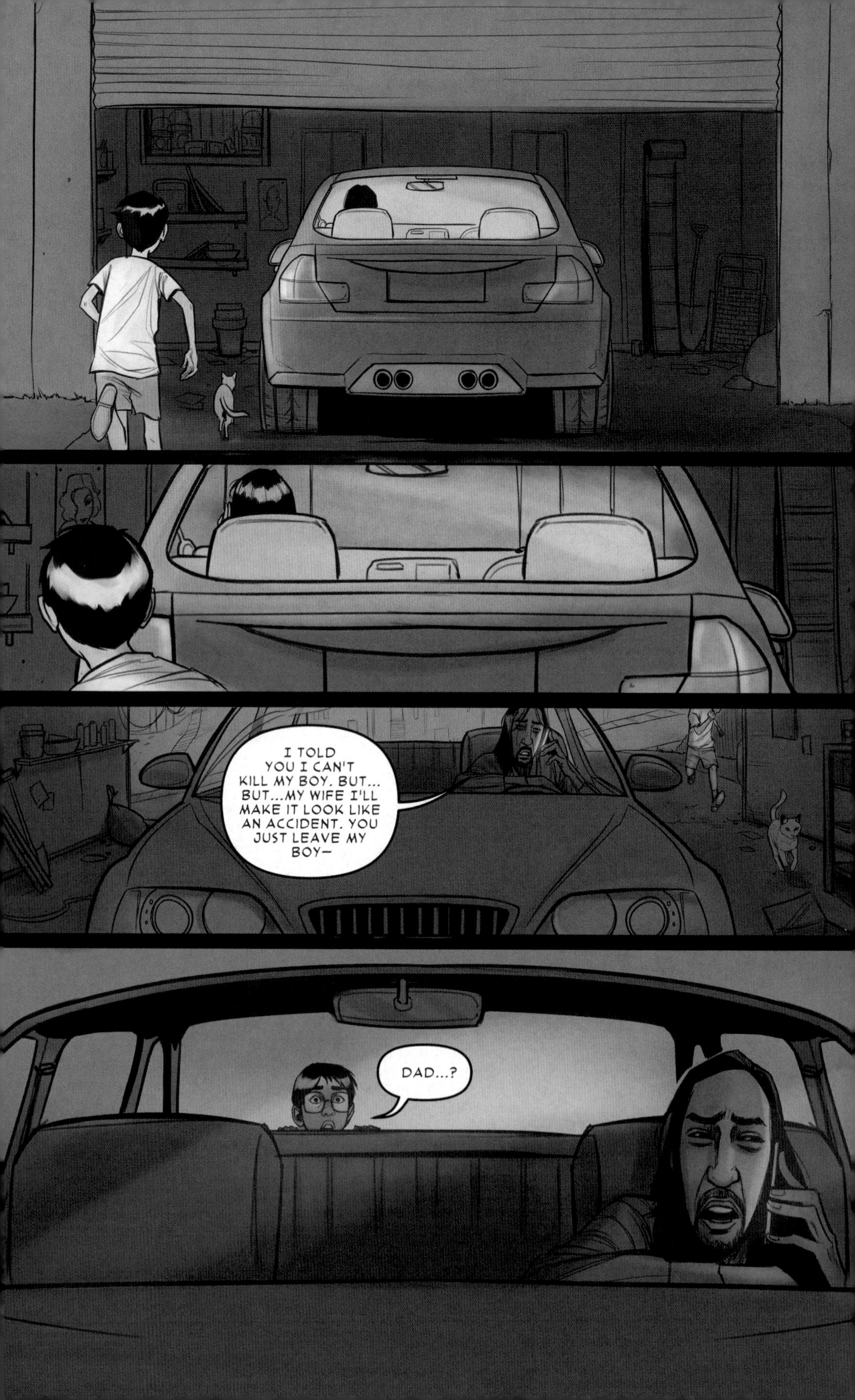
I TOLD YOU I CAN'T KILL MY BOY. BUT... BUT...MY WIFE I'LL MAKE IT LOOK LIKE AN ACCIDENT. YOU JUST LEAVE MY BOY—
DAD...?

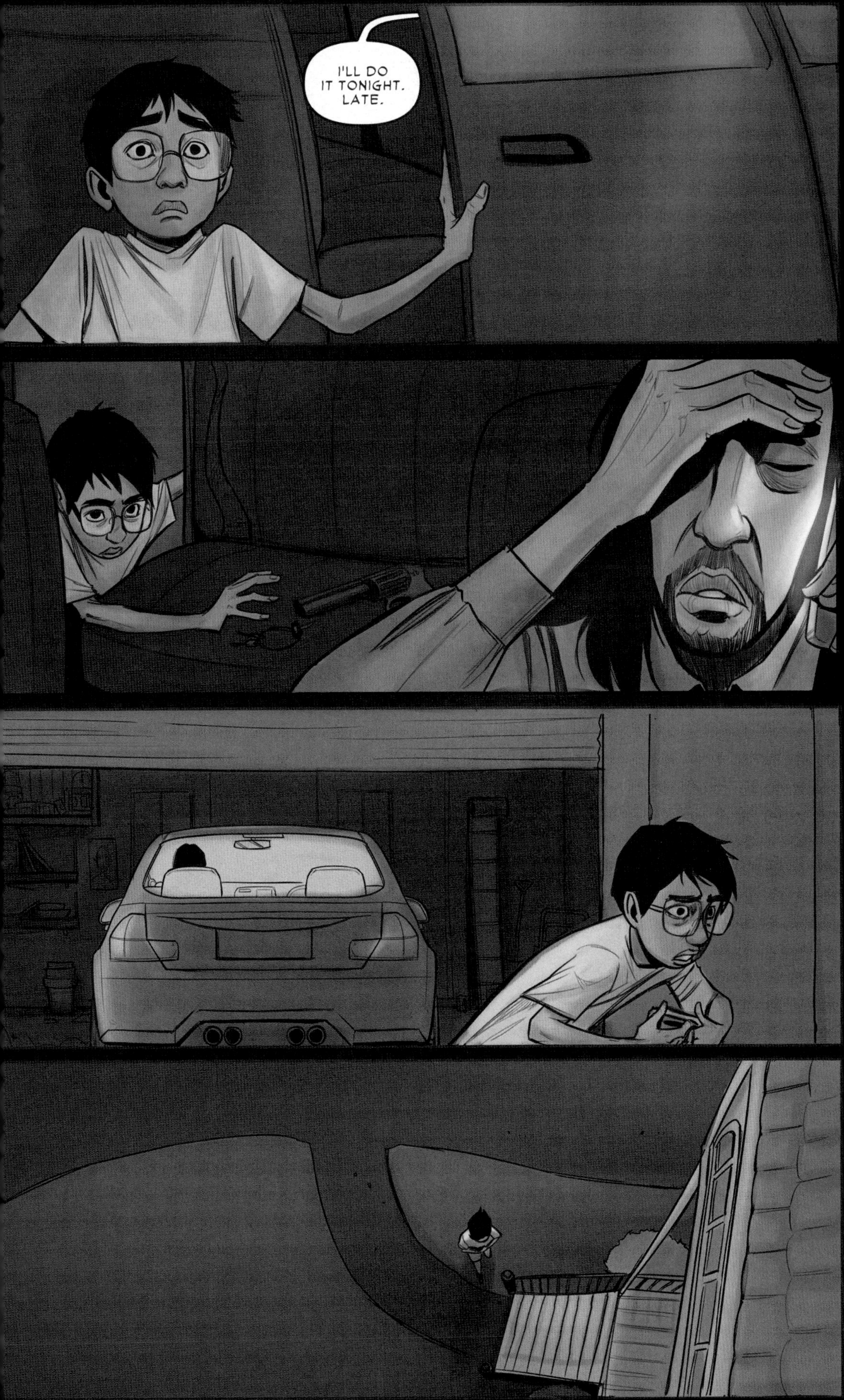
I'LL DO IT TONIGHT. LATE.

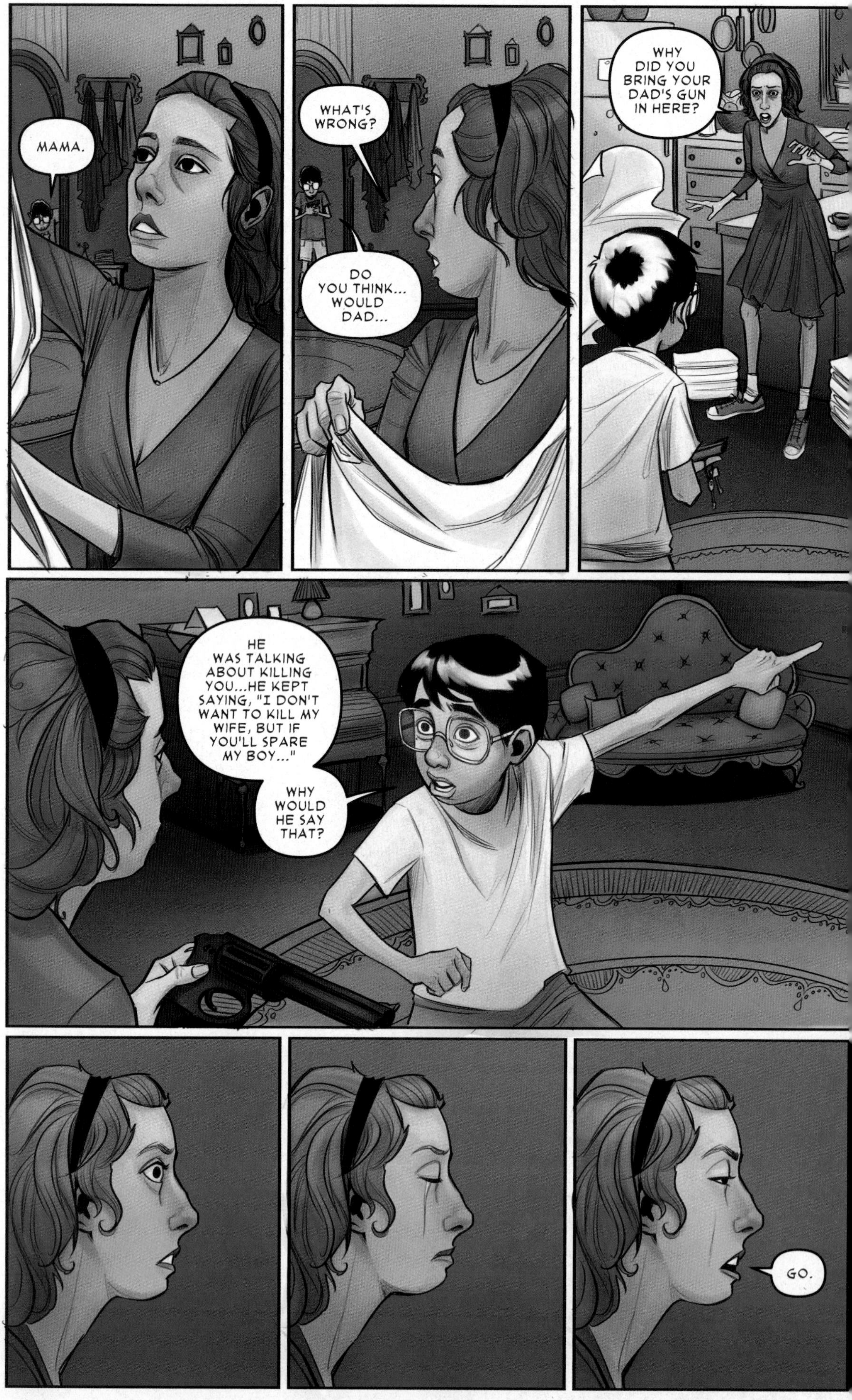
MAMA.
WHAT'S WRONG?
DO YOU THINK... WOULD DAD...
WHY DID YOU BRING YOUR DAD'S GUN IN HERE?
HE WAS TALKING ABOUT KILLING YOU...HE KEPT SAYING, "I DON'T WANT TO KILL MY WIFE, BUT IF YOU'LL SPARE MY BOY..."
WHY WOULD HE SAY THAT?
GO.

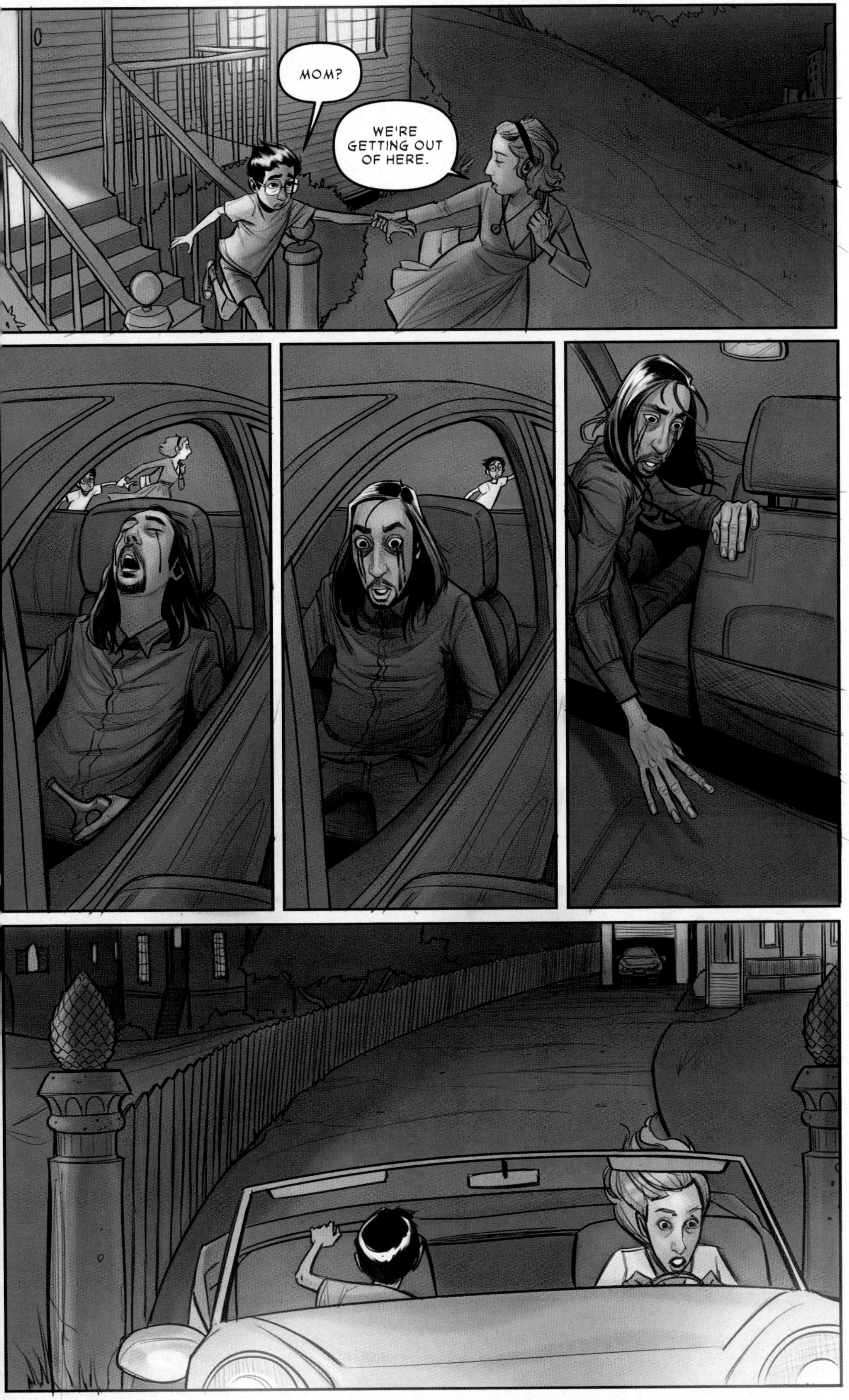

MOM?
WE'RE GETTING OUT OF HERE.

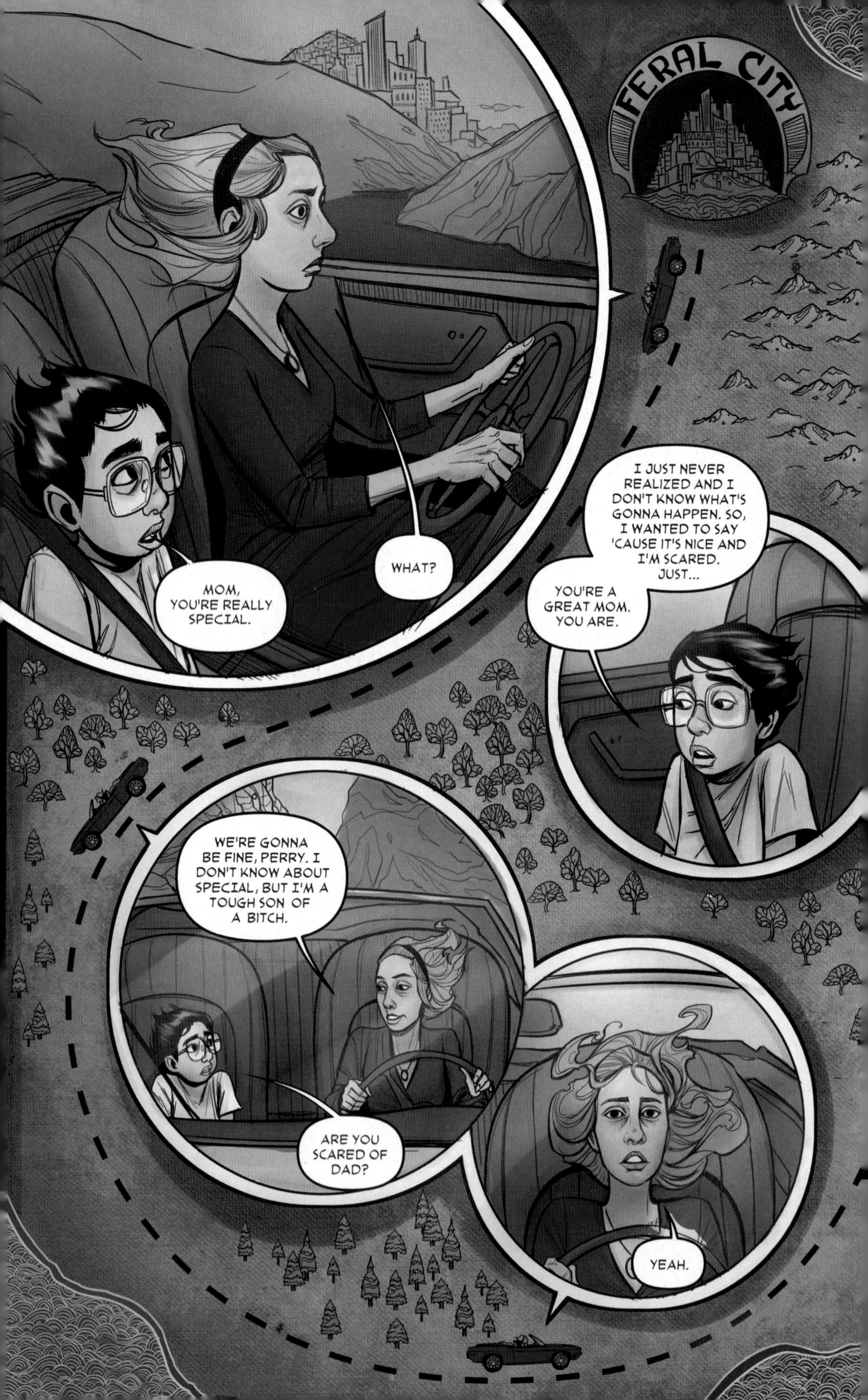
FERAL CITY
MOM, YOU'RE REALLY SPECIAL.
WHAT?
I JUST NEVER REALIZED AND I DON'T KNOW WHAT'S GONNA HAPPEN. SO, I WANTED TO SAY 'CAUSE IT'S NICE AND I'M SCARED. JUST...
YOU'RE A GREAT MOM. YOU ARE.
WE'RE GONNA BE FINE, PERRY. I DON'T KNOW ABOUT SPECIAL, BUT I'M A TOUGH SON OF A BITCH.
ARE YOU SCARED OF DAD?
YEAH.

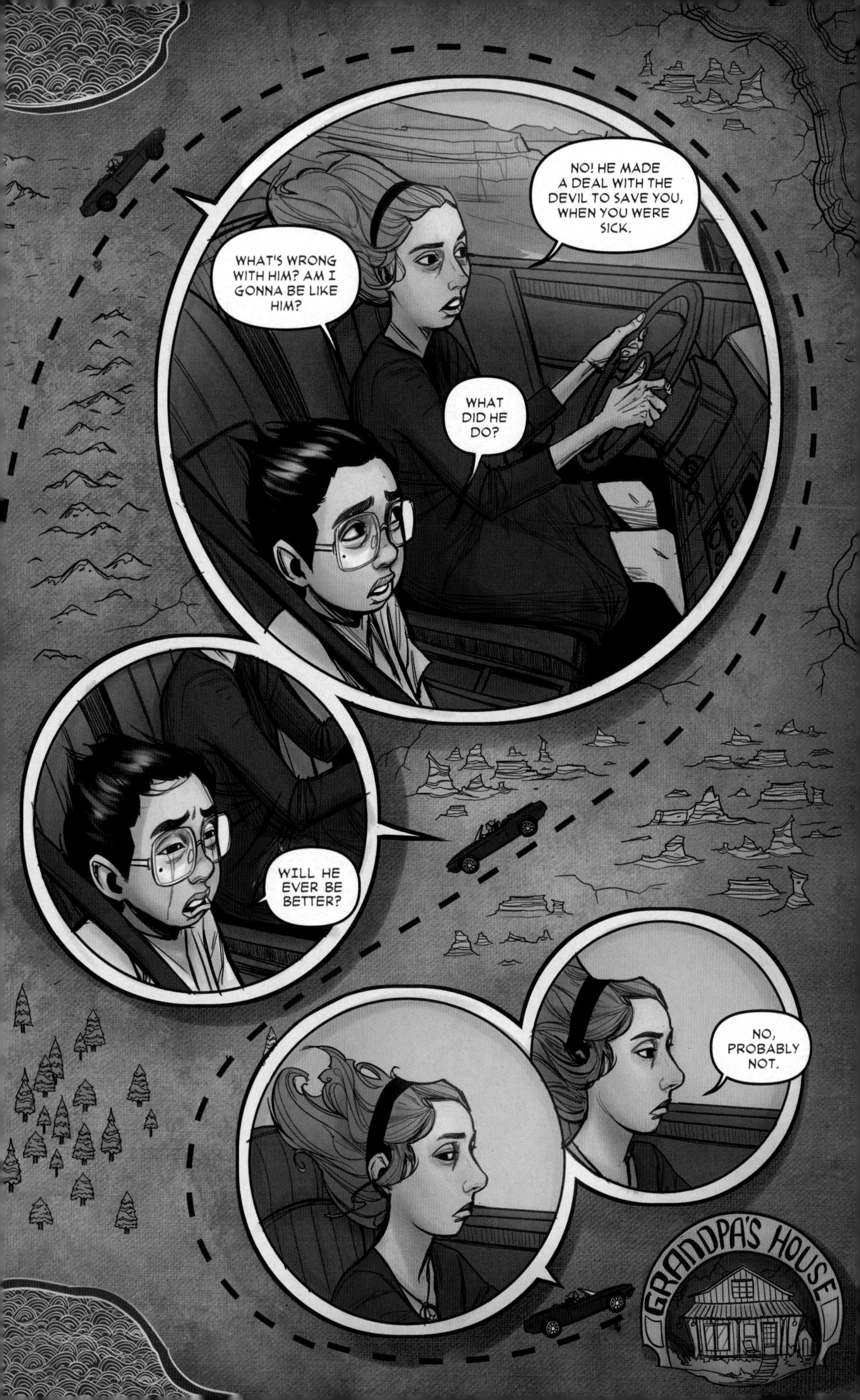
WHAT'S WRONG WITH HIM? AM I GONNA BE LIKE HIM?
NO! HE MADE A DEAL WITH THE DEVIL TO SAVE YOU, WHEN YOU WERE SICK.
WHAT DID HE DO?
WILL HE EVER BE BETTER?
NO, PROBABLY NOT.
GRANDPA'S HOUSE

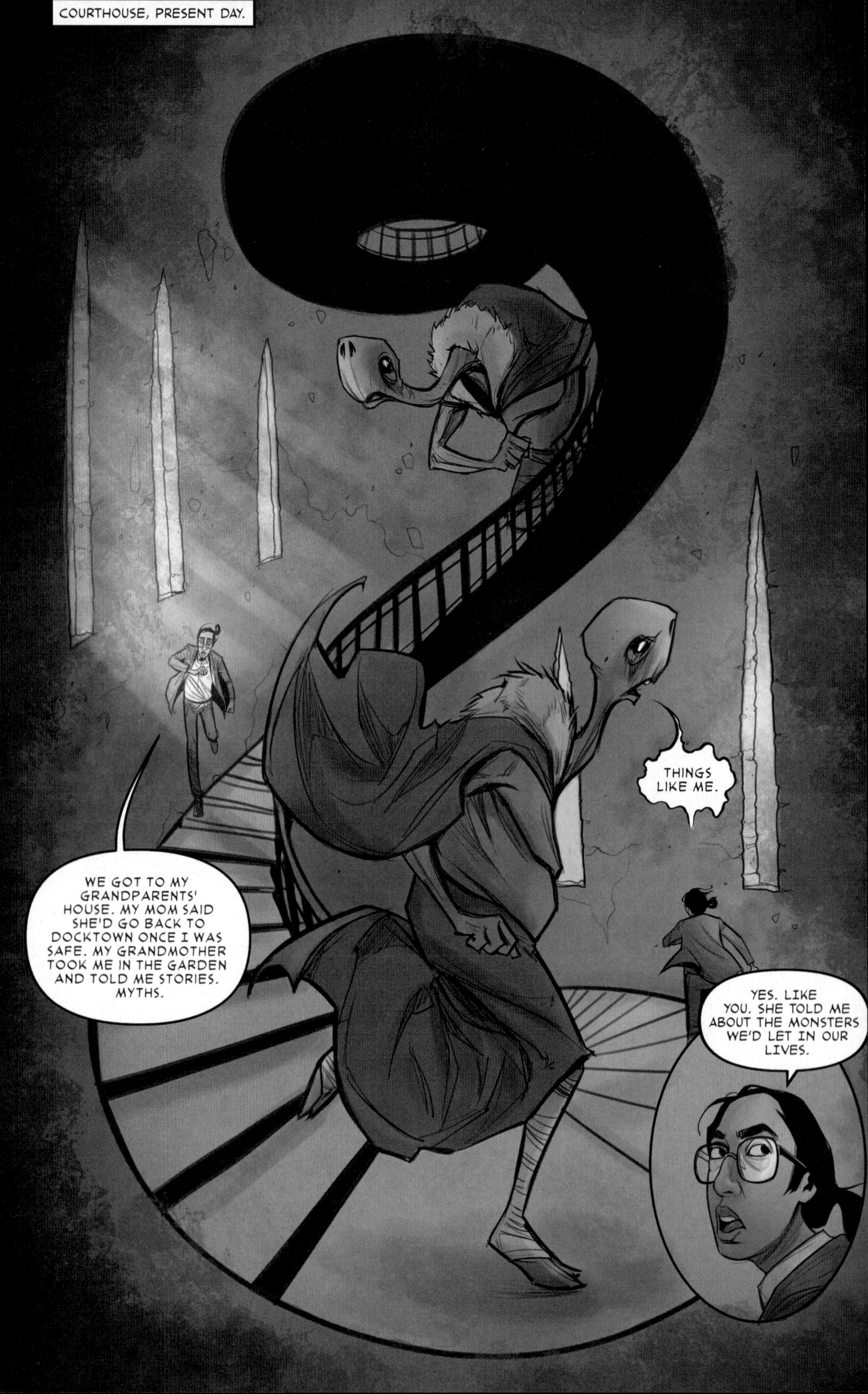
COURTHOUSE, PRESENT DAY.
WE GOT TO MY GRANDPARENTS' HOUSE. MY MOM SAID SHE'D GO BACK TO DOCKTOWN ONCE I WAS SAFE. MY GRANDMOTHER TOOK ME IN THE GARDEN AND TOLD ME STORIES. MYTHS.
THINGS LIKE ME.
YES. LIKE YOU. SHE TOLD ME ABOUT THE MONSTERS WE'D LET IN OUR LIVES.

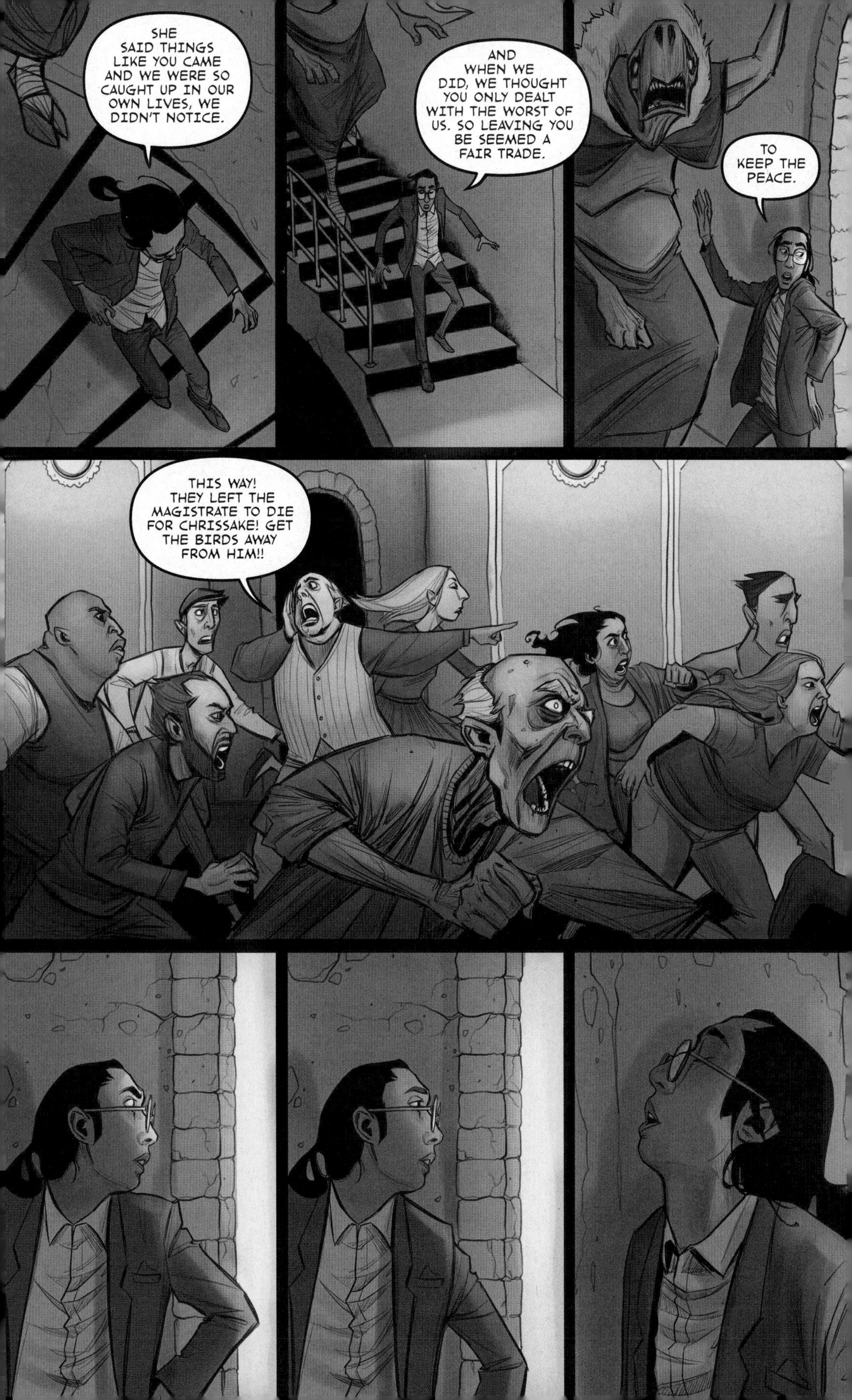
SHE SAID THINGS LIKE YOU CAME AND WE WERE SO CAUGHT UP IN OUR OWN LIVES, WE DIDN'T NOTICE.
AND WHEN WE DID, WE THOUGHT YOU ONLY DEALT WITH THE WORST OF US. SO LEAVING YOU BE SEEMED A FAIR TRADE.
TO KEEP THE PEACE.
THIS WAY! THEY LEFT THE MAGISTRATE TO DIE FOR CHRISSAKE! GET THE BIRDS AWAY FROM HIM!!

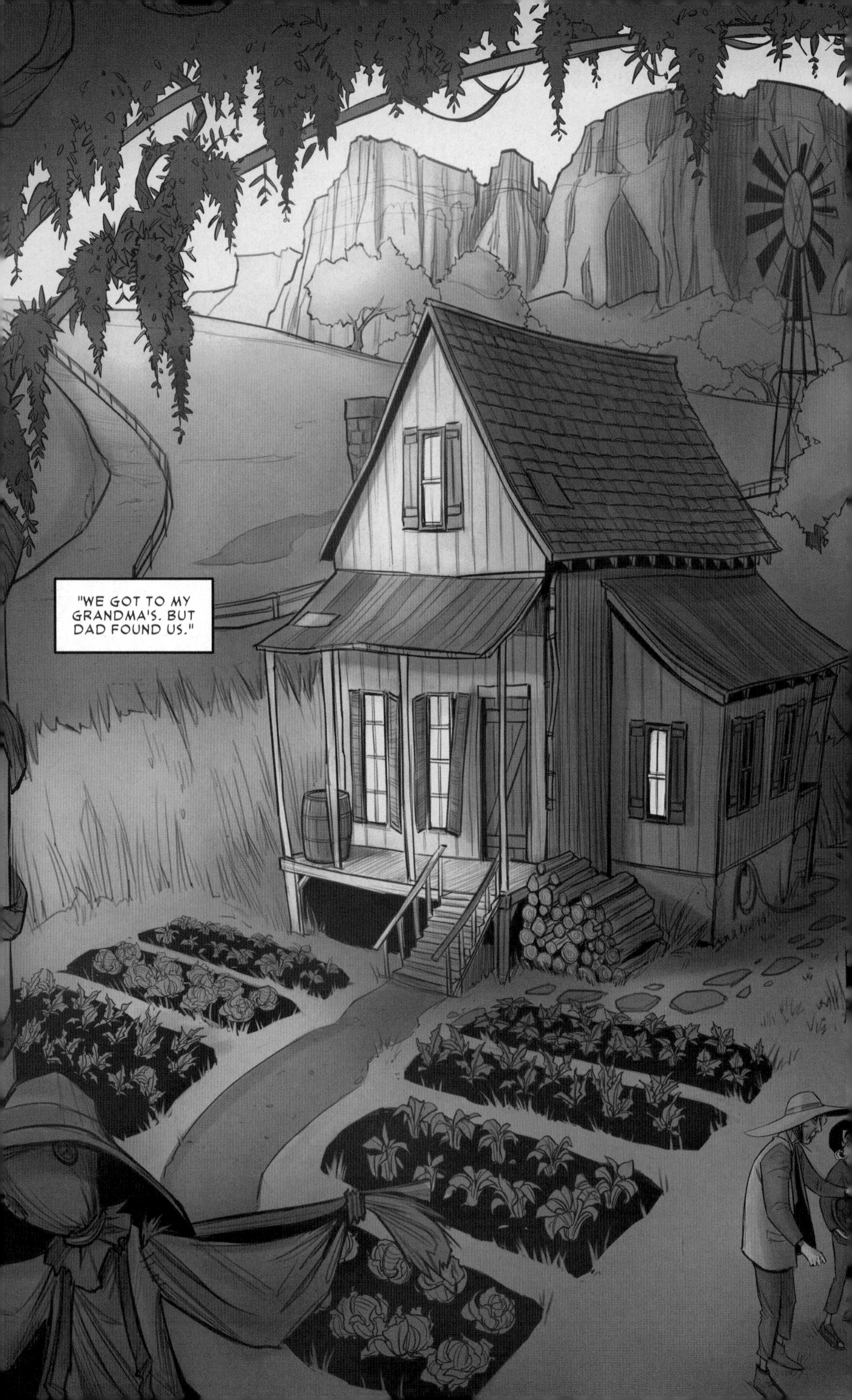
"WE GOT TO MY GRANDMA'S. BUT DAD FOUND US."

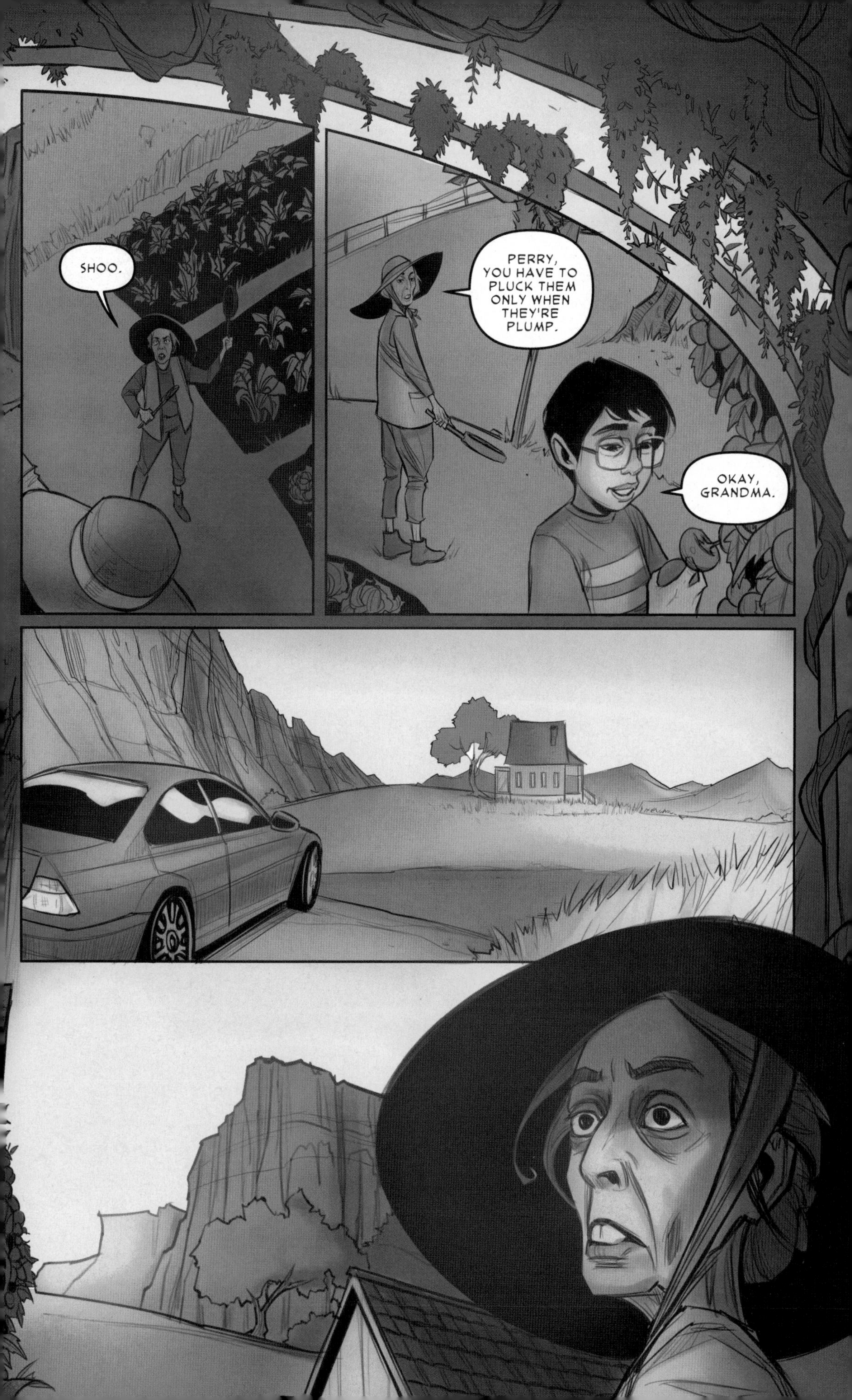
SHOO.
PERRY, YOU HAVE TO PLUCK THEM ONLY WHEN THEY'RE PLUMP.
OKAY, GRANDMA.

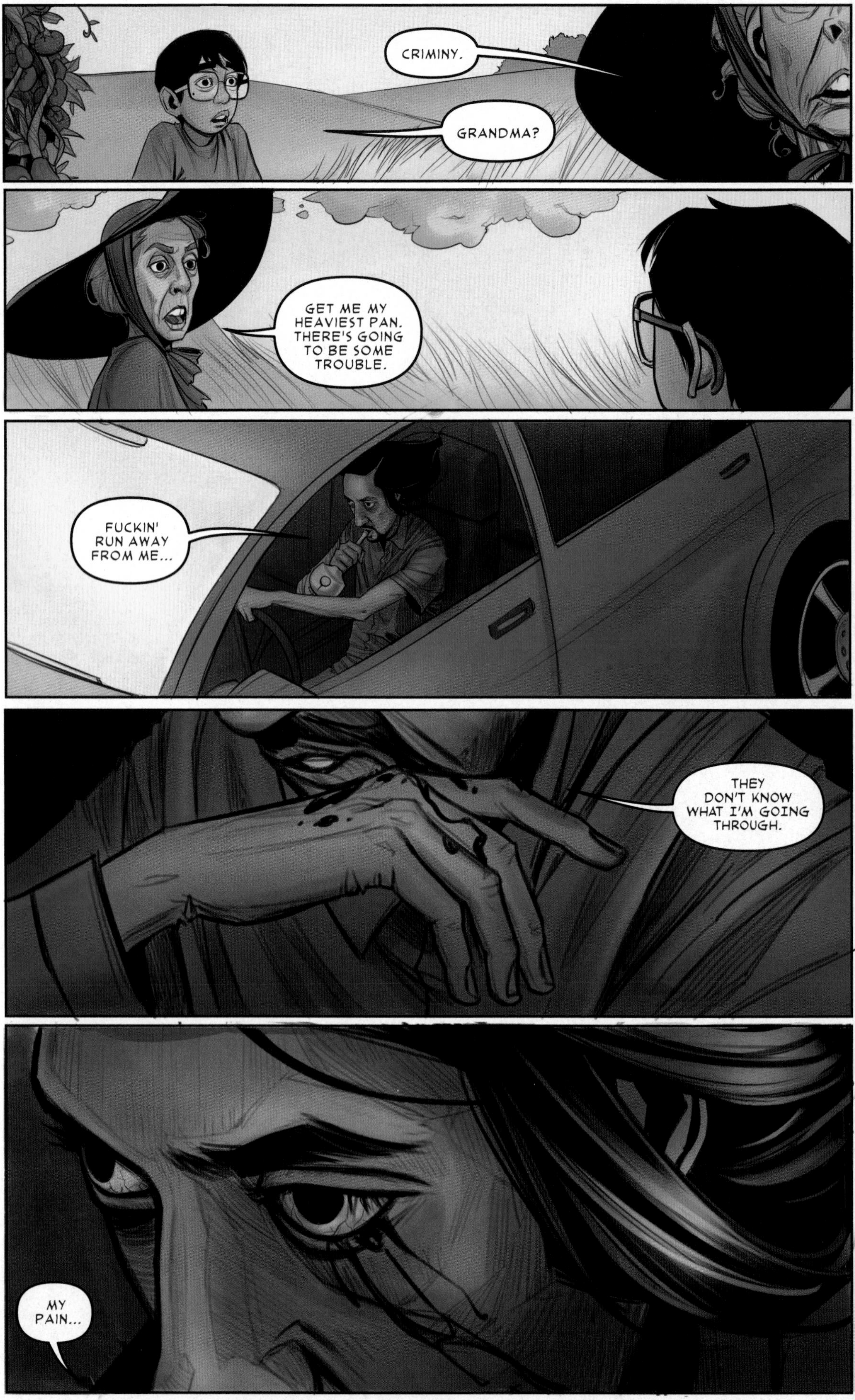
CRIMINY.
GRANDMA?
GET ME MY HEAVIEST PAN. THERE'S GOING TO BE SOME TROUBLE.
FUCKIN' RUN AWAY FROM ME...
THEY DON'T KNOW WHAT I'M GOING THROUGH.
MY PAIN...

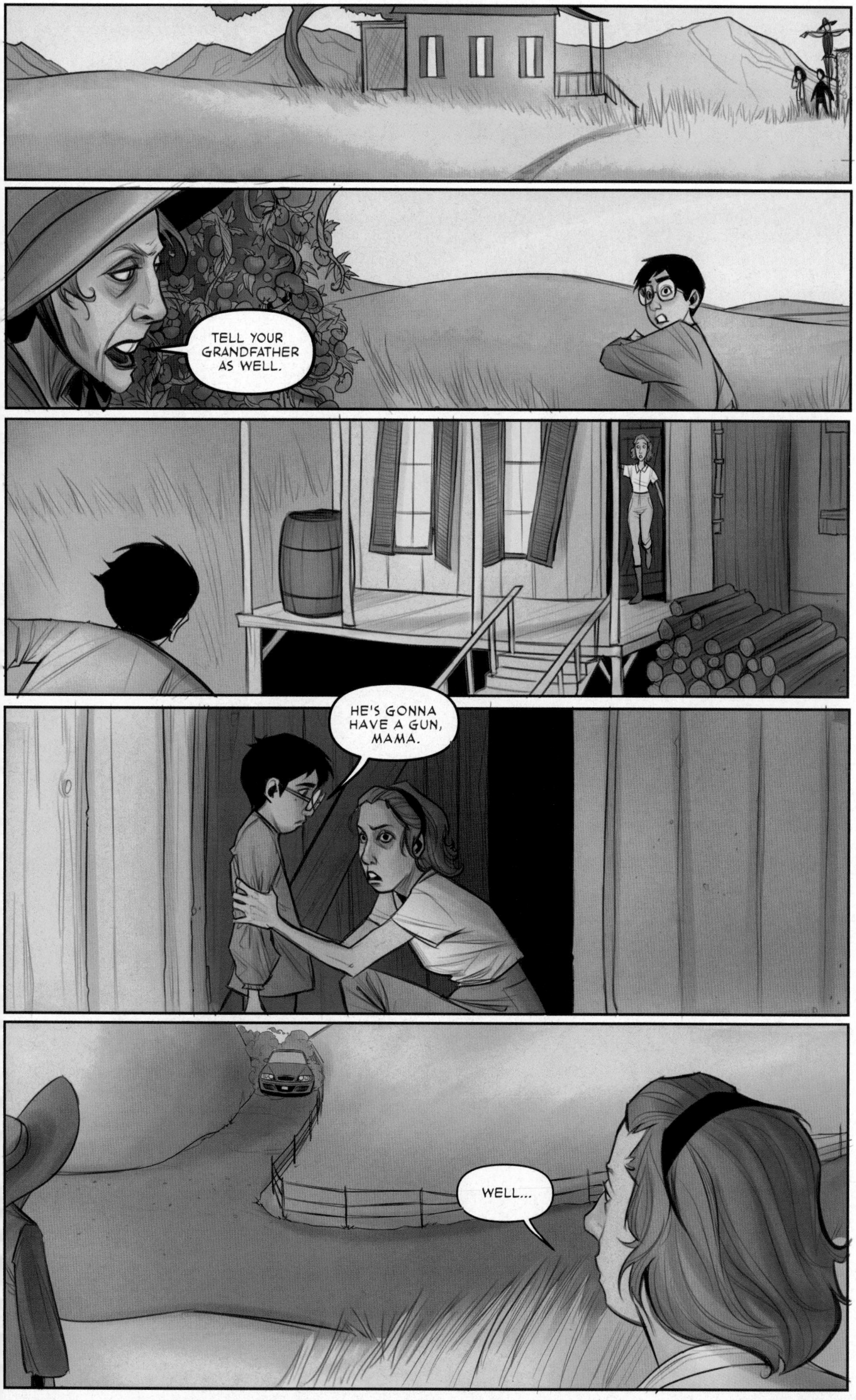
TELL YOUR GRANDFATHER AS WELL.
HE'S GONNA HAVE A GUN, MAMA.
WELL...

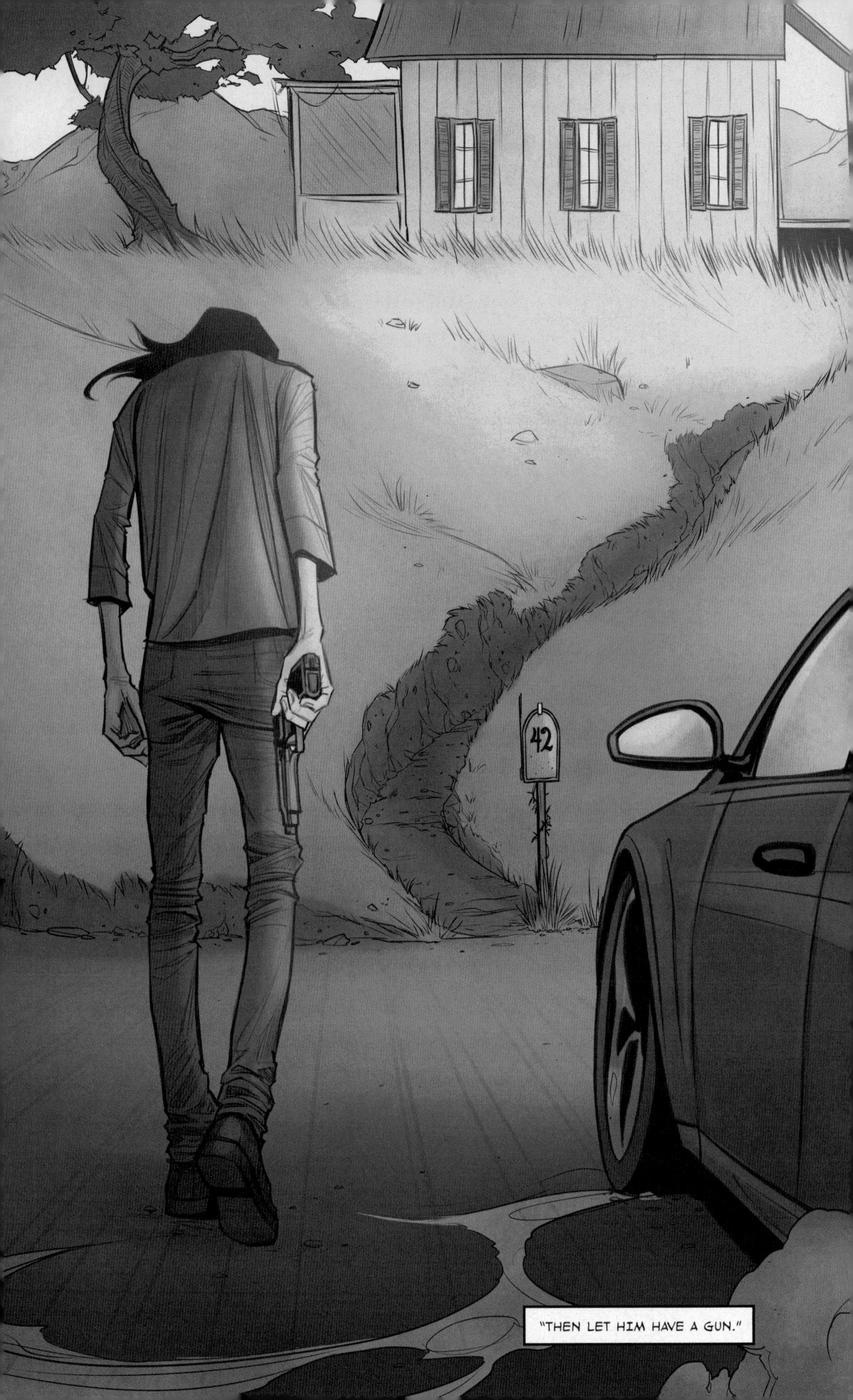
42
"THEN LET HIM HAVE A GUN."

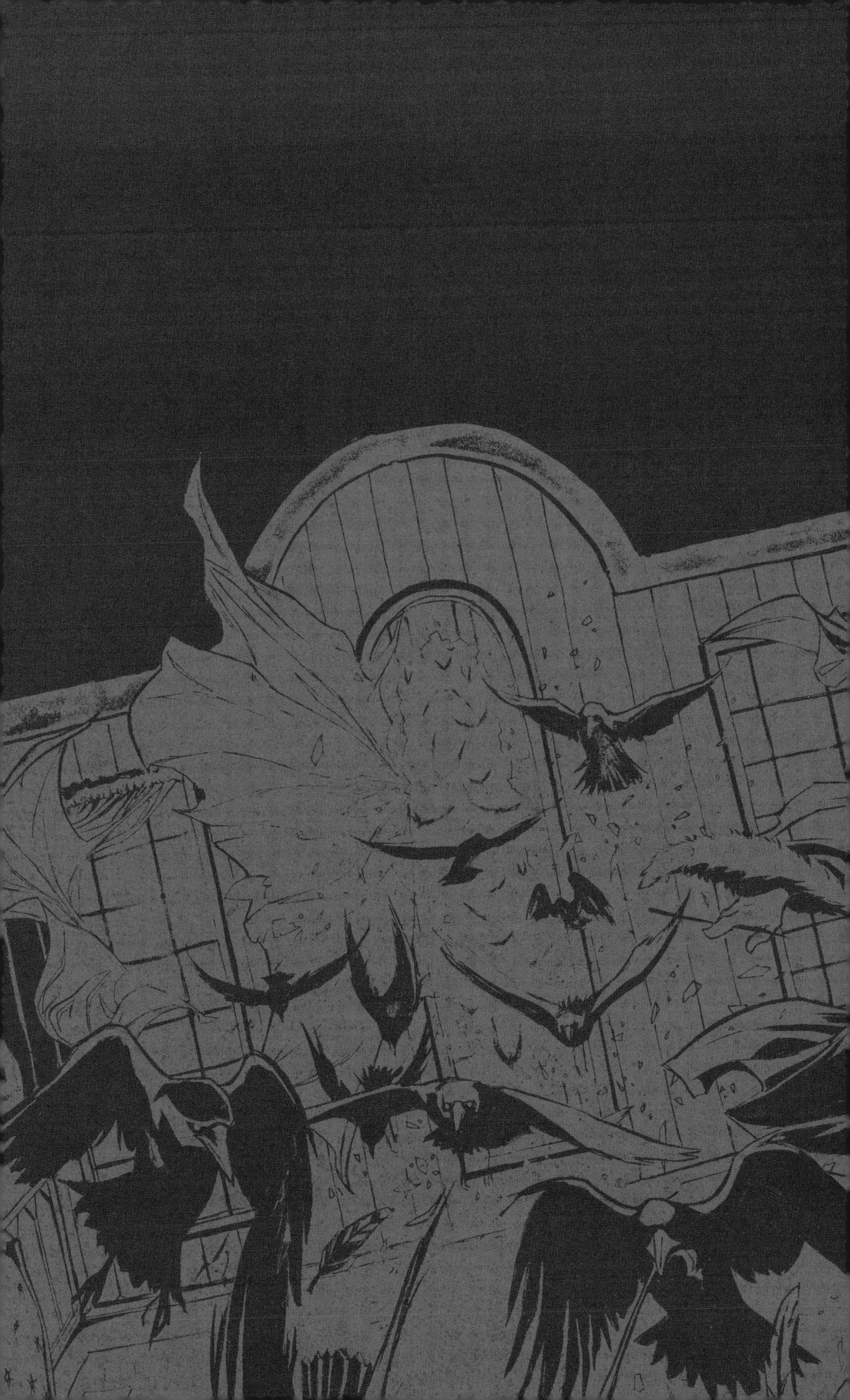

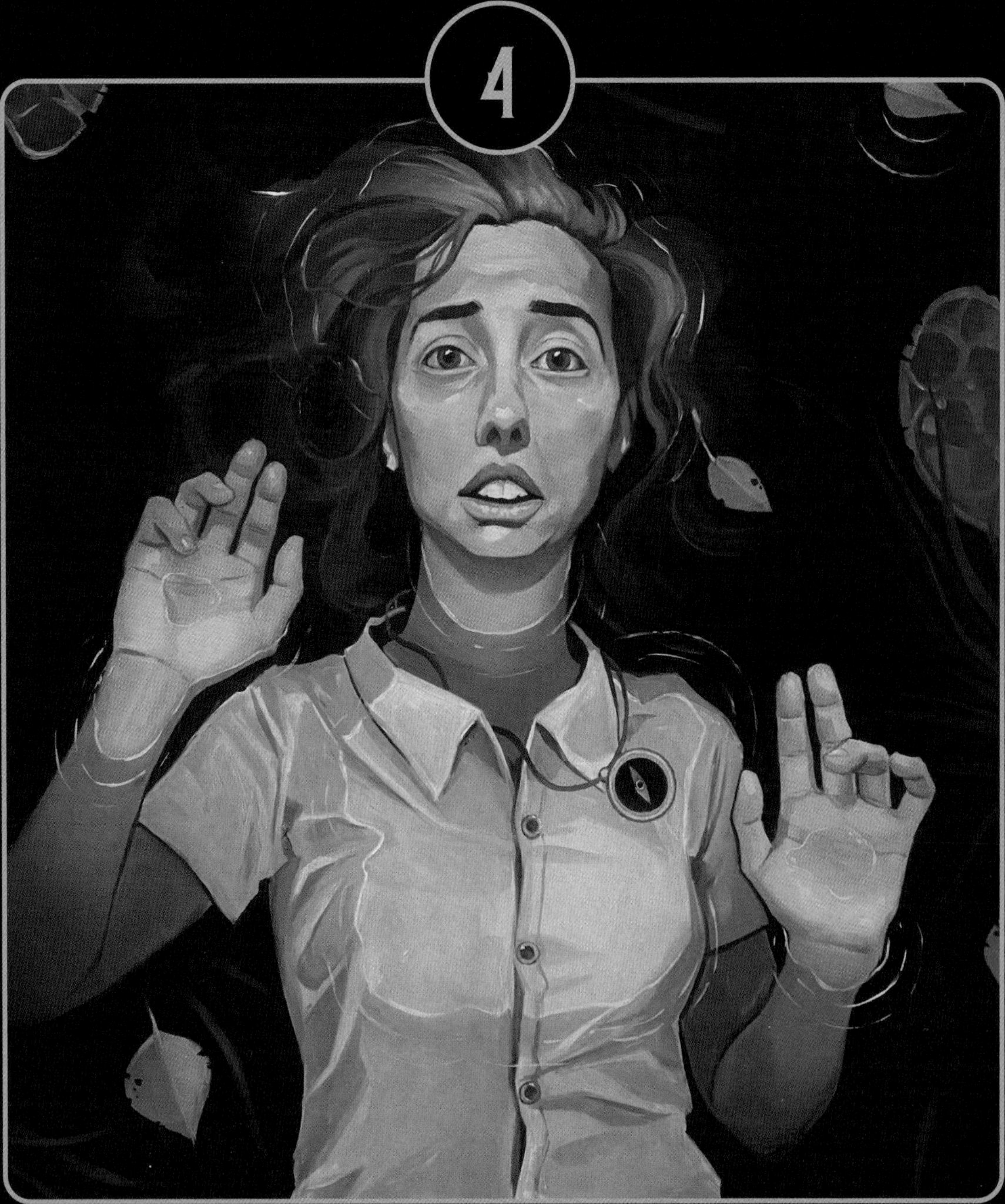
4

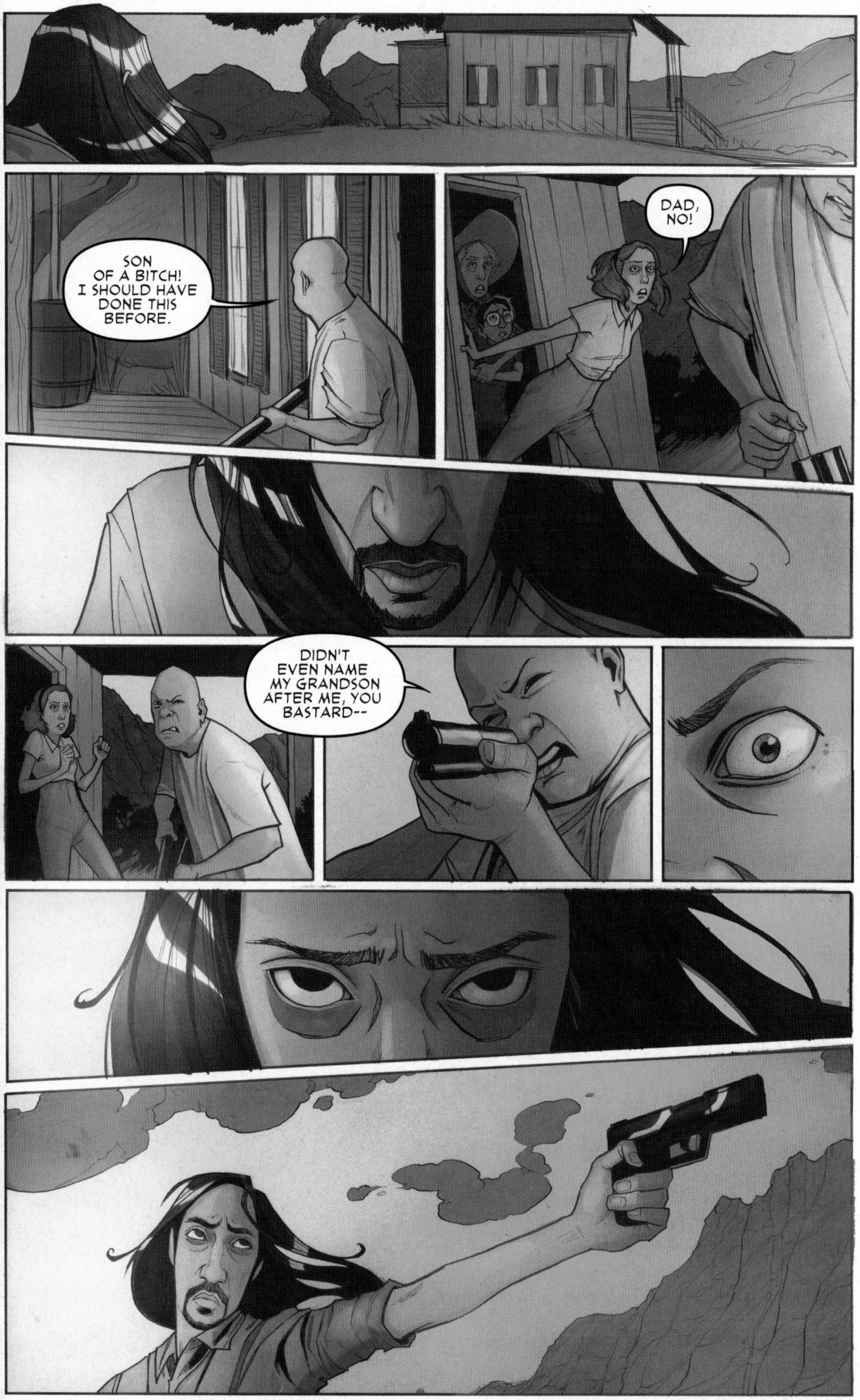
SON OF A BITCH! I SHOULD HAVE DONE THIS BEFORE.
DAD, NO!
DIDN'T EVEN NAME MY GRANDSON AFTER ME, YOU BASTARD--

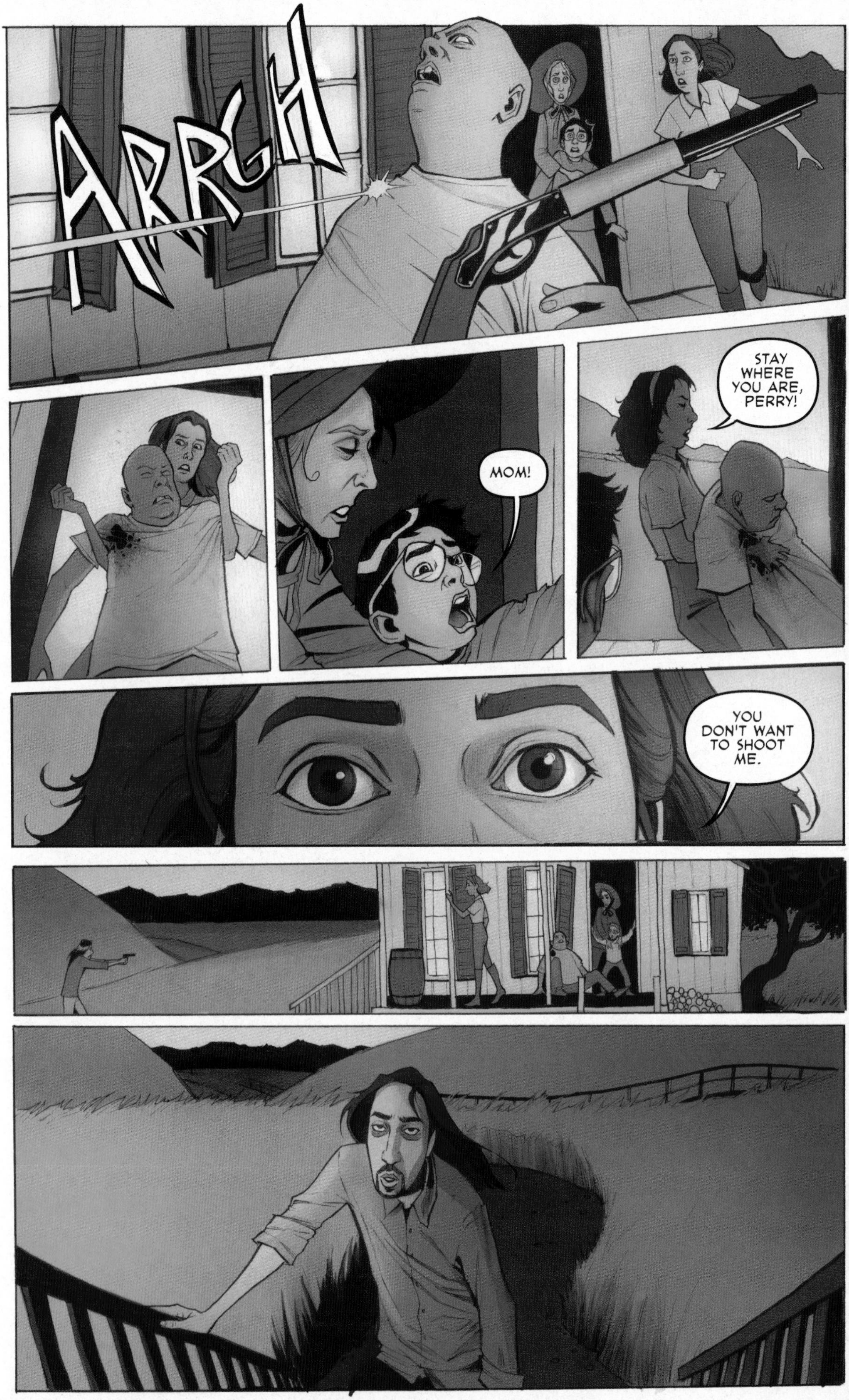
ARRGH
MOM!
STAY WHERE YOU ARE, PERRY!
YOU DON'T WANT TO SHOOT ME.

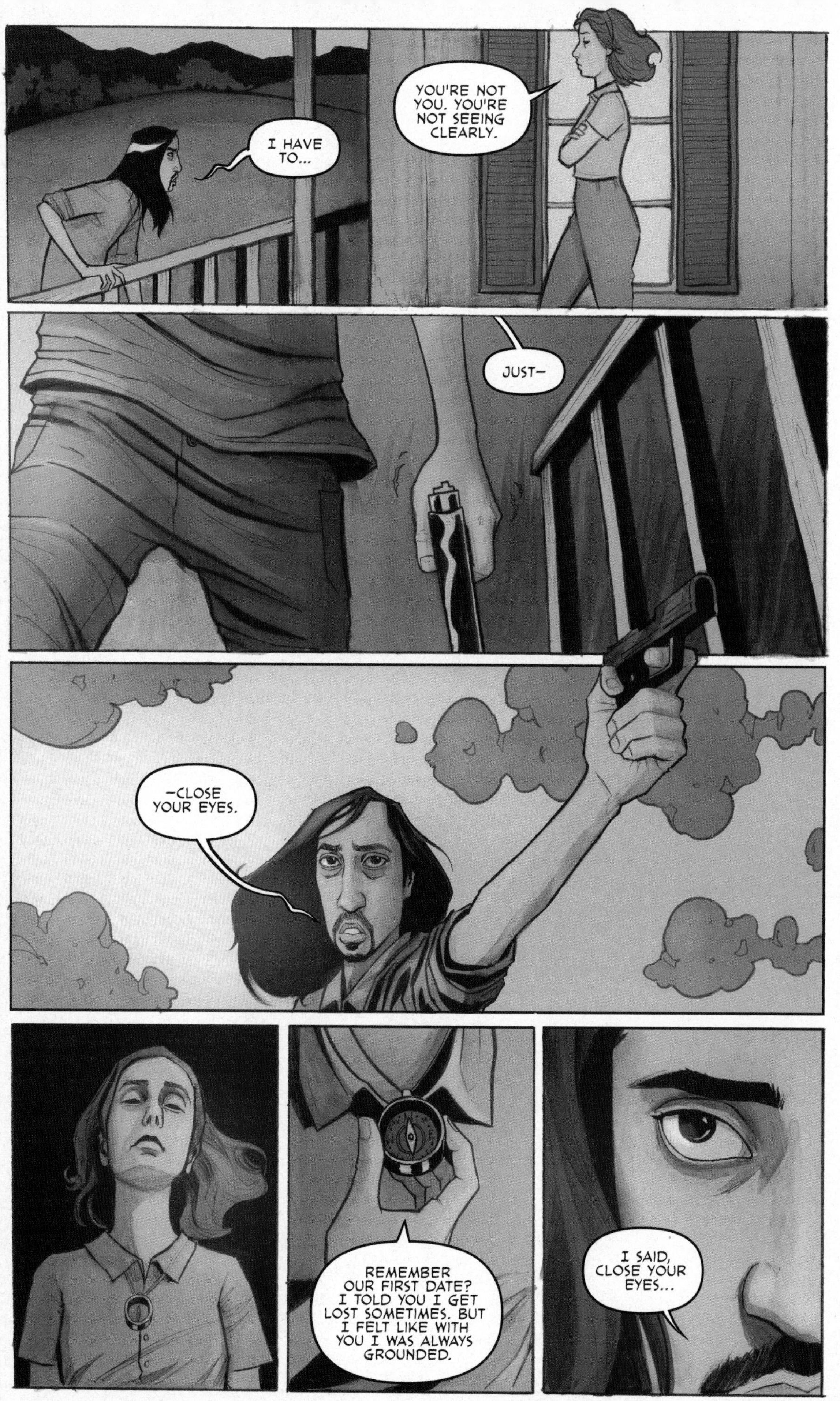
YOU'RE NOT YOU. YOU'RE NOT SEEING CLEARLY.
I HAVE TO...
JUST—
—CLOSE YOUR EYES.
REMEMBER OUR FIRST DATE? I TOLD YOU I GET LOST SOMETIMES. BUT I FELT LIKE WITH YOU I WAS ALWAYS GROUNDED.
I SAID, CLOSE YOUR EYES...

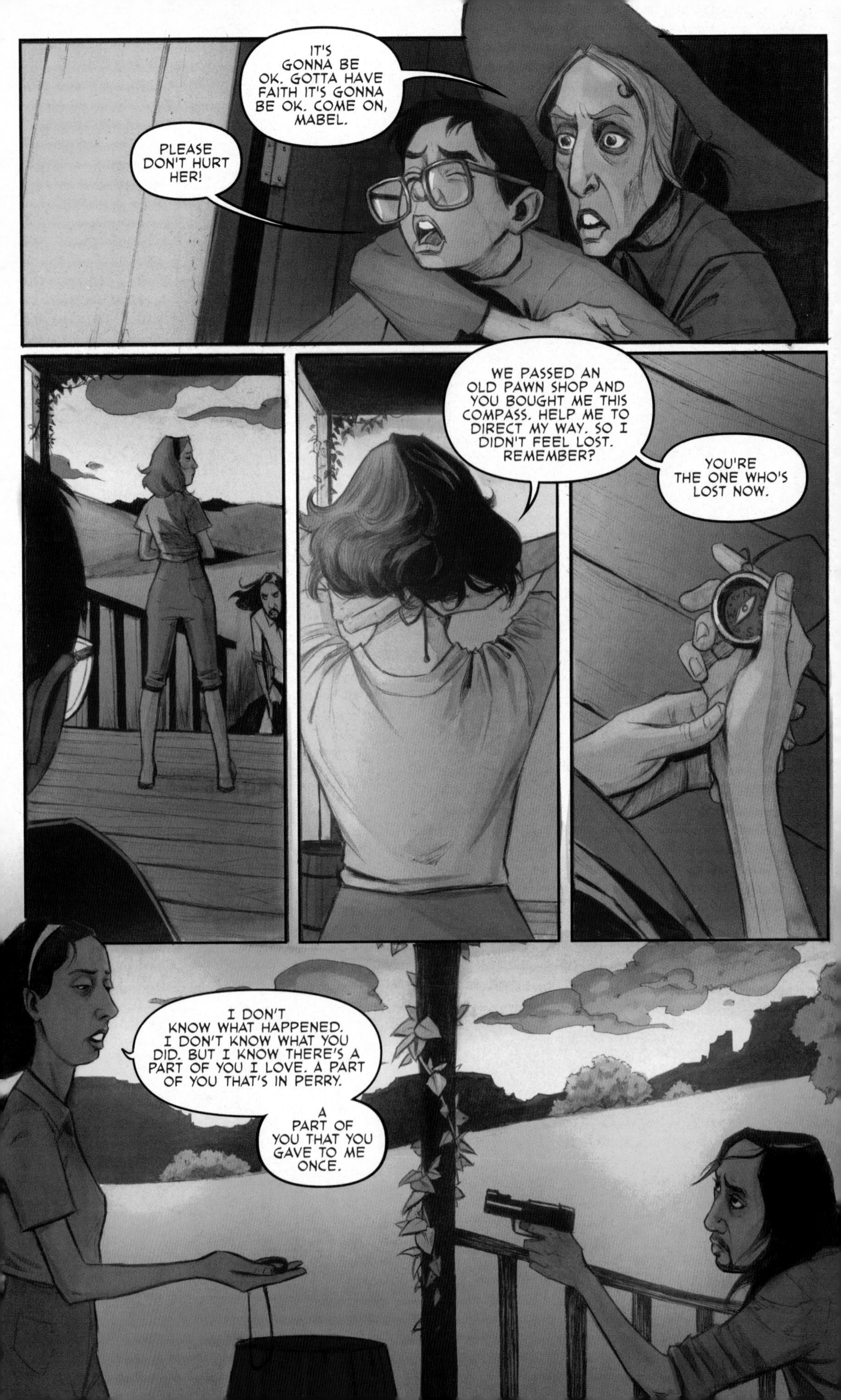
IT'S GONNA BE OK. GOTTA HAVE FAITH IT'S GONNA BE OK. COME ON, MABEL.
PLEASE DON'T HURT HER!
WE PASSED AN OLD PAWN SHOP AND YOU BOUGHT ME THIS COMPASS. HELP ME TO DIRECT MY WAY. SO I DIDN'T FEEL LOST. REMEMBER?
YOU'RE THE ONE WHO'S LOST NOW.
I DON'T KNOW WHAT HAPPENED. I DON'T KNOW WHAT YOU DID. BUT I KNOW THERE'S A PART OF YOU I LOVE. A PART OF YOU THAT'S IN PERRY.
A PART OF YOU THAT YOU GAVE TO ME ONCE.

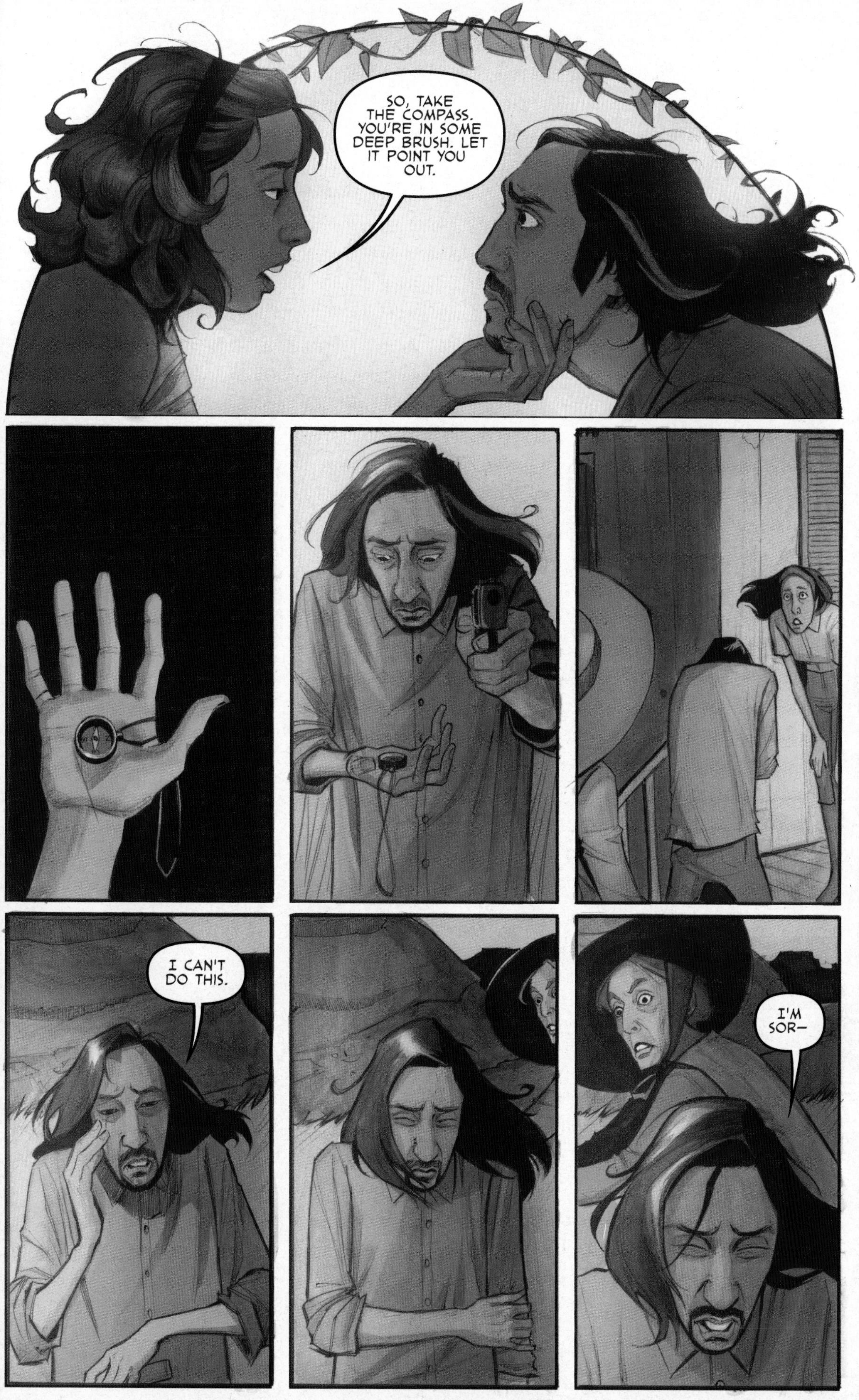
SO, TAKE THE COMPASS. YOU'RE IN SOME DEEP BRUSH. LET IT POINT YOU OUT.
I CAN'T DO THIS.
I'M SOR—

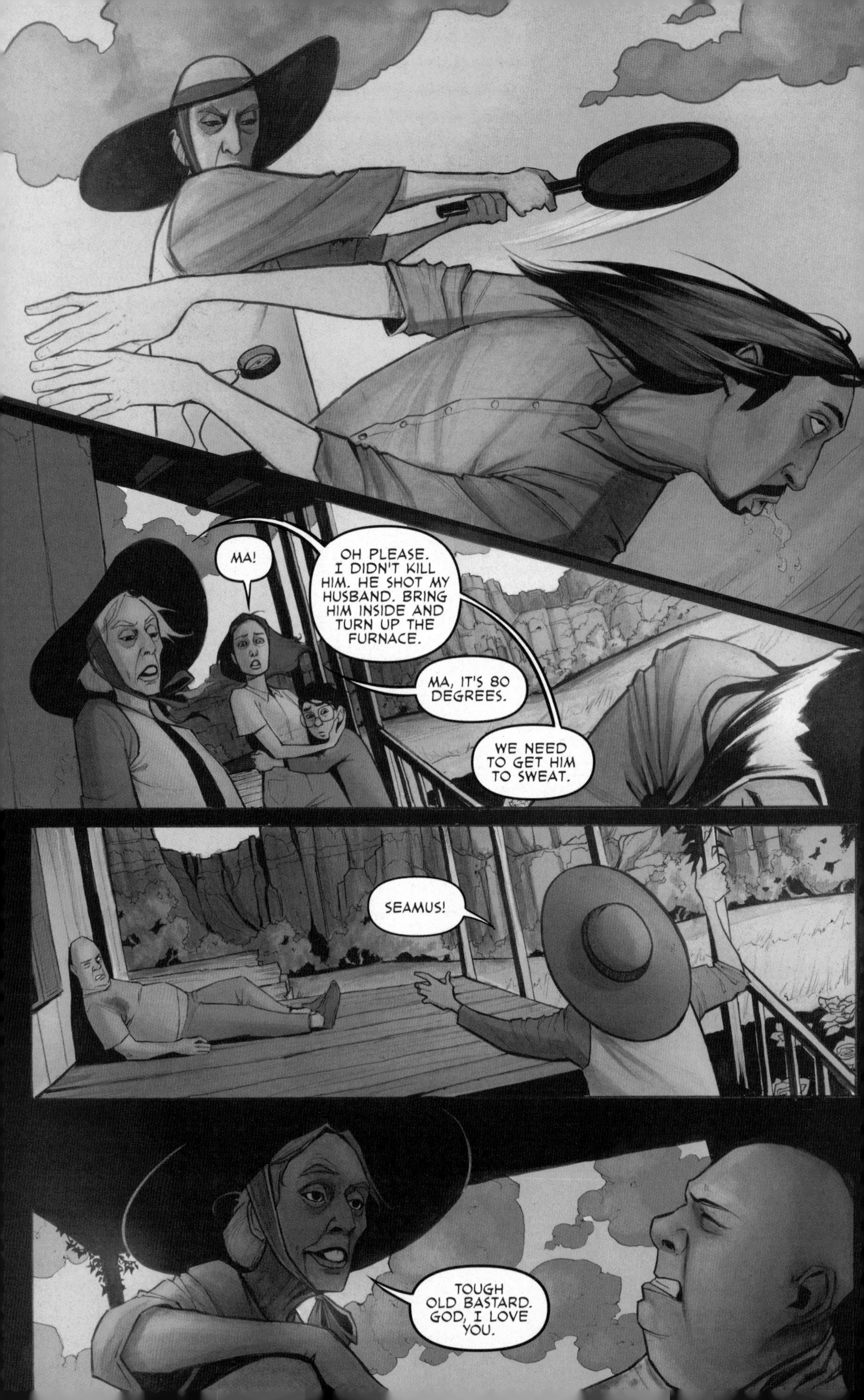
MA!
OH PLEASE. I DIDN'T KILL HIM. HE SHOT MY HUSBAND. BRING HIM INSIDE AND TURN UP THE FURNACE.
MA, IT'S 80 DEGREES.
WE NEED TO GET HIM TO SWEAT.
SEAMUS!
TOUGH OLD BASTARD. GOD, I LOVE YOU.

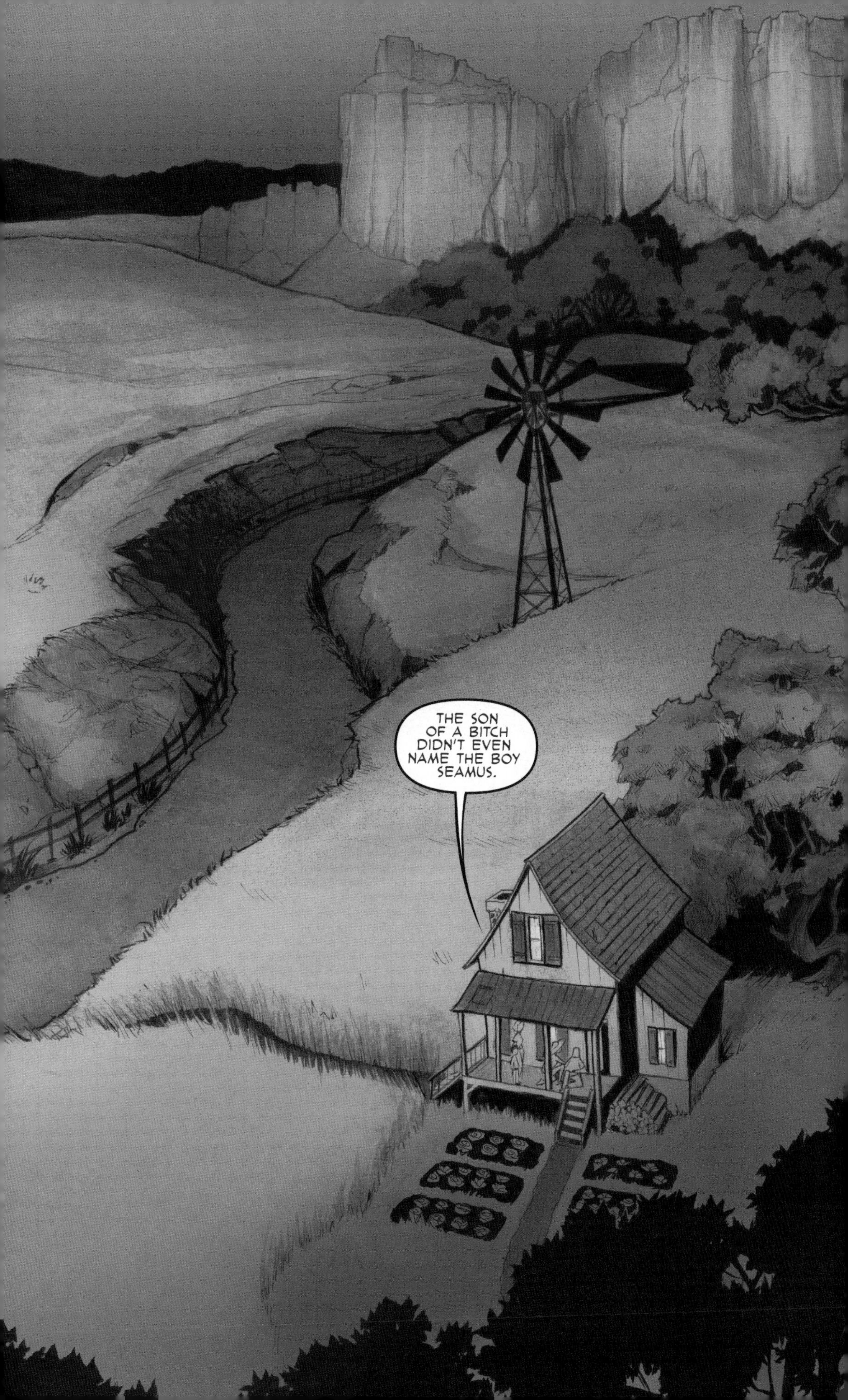
THE SON OF A BITCH DIDN'T EVEN NAME THE BOY SEAMUS.

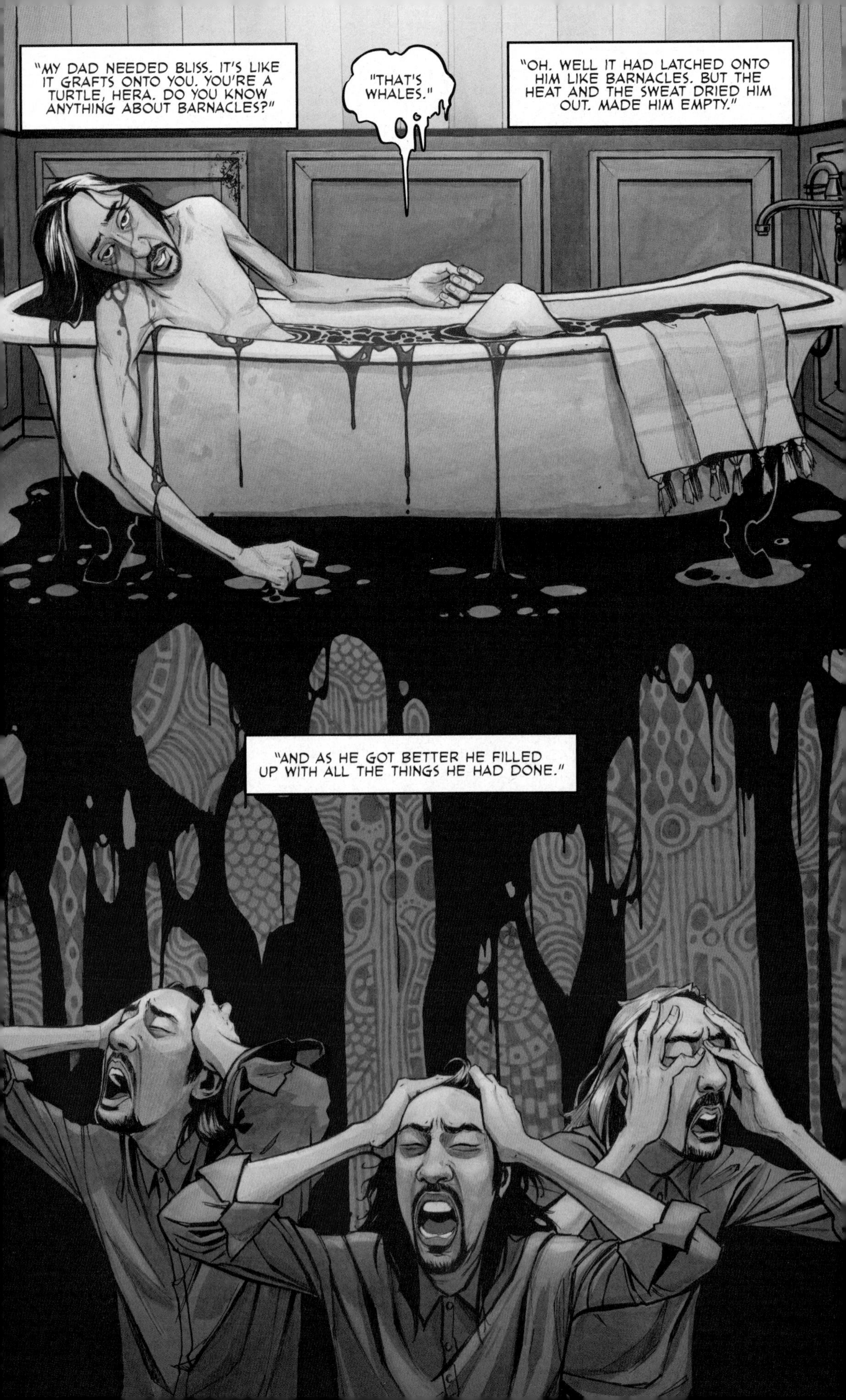
"MY DAD NEEDED BLISS. IT'S LIKE IT GRAFTS ONTO YOU. YOU'RE A TURTLE, HERA. DO YOU KNOW ANYTHING ABOUT BARNACLES?"
"THAT'S WHALES."
"OH. WELL IT HAD LATCHED ONTO HIM LIKE BARNACLES. BUT THE HEAT AND THE SWEAT DRIED HIM OUT. MADE HIM EMPTY."
"AND AS HE GOT BETTER HE FILLED UP WITH ALL THE THINGS HE HAD DONE."

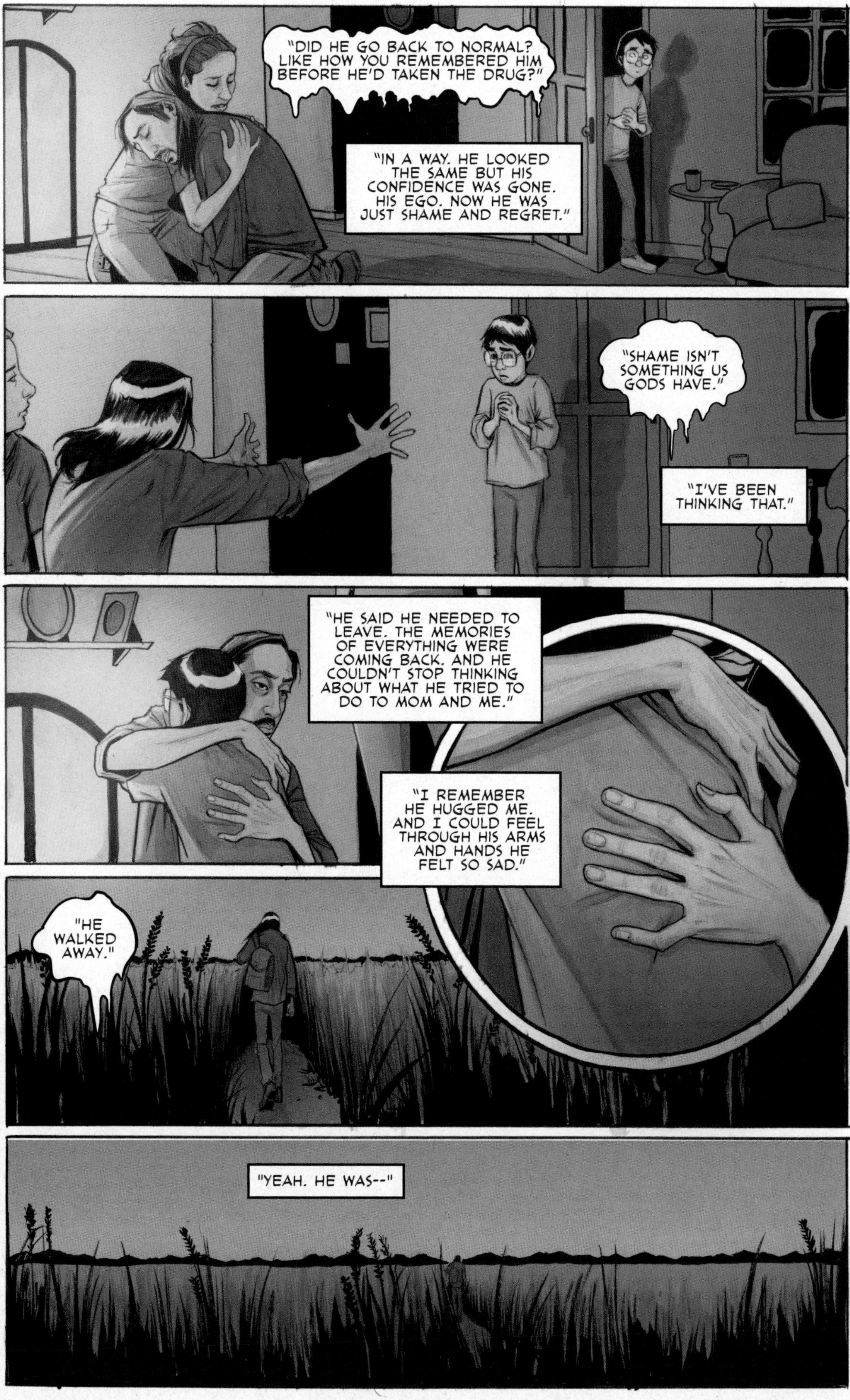
"DID HE GO BACK TO NORMAL? LIKE HOW YOU REMEMBERED HIM BEFORE HE'D TAKEN THE DRUG?"
"IN A WAY. HE LOOKED THE SAME BUT HIS CONFIDENCE WAS GONE. HIS EGO. NOW HE WAS JUST SHAME AND REGRET."
"SHAME ISN'T SOMETHING US GODS HAVE."
"I'VE BEEN THINKING THAT."
"HE SAID HE NEEDED TO LEAVE. THE MEMORIES OF EVERYTHING WERE COMING BACK. AND HE COULDN'T STOP THINKING ABOUT WHAT HE TRIED TO DO TO MOM AND ME."
"I REMEMBER HE HUGGED ME. AND I COULD FEEL THROUGH HIS ARMS AND HANDS HE FELT SO SAD."
"HE WALKED AWAY."
"YEAH. HE WAS--"

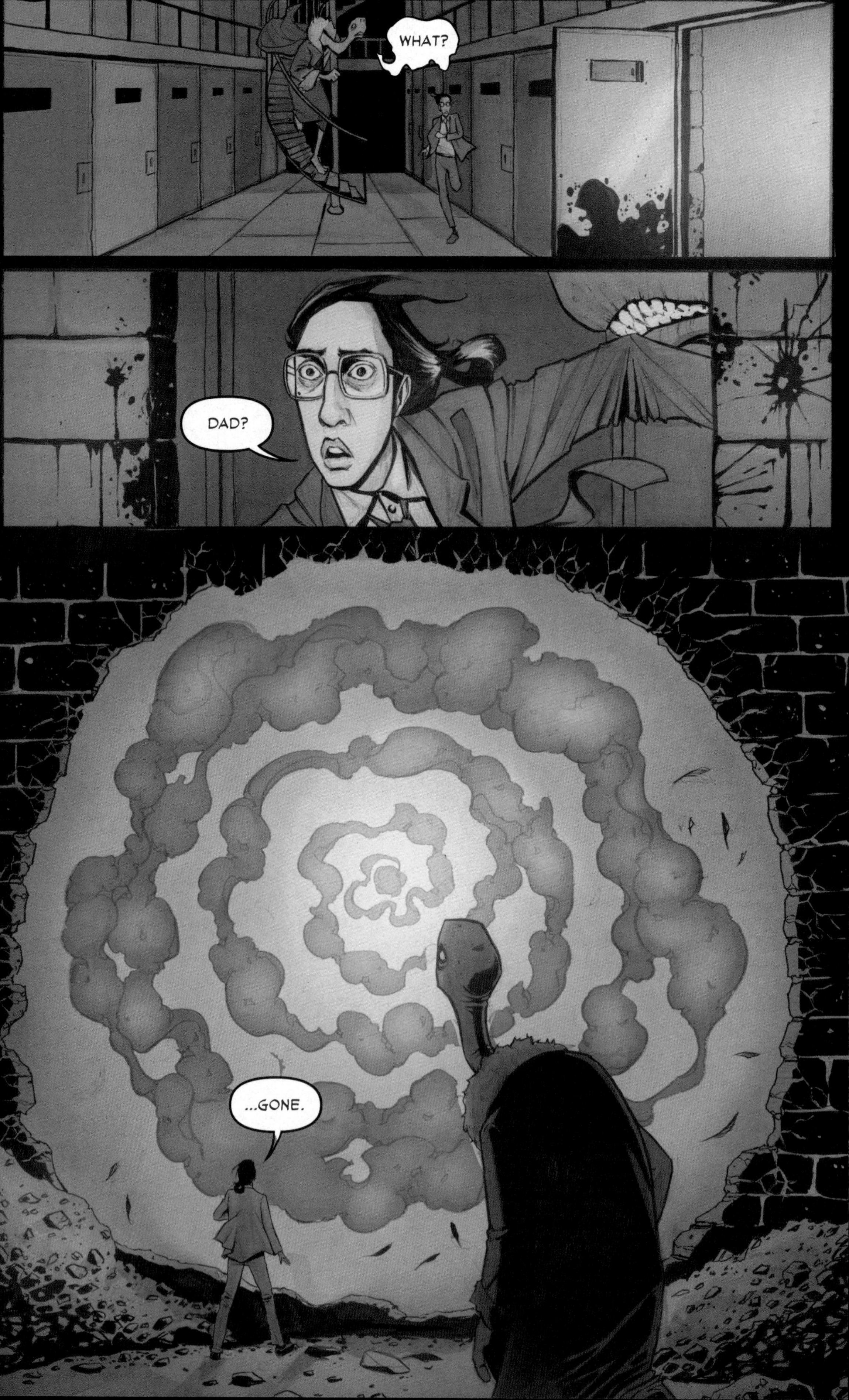
WHAT?
DAD?
...GONE.

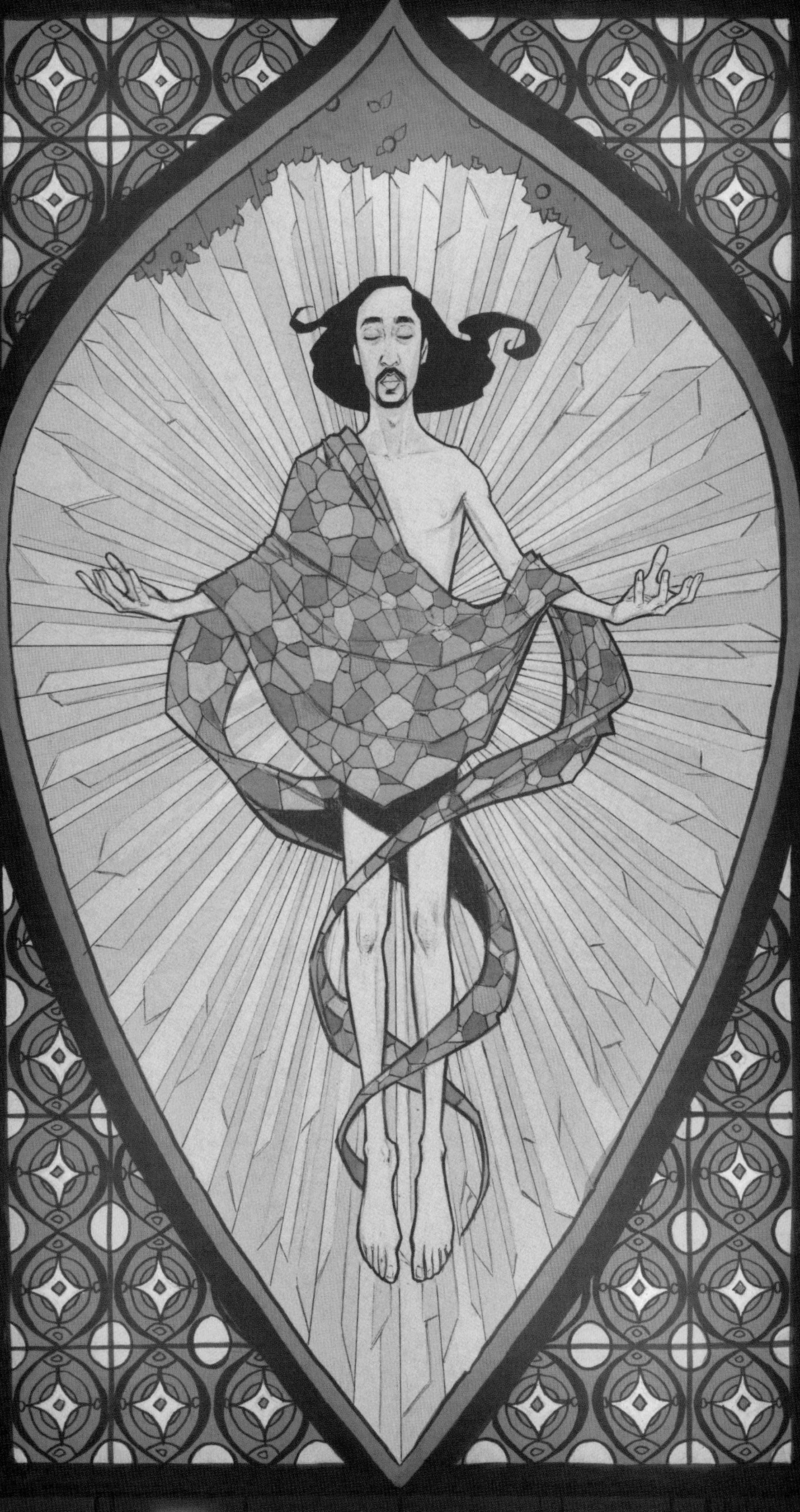

BENTON

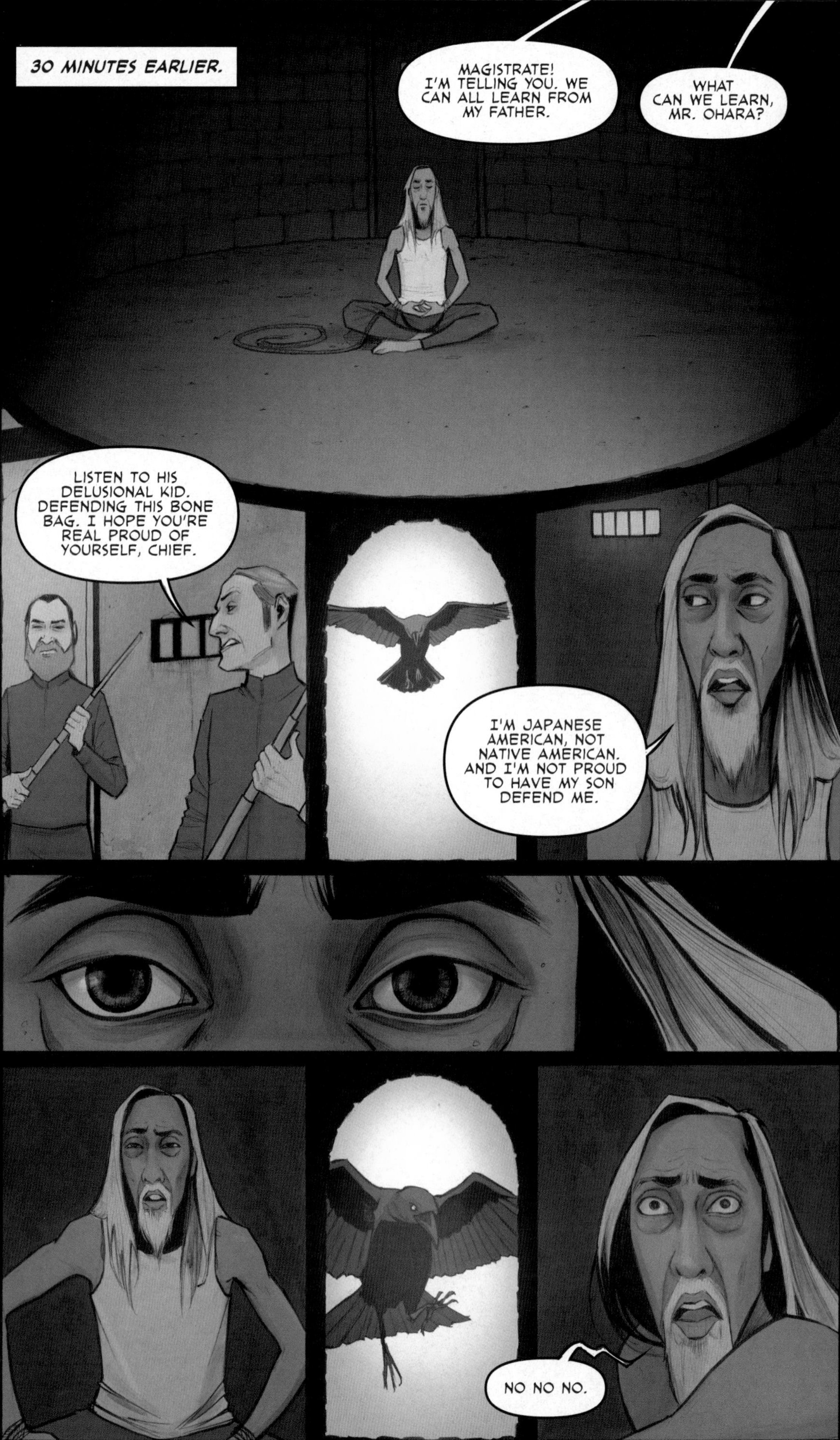

30 MINUTES EARLIER.
MAGISTRATE! I'M TELLING YOU. WE CAN ALL LEARN FROM MY FATHER.
WHAT CAN WE LEARN, MR. OHARA?
LISTEN TO HIS DELUSIONAL KID. DEFENDING THIS BONE BAG. I HOPE YOU'RE REAL PROUD OF YOURSELF, CHIEF.
I'M JAPANESE AMERICAN, NOT NATIVE AMERICAN. AND I'M NOT PROUD TO HAVE MY SON DEFEND ME.
NO NO NO.

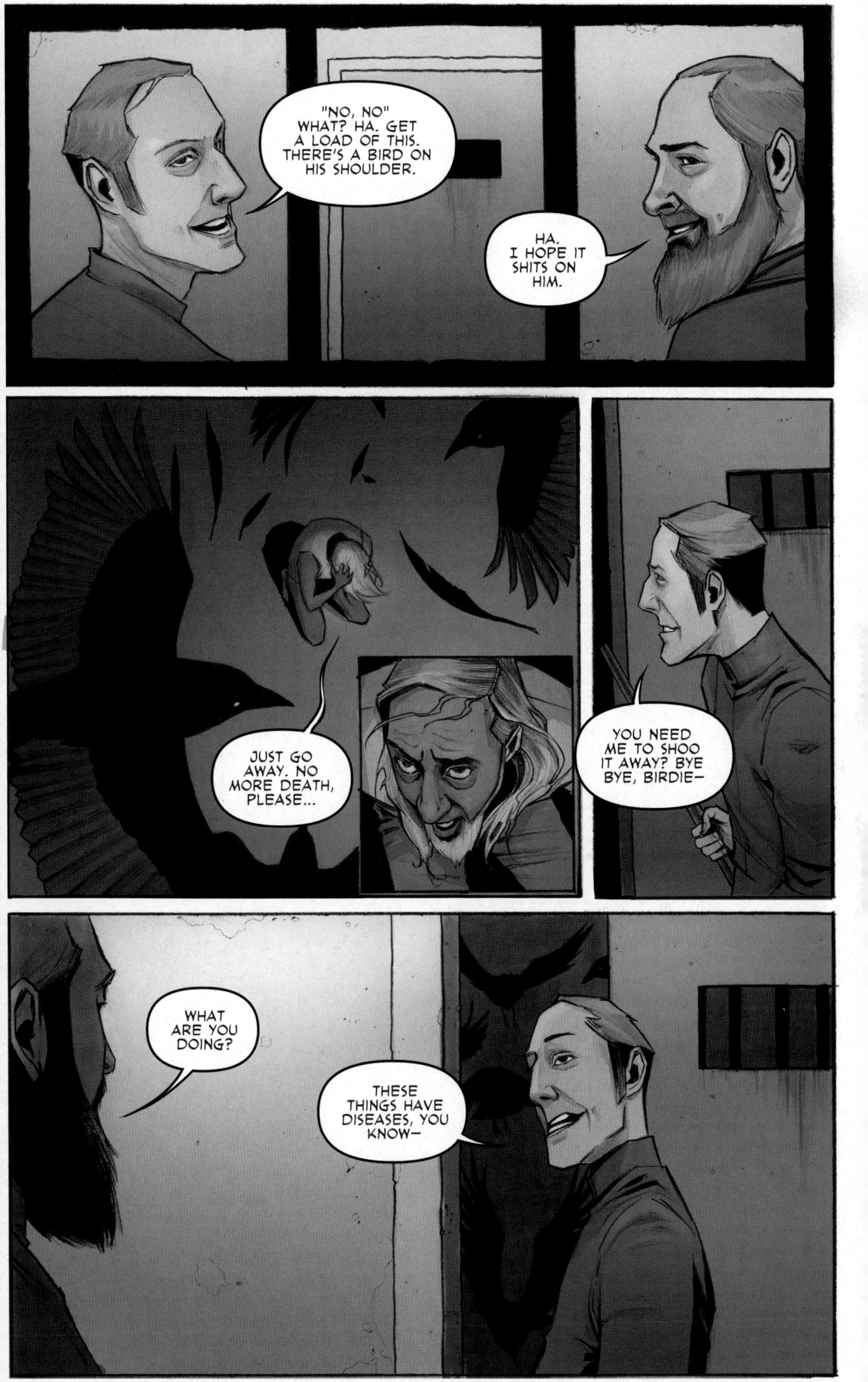
"NO, NO" WHAT? HA. GET A LOAD OF THIS. THERE'S A BIRD ON HIS SHOULDER.
HA. I HOPE IT SHITS ON HIM.
JUST GO AWAY. NO MORE DEATH, PLEASE...
YOU NEED ME TO SHOO IT AWAY? BYE BYE, BIRDIE–
WHAT ARE YOU DOING?
THESE THINGS HAVE DISEASES, YOU KNOW–

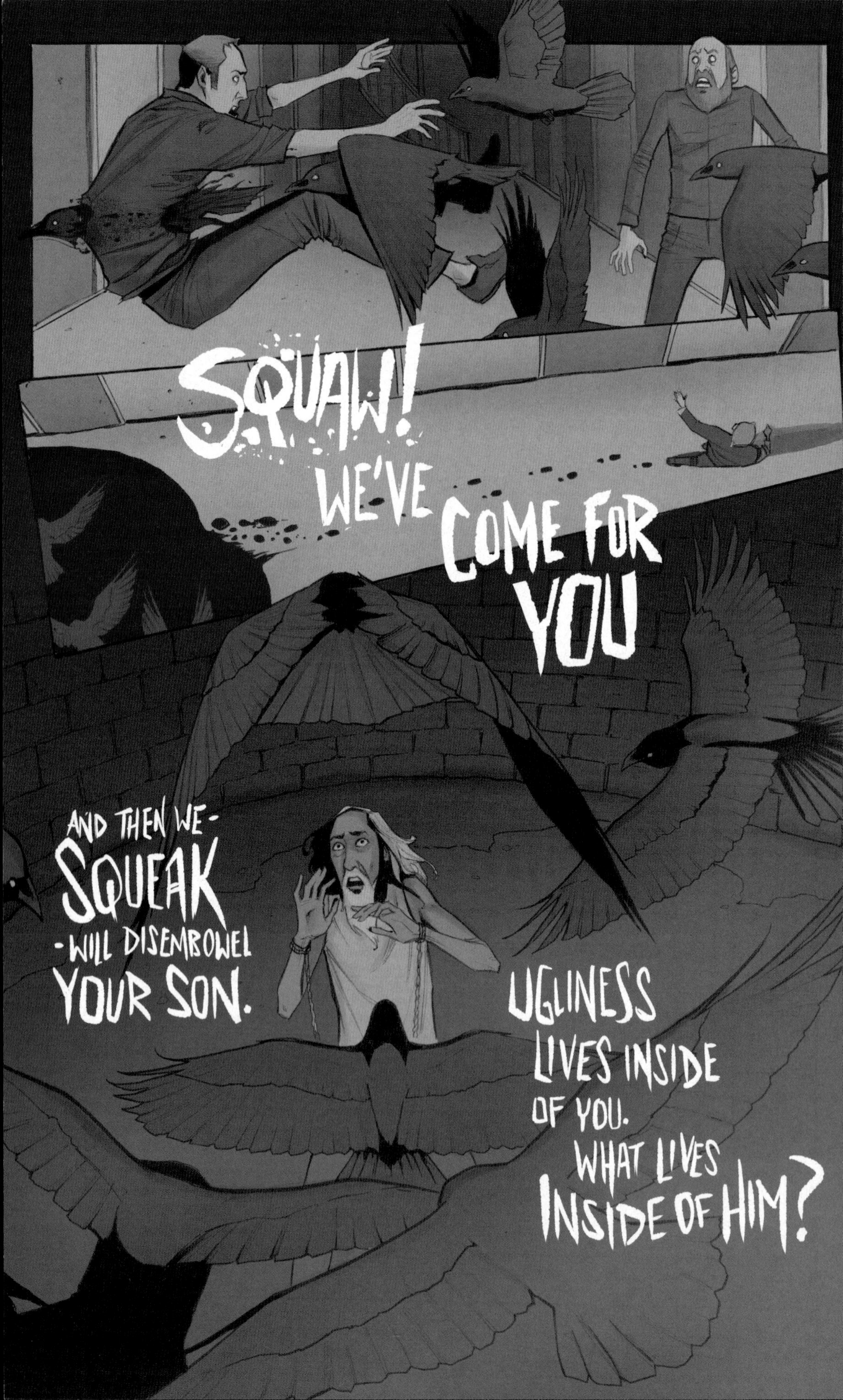
SQUAW!
WE'VE COME FOR YOU
AND THEN WE-
SQUEAK
-WILL DISEMBOWEL YOUR SON.
UGLINESS LIVES INSIDE OF YOU.
WHAT LIVES INSIDE OF HIM?

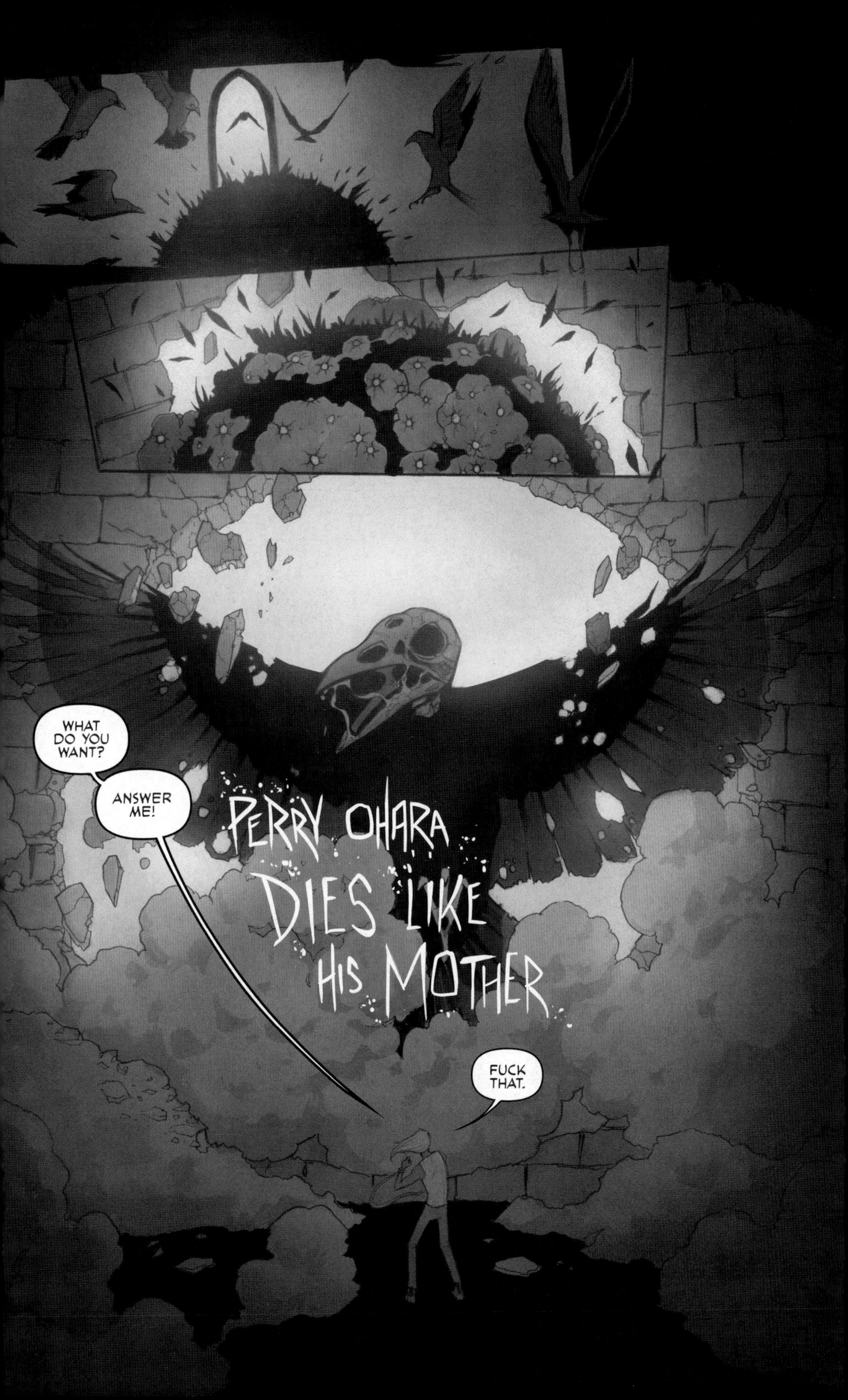
WHAT DO YOU WANT?
ANSWER ME!
PERRY OHARA DIES LIKE HIS MOTHER
FUCK THAT.

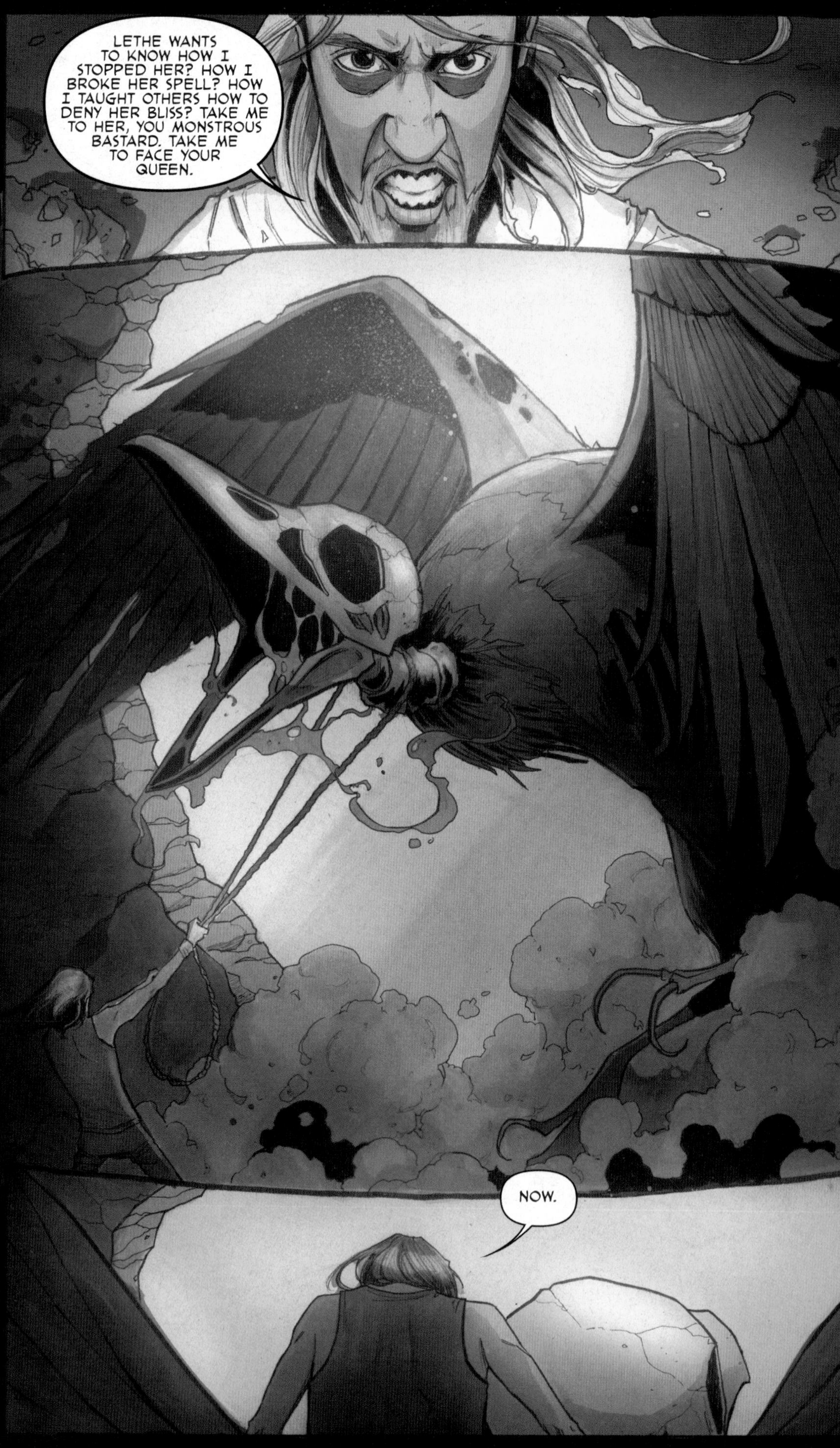
LETHE WANTS TO KNOW HOW I STOPPED HER? HOW I BROKE HER SPELL? HOW I TAUGHT OTHERS HOW TO DENY HER BLISS? TAKE ME TO HER, YOU MONSTROUS BASTARD. TAKE ME TO FACE YOUR QUEEN.
NOW.

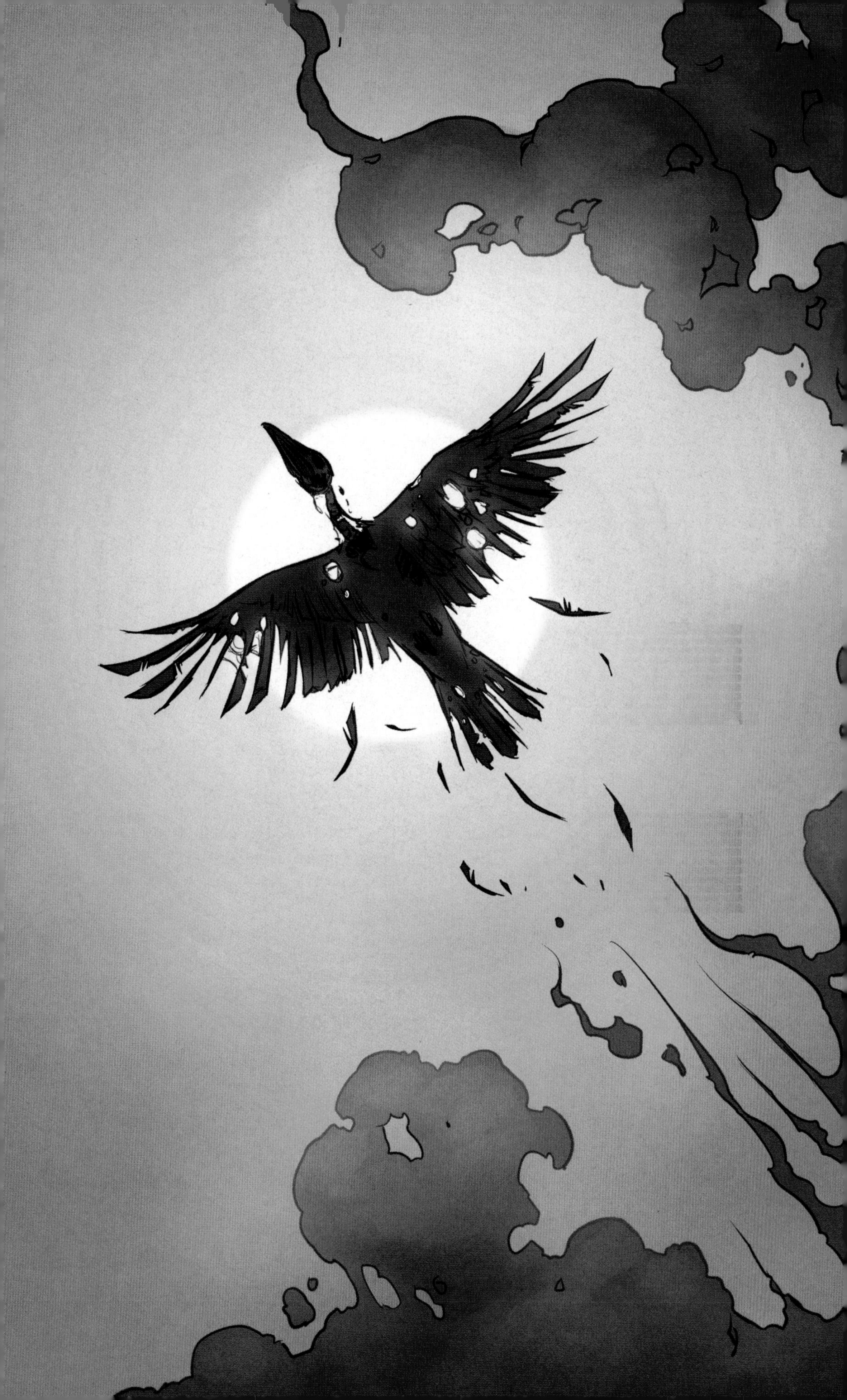

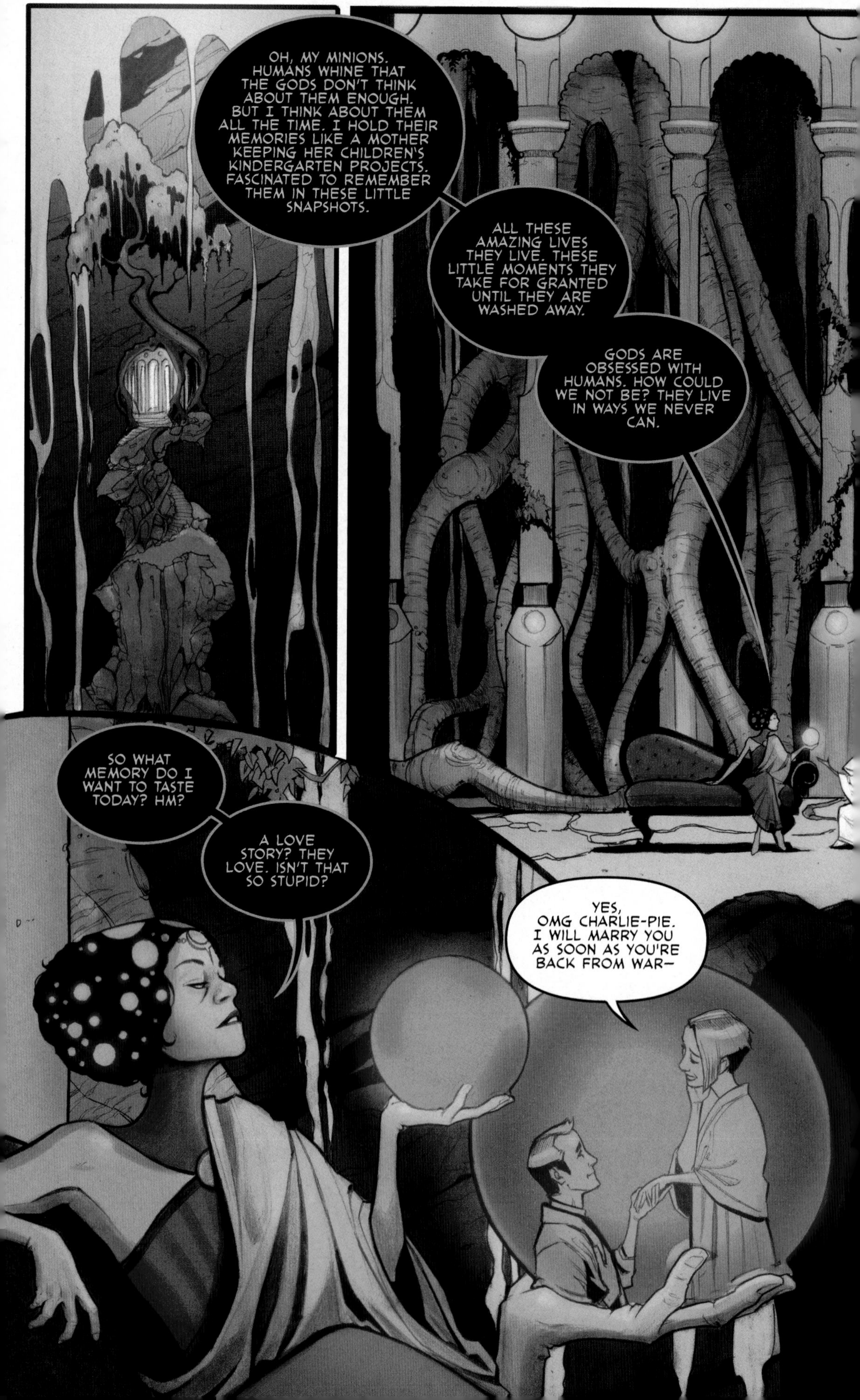
OH, MY MINIONS. HUMANS WHINE THAT THE GODS DON'T THINK ABOUT THEM ENOUGH. BUT I THINK ABOUT THEM ALL THE TIME. I HOLD THEIR MEMORIES LIKE A MOTHER KEEPING HER CHILDREN'S KINDERGARTEN PROJECTS. FASCINATED TO REMEMBER THEM IN THESE LITTLE SNAPSHOTS.
ALL THESE AMAZING LIVES THEY LIVE. THESE LITTLE MOMENTS THEY TAKE FOR GRANTED UNTIL THEY ARE WASHED AWAY.
GODS ARE OBSESSED WITH HUMANS. HOW COULD WE NOT BE? THEY LIVE IN WAYS WE NEVER CAN.
SO WHAT MEMORY DO I WANT TO TASTE TODAY? HM?
A LOVE STORY? THEY LOVE. ISN'T THAT SO STUPID?
YES, OMG CHARLIE-PIE. I WILL MARRY YOU AS SOON AS YOU'RE BACK FROM WAR–

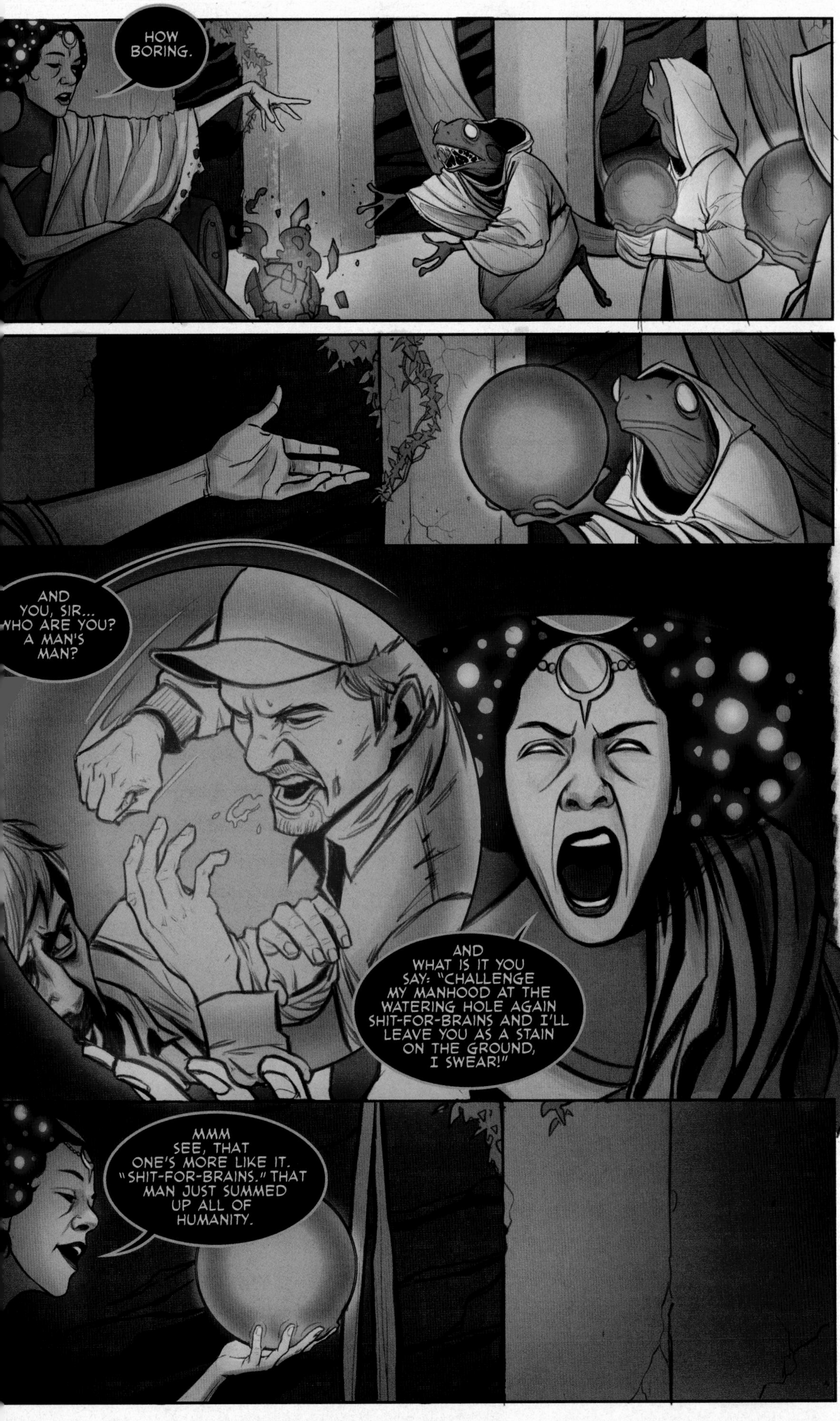
HOW BORING.
AND YOU, SIR... WHO ARE YOU? A MAN'S MAN?
AND WHAT IS IT YOU SAY: "CHALLENGE MY MANHOOD AT THE WATERING HOLE AGAIN SHIT-FOR-BRAINS AND I'LL LEAVE YOU AS A STAIN ON THE GROUND, I SWEAR!"
MMM SEE, THAT ONE'S MORE LIKE IT. "SHIT-FOR-BRAINS." THAT MAN JUST SUMMED UP ALL OF HUMANITY.

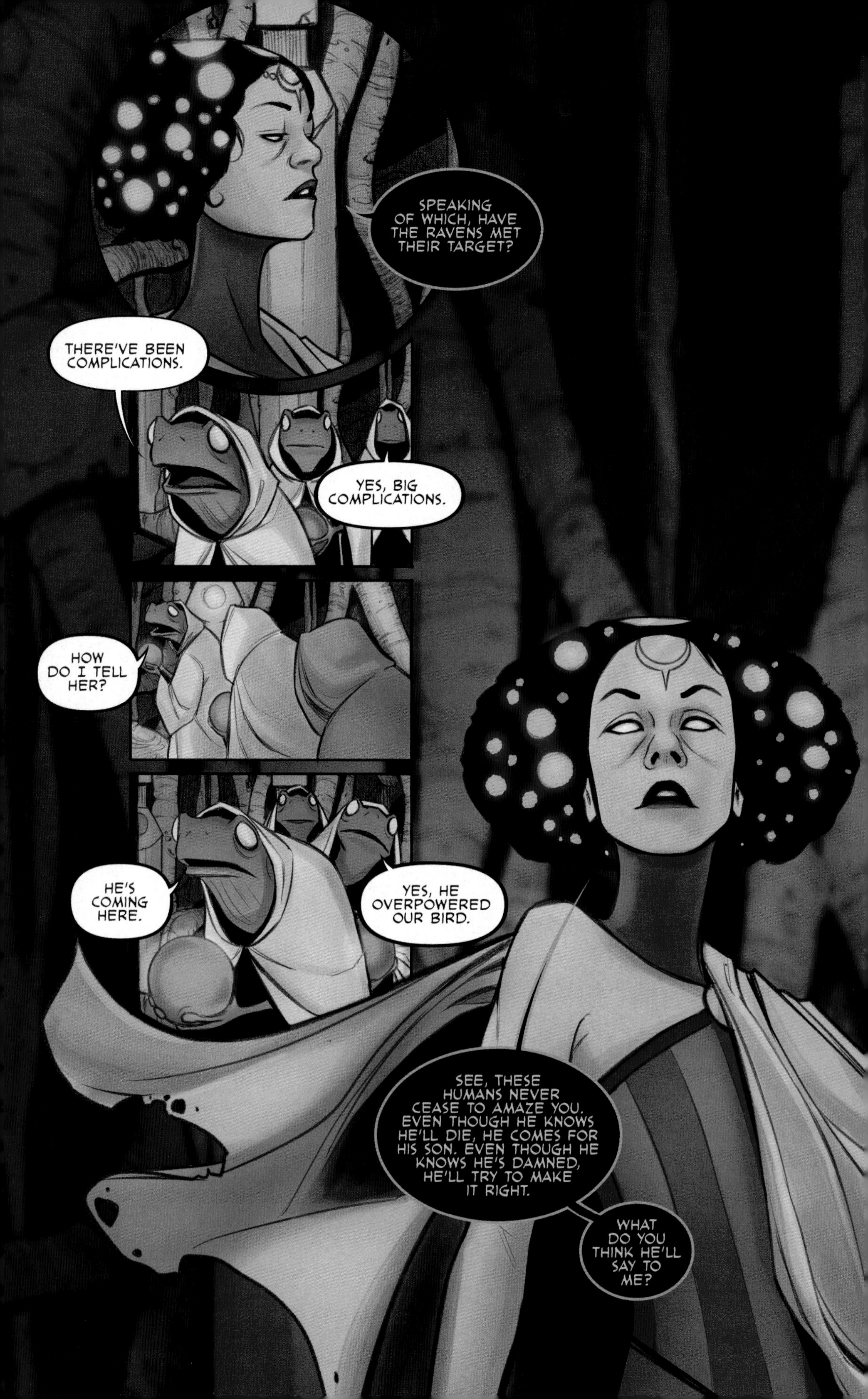
SPEAKING OF WHICH, HAVE THE RAVENS MET THEIR TARGET?
THERE'VE BEEN COMPLICATIONS.
YES, BIG COMPLICATIONS.
HOW DO I TELL HER?
HE'S COMING HERE.
YES, HE OVERPOWERED OUR BIRD.
SEE, THESE HUMANS NEVER CEASE TO AMAZE YOU. EVEN THOUGH HE KNOWS HE'LL DIE, HE COMES FOR HIS SON. EVEN THOUGH HE KNOWS HE'S DAMNED, HE'LL TRY TO MAKE IT RIGHT.
WHAT DO YOU THINK HE'LL SAY TO ME?

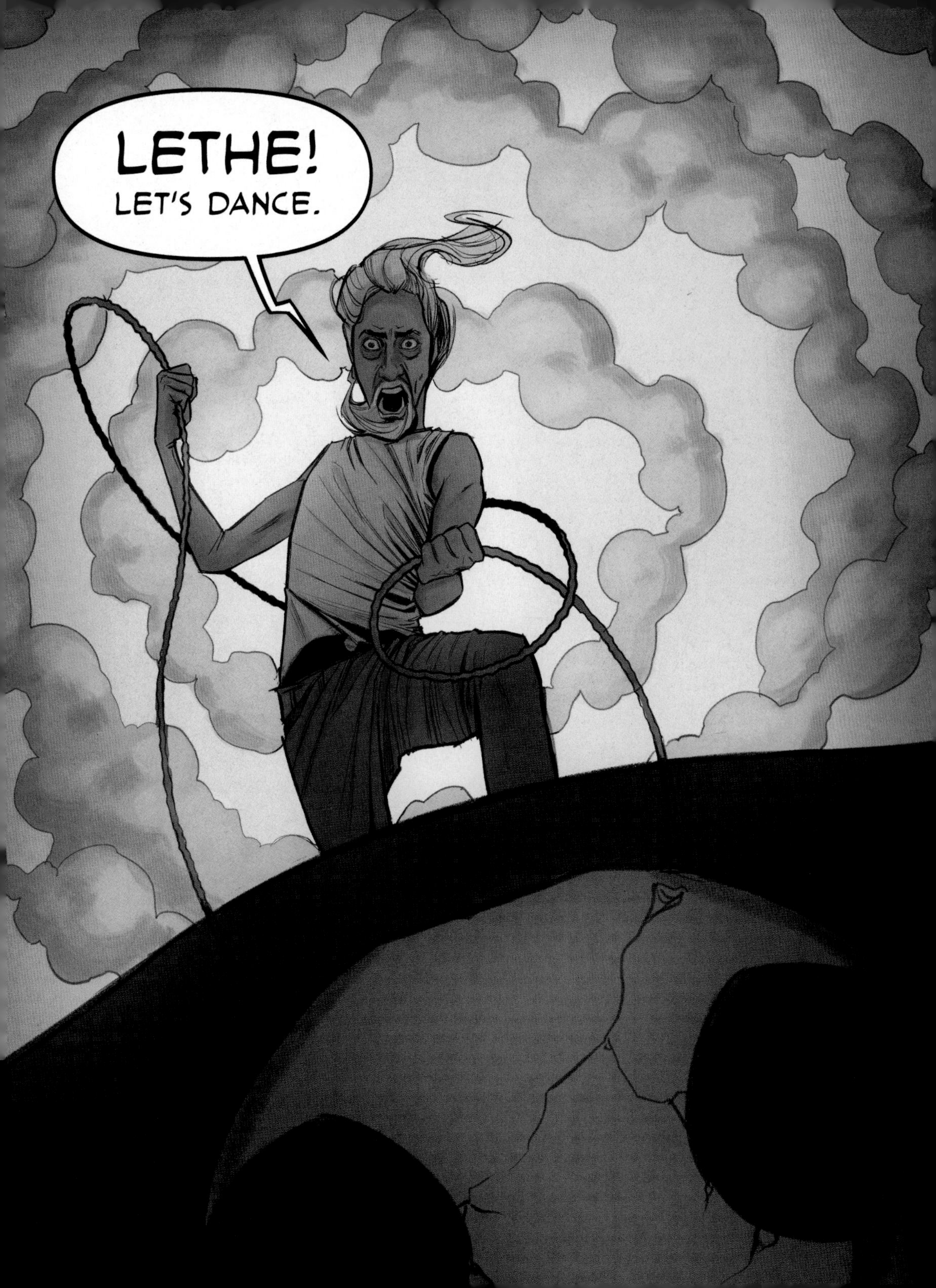
LETHE!
LET'S DANCE.

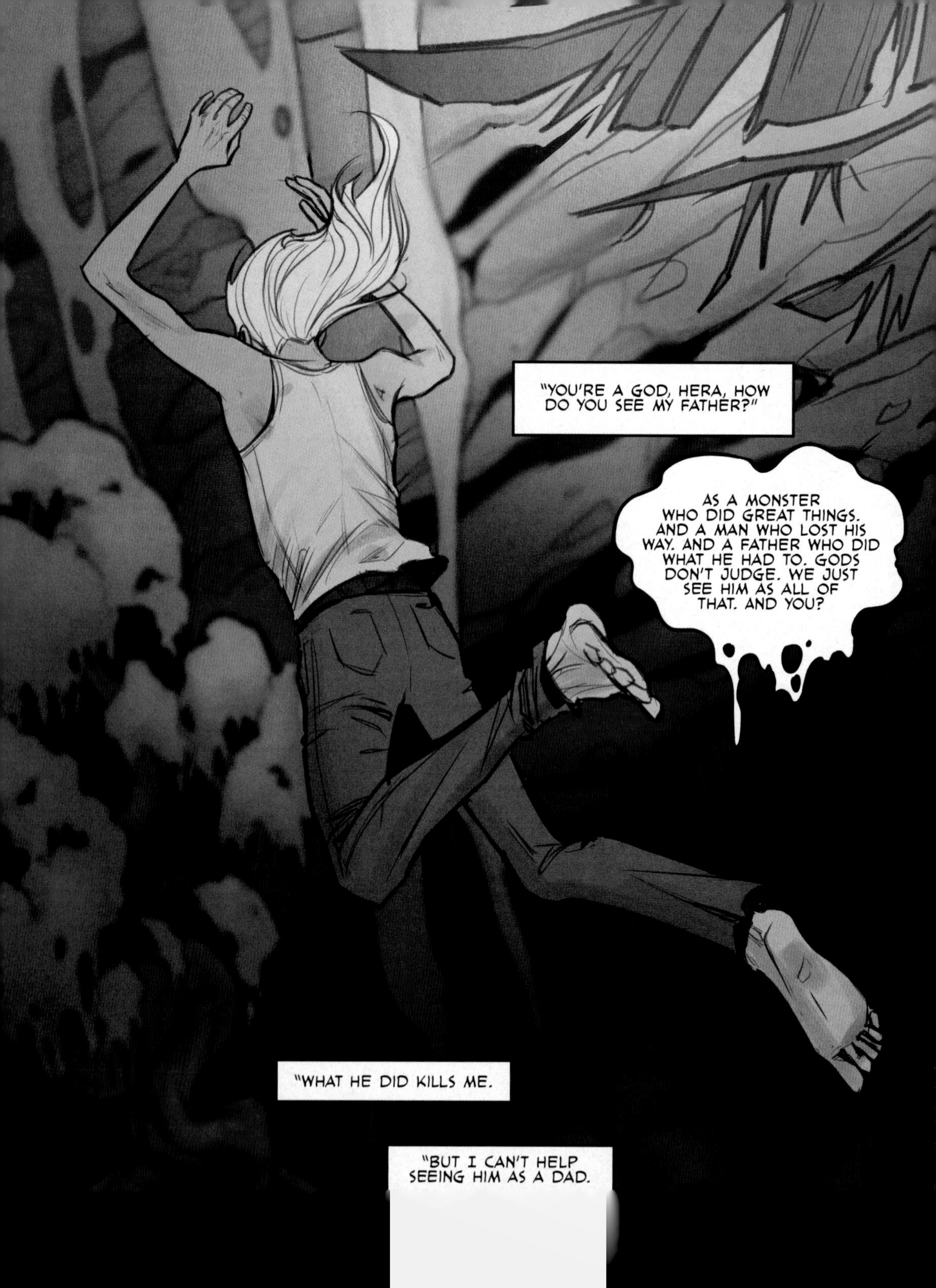
"YOU'RE A GOD, HERA, HOW DO YOU SEE MY FATHER?"
AS A MONSTER WHO DID GREAT THINGS. AND A MAN WHO LOST HIS WAY. AND A FATHER WHO DID WHAT HE HAD TO. GODS DON'T JUDGE. WE JUST SEE HIM AS ALL OF THAT. AND YOU?
"WHAT HE DID KILLS ME.
"BUT I CAN'T HELP SEEING HIM AS A DAD.

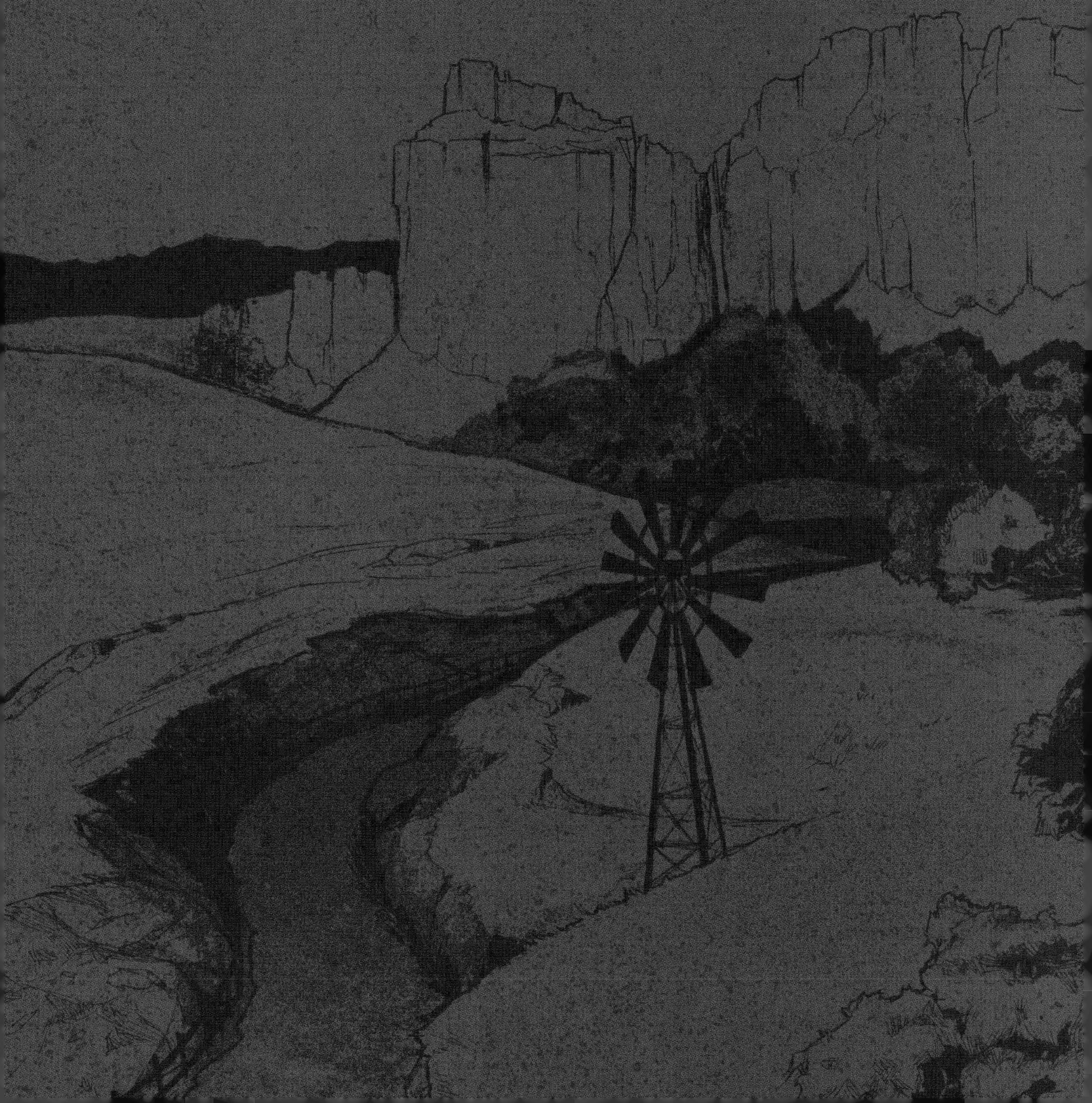

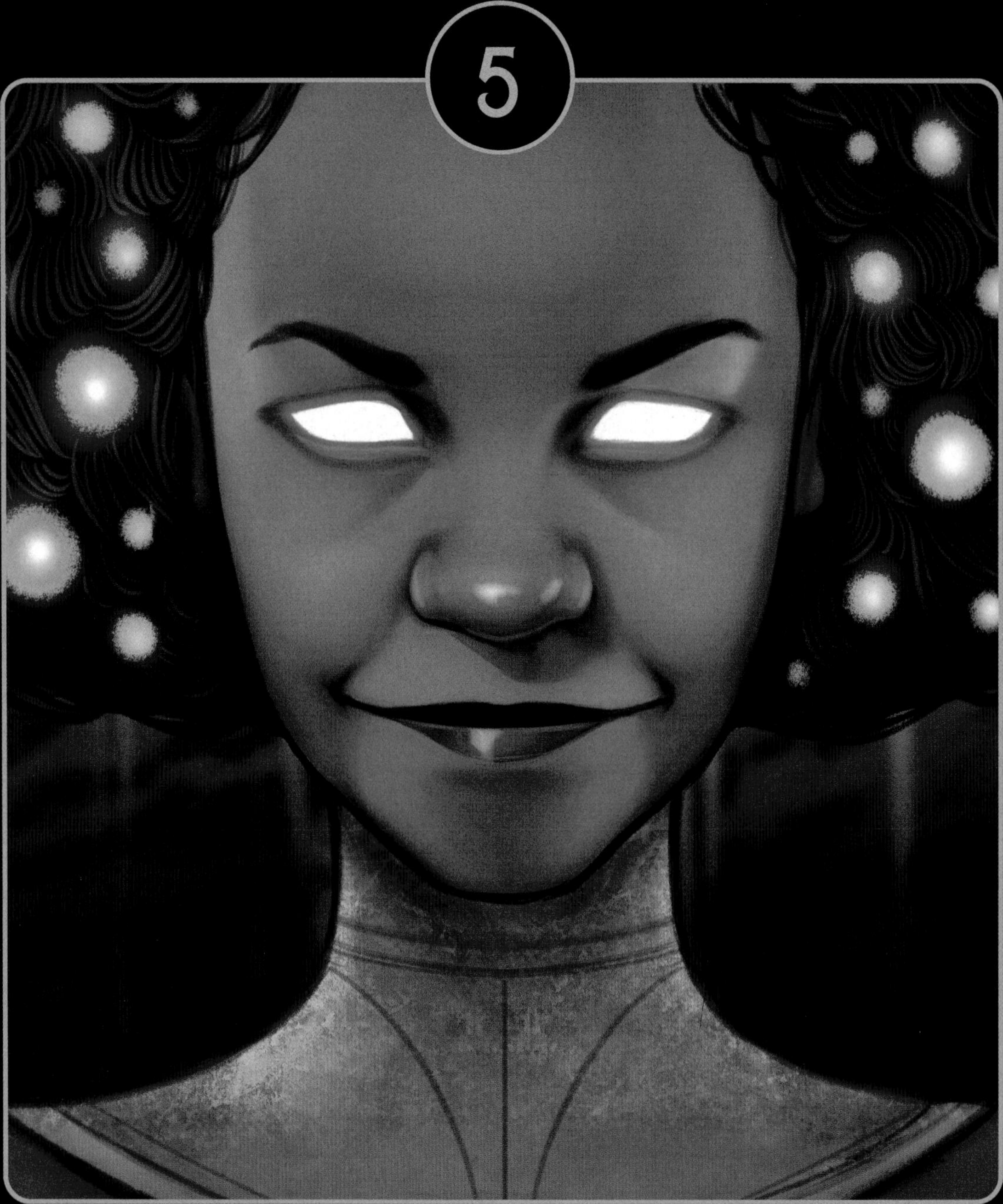
5

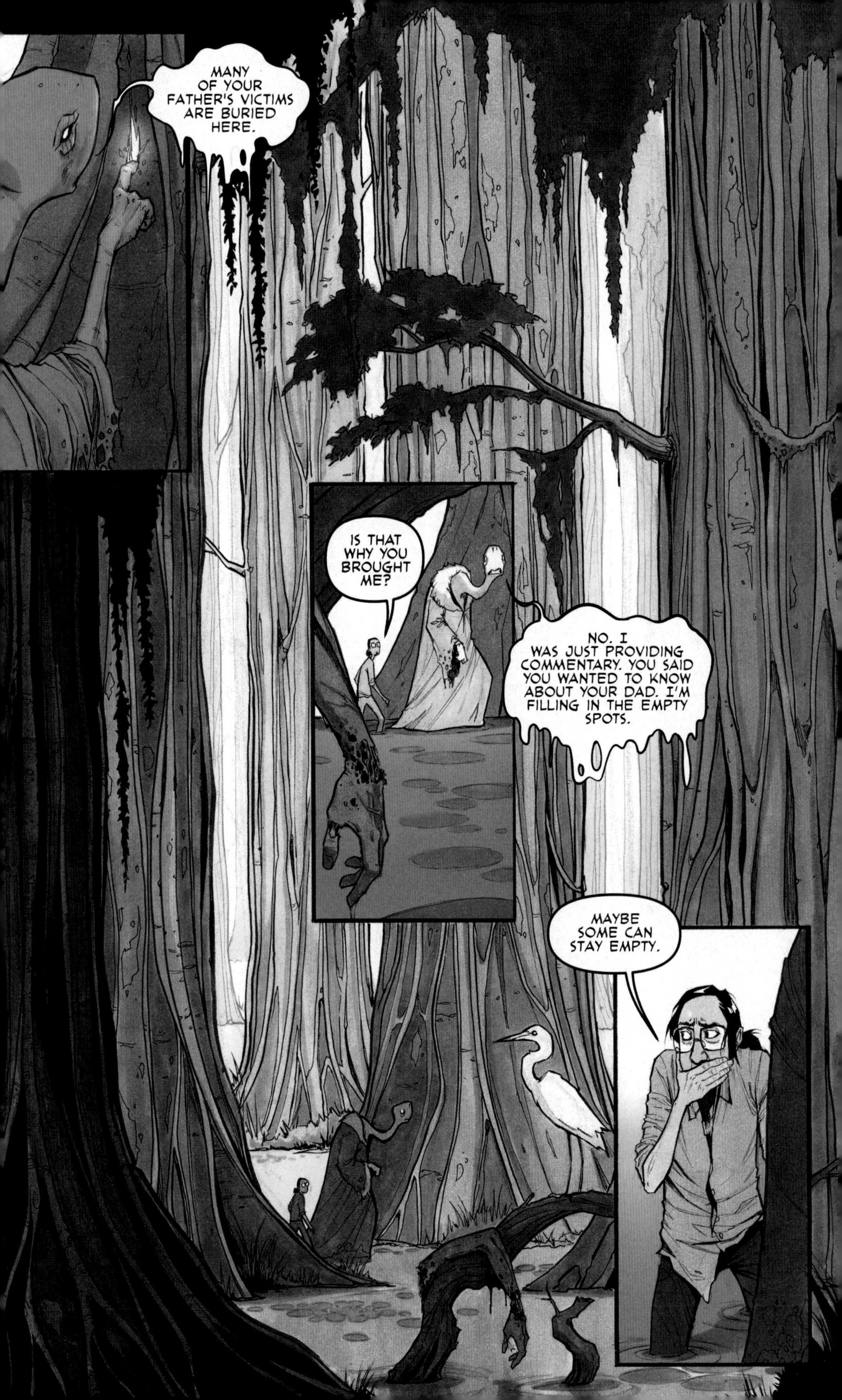
MANY OF YOUR FATHER'S VICTIMS ARE BURIED HERE.
IS THAT WHY YOU BROUGHT ME?
NO. I WAS JUST PROVIDING COMMENTARY. YOU SAID YOU WANTED TO KNOW ABOUT YOUR DAD. I'M FILLING IN THE EMPTY SPOTS.
MAYBE SOME CAN STAY EMPTY.

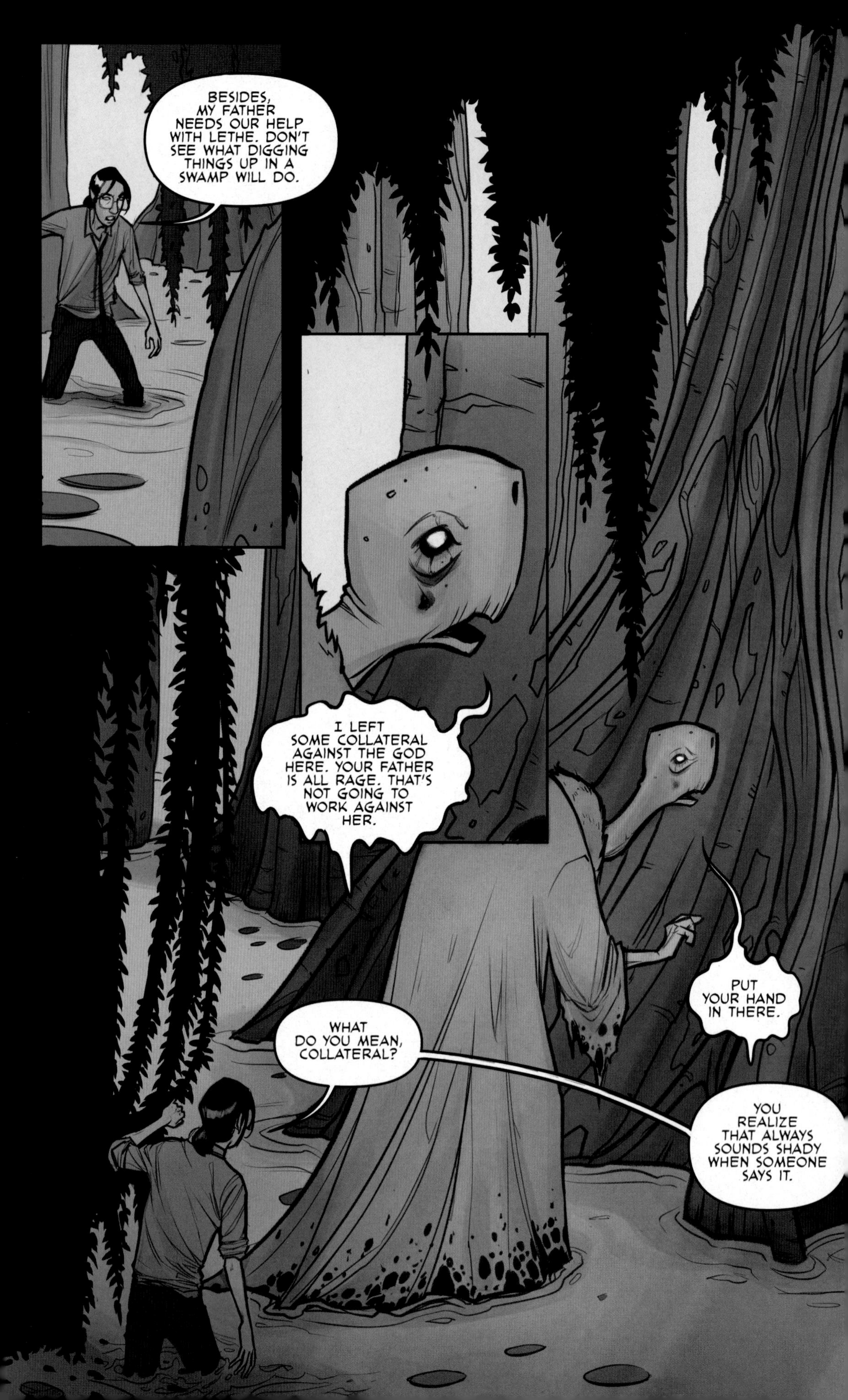
BESIDES, MY FATHER NEEDS OUR HELP WITH LETHE. DON'T SEE WHAT DIGGING THINGS UP IN A SWAMP WILL DO.
I LEFT SOME COLLATERAL AGAINST THE GOD HERE. YOUR FATHER IS ALL RAGE. THAT'S NOT GOING TO WORK AGAINST HER.
PUT YOUR HAND IN THERE.
WHAT DO YOU MEAN, COLLATERAL?
YOU REALIZE THAT ALWAYS SOUNDS SHADY WHEN SOMEONE SAYS IT.

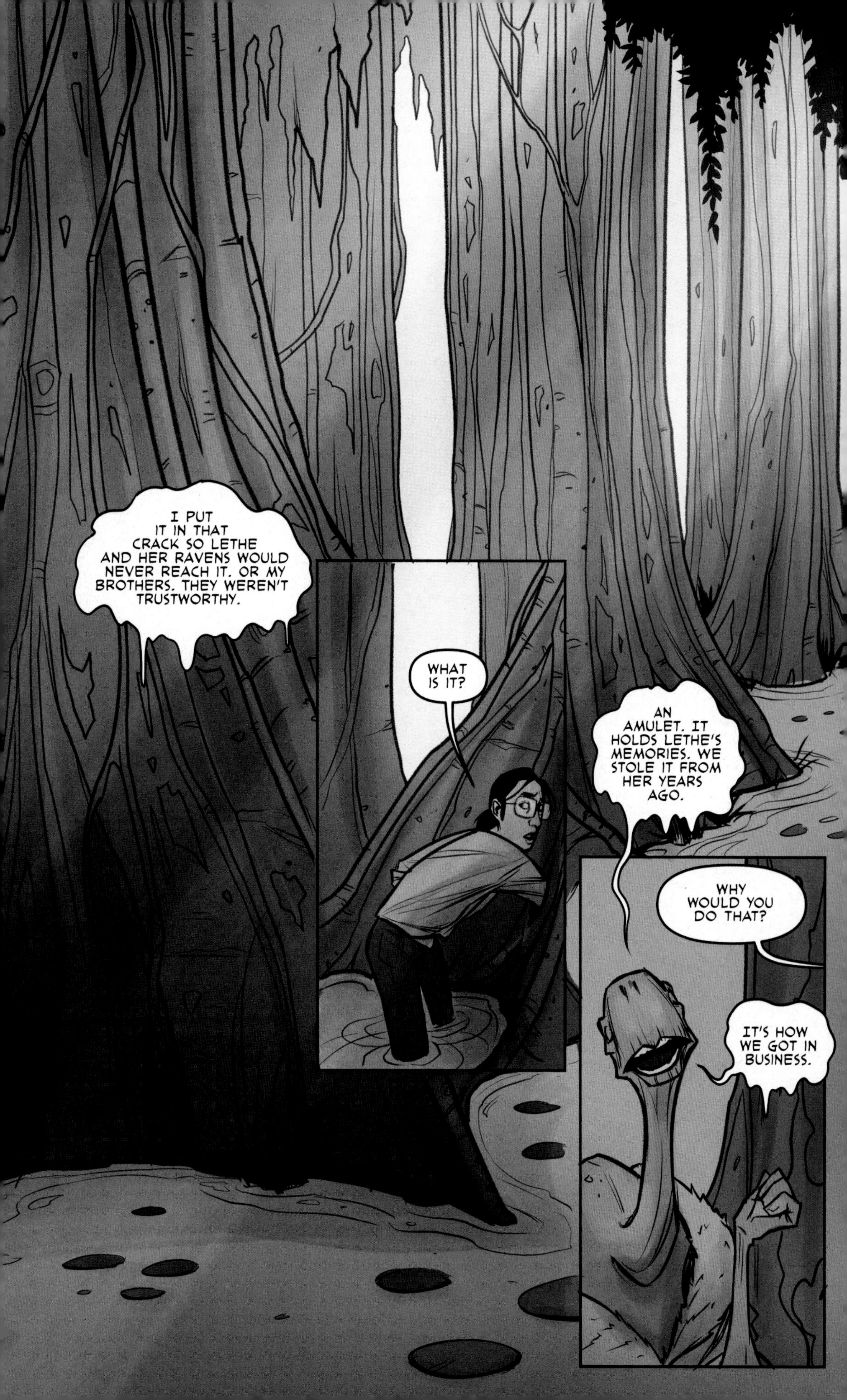
I PUT IT IN THAT CRACK SO LETHE AND HER RAVENS WOULD NEVER REACH IT. OR MY BROTHERS. THEY WEREN'T TRUSTWORTHY.
WHAT IS IT?
AN AMULET. IT HOLDS LETHE'S MEMORIES. WE STOLE IT FROM HER YEARS AGO.
WHY WOULD YOU DO THAT?
IT'S HOW WE GOT IN BUSINESS.

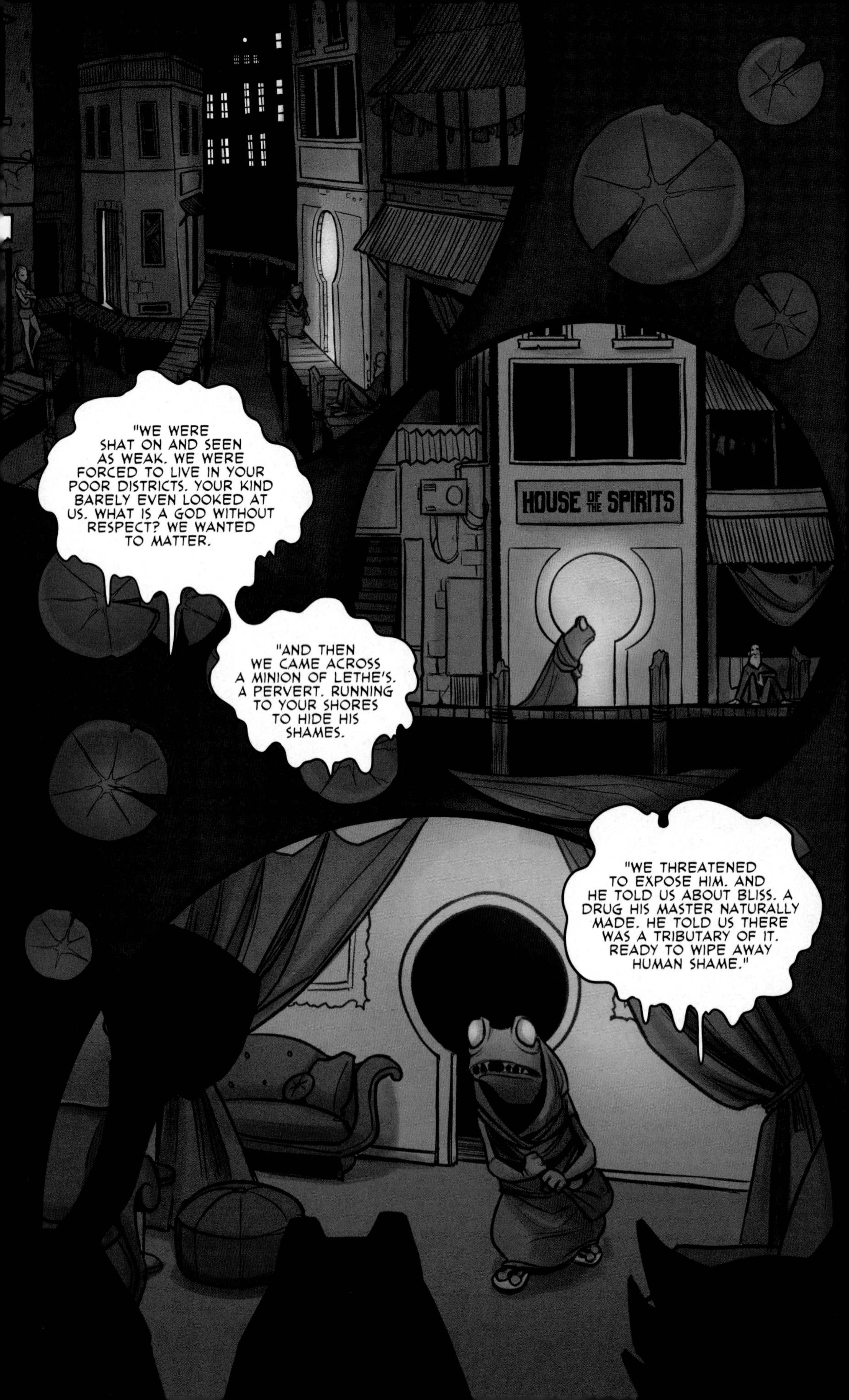
"WE WERE SHAT ON AND SEEN AS WEAK. WE WERE FORCED TO LIVE IN YOUR POOR DISTRICTS. YOUR KIND BARELY EVEN LOOKED AT US. WHAT IS A GOD WITHOUT RESPECT? WE WANTED TO MATTER.
HOUSE OF THE SPIRITS
"AND THEN WE CAME ACROSS A MINION OF LETHE'S. A PERVERT. RUNNING TO YOUR SHORES TO HIDE HIS SHAMES.
"WE THREATENED TO EXPOSE HIM. AND HE TOLD US ABOUT BLISS. A DRUG HIS MASTER NATURALLY MADE. HE TOLD US THERE WAS A TRIBUTARY OF IT. READY TO WIPE AWAY HUMAN SHAME."

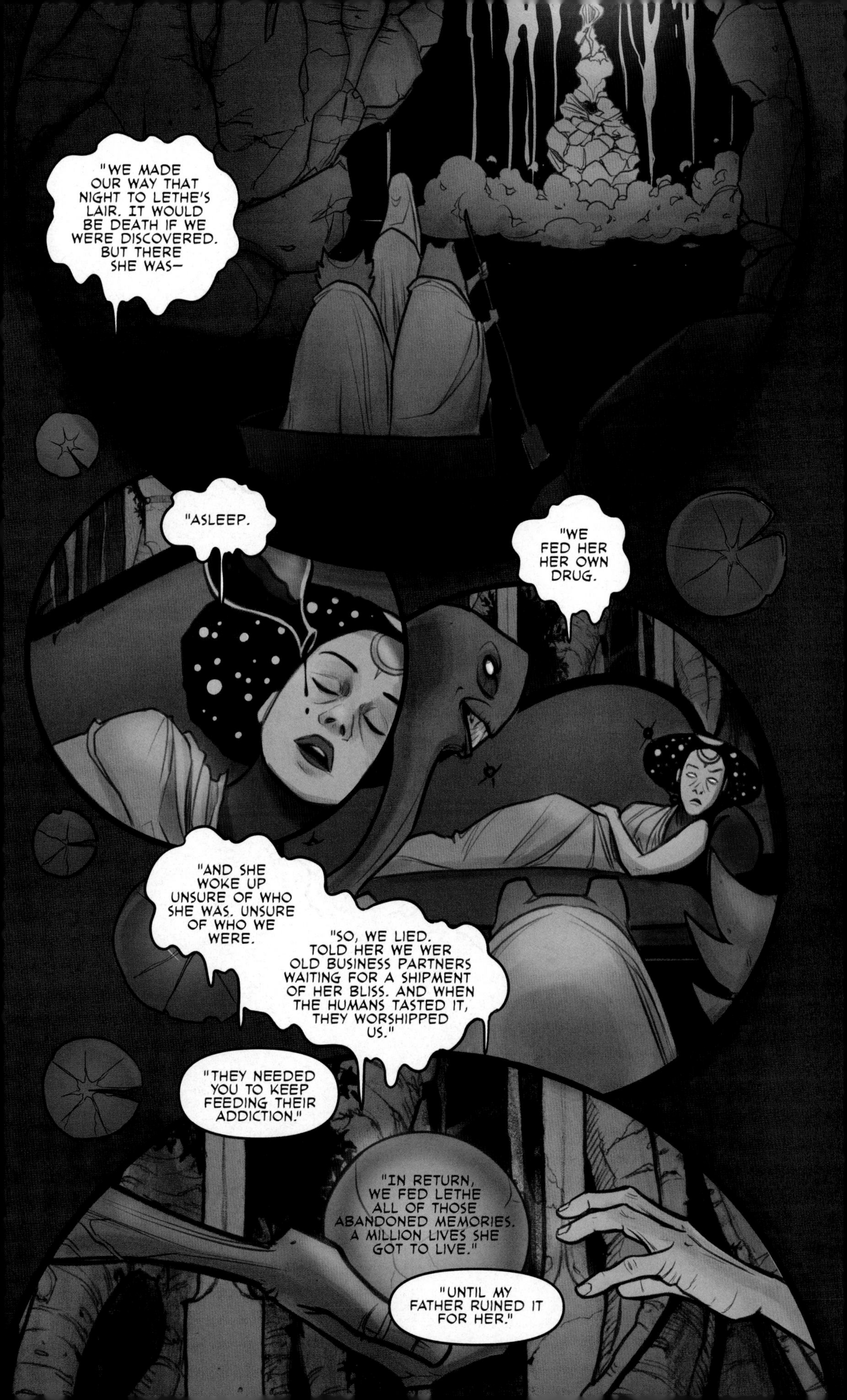
"WE MADE OUR WAY THAT NIGHT TO LETHE'S LAIR. IT WOULD BE DEATH IF WE WERE DISCOVERED. BUT THERE SHE WAS—
"ASLEEP.
"WE FED HER HER OWN DRUG.
"AND SHE WOKE UP UNSURE OF WHO SHE WAS. UNSURE OF WHO WE WERE.
"SO, WE LIED. TOLD HER WE WER OLD BUSINESS PARTNERS WAITING FOR A SHIPMENT OF HER BLISS. AND WHEN THE HUMANS TASTED IT, THEY WORSHIPPED US."
"THEY NEEDED YOU TO KEEP FEEDING THEIR ADDICTION."
"IN RETURN, WE FED LETHE ALL OF THOSE ABANDONED MEMORIES. A MILLION LIVES SHE GOT TO LIVE."
"UNTIL MY FATHER RUINED IT FOR HER."

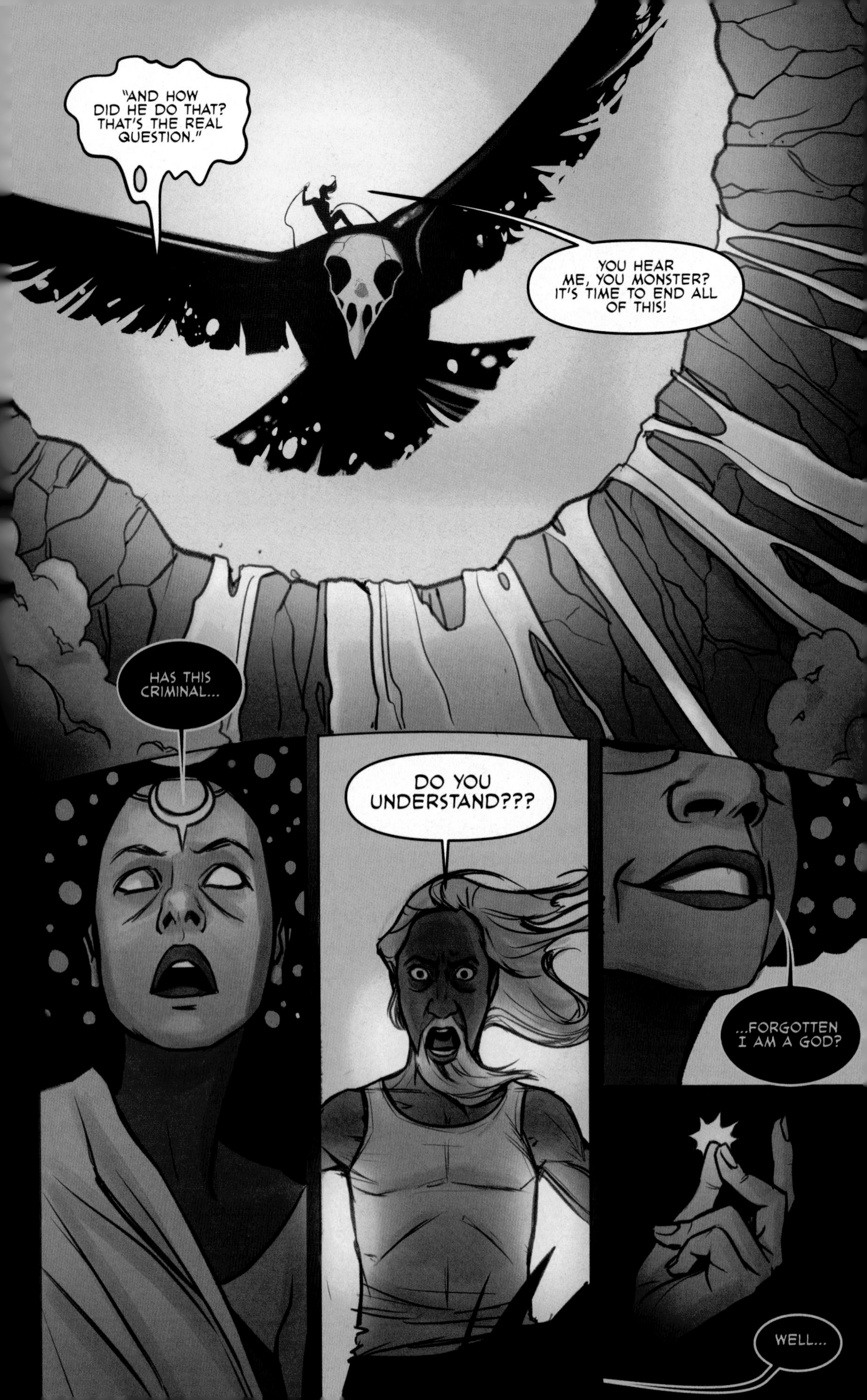
"AND HOW DID HE DO THAT? THAT'S THE REAL QUESTION."
YOU HEAR ME, YOU MONSTER? IT'S TIME TO END ALL OF THIS!
HAS THIS CRIMINAL...
DO YOU UNDERSTAND???
...FORGOTTEN I AM A GOD?
WELL...

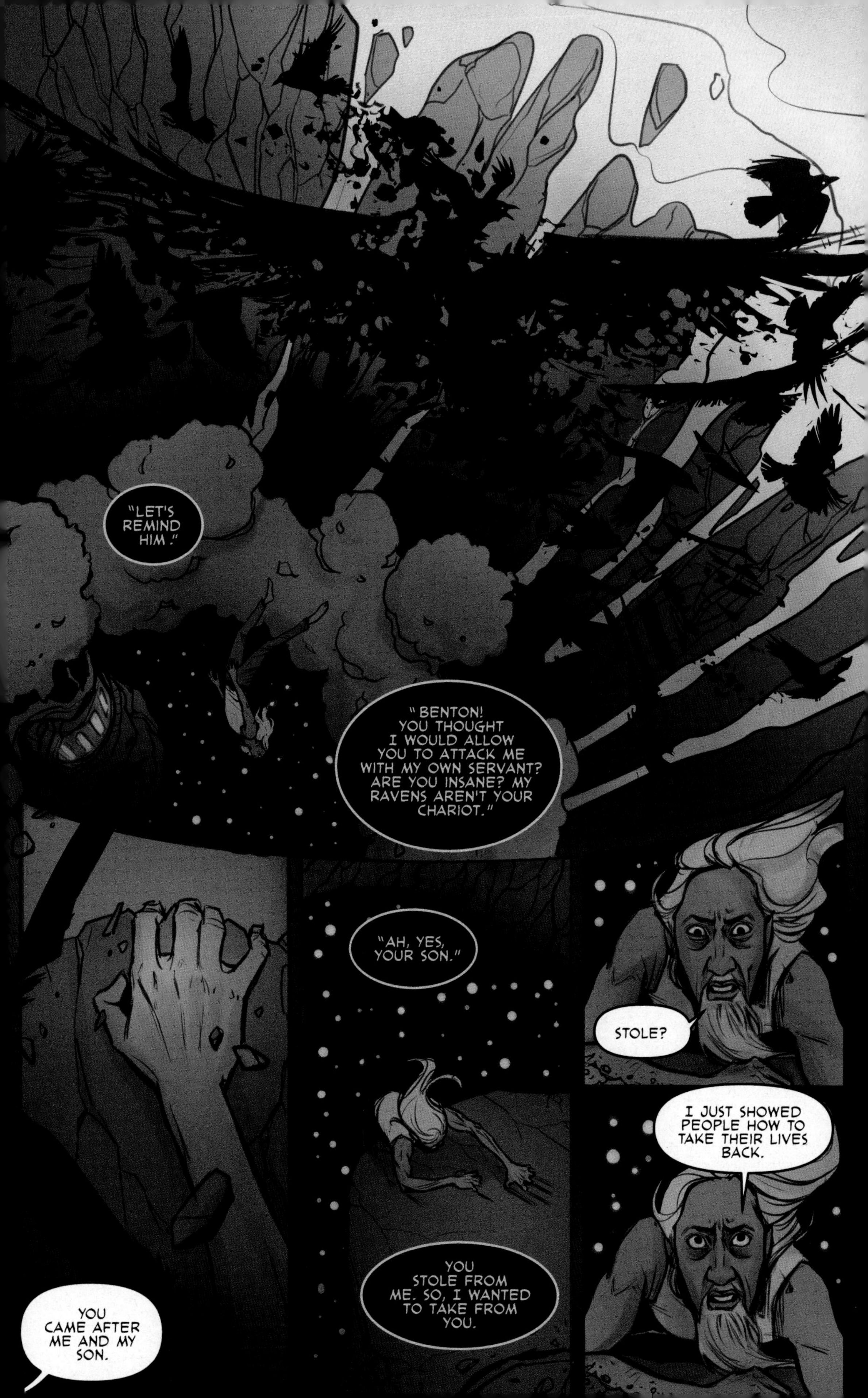
"LET'S REMIND HIM."
"BENTON! YOU THOUGHT I WOULD ALLOW YOU TO ATTACK ME WITH MY OWN SERVANT? ARE YOU INSANE? MY RAVENS AREN'T YOUR CHARIOT."
YOU CAME AFTER ME AND MY SON.
"AH, YES, YOUR SON."
YOU STOLE FROM ME. SO, I WANTED TO TAKE FROM YOU.
STOLE?
I JUST SHOWED PEOPLE HOW TO TAKE THEIR LIVES BACK.

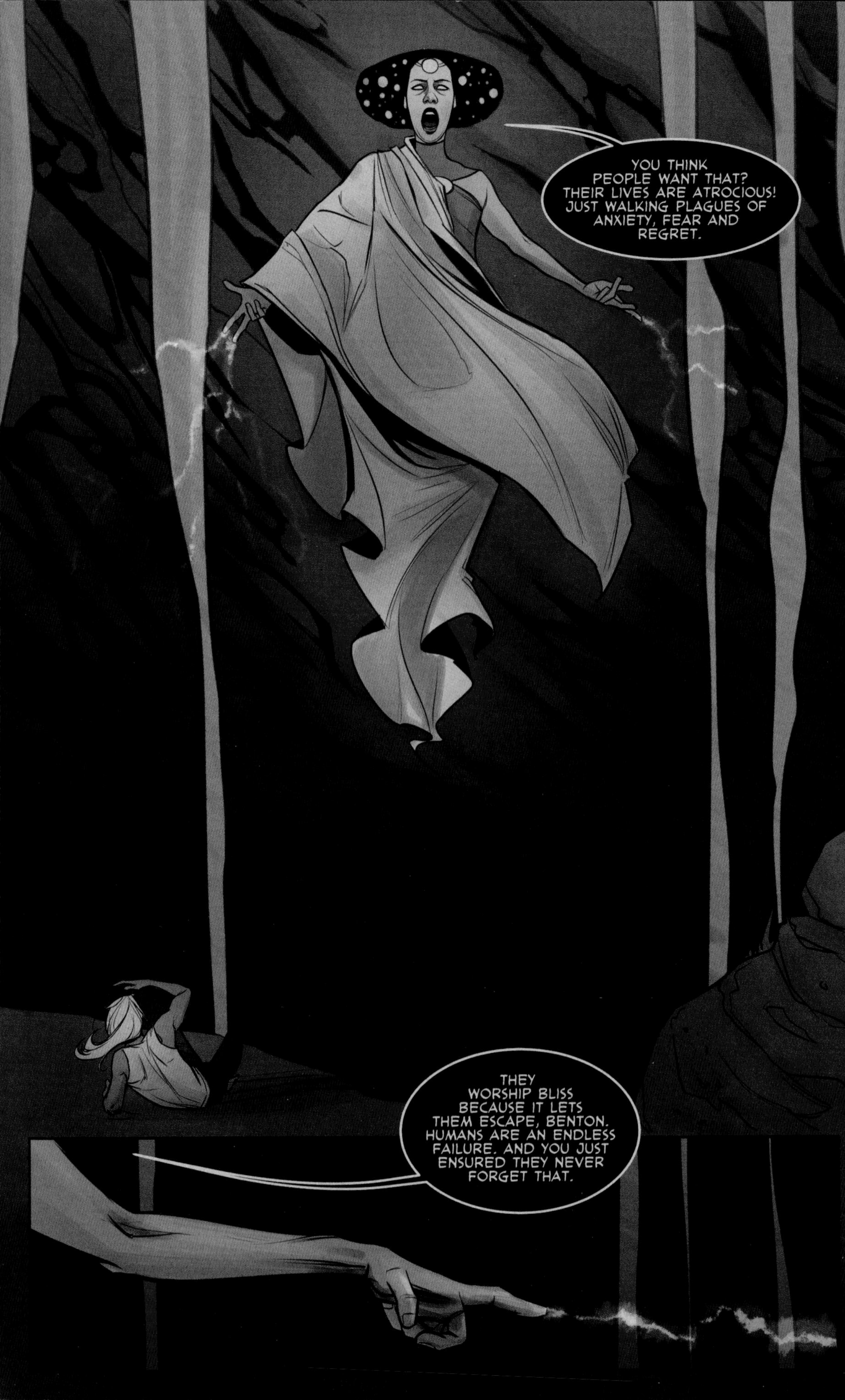
YOU THINK PEOPLE WANT THAT? THEIR LIVES ARE ATROCIOUS! JUST WALKING PLAGUES OF ANXIETY, FEAR AND REGRET.
THEY WORSHIP BLISS BECAUSE IT LETS THEM ESCAPE, BENTON. HUMANS ARE AN ENDLESS FAILURE. AND YOU JUST ENSURED THEY NEVER FORGET THAT.

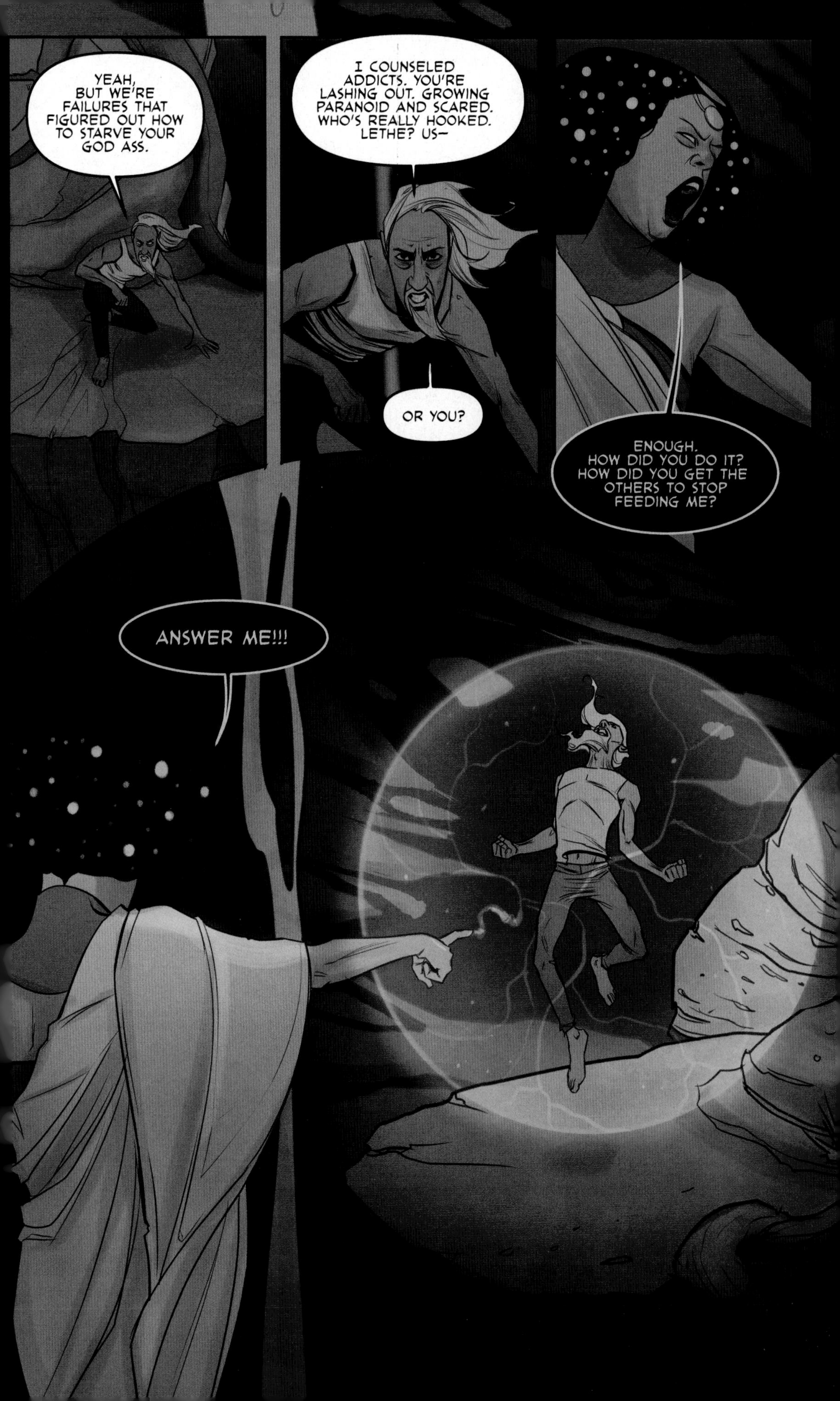
YEAH, BUT WE'RE FAILURES THAT FIGURED OUT HOW TO STARVE YOUR GOD ASS.
I COUNSELED ADDICTS. YOU'RE LASHING OUT. GROWING PARANOID AND SCARED. WHO'S REALLY HOOKED. LETHE? US—
OR YOU?
ENOUGH. HOW DID YOU DO IT? HOW DID YOU GET THE OTHERS TO STOP FEEDING ME?
ANSWER ME!!!

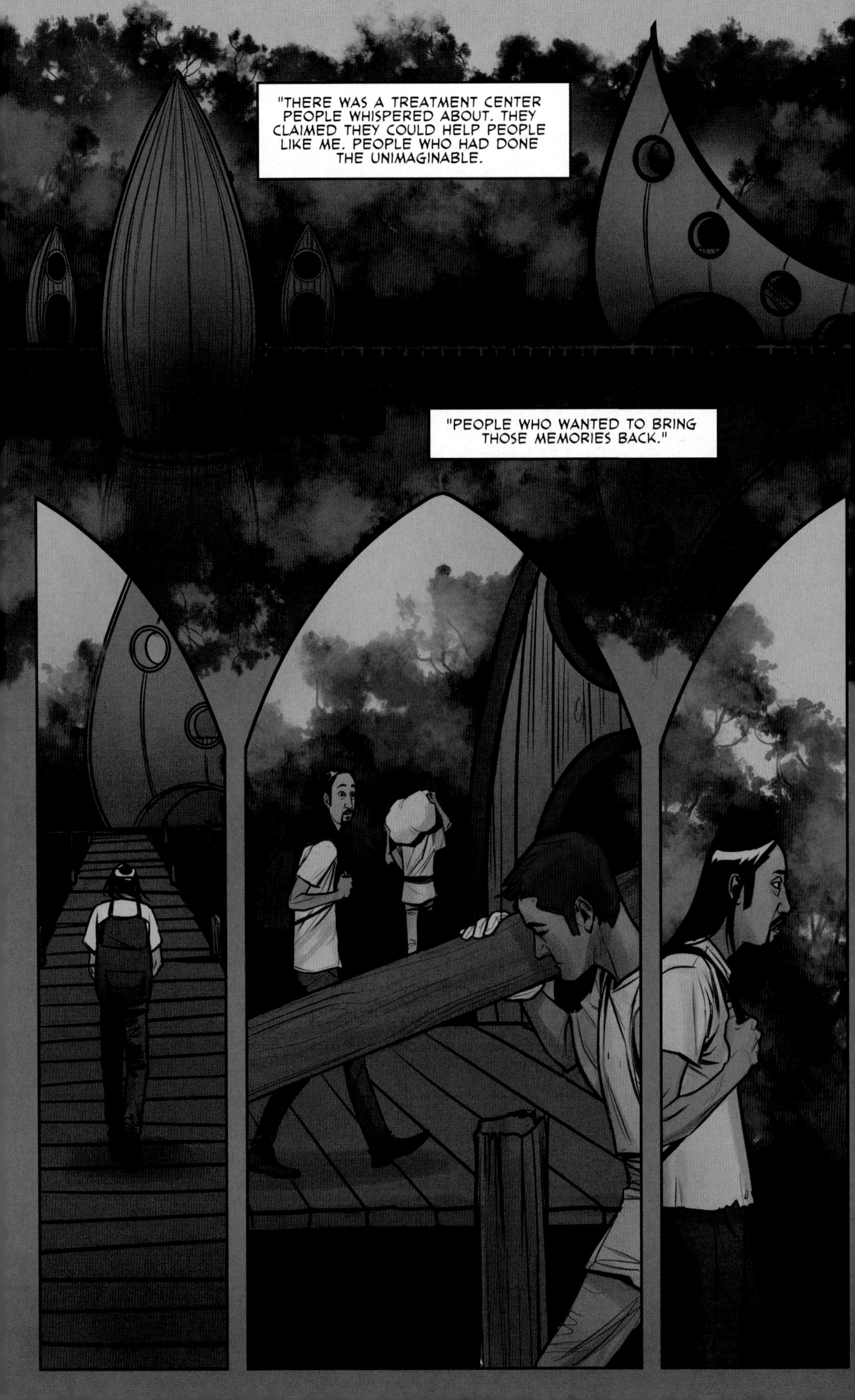
"THERE WAS A TREATMENT CENTER PEOPLE WHISPERED ABOUT. THEY CLAIMED THEY COULD HELP PEOPLE LIKE ME. PEOPLE WHO HAD DONE THE UNIMAGINABLE.
"PEOPLE WHO WANTED TO BRING THOSE MEMORIES BACK."

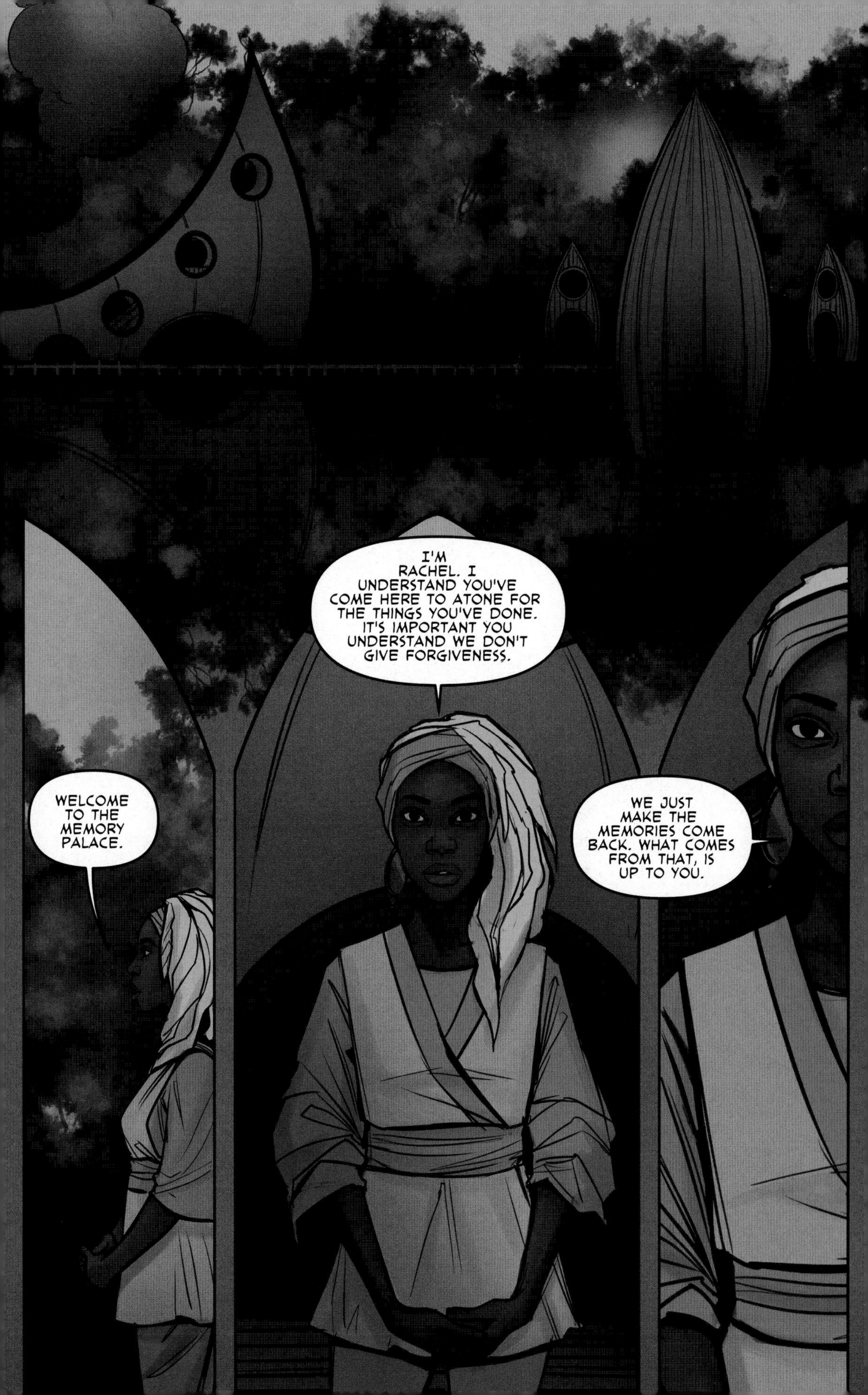
WELCOME TO THE MEMORY PALACE.
I'M RACHEL. I UNDERSTAND YOU'VE COME HERE TO ATONE FOR THE THINGS YOU'VE DONE. IT'S IMPORTANT YOU UNDERSTAND WE DON'T GIVE FORGIVENESS.
WE JUST MAKE THE MEMORIES COME BACK. WHAT COMES FROM THAT, IS UP TO YOU.

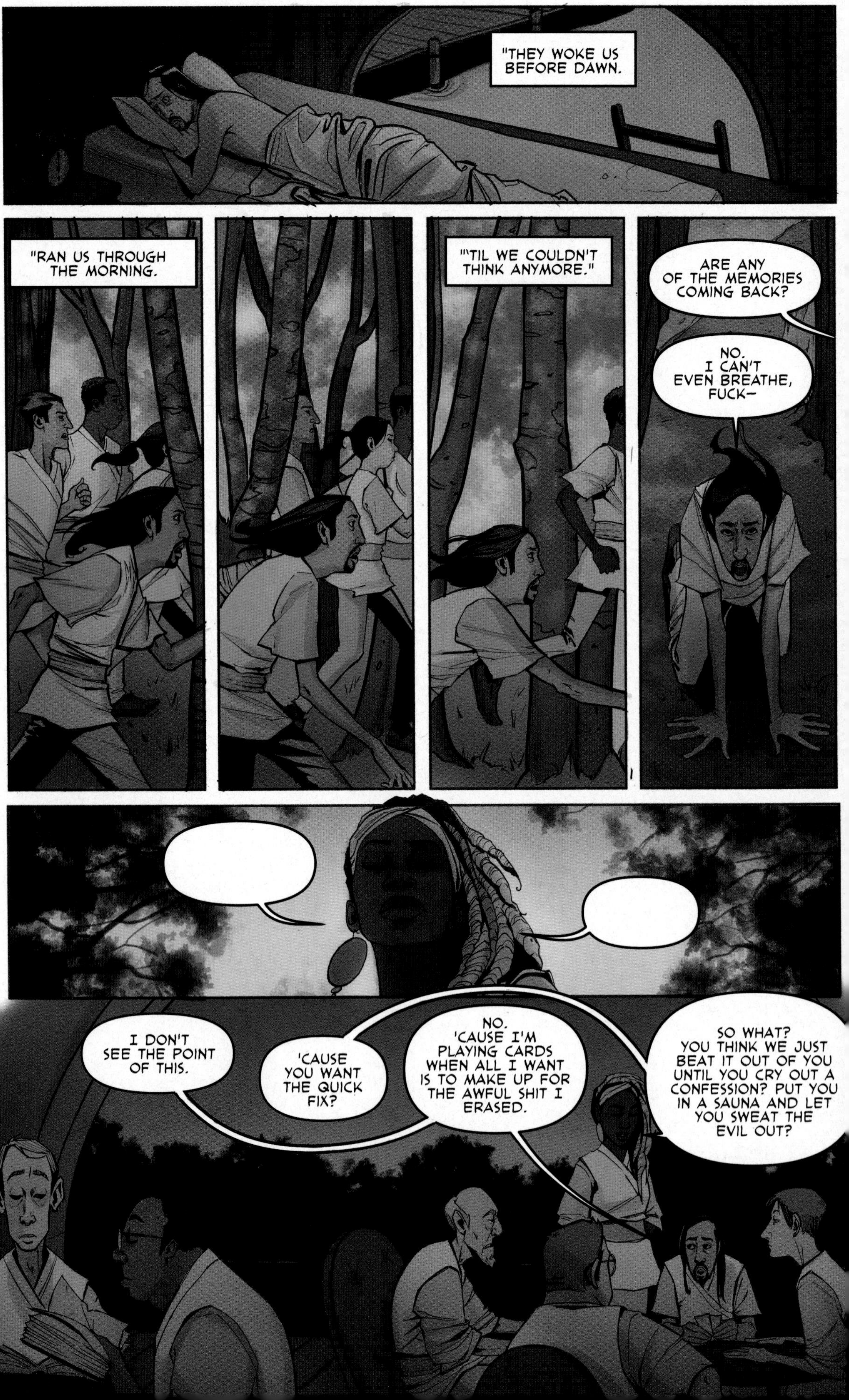
"THEY WOKE US BEFORE DAWN.
"RAN US THROUGH THE MORNING.
"'TIL WE COULDN'T THINK ANYMORE."
ARE ANY OF THE MEMORIES COMING BACK?
NO. I CAN'T EVEN BREATHE, FUCK—
I DON'T SEE THE POINT OF THIS.
'CAUSE YOU WANT THE QUICK FIX?
NO. 'CAUSE I'M PLAYING CARDS WHEN ALL I WANT IS TO MAKE UP FOR THE AWFUL SHIT I ERASED.
SO WHAT? YOU THINK WE JUST BEAT IT OUT OF YOU UNTIL YOU CRY OUT A CONFESSION? PUT YOU IN A SAUNA AND LET YOU SWEAT THE EVIL OUT?

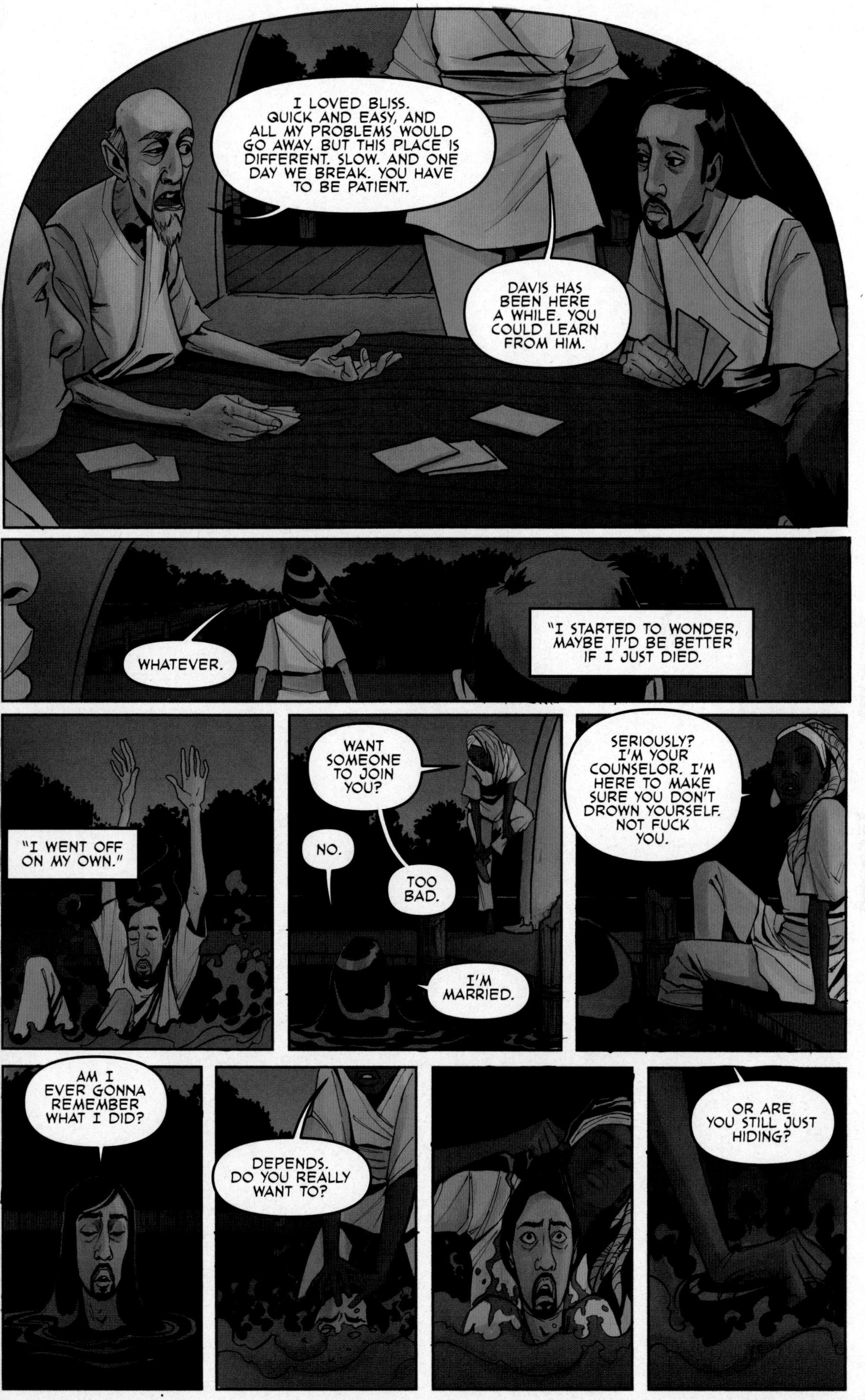
I LOVED BLISS. QUICK AND EASY, AND ALL MY PROBLEMS WOULD GO AWAY. BUT THIS PLACE IS DIFFERENT. SLOW. AND ONE DAY WE BREAK. YOU HAVE TO BE PATIENT.
DAVIS HAS BEEN HERE A WHILE. YOU COULD LEARN FROM HIM.
WHATEVER.
"I STARTED TO WONDER, MAYBE IT'D BE BETTER IF I JUST DIED.
"I WENT OFF ON MY OWN."
WANT SOMEONE TO JOIN YOU?
NO.
TOO BAD.
I'M MARRIED.
SERIOUSLY? I'M YOUR COUNSELOR. I'M HERE TO MAKE SURE YOU DON'T DROWN YOURSELF. NOT FUCK YOU.
AM I EVER GONNA REMEMBER WHAT I DID?
DEPENDS. DO YOU REALLY WANT TO?
OR ARE YOU STILL JUST HIDING?

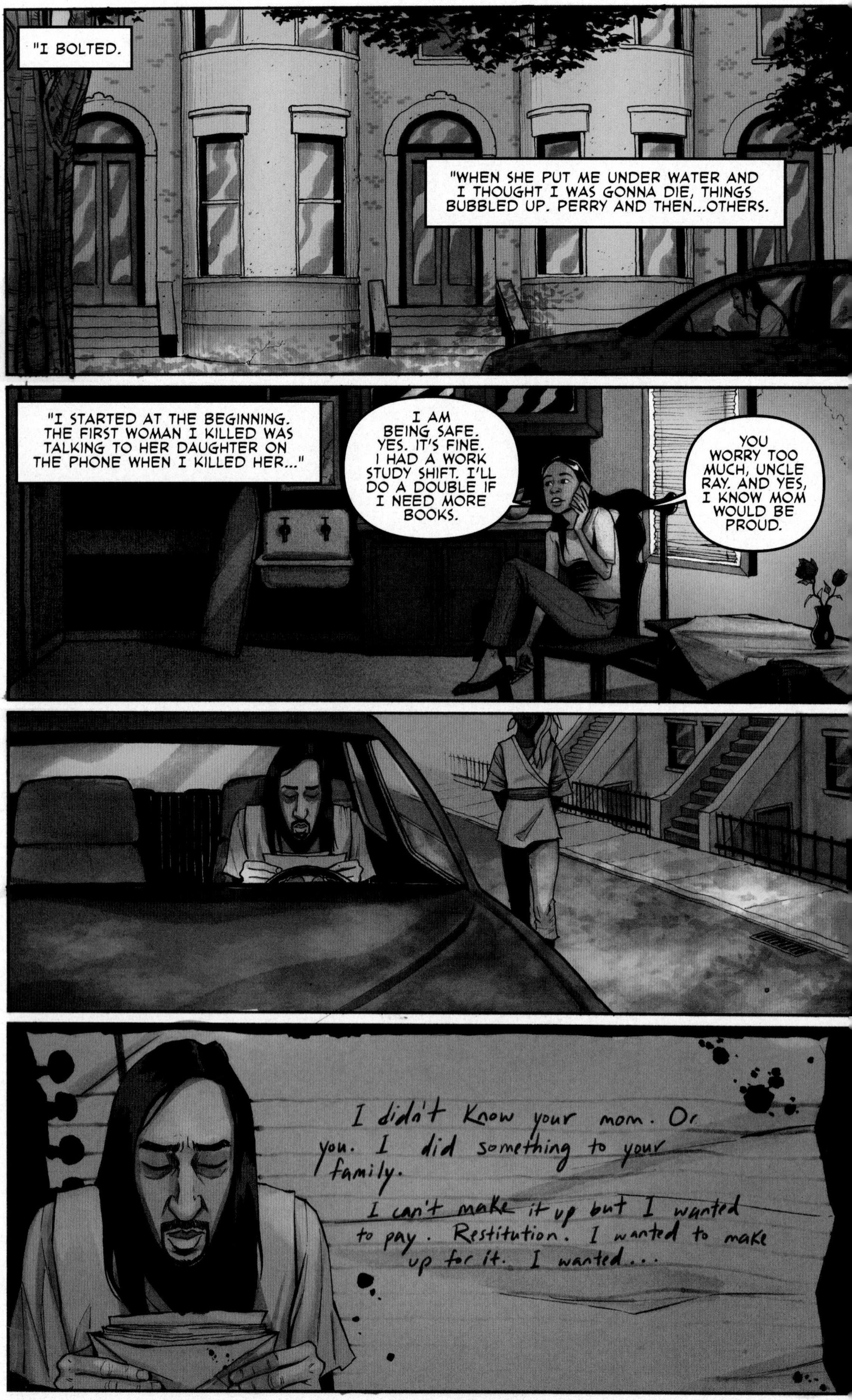
"I BOLTED.
"WHEN SHE PUT ME UNDER WATER AND I THOUGHT I WAS GONNA DIE, THINGS BUBBLED UP. PERRY AND THEN...OTHERS.
"I STARTED AT THE BEGINNING. THE FIRST WOMAN I KILLED WAS TALKING TO HER DAUGHTER ON THE PHONE WHEN I KILLED HER..."
I AM BEING SAFE. YES. IT'S FINE. I HAD A WORK STUDY SHIFT. I'LL DO A DOUBLE IF I NEED MORE BOOKS.
YOU WORRY TOO MUCH, UNCLE RAY. AND YES, I KNOW MOM WOULD BE PROUD.
I didn't know your mom. Or you. I did something to your family.
I can't make it up but I wanted to pay. Restitution. I wanted to make up for it. I wanted...

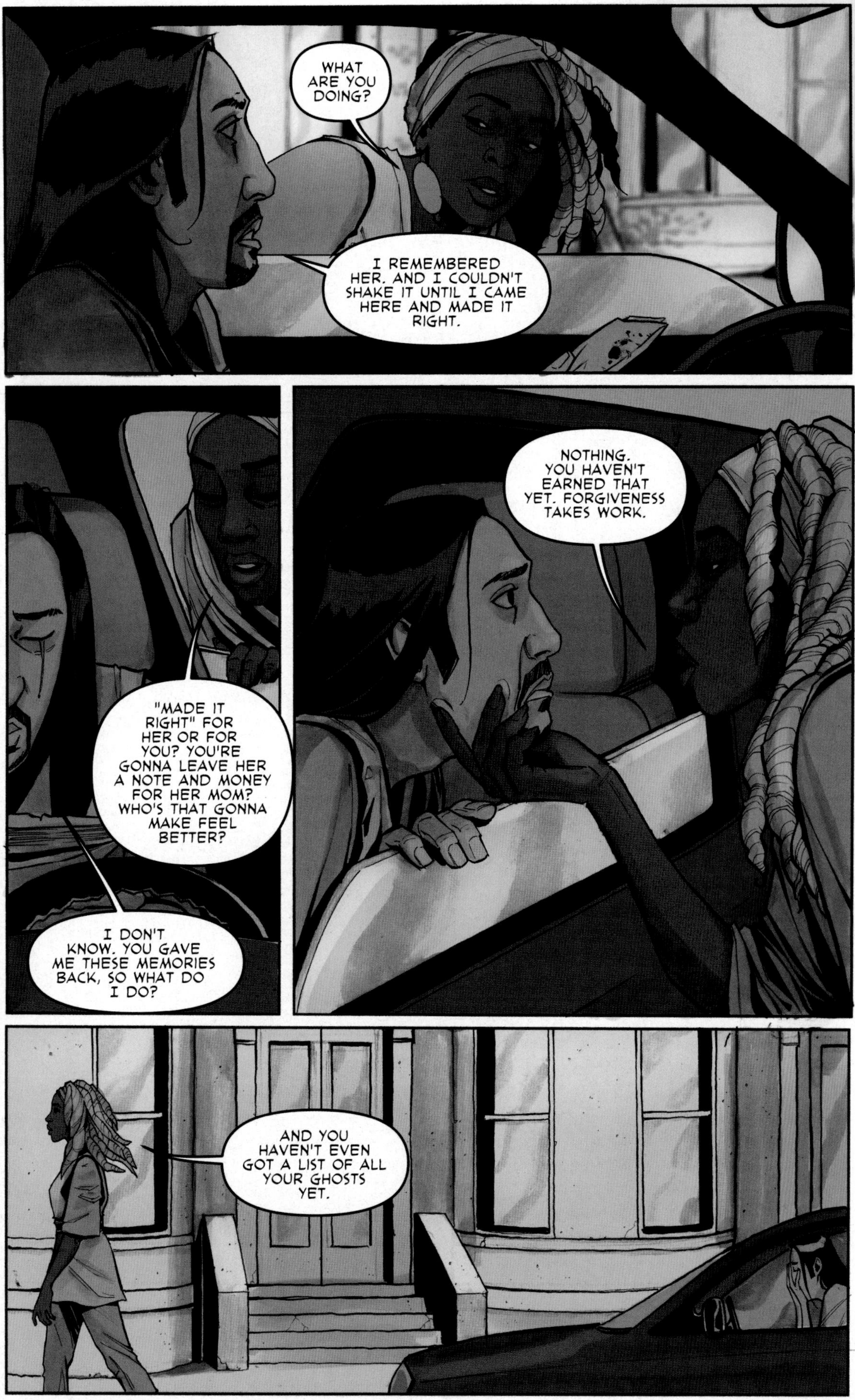
WHAT ARE YOU DOING?
I REMEMBERED HER. AND I COULDN'T SHAKE IT UNTIL I CAME HERE AND MADE IT RIGHT.
"MADE IT RIGHT" FOR HER OR FOR YOU? YOU'RE GONNA LEAVE HER A NOTE AND MONEY FOR HER MOM? WHO'S THAT GONNA MAKE FEEL BETTER?
I DON'T KNOW. YOU GAVE ME THESE MEMORIES BACK, SO WHAT DO I DO?
NOTHING. YOU HAVEN'T EARNED THAT YET. FORGIVENESS TAKES WORK.
AND YOU HAVEN'T EVEN GOT A LIST OF ALL YOUR GHOSTS YET.

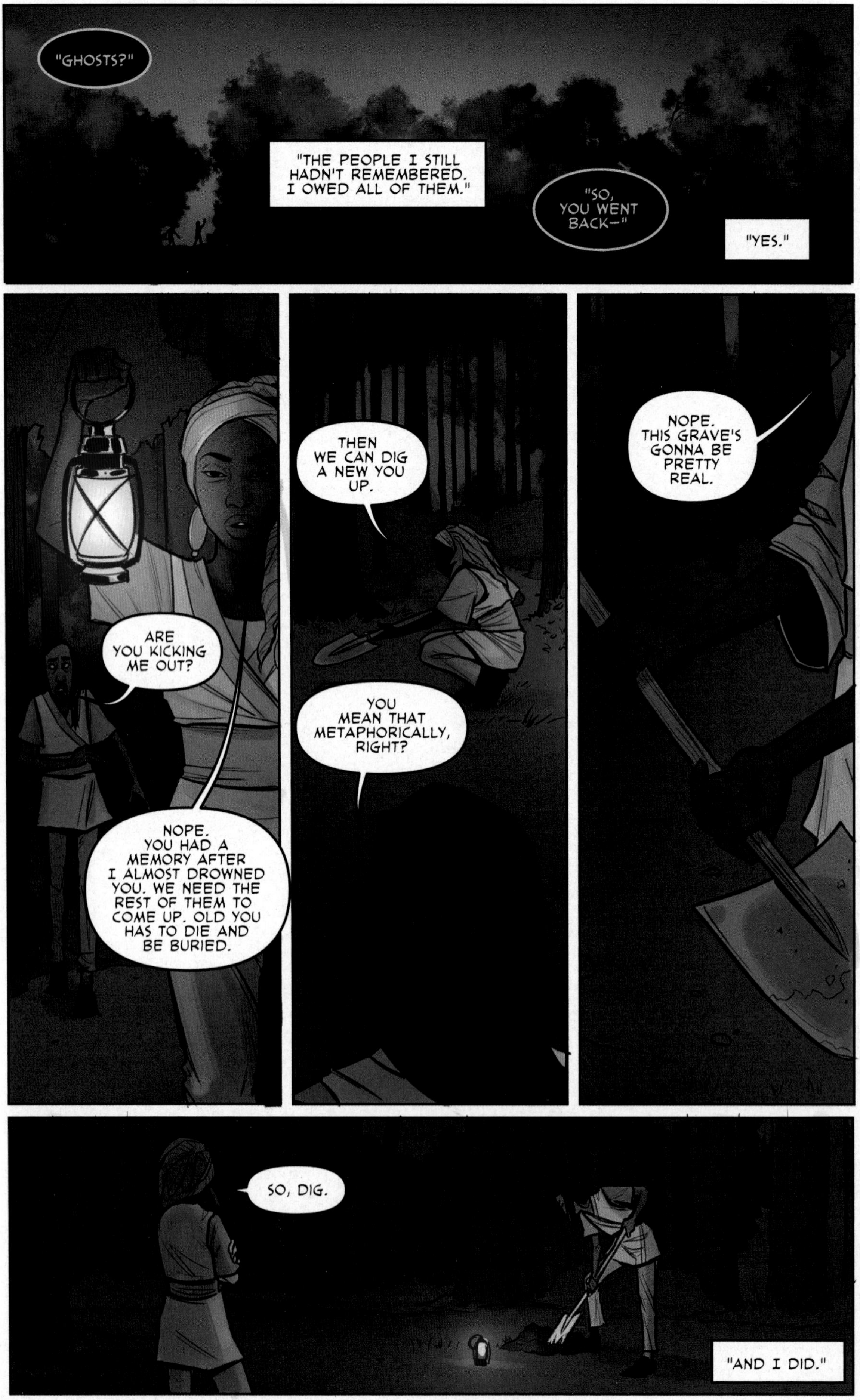
"GHOSTS?"
"THE PEOPLE I STILL HADN'T REMEMBERED. I OWED ALL OF THEM."
"SO, YOU WENT BACK—"
"YES."
ARE YOU KICKING ME OUT?
NOPE. YOU HAD A MEMORY AFTER I ALMOST DROWNED YOU. WE NEED THE REST OF THEM TO COME UP. OLD YOU HAS TO DIE AND BE BURIED.
THEN WE CAN DIG A NEW YOU UP.
YOU MEAN THAT METAPHORICALLY, RIGHT?
NOPE. THIS GRAVE'S GONNA BE PRETTY REAL.
SO, DIG.
"AND I DID."

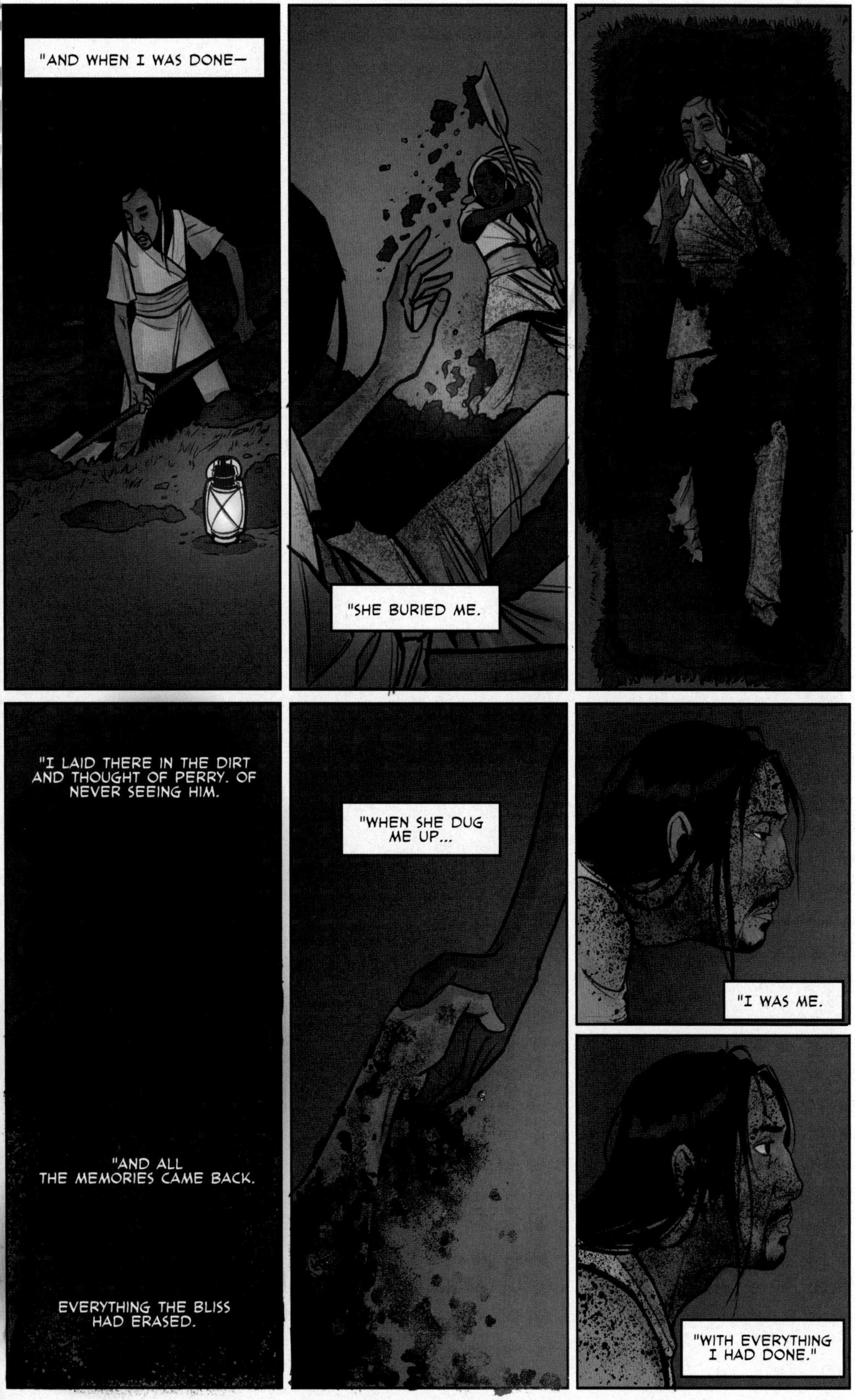
"AND WHEN I WAS DONE—
"SHE BURIED ME.
"I LAID THERE IN THE DIRT AND THOUGHT OF PERRY. OF NEVER SEEING HIM.
"AND ALL THE MEMORIES CAME BACK.
EVERYTHING THE BLISS HAD ERASED.
"WHEN SHE DUG ME UP...
"I WAS ME.
"WITH EVERYTHING I HAD DONE."

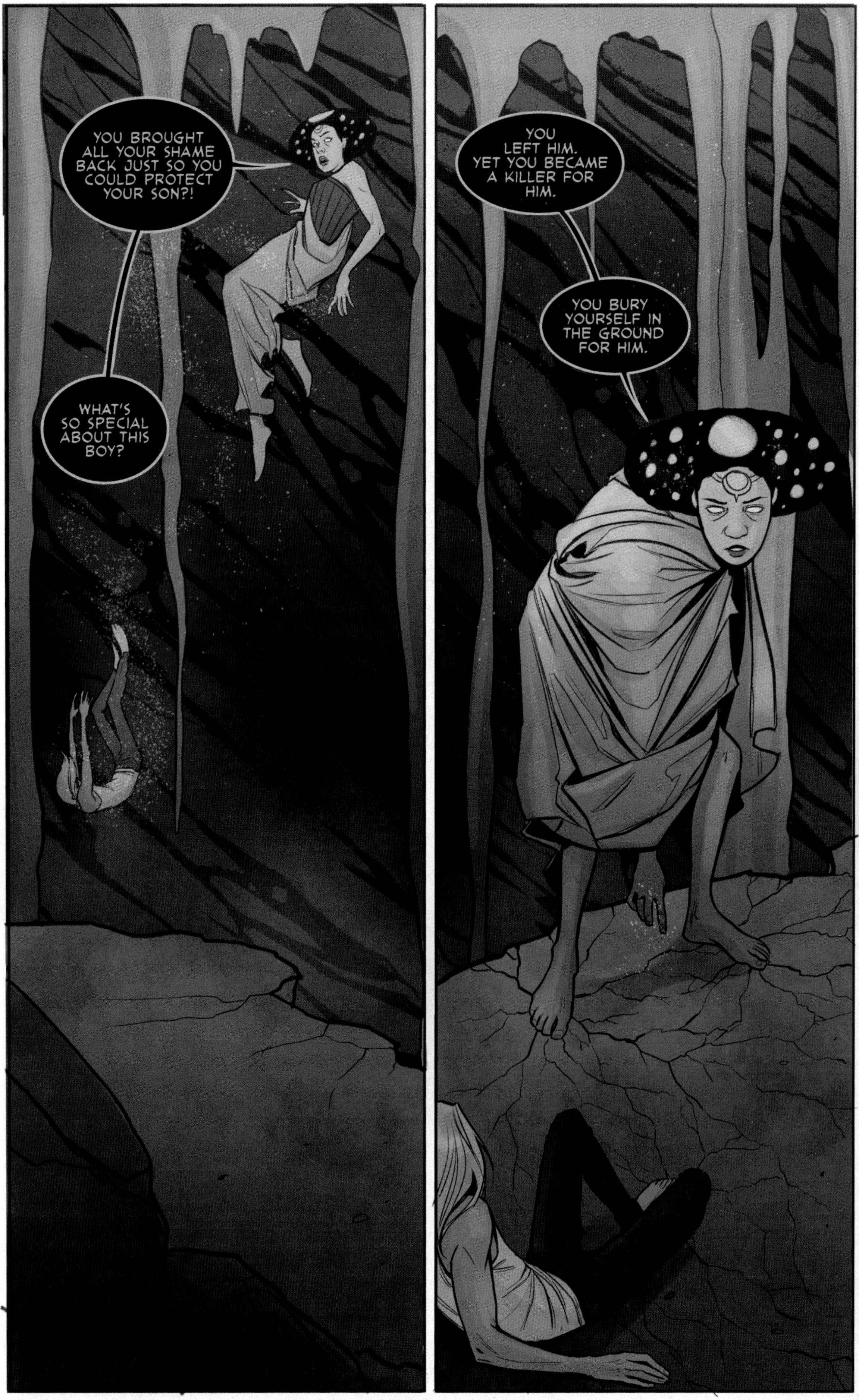
YOU BROUGHT ALL YOUR SHAME BACK JUST SO YOU COULD PROTECT YOUR SON?!
WHAT'S SO SPECIAL ABOUT THIS BOY?
YOU LEFT HIM. YET YOU BECAME A KILLER FOR HIM.
YOU BURY YOURSELF IN THE GROUND FOR HIM.

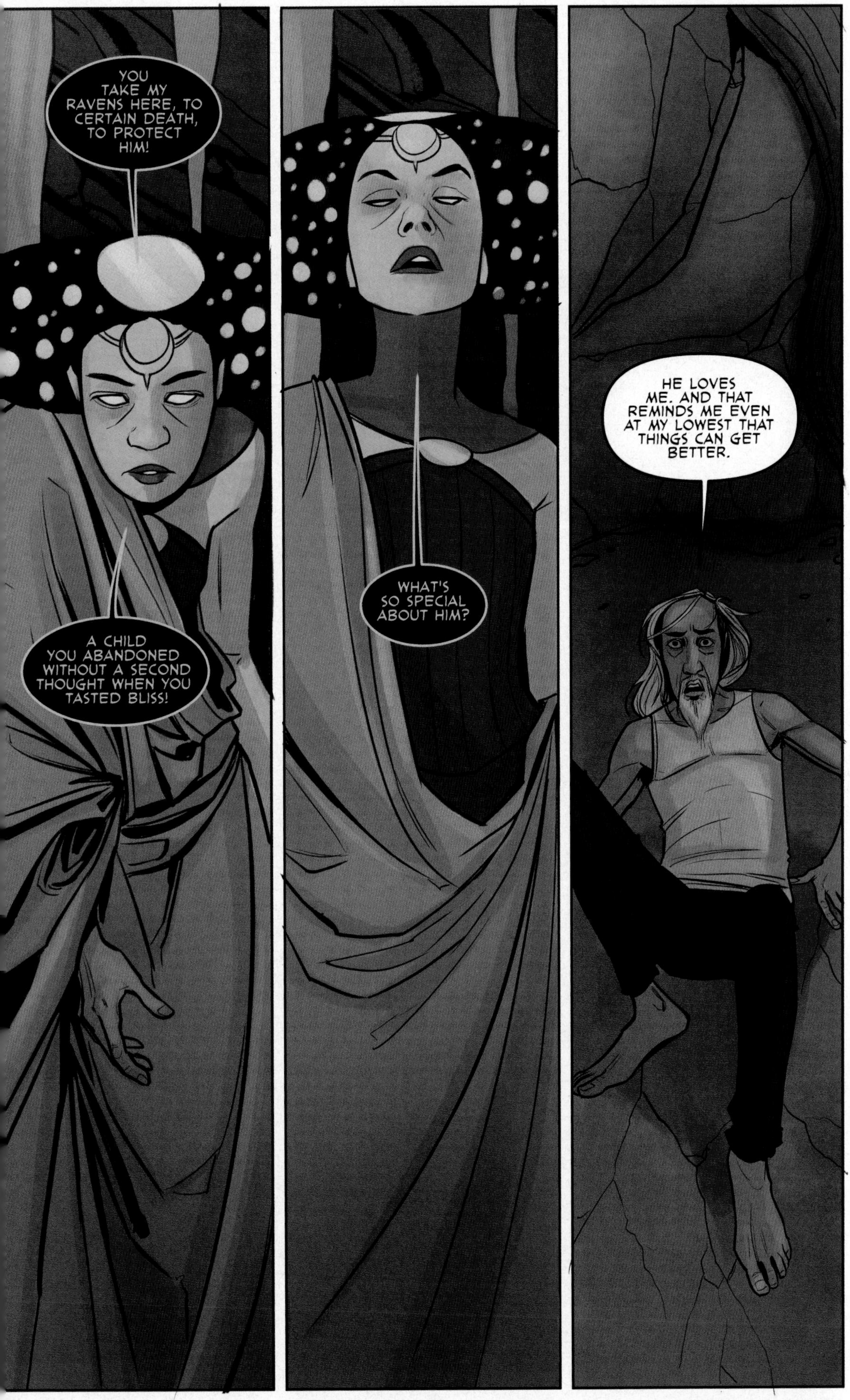
YOU TAKE MY RAVENS HERE, TO CERTAIN DEATH, TO PROTECT HIM!
A CHILD YOU ABANDONED WITHOUT A SECOND THOUGHT WHEN YOU TASTED BLISS!
WHAT'S SO SPECIAL ABOUT HIM?
HE LOVES ME. AND THAT REMINDS ME EVEN AT MY LOWEST THAT THINGS CAN GET BETTER.

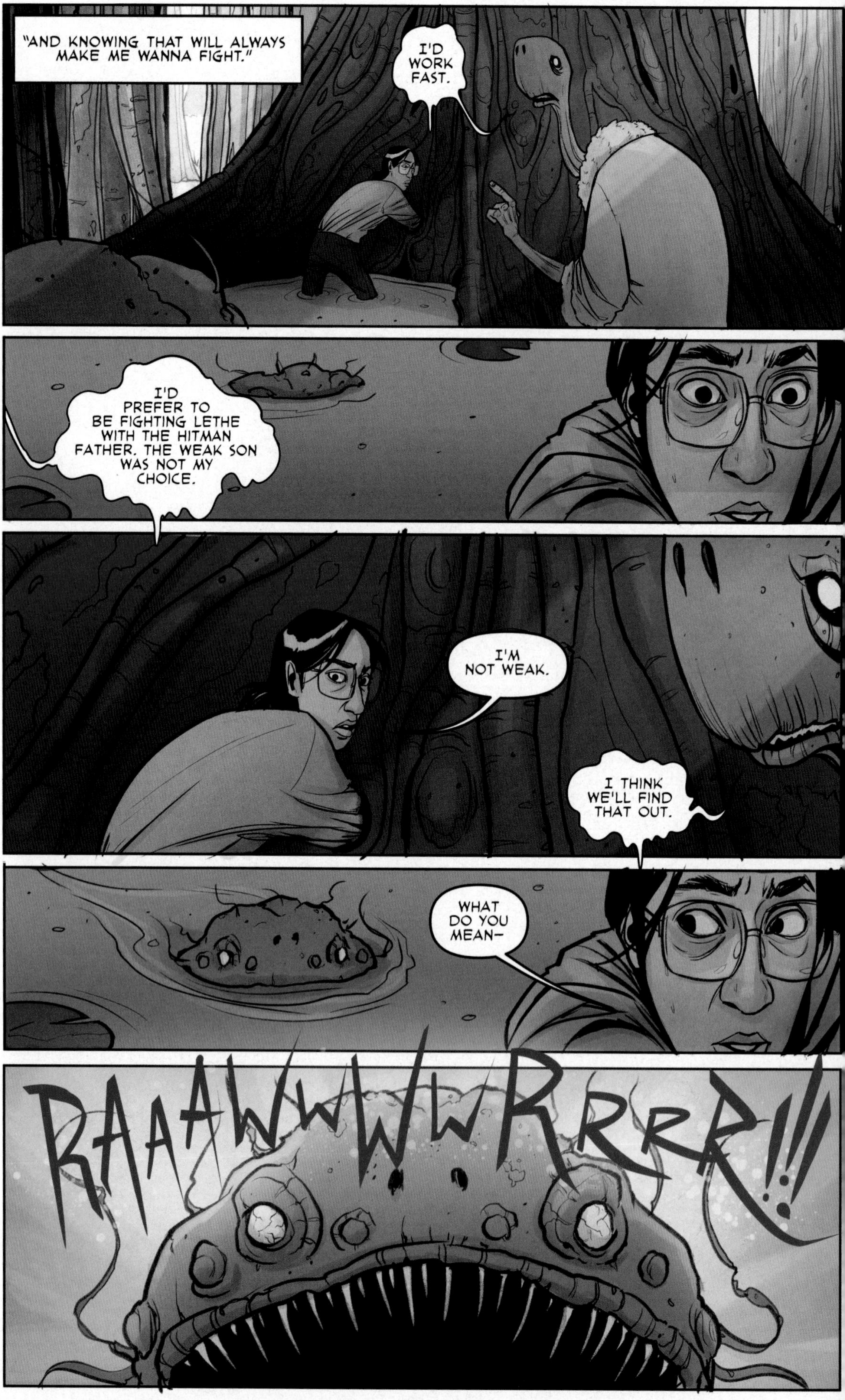
"AND KNOWING THAT WILL ALWAYS MAKE ME WANNA FIGHT."
I'D WORK FAST.
I'D PREFER TO BE FIGHTING LETHE WITH THE HITMAN FATHER. THE WEAK SON WAS NOT MY CHOICE.
I'M NOT WEAK.
I THINK WE'LL FIND THAT OUT.
WHAT DO YOU MEAN—
RAAAWWWWRRRR!!

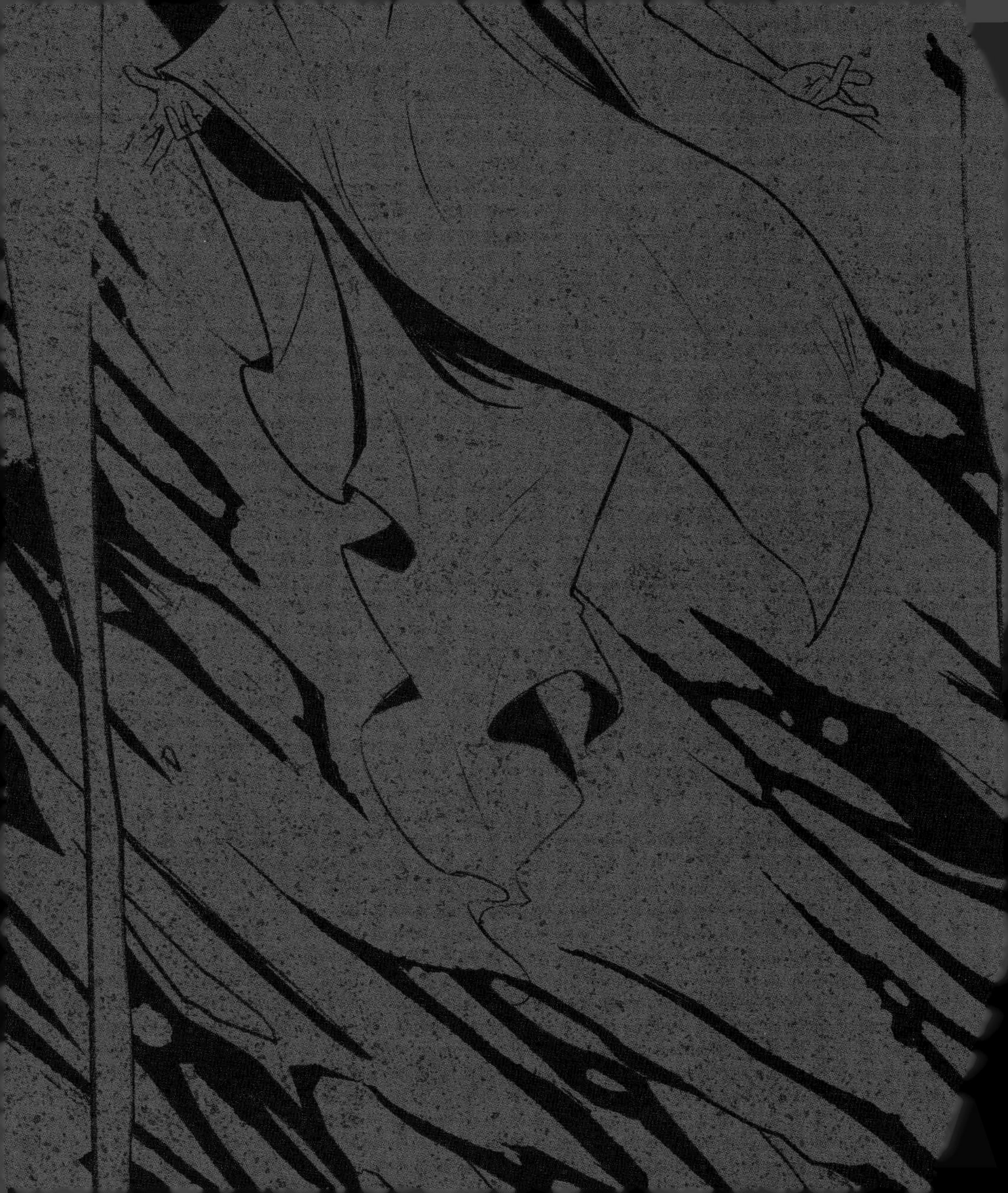

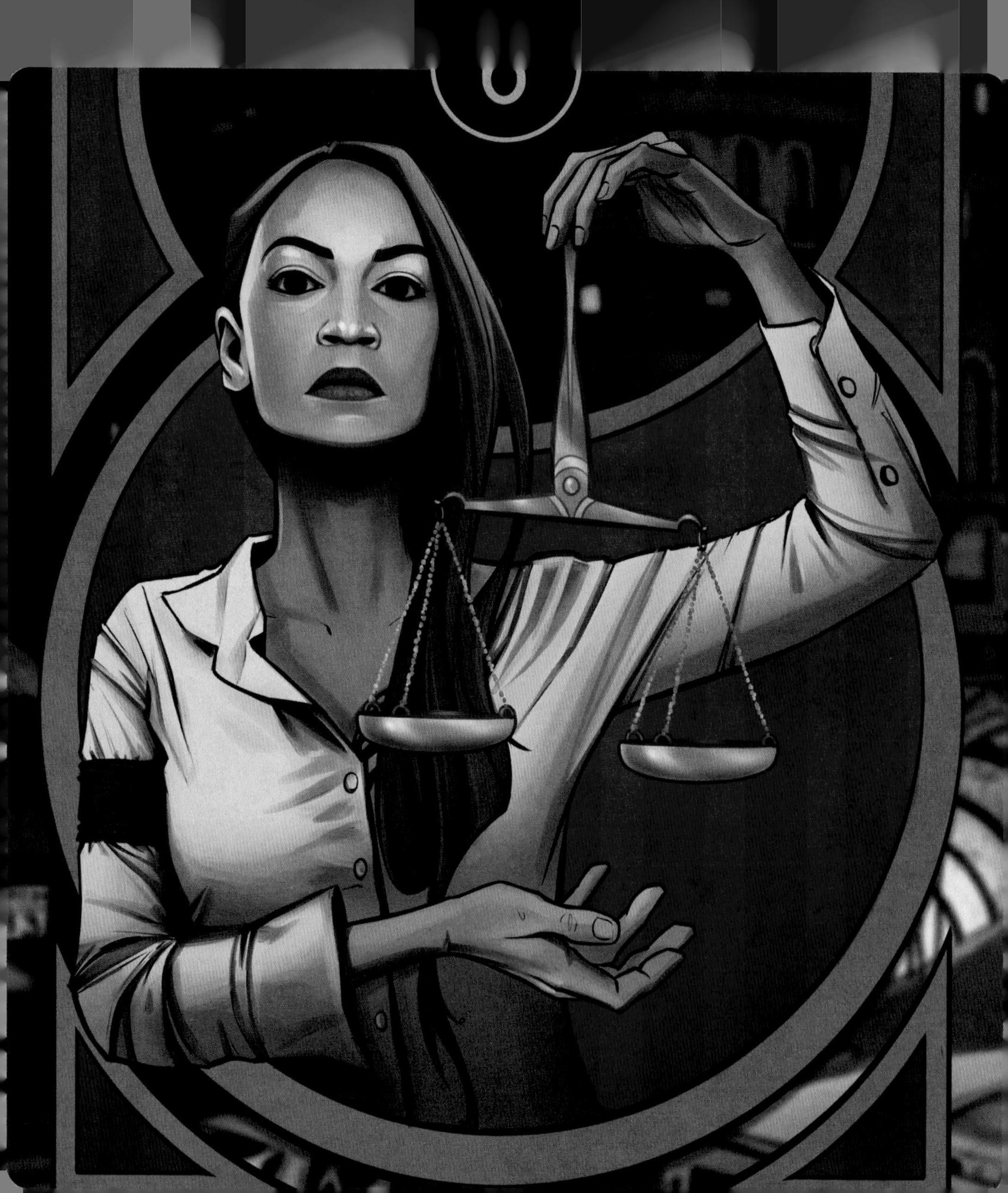

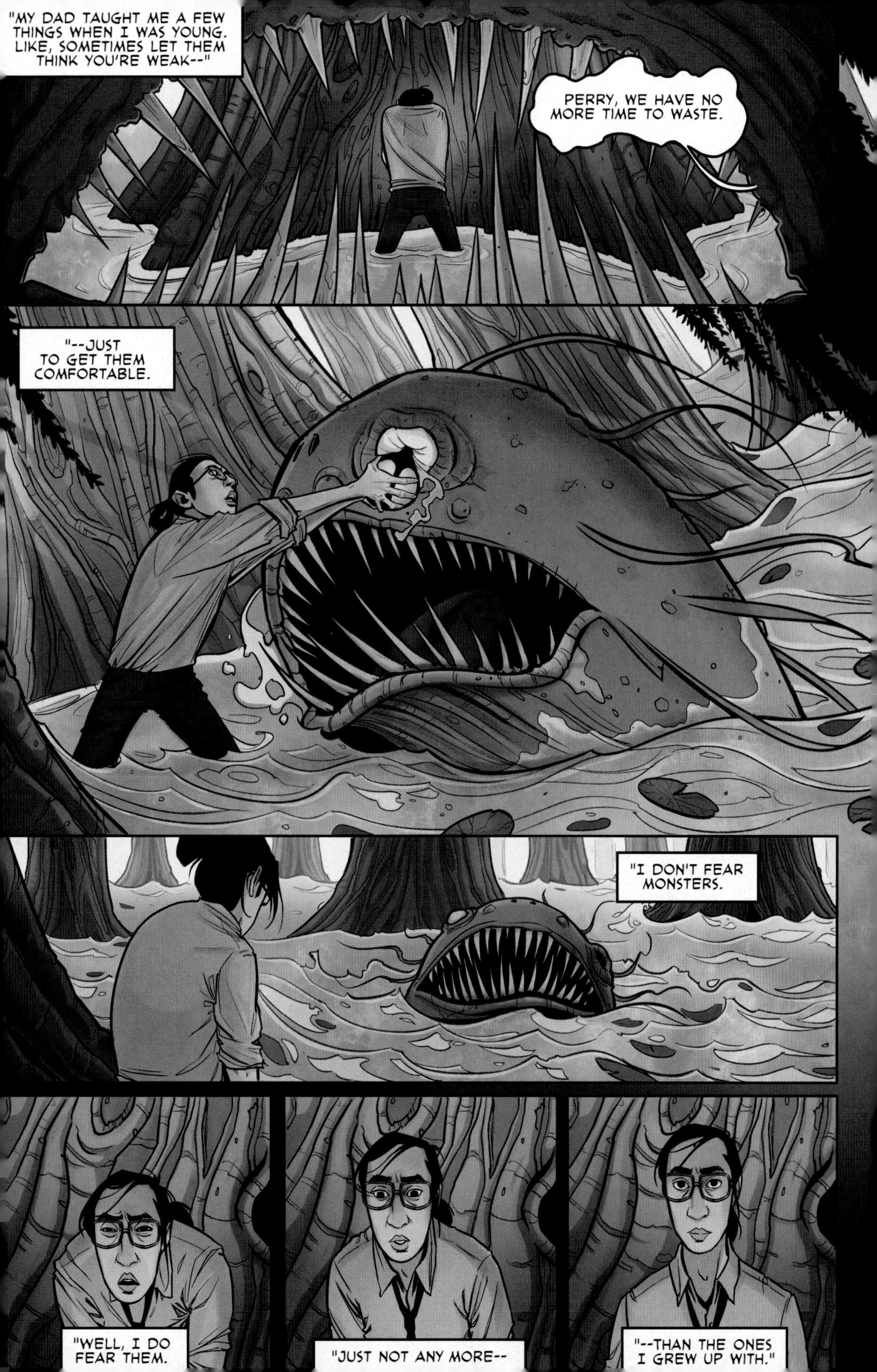
"MY DAD TAUGHT ME A FEW THINGS WHEN I WAS YOUNG. LIKE, SOMETIMES LET THEM THINK YOU'RE WEAK--"
PERRY, WE HAVE NO MORE TIME TO WASTE.
"--JUST TO GET THEM COMFORTABLE.
"I DON'T FEAR MONSTERS.
"WELL, I DO FEAR THEM.
"JUST NOT ANY MORE--
"--THAN THE ONES I GREW UP WITH."

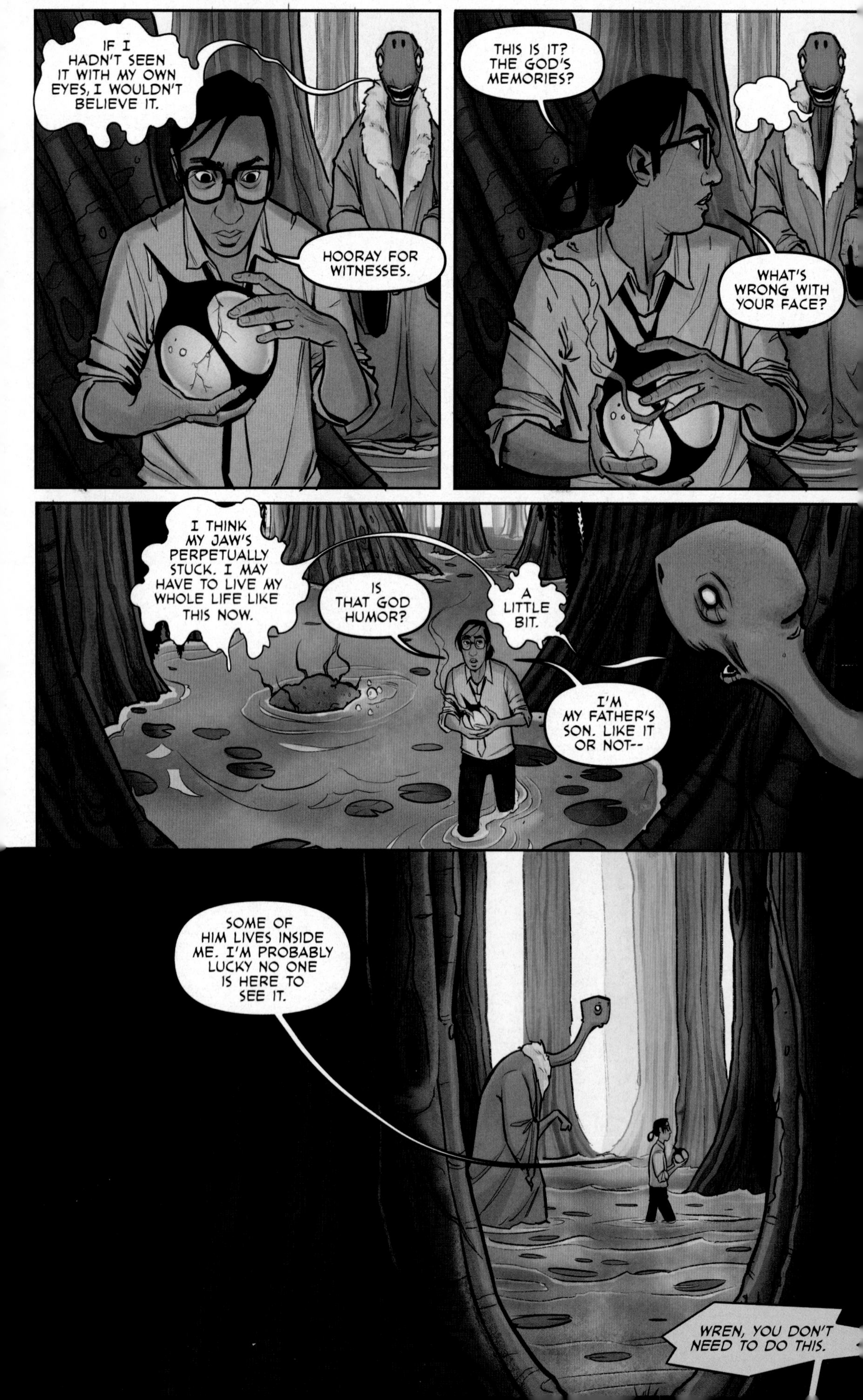
IF I HADN'T SEEN IT WITH MY OWN EYES, I WOULDN'T BELIEVE IT.
HOORAY FOR WITNESSES.
THIS IS IT? THE GOD'S MEMORIES?
WHAT'S WRONG WITH YOUR FACE?
I THINK MY JAW'S PERPETUALLY STUCK. I MAY HAVE TO LIVE MY WHOLE LIFE LIKE THIS NOW.
IS THAT GOD HUMOR?
A LITTLE BIT.
I'M MY FATHER'S SON. LIKE IT OR NOT--
SOME OF HIM LIVES INSIDE ME. I'M PROBABLY LUCKY NO ONE IS HERE TO SEE IT.
WREN, YOU DON'T NEED TO DO THIS.

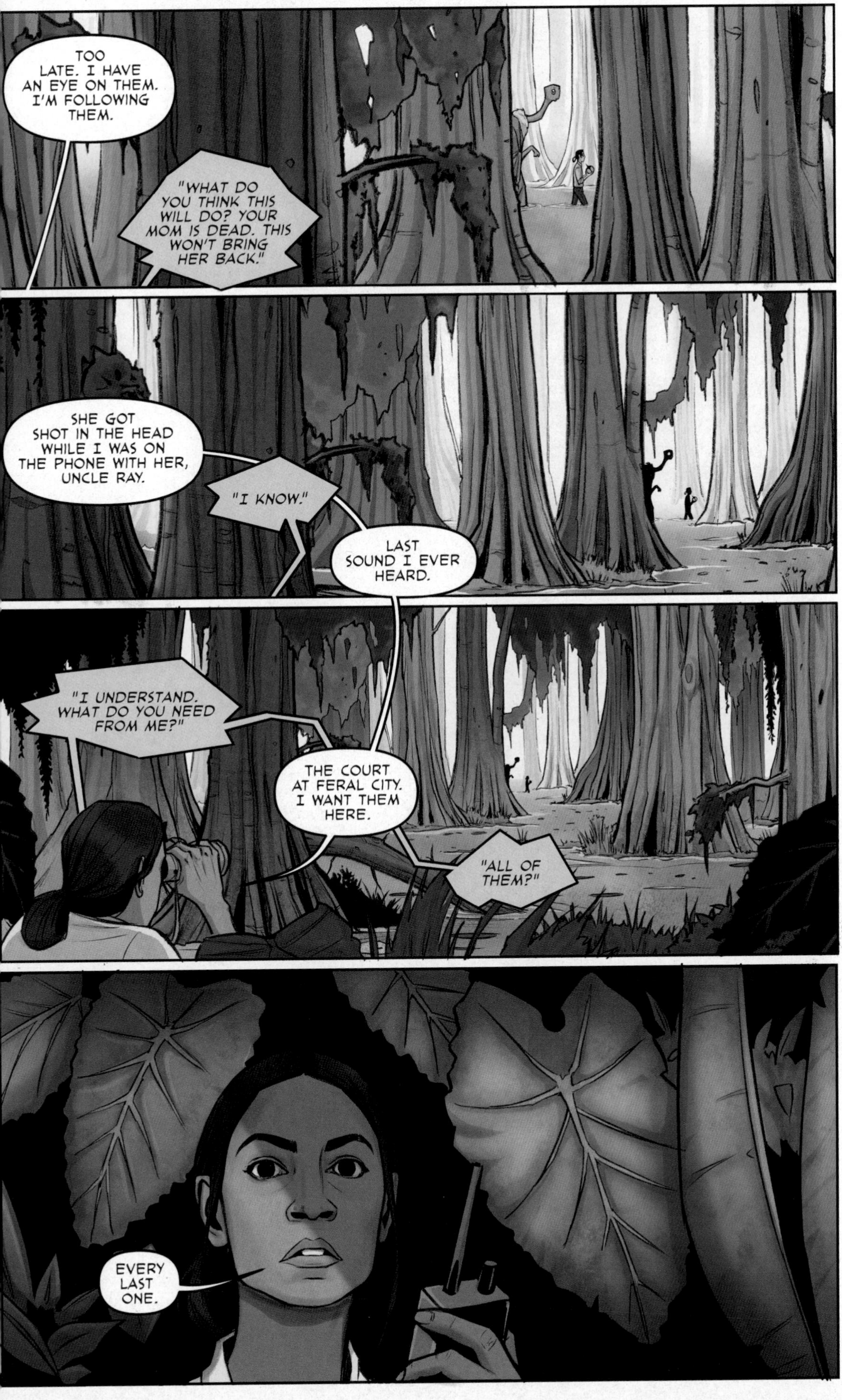
TOO LATE. I HAVE AN EYE ON THEM. I'M FOLLOWING THEM.
"WHAT DO YOU THINK THIS WILL DO? YOUR MOM IS DEAD. THIS WON'T BRING HER BACK."
SHE GOT SHOT IN THE HEAD WHILE I WAS ON THE PHONE WITH HER, UNCLE RAY.
"I KNOW."
LAST SOUND I EVER HEARD.
"I UNDERSTAND. WHAT DO YOU NEED FROM ME?"
THE COURT AT FERAL CITY. I WANT THEM HERE.
"ALL OF THEM?"
EVERY LAST ONE.

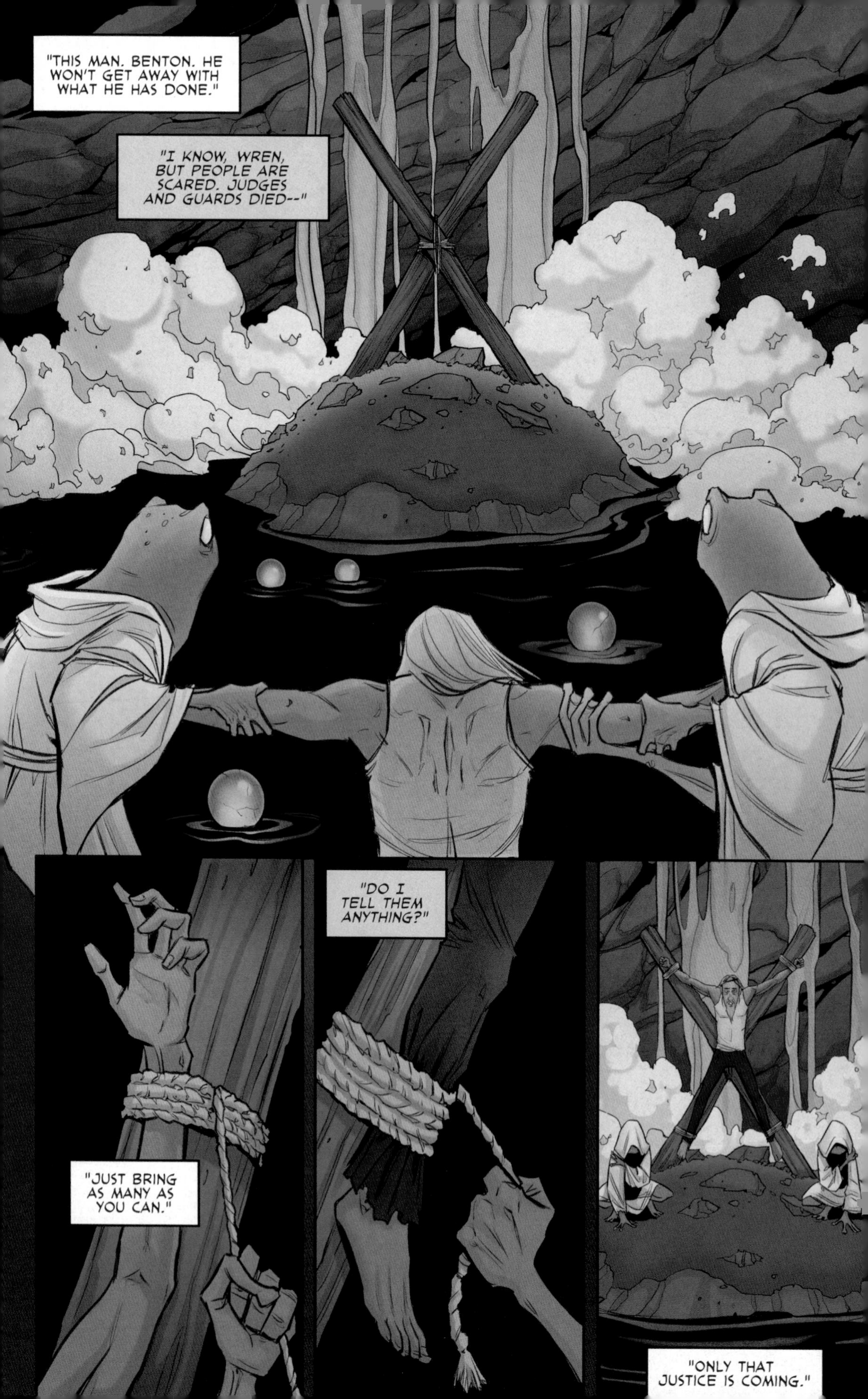
"THIS MAN. BENTON. HE WON'T GET AWAY WITH WHAT HE HAS DONE."
"I KNOW, WREN, BUT PEOPLE ARE SCARED. JUDGES AND GUARDS DIED--"
"JUST BRING AS MANY AS YOU CAN."
"DO I TELL THEM ANYTHING?"
"ONLY THAT JUSTICE IS COMING."

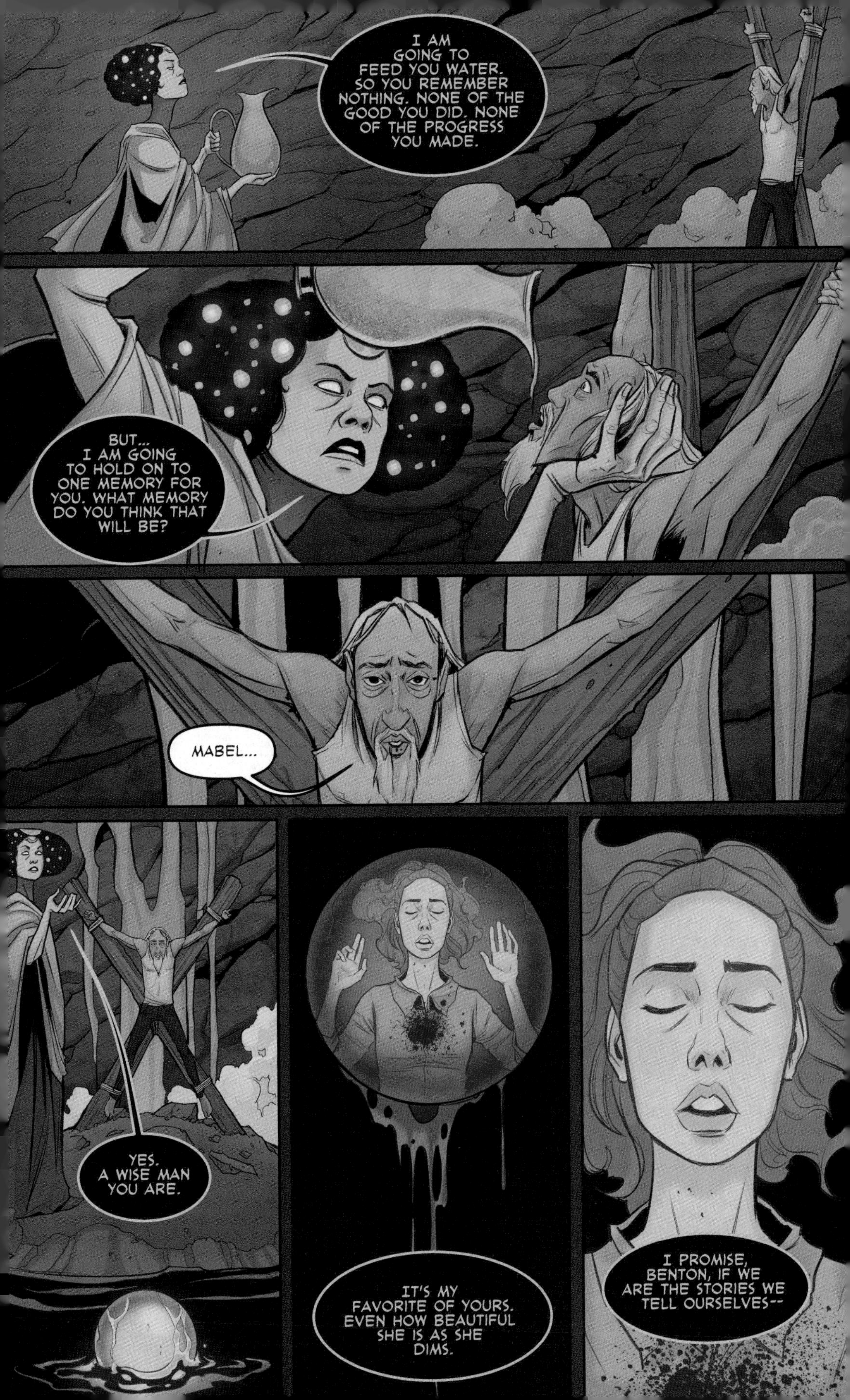
I AM GOING TO FEED YOU WATER. SO YOU REMEMBER NOTHING. NONE OF THE GOOD YOU DID. NONE OF THE PROGRESS YOU MADE.
BUT... I AM GOING TO HOLD ON TO ONE MEMORY FOR YOU. WHAT MEMORY DO YOU THINK THAT WILL BE?
MABEL...
YES. A WISE MAN YOU ARE.
IT'S MY FAVORITE OF YOURS. EVEN HOW BEAUTIFUL SHE IS AS SHE DIMS.
I PROMISE, BENTON, IF WE ARE THE STORIES WE TELL OURSELVES--

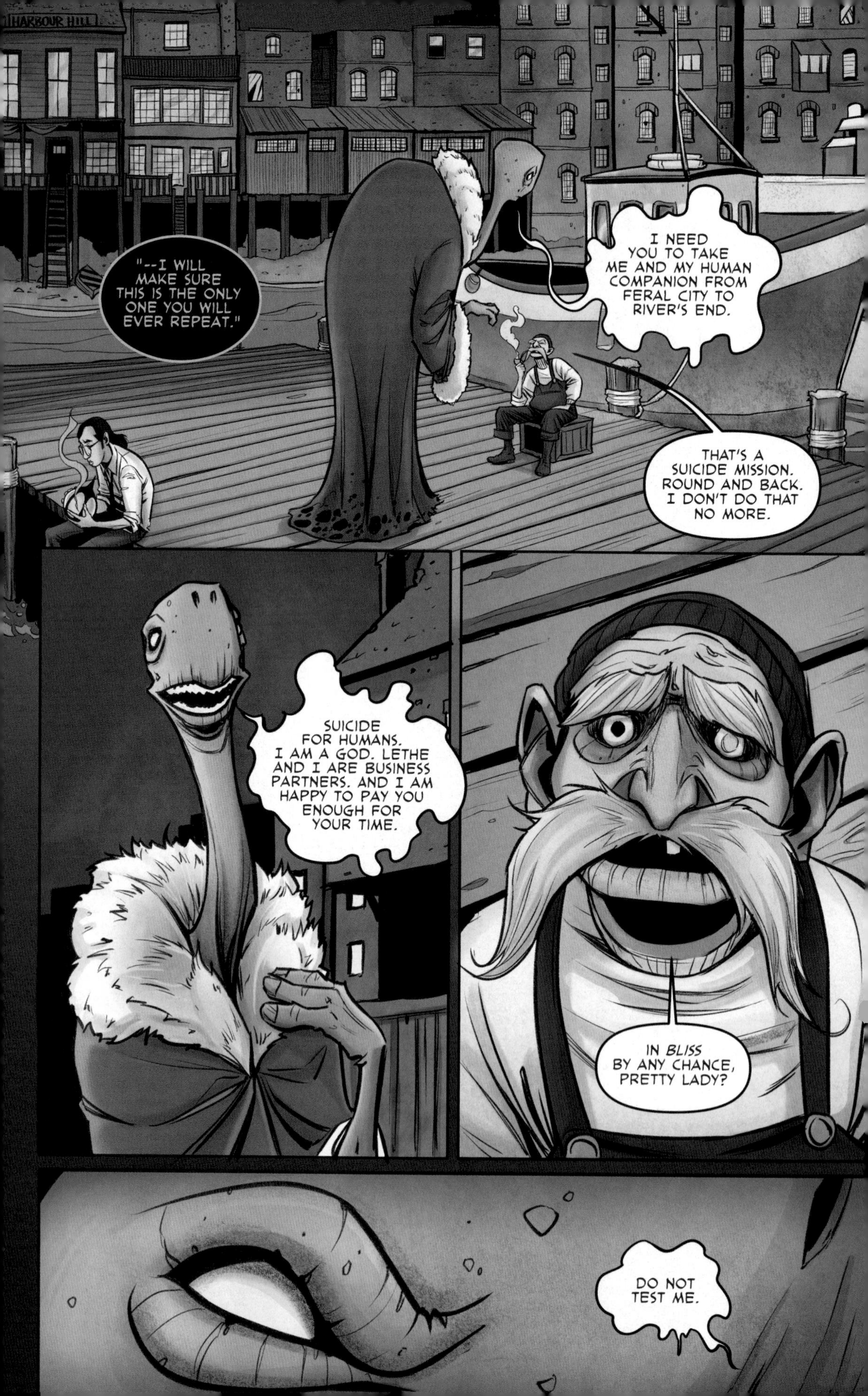
HARBOUR HILL
"--I WILL MAKE SURE THIS IS THE ONLY ONE YOU WILL EVER REPEAT."
I NEED YOU TO TAKE ME AND MY HUMAN COMPANION FROM FERAL CITY TO RIVER'S END.
THAT'S A SUICIDE MISSION. ROUND AND BACK. I DON'T DO THAT NO MORE.
SUICIDE FOR HUMANS. I AM A GOD. LETHE AND I ARE BUSINESS PARTNERS. AND I AM HAPPY TO PAY YOU ENOUGH FOR YOUR TIME.
IN *BLISS* BY ANY CHANCE, PRETTY LADY?
DO NOT TEST ME.

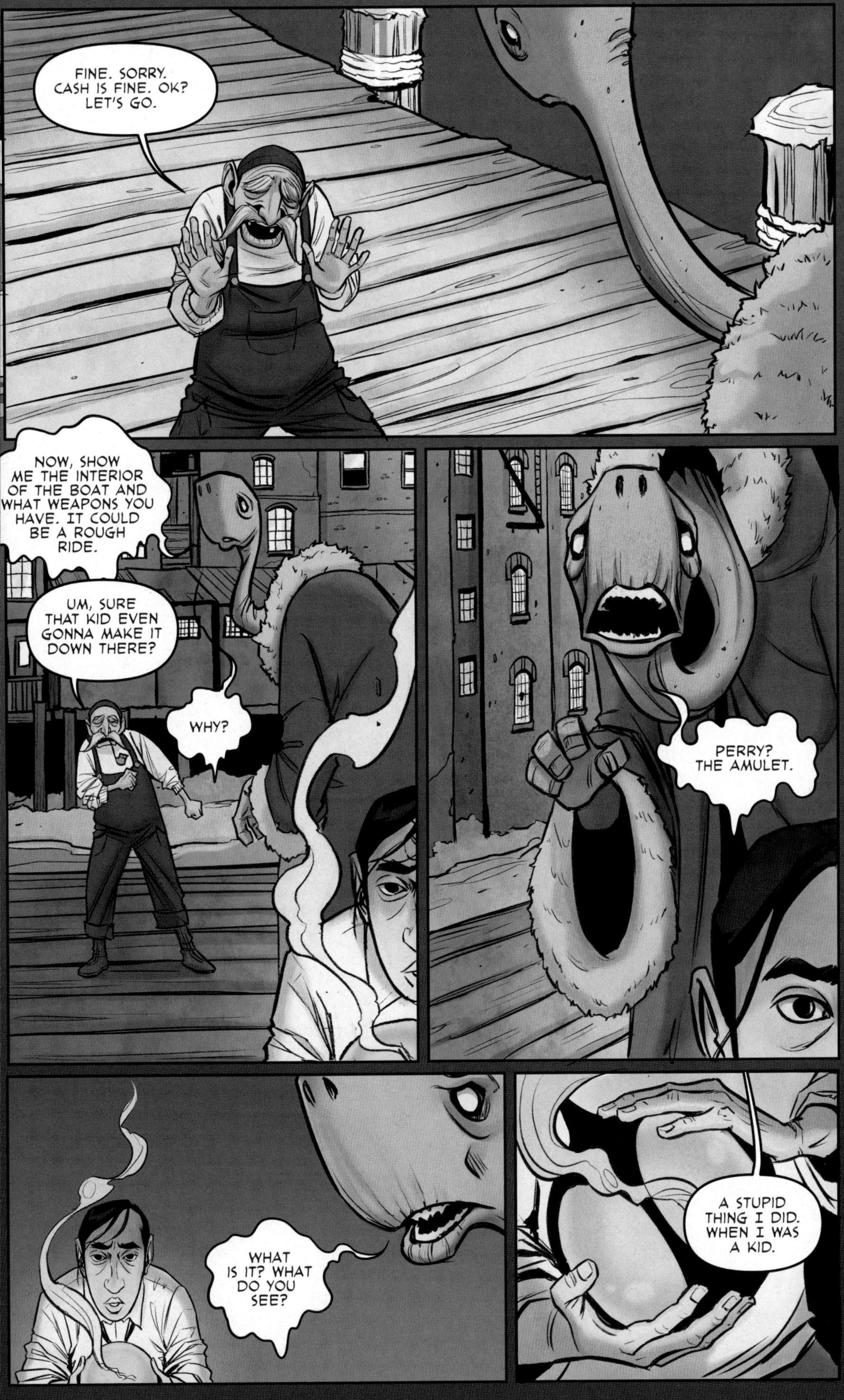
FINE. SORRY. CASH IS FINE. OK? LET'S GO.
NOW, SHOW ME THE INTERIOR OF THE BOAT AND WHAT WEAPONS YOU HAVE. IT COULD BE A ROUGH RIDE.
UM, SURE THAT KID EVEN GONNA MAKE IT DOWN THERE?
WHY?
PERRY? THE AMULET.
WHAT IS IT? WHAT DO YOU SEE?
A STUPID THING I DID. WHEN I WAS A KID.

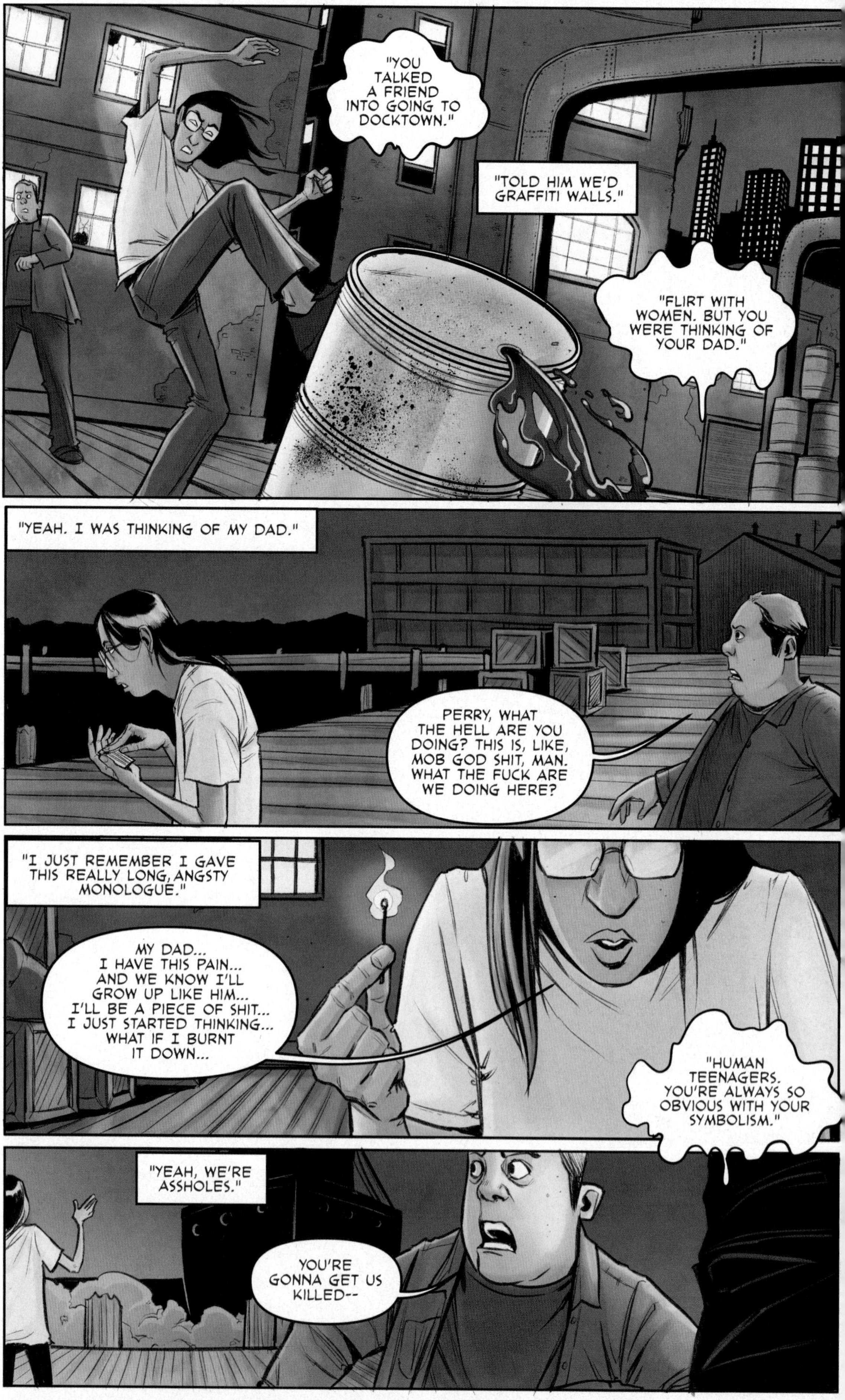
"YOU TALKED A FRIEND INTO GOING TO DOCKTOWN."
"TOLD HIM WE'D GRAFFITI WALLS."
"FLIRT WITH WOMEN. BUT YOU WERE THINKING OF YOUR DAD."
"YEAH. I WAS THINKING OF MY DAD."
PERRY, WHAT THE HELL ARE YOU DOING? THIS IS, LIKE, MOB GOD SHIT, MAN. WHAT THE FUCK ARE WE DOING HERE?
"I JUST REMEMBER I GAVE THIS REALLY LONG, ANGSTY MONOLOGUE."
MY DAD... I HAVE THIS PAIN... AND WE KNOW I'LL GROW UP LIKE HIM... I'LL BE A PIECE OF SHIT... I JUST STARTED THINKING... WHAT IF I BURNT IT DOWN...
"HUMAN TEENAGERS. YOU'RE ALWAYS SO OBVIOUS WITH YOUR SYMBOLISM."
"YEAH, WE'RE ASSHOLES."
YOU'RE GONNA GET US KILLED--

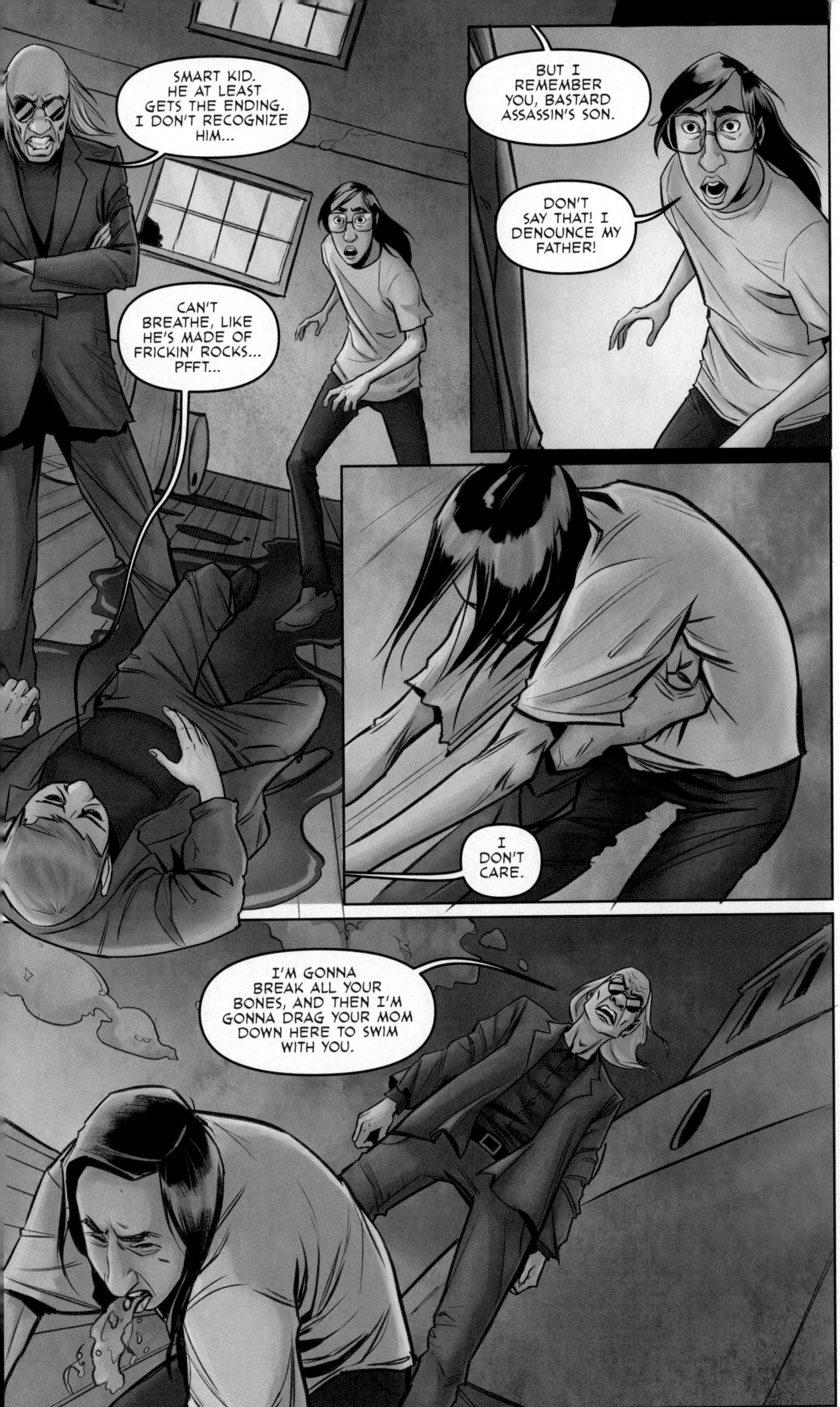
SMART KID. HE AT LEAST GETS THE ENDING. I DON'T RECOGNIZE HIM...
CAN'T BREATHE, LIKE HE'S MADE OF FRICKIN' ROCKS... PFFT...
BUT I REMEMBER YOU, BASTARD ASSASSIN'S SON.
DON'T SAY THAT! I DENOUNCE MY FATHER!
I DON'T CARE.
I'M GONNA BREAK ALL YOUR BONES, AND THEN I'M GONNA DRAG YOUR MOM DOWN HERE TO SWIM WITH YOU.

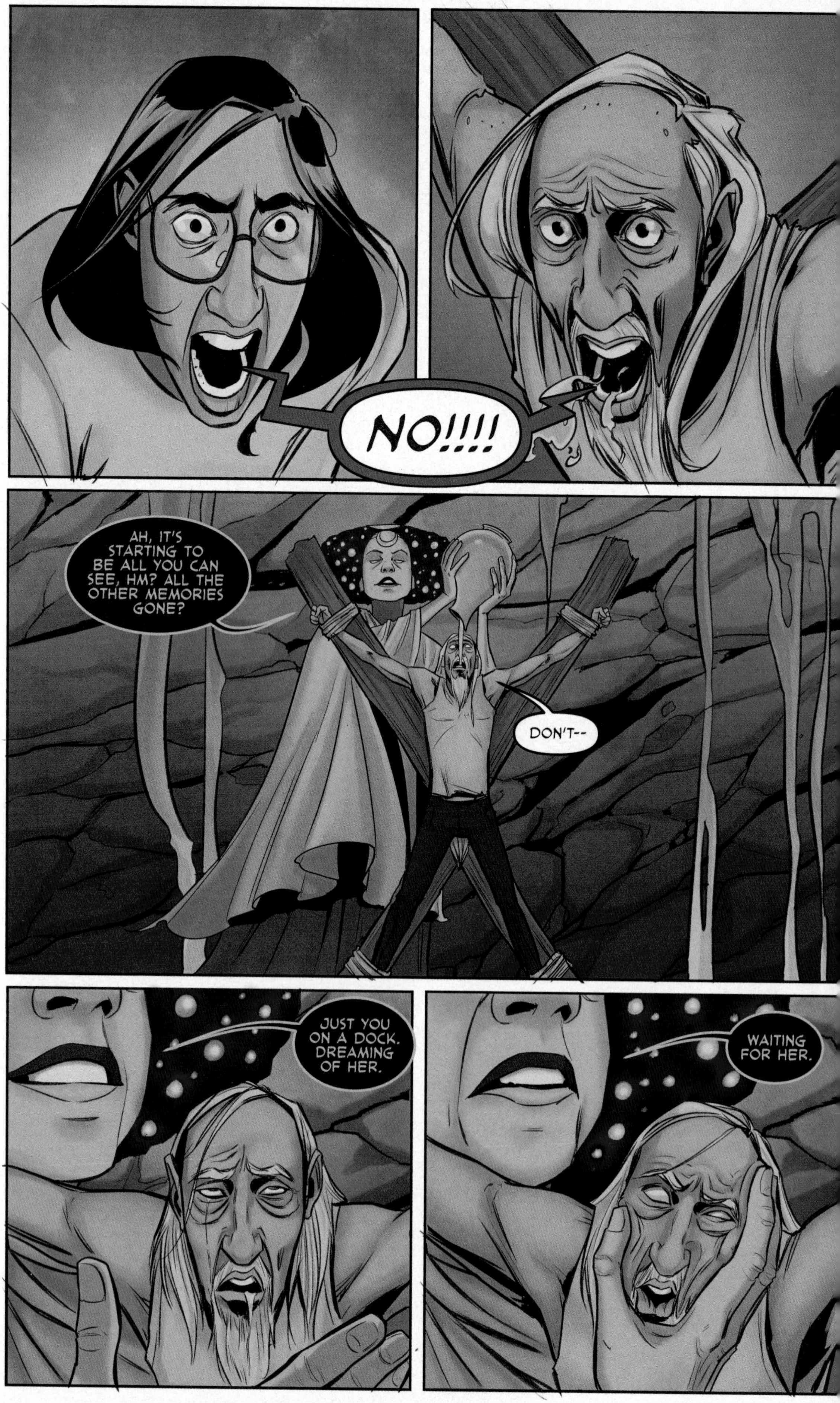
NO!!!!
AH, IT'S STARTING TO BE ALL YOU CAN SEE, HM? ALL THE OTHER MEMORIES GONE?
DON'T--
JUST YOU ON A DOCK. DREAMING OF HER.
WAITING FOR HER.

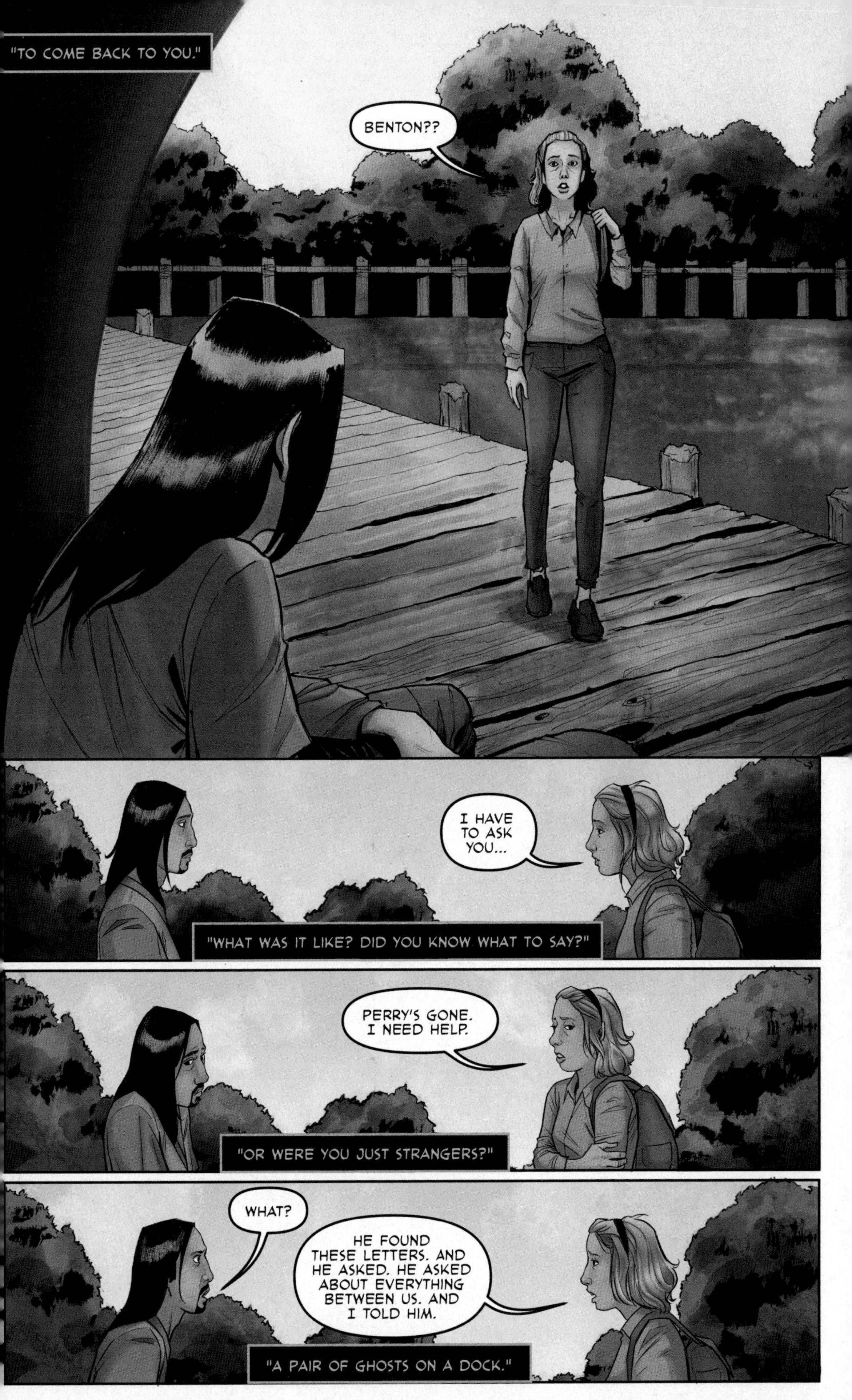
"TO COME BACK TO YOU."
BENTON??
I HAVE TO ASK YOU...
"WHAT WAS IT LIKE? DID YOU KNOW WHAT TO SAY?"
PERRY'S GONE. I NEED HELP.
"OR WERE YOU JUST STRANGERS?"
WHAT?
HE FOUND THESE LETTERS. AND HE ASKED. HE ASKED ABOUT EVERYTHING BETWEEN US. AND I TOLD HIM.
"A PAIR OF GHOSTS ON A DOCK."

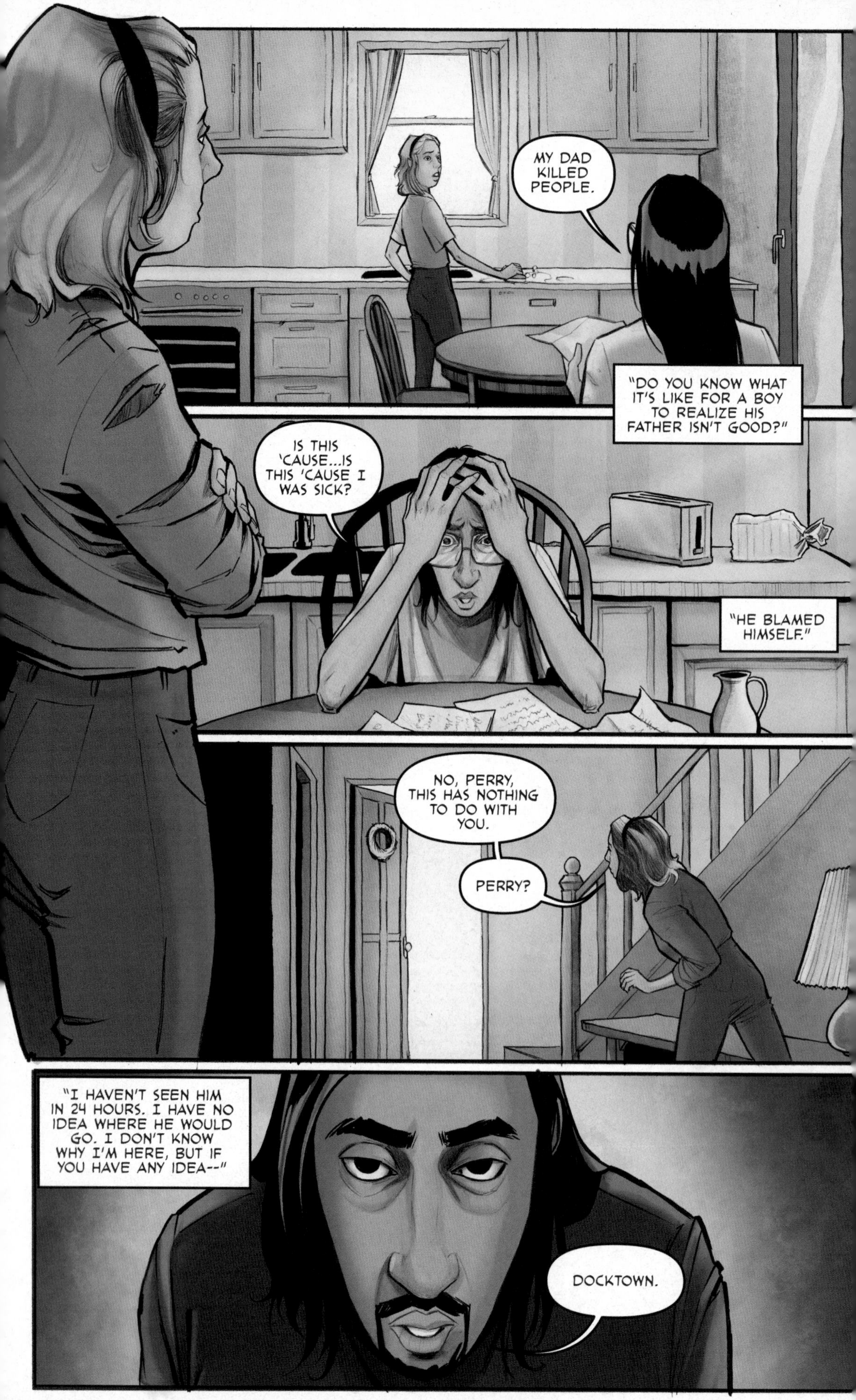
MY DAD KILLED PEOPLE.
"DO YOU KNOW WHAT IT'S LIKE FOR A BOY TO REALIZE HIS FATHER ISN'T GOOD?"
IS THIS 'CAUSE...IS THIS 'CAUSE I WAS SICK?
"HE BLAMED HIMSELF."
NO, PERRY, THIS HAS NOTHING TO DO WITH YOU.
PERRY?
"I HAVEN'T SEEN HIM IN 24 HOURS. I HAVE NO IDEA WHERE HE WOULD GO. I DON'T KNOW WHY I'M HERE, BUT IF YOU HAVE ANY IDEA--"
DOCKTOWN.

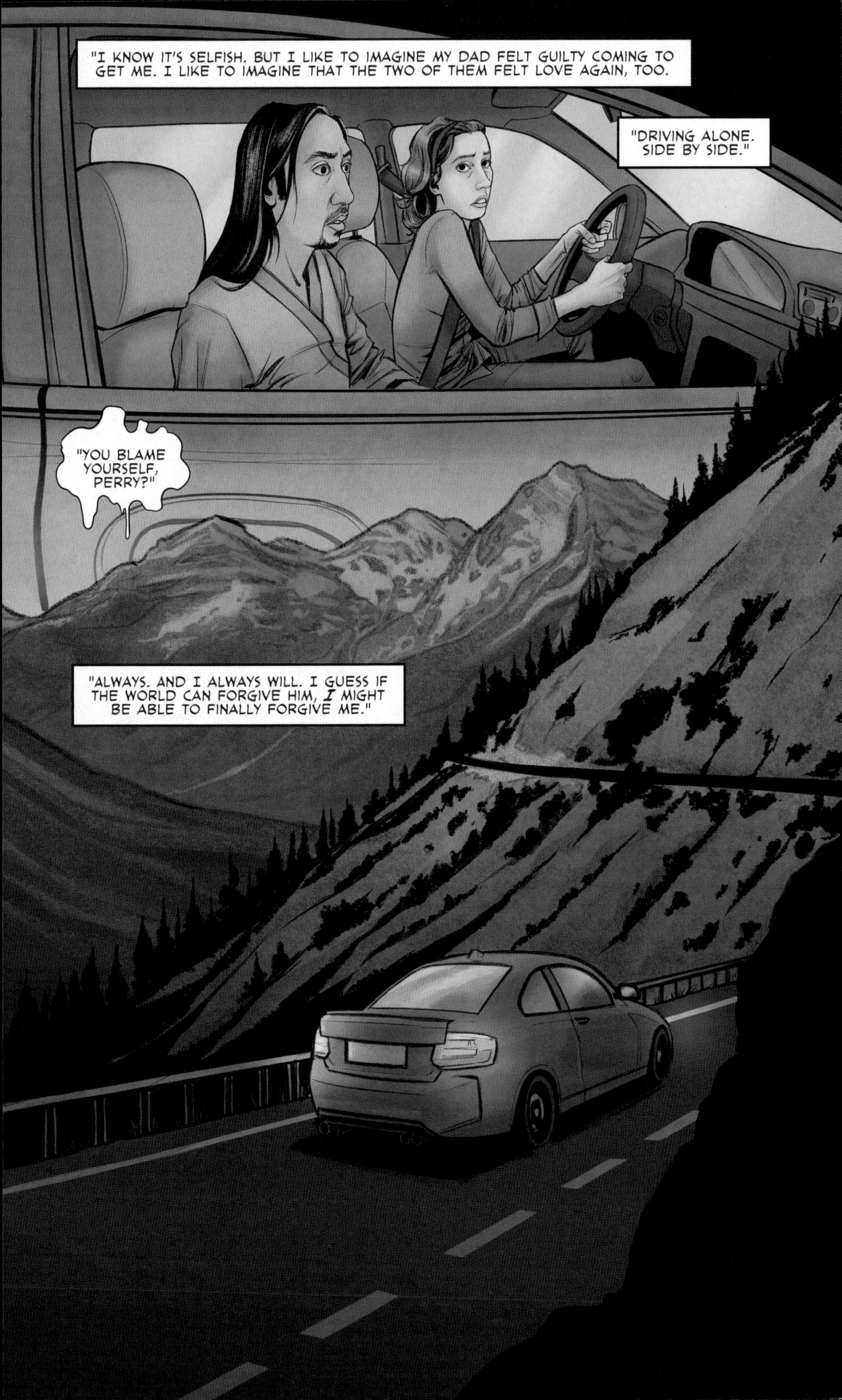
"I KNOW IT'S SELFISH. BUT I LIKE TO IMAGINE MY DAD FELT GUILTY COMING TO GET ME. I LIKE TO IMAGINE THAT THE TWO OF THEM FELT LOVE AGAIN, TOO.
"DRIVING ALONE. SIDE BY SIDE."
"YOU BLAME YOURSELF, PERRY?"
"ALWAYS. AND I ALWAYS WILL. I GUESS IF THE WORLD CAN FORGIVE HIM, *I* MIGHT BE ABLE TO FINALLY FORGIVE ME."

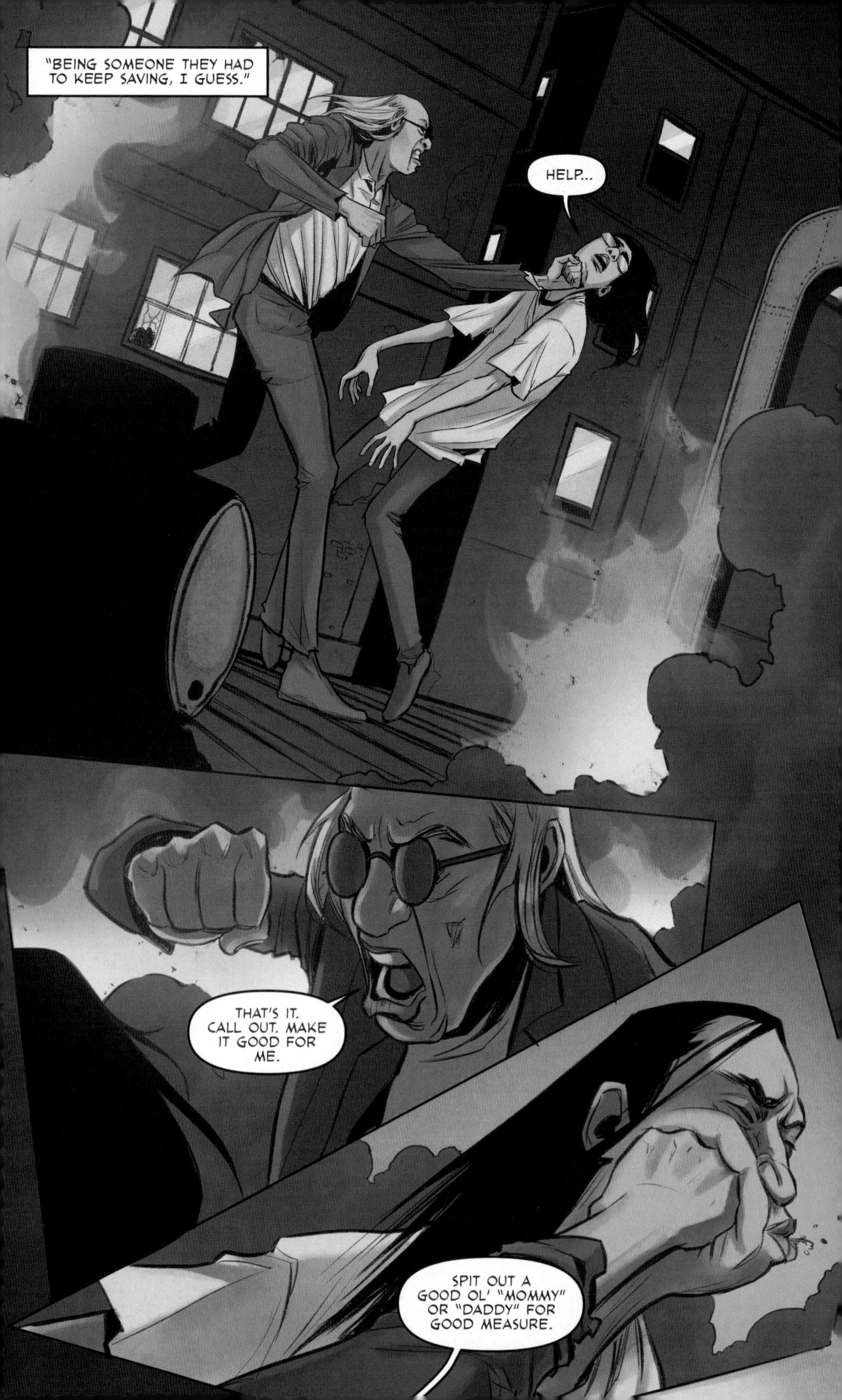
"BEING SOMEONE THEY HAD TO KEEP SAVING, I GUESS."
HELP...
THAT'S IT. CALL OUT. MAKE IT GOOD FOR ME.
SPIT OUT A GOOD OL' "MOMMY" OR "DADDY" FOR GOOD MEASURE.

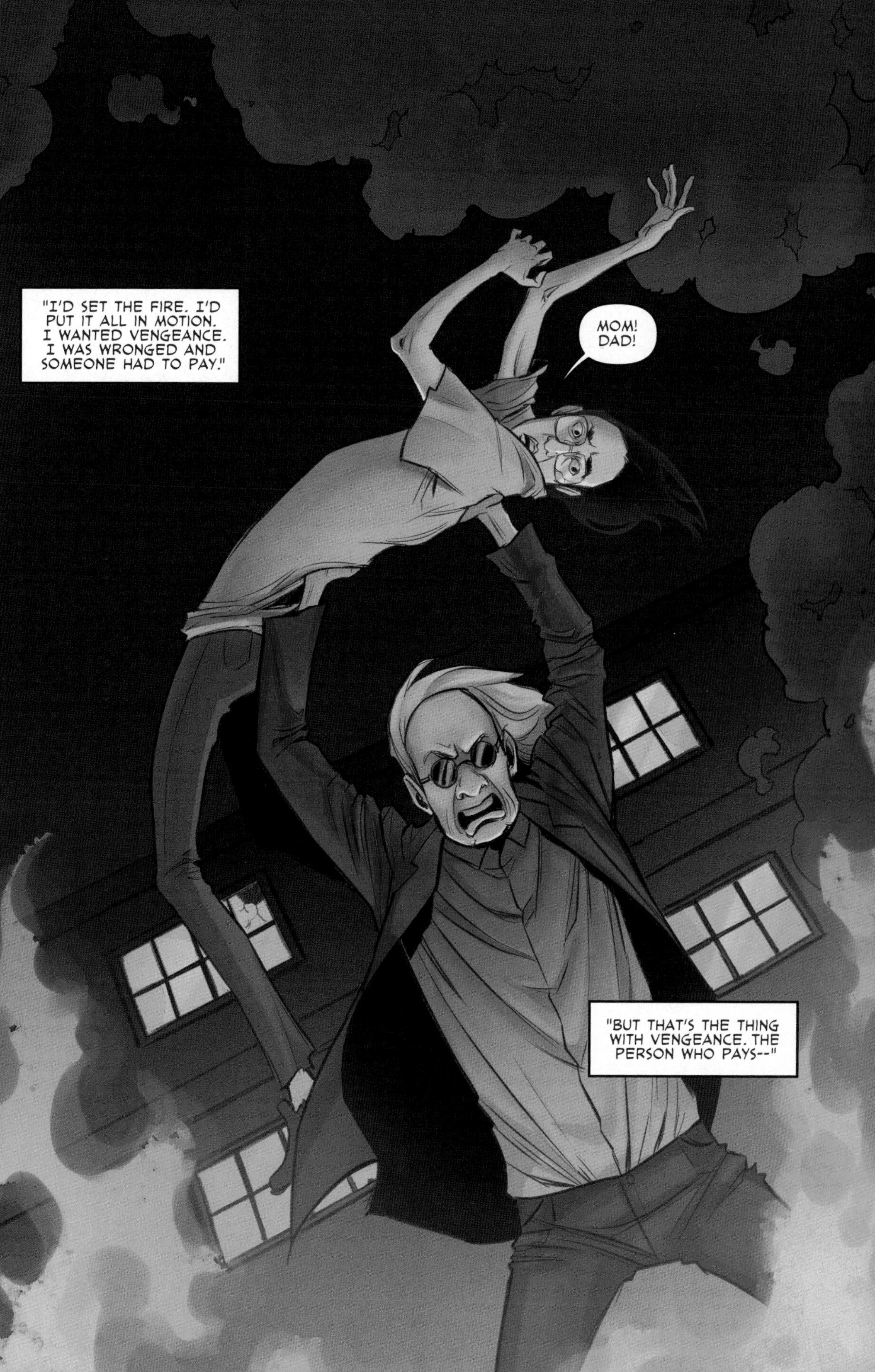
"I'D SET THE FIRE. I'D PUT IT ALL IN MOTION. I WANTED VENGEANCE. I WAS WRONGED AND SOMEONE HAD TO PAY."
MOM! DAD!
"BUT THAT'S THE THING WITH VENGEANCE. THE PERSON WHO PAYS--"

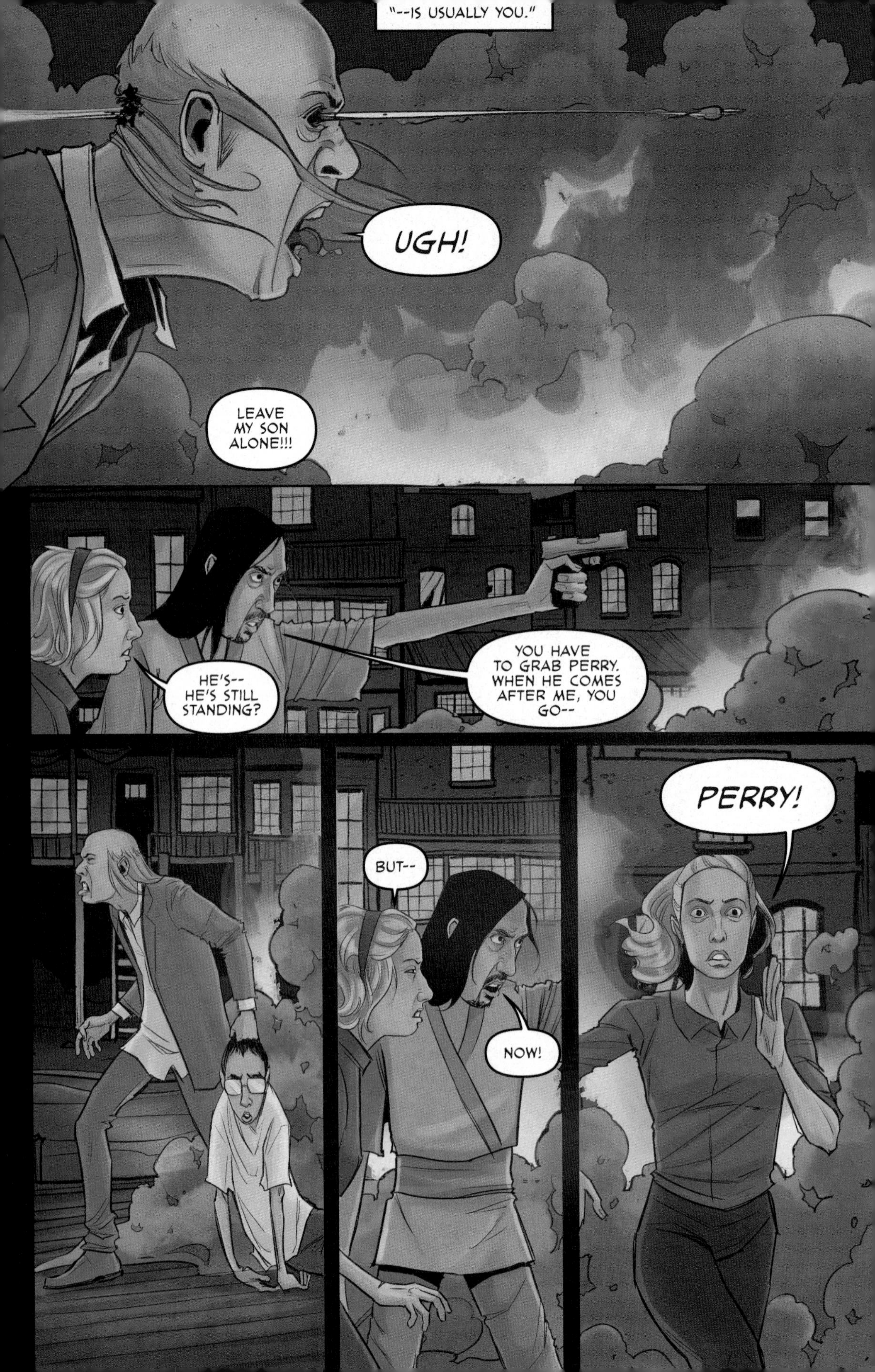
"--IS USUALLY YOU."
UGH!
LEAVE MY SON ALONE!!!
HE'S-- HE'S STILL STANDING?
YOU HAVE TO GRAB PERRY. WHEN HE COMES AFTER ME, YOU GO--
BUT--
NOW!
PERRY!

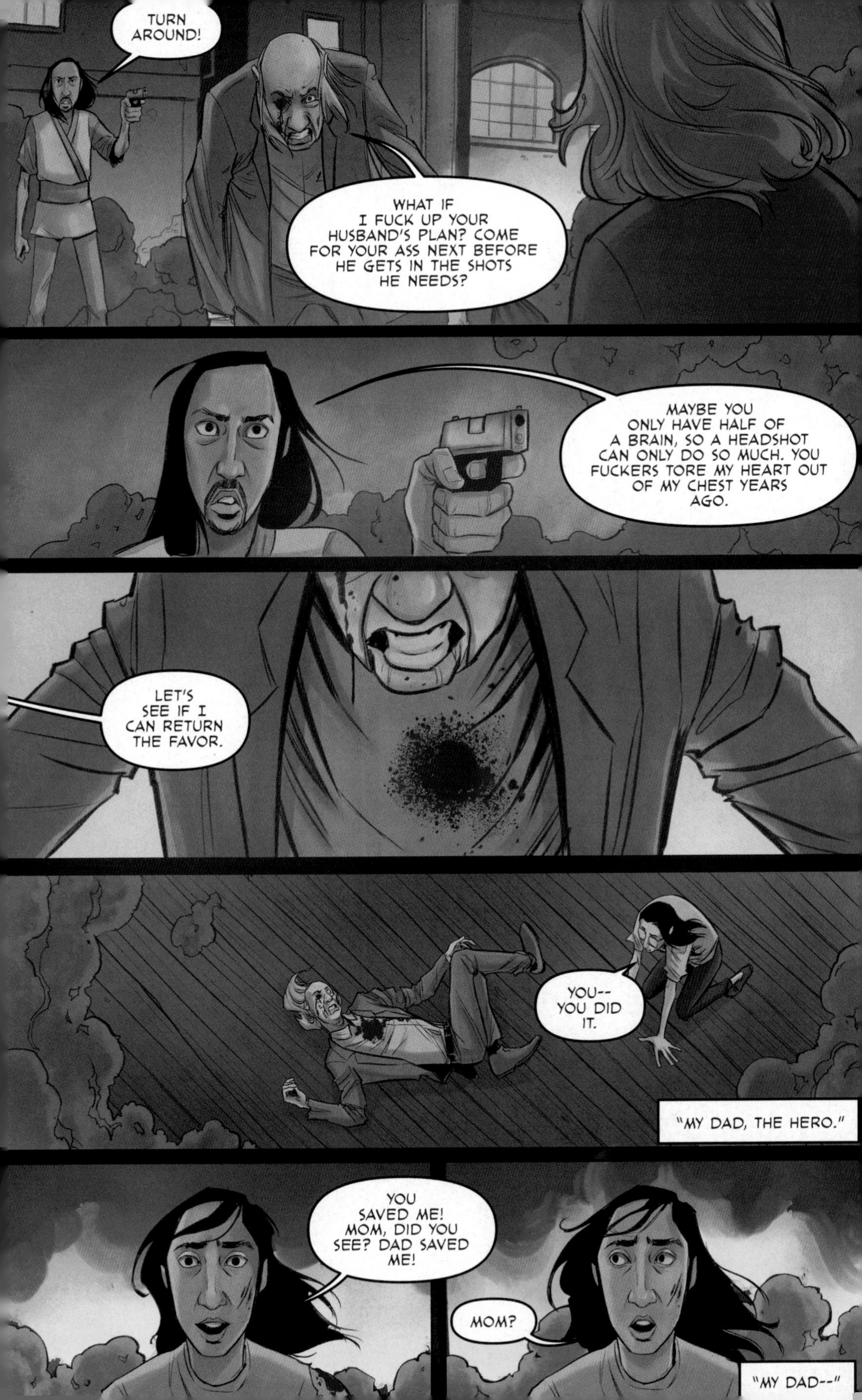
TURN AROUND!
WHAT IF I FUCK UP YOUR HUSBAND'S PLAN? COME FOR YOUR ASS NEXT BEFORE HE GETS IN THE SHOTS HE NEEDS?
MAYBE YOU ONLY HAVE HALF OF A BRAIN, SO A HEADSHOT CAN ONLY DO SO MUCH. YOU FUCKERS TORE MY HEART OUT OF MY CHEST YEARS AGO.
LET'S SEE IF I CAN RETURN THE FAVOR.
YOU-- YOU DID IT.
"MY DAD, THE HERO."
YOU SAVED ME! MOM, DID YOU SEE? DAD SAVED ME!
MOM?
"MY DAD--"

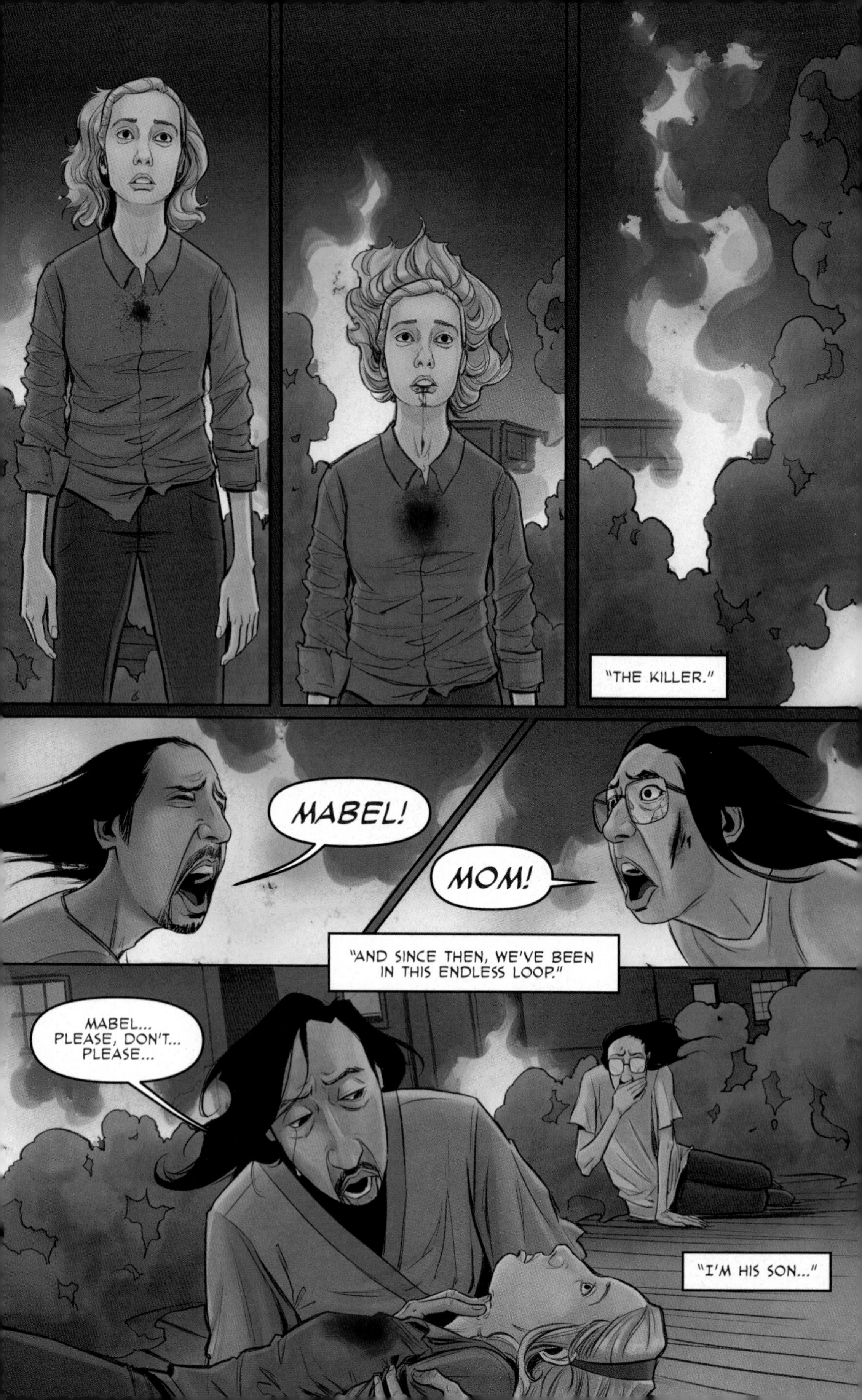
"THE KILLER."
MABEL!
MOM!
"AND SINCE THEN, WE'VE BEEN IN THIS ENDLESS LOOP."
MABEL... PLEASE, DON'T... PLEASE...
"I'M HIS SON..."

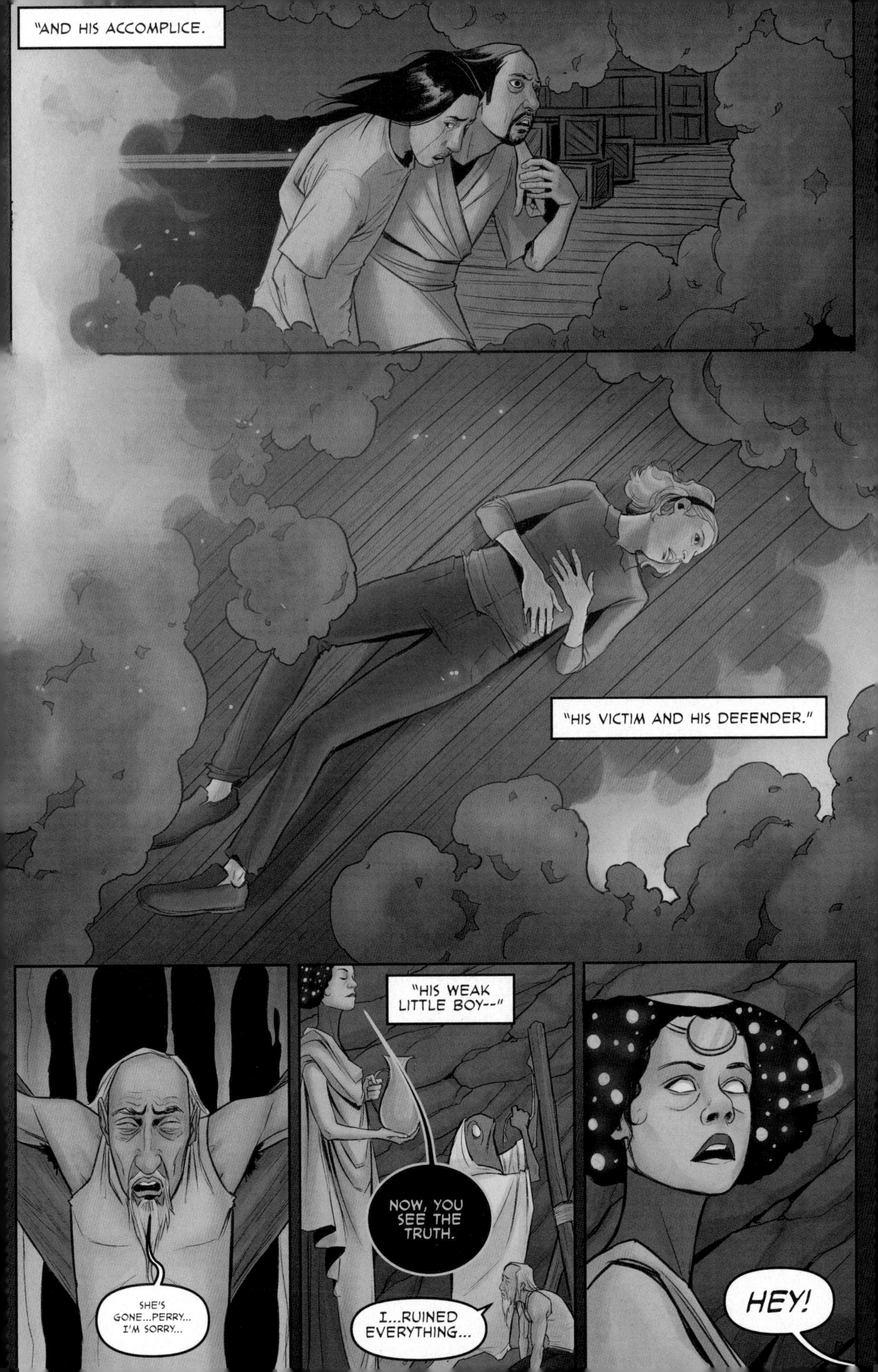
"AND HIS ACCOMPLICE.
"HIS VICTIM AND HIS DEFENDER."
SHE'S GONE...PERRY... I'M SORRY...
"HIS WEAK LITTLE BOY--"
NOW, YOU SEE THE TRUTH.
I...RUINED EVERYTHING...
HEY!

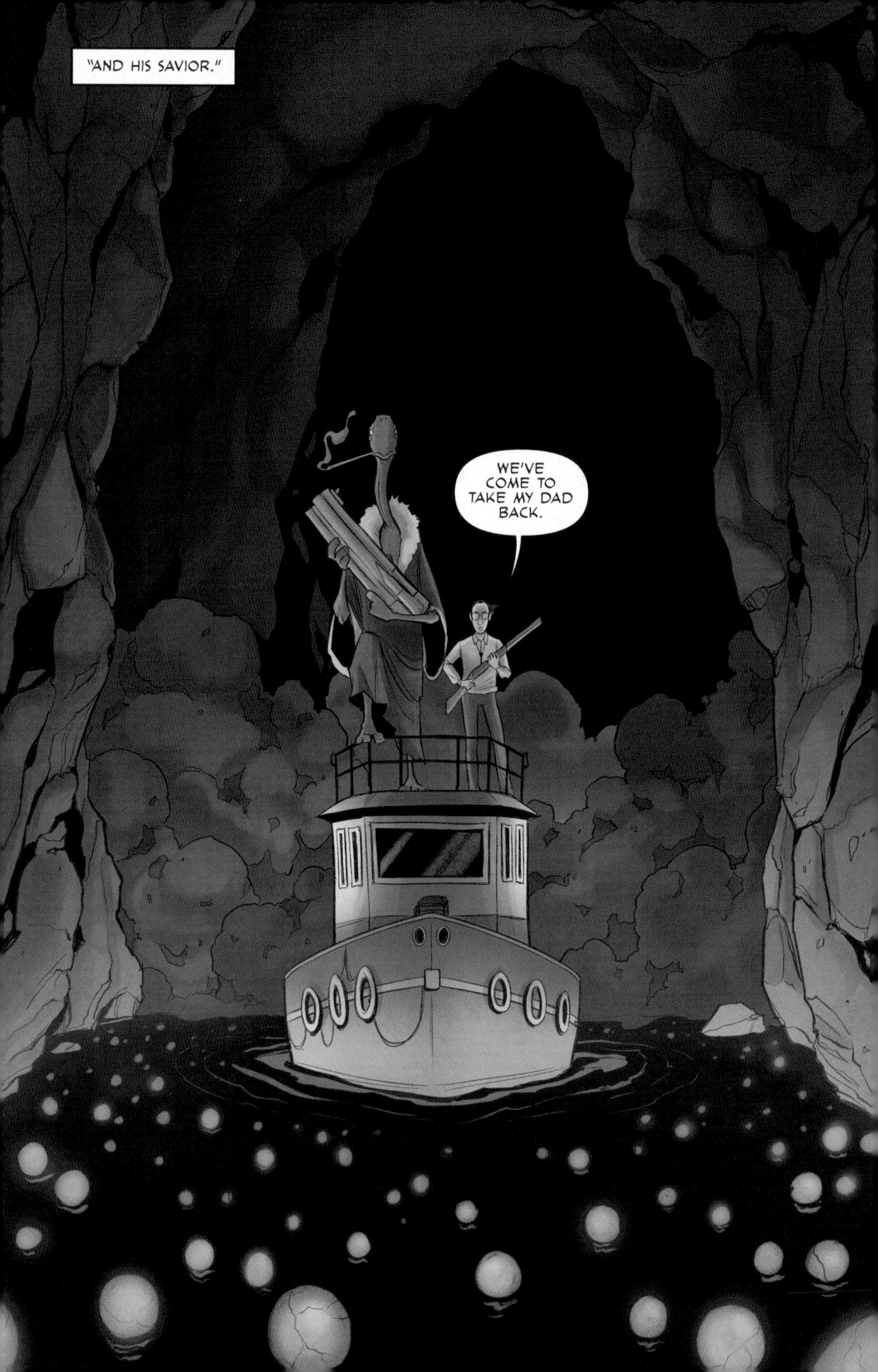
"AND HIS SAVIOR."
WE'VE COME TO TAKE MY DAD BACK.

7

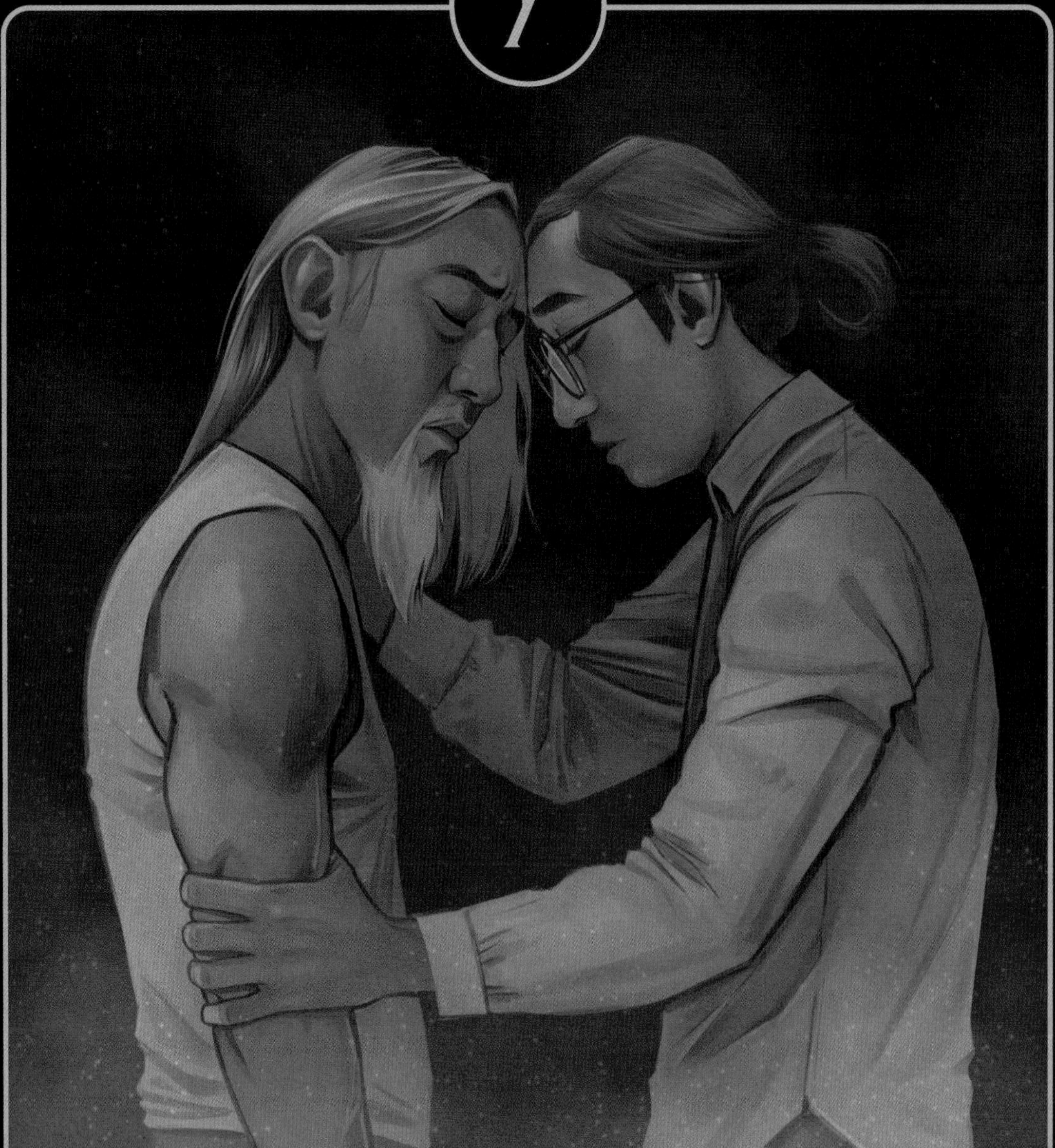

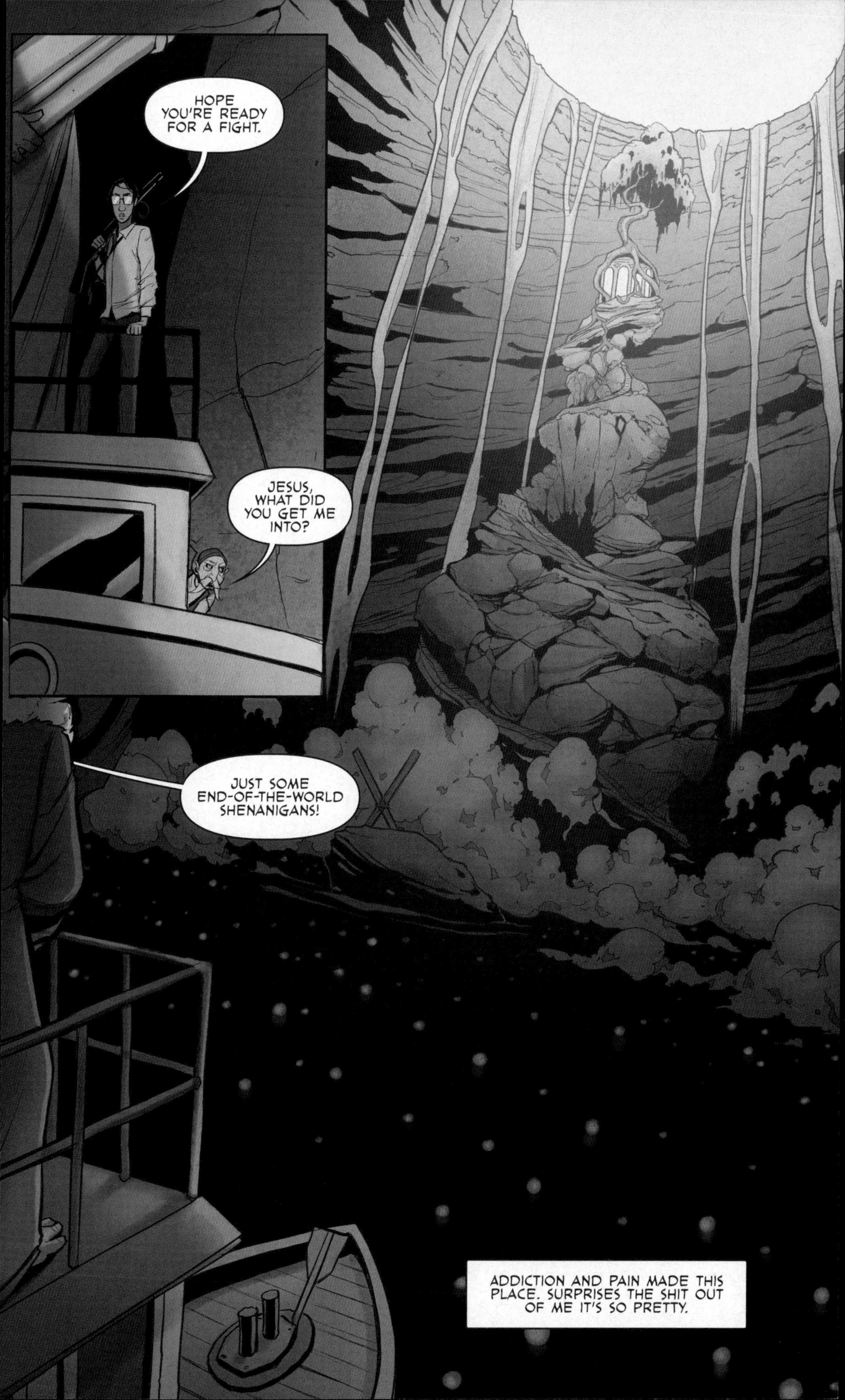
HOPE YOU'RE READY FOR A FIGHT.
JESUS, WHAT DID YOU GET ME INTO?
JUST SOME END-OF-THE-WORLD SHENANIGANS!
ADDICTION AND PAIN MADE THIS PLACE. SURPRISES THE SHIT OUT OF ME IT'S SO PRETTY.

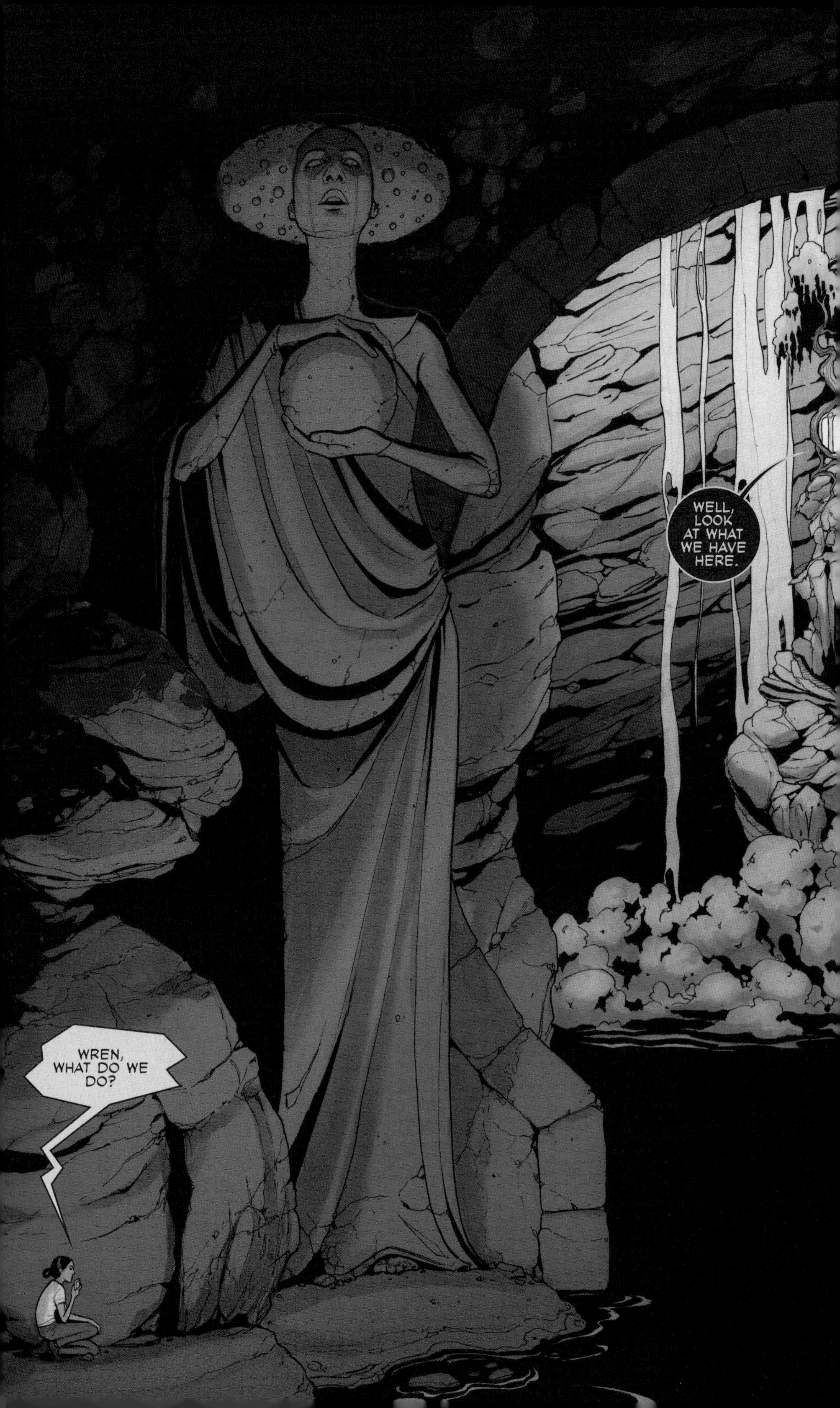
WELL, LOOK AT WHAT WE HAVE HERE.
WREN, WHAT DO WE DO?

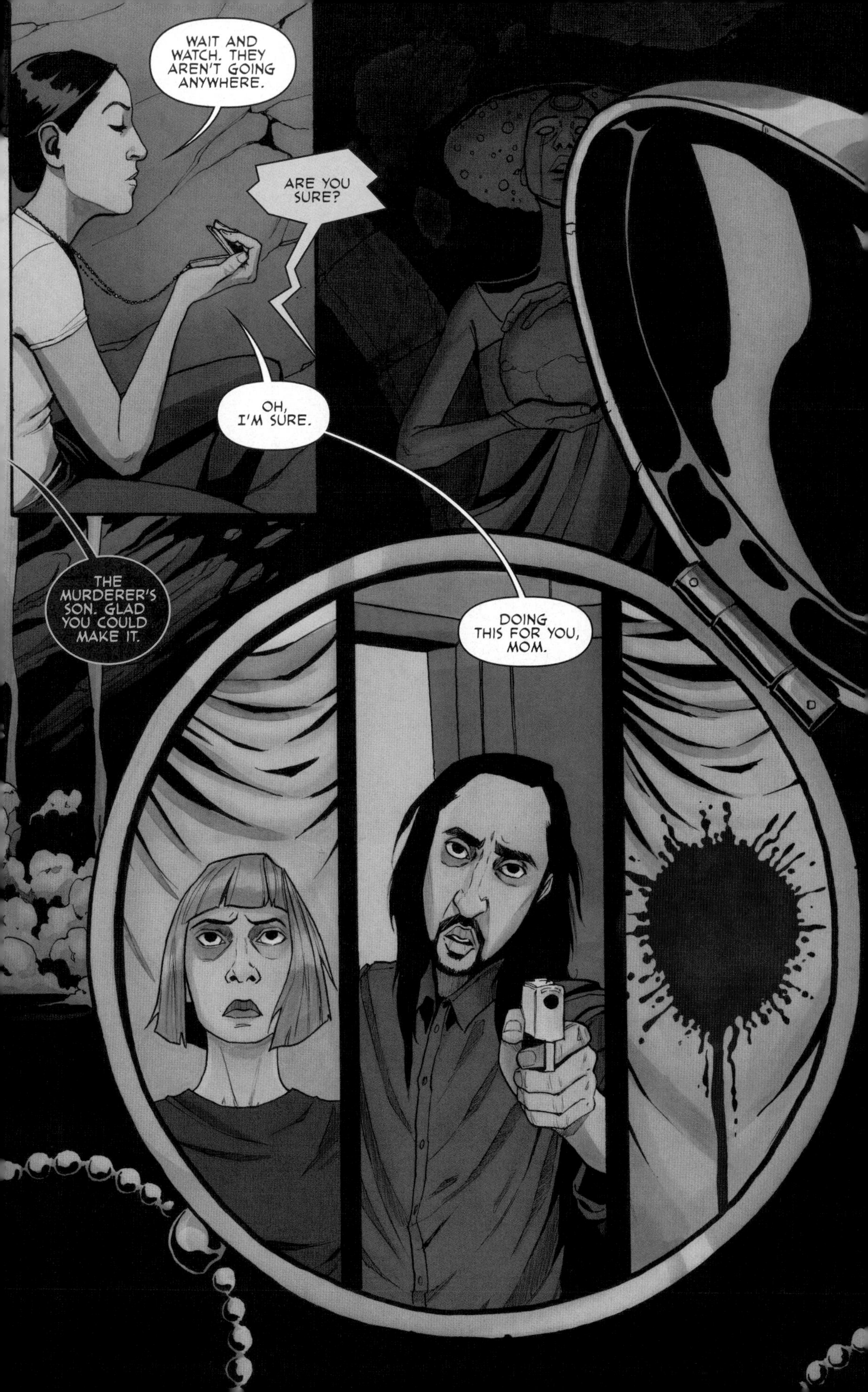
WAIT AND WATCH. THEY AREN'T GOING ANYWHERE.
ARE YOU SURE?
OH, I'M SURE.
THE MURDERER'S SON. GLAD YOU COULD MAKE IT.
DOING THIS FOR YOU, MOM.

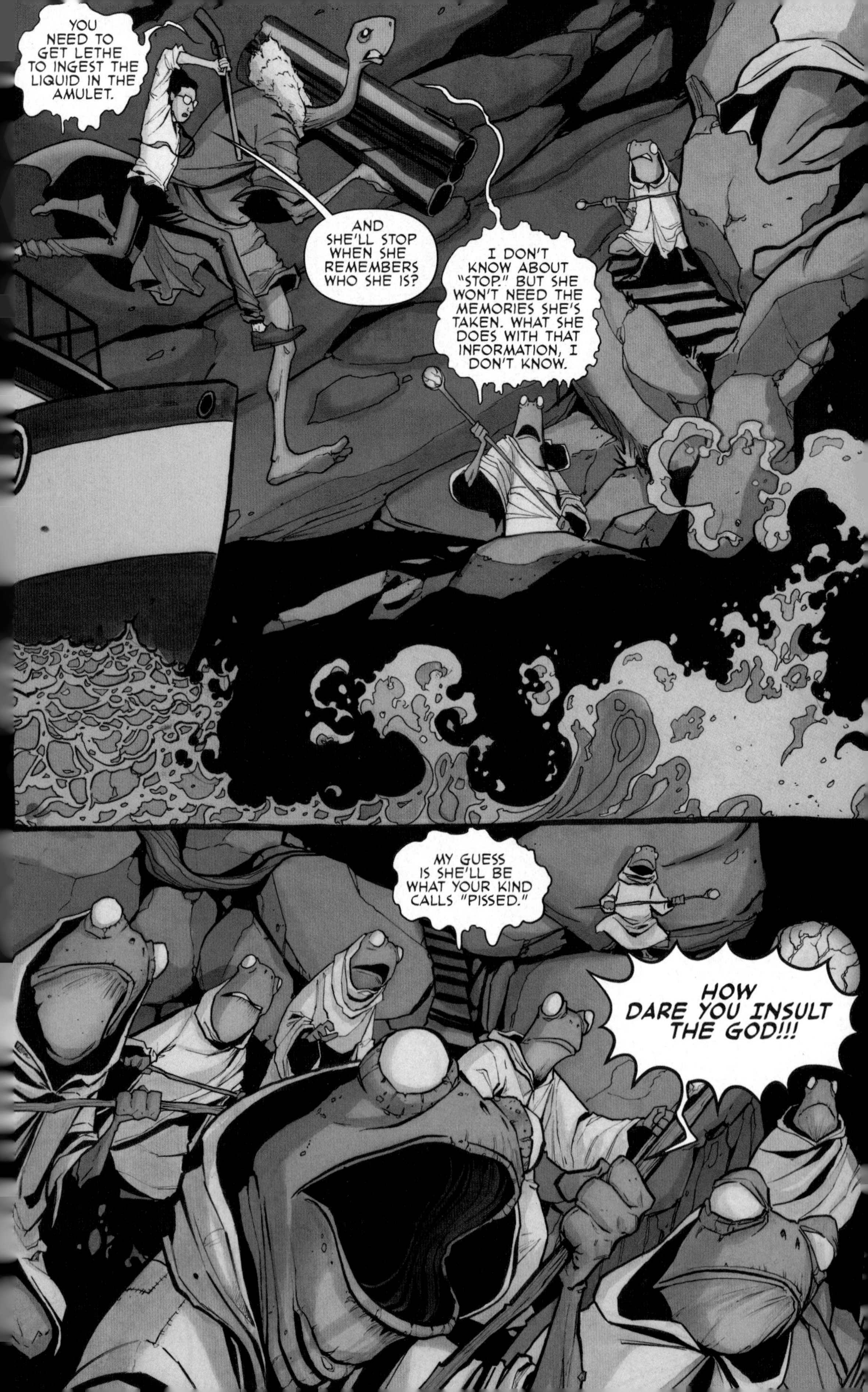
YOU NEED TO GET LETHE TO INGEST THE LIQUID IN THE AMULET.
AND SHE'LL STOP WHEN SHE REMEMBERS WHO SHE IS?
I DON'T KNOW ABOUT "STOP." BUT SHE WON'T NEED THE MEMORIES SHE'S TAKEN. WHAT SHE DOES WITH THAT INFORMATION, I DON'T KNOW.
MY GUESS IS SHE'LL BE WHAT YOUR KIND CALLS "PISSED."
HOW DARE YOU INSULT THE GOD!!!

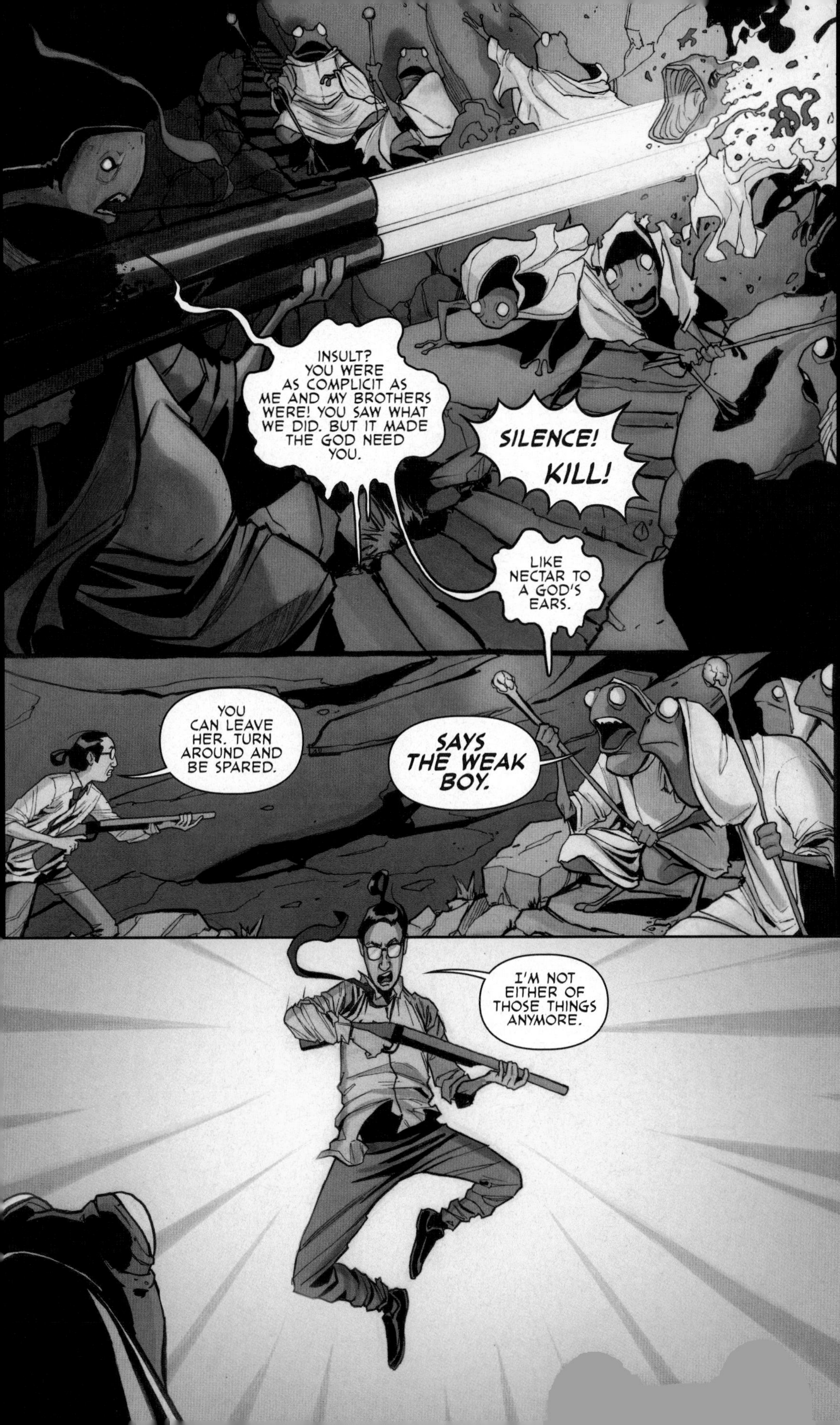
INSULT? YOU WERE AS COMPLICIT AS ME AND MY BROTHERS WERE! YOU SAW WHAT WE DID. BUT IT MADE THE GOD NEED YOU.
SILENCE!
KILL!
LIKE NECTAR TO A GOD'S EARS.
YOU CAN LEAVE HER. TURN AROUND AND BE SPARED.
SAYS THE WEAK BOY.
I'M NOT EITHER OF THOSE THINGS ANYMORE.

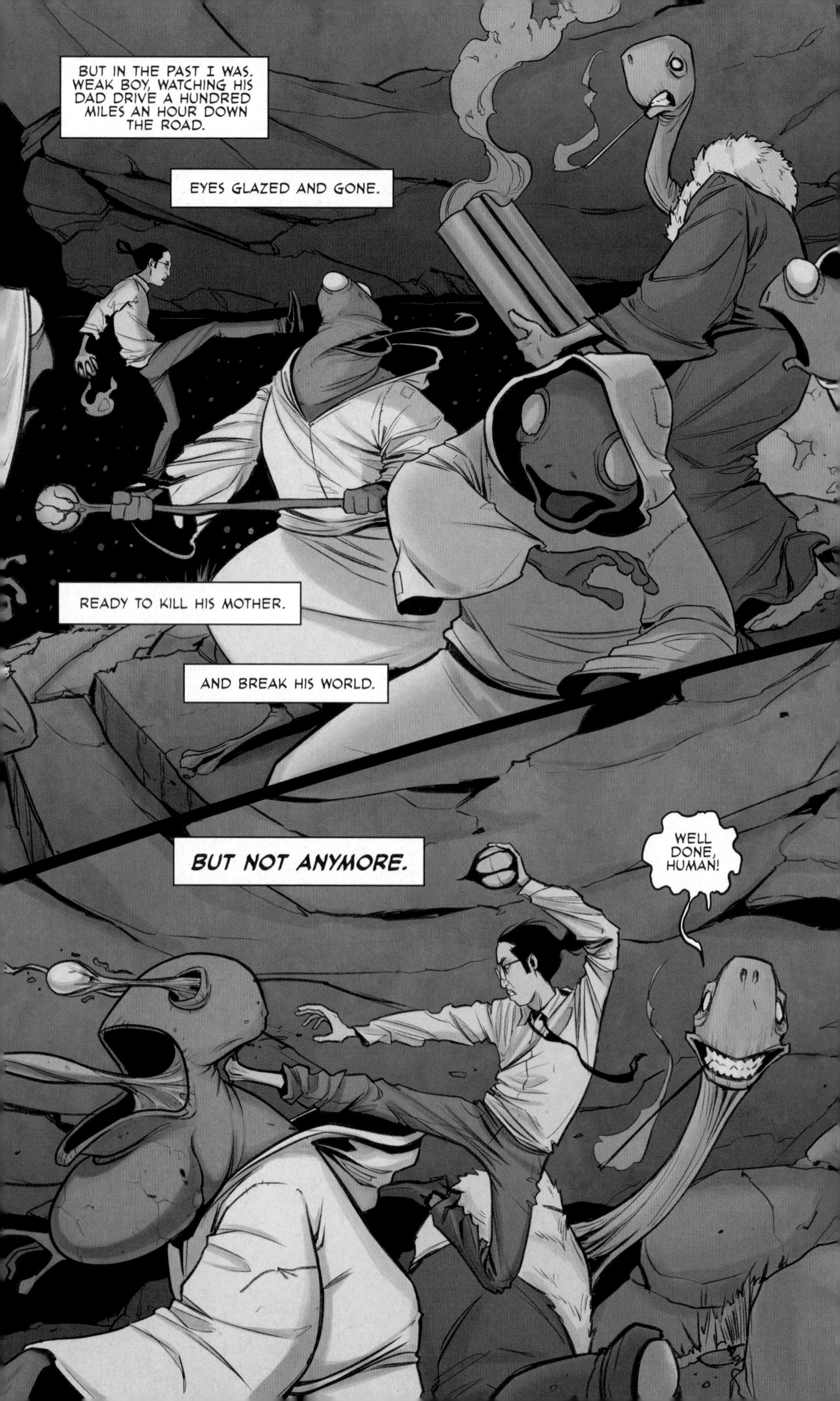
BUT IN THE PAST I WAS. WEAK BOY, WATCHING HIS DAD DRIVE A HUNDRED MILES AN HOUR DOWN THE ROAD.
EYES GLAZED AND GONE.
READY TO KILL HIS MOTHER.
AND BREAK HIS WORLD.
BUT NOT ANYMORE.
WELL DONE, HUMAN!

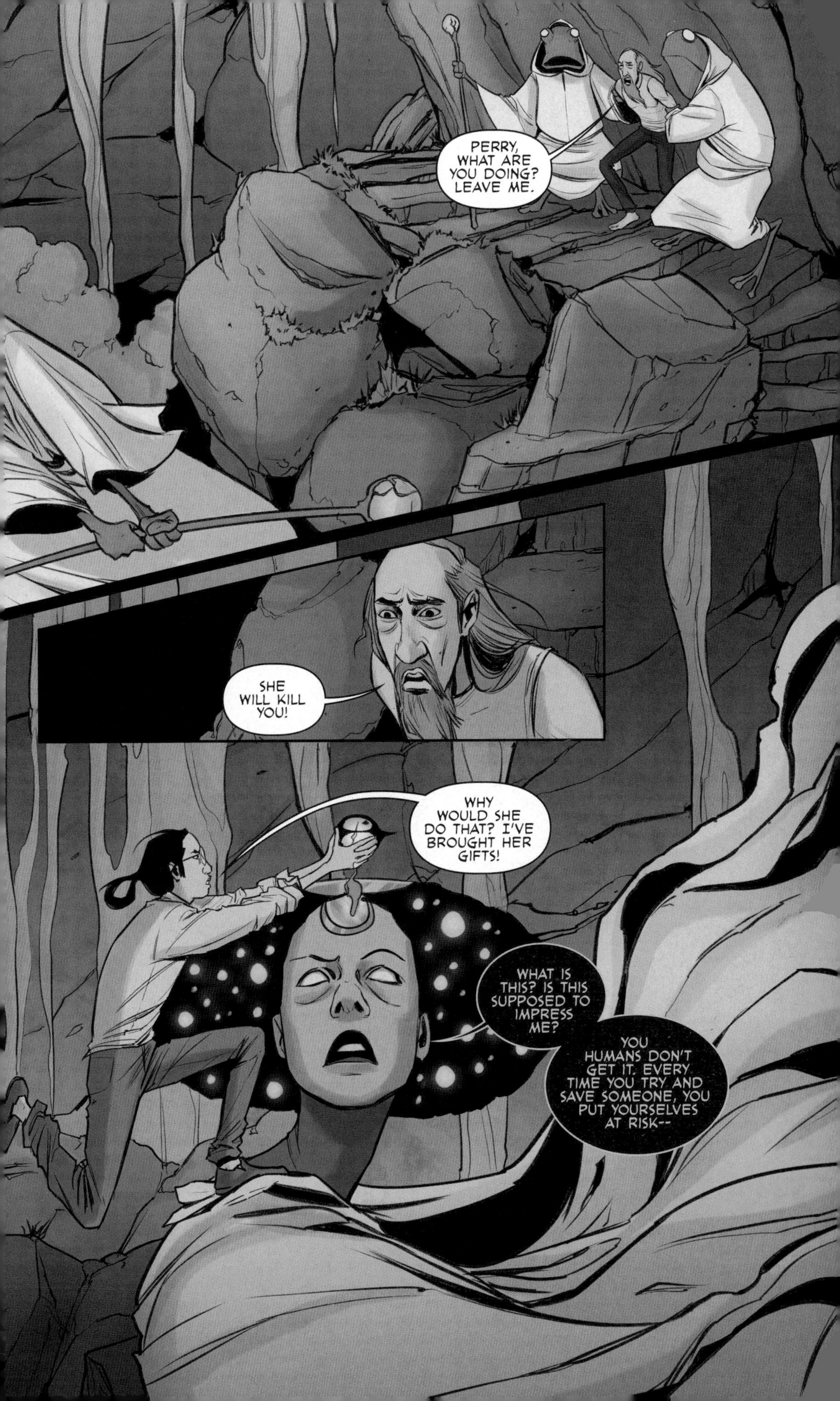
PERRY, WHAT ARE YOU DOING? LEAVE ME.
SHE WILL KILL YOU!
WHY WOULD SHE DO THAT? I'VE BROUGHT HER GIFTS!
WHAT IS THIS? IS THIS SUPPOSED TO IMPRESS ME?
YOU HUMANS DON'T GET IT. EVERY TIME YOU TRY AND SAVE SOMEONE, YOU PUT YOURSELVES AT RISK--

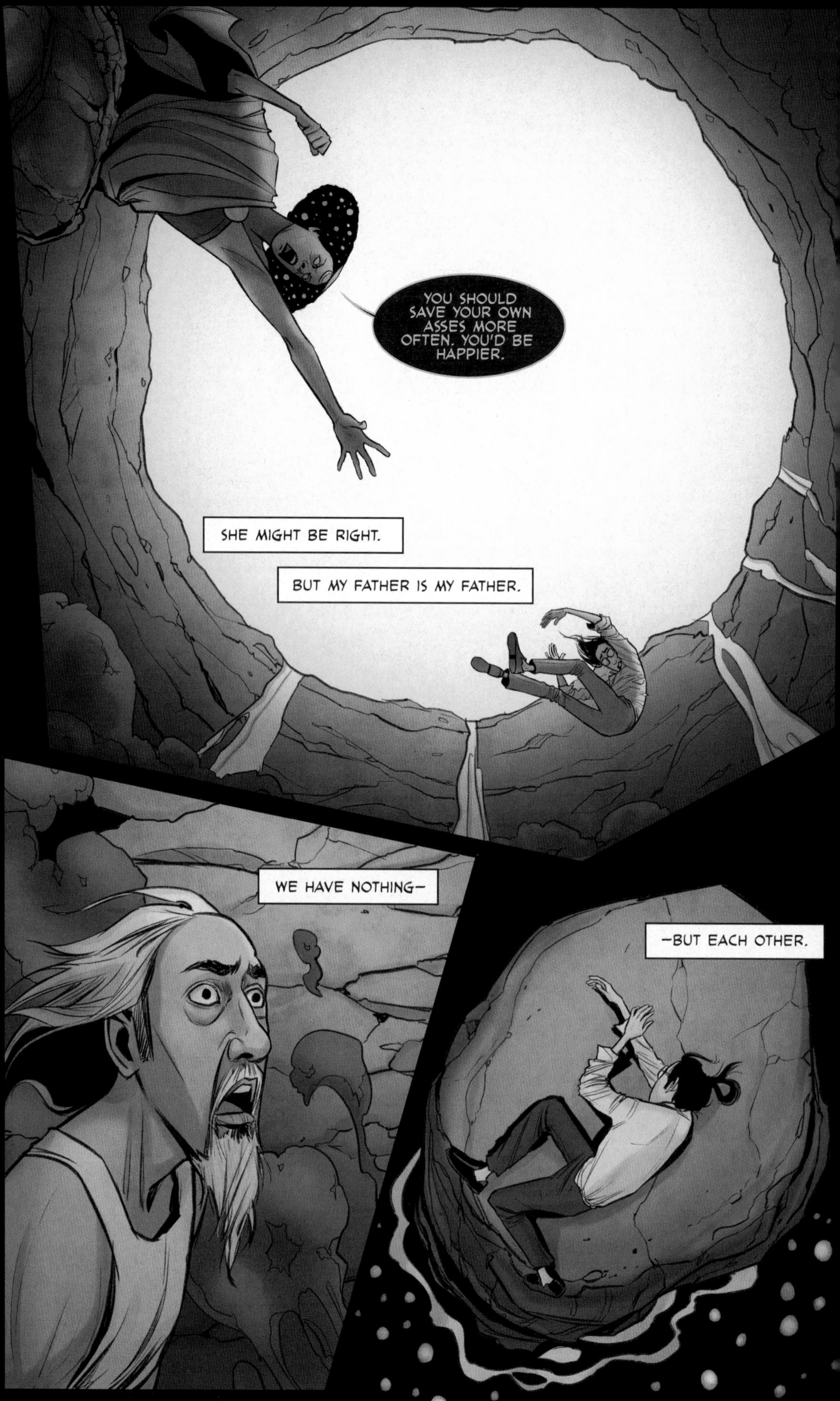
YOU SHOULD SAVE YOUR OWN ASSES MORE OFTEN. YOU'D BE HAPPIER.
SHE MIGHT BE RIGHT.
BUT MY FATHER IS MY FATHER.
WE HAVE NOTHING–
–BUT EACH OTHER.

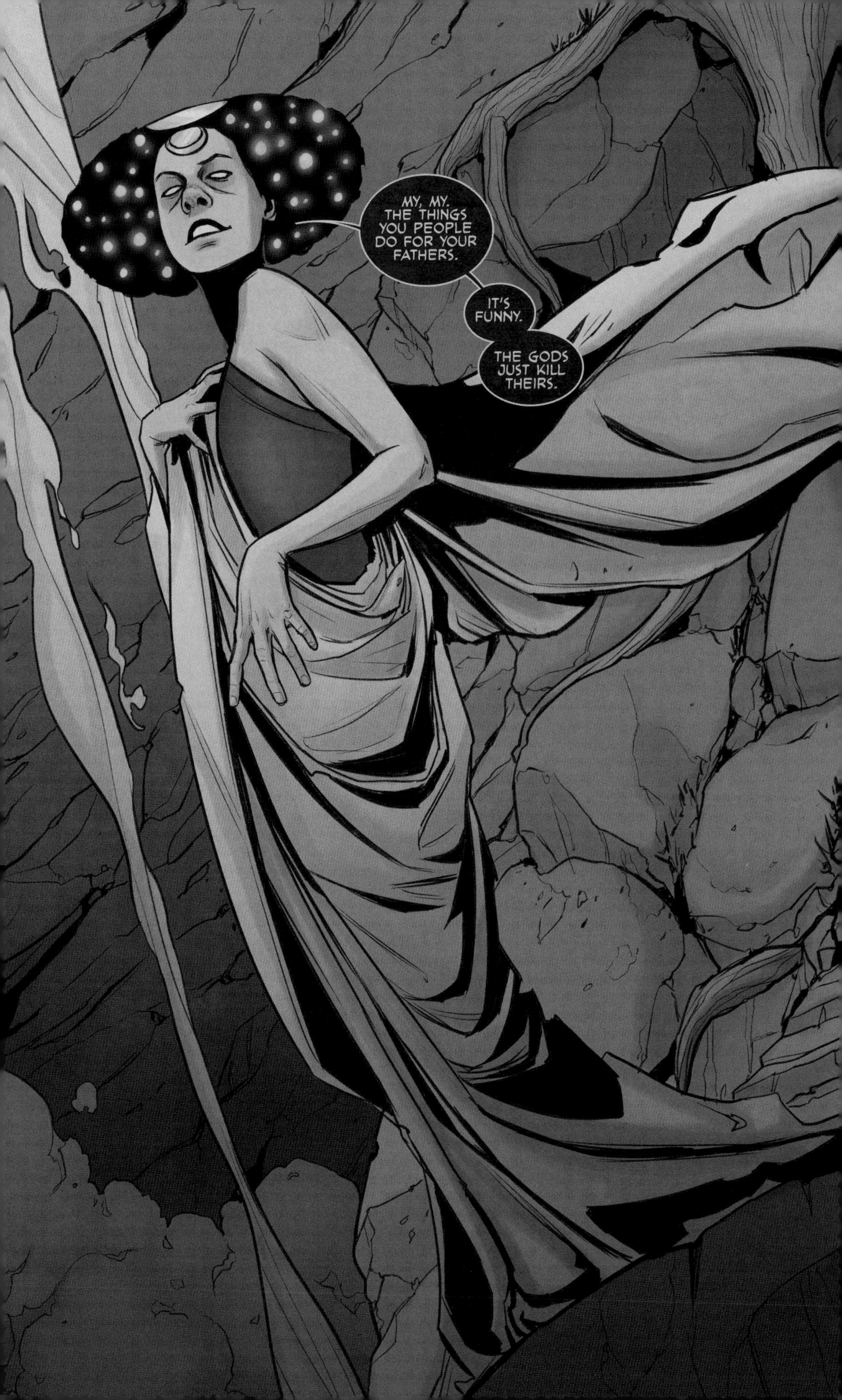
MY, MY. THE THINGS YOU PEOPLE DO FOR YOUR FATHERS.
IT'S FUNNY.
THE GODS JUST KILL THEIRS.

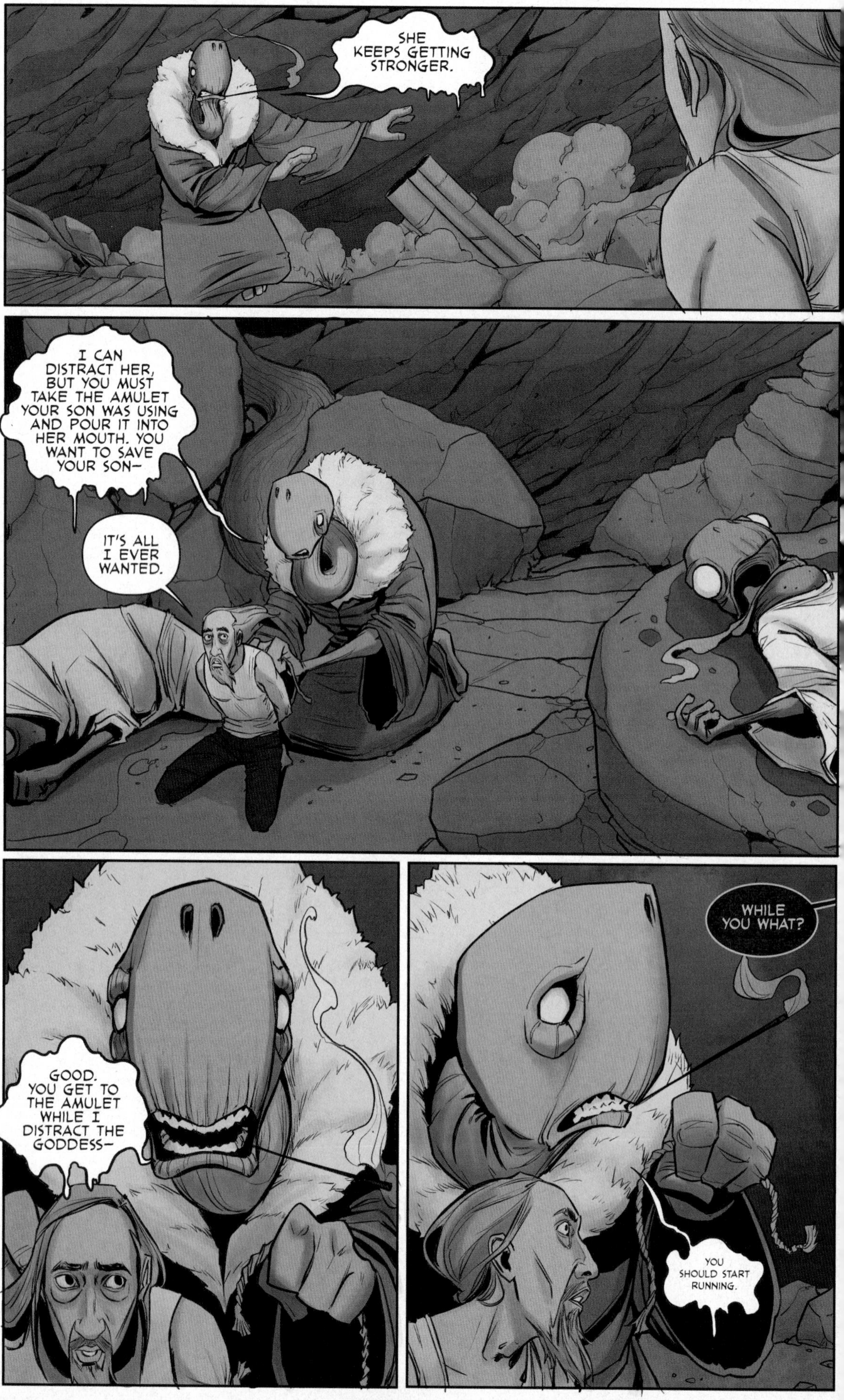
SHE KEEPS GETTING STRONGER.
I CAN DISTRACT HER, BUT YOU MUST TAKE THE AMULET YOUR SON WAS USING AND POUR IT INTO HER MOUTH. YOU WANT TO SAVE YOUR SON–
IT'S ALL I EVER WANTED.
GOOD. YOU GET TO THE AMULET WHILE I DISTRACT THE GODDESS–
WHILE YOU WHAT?
YOU SHOULD START RUNNING.

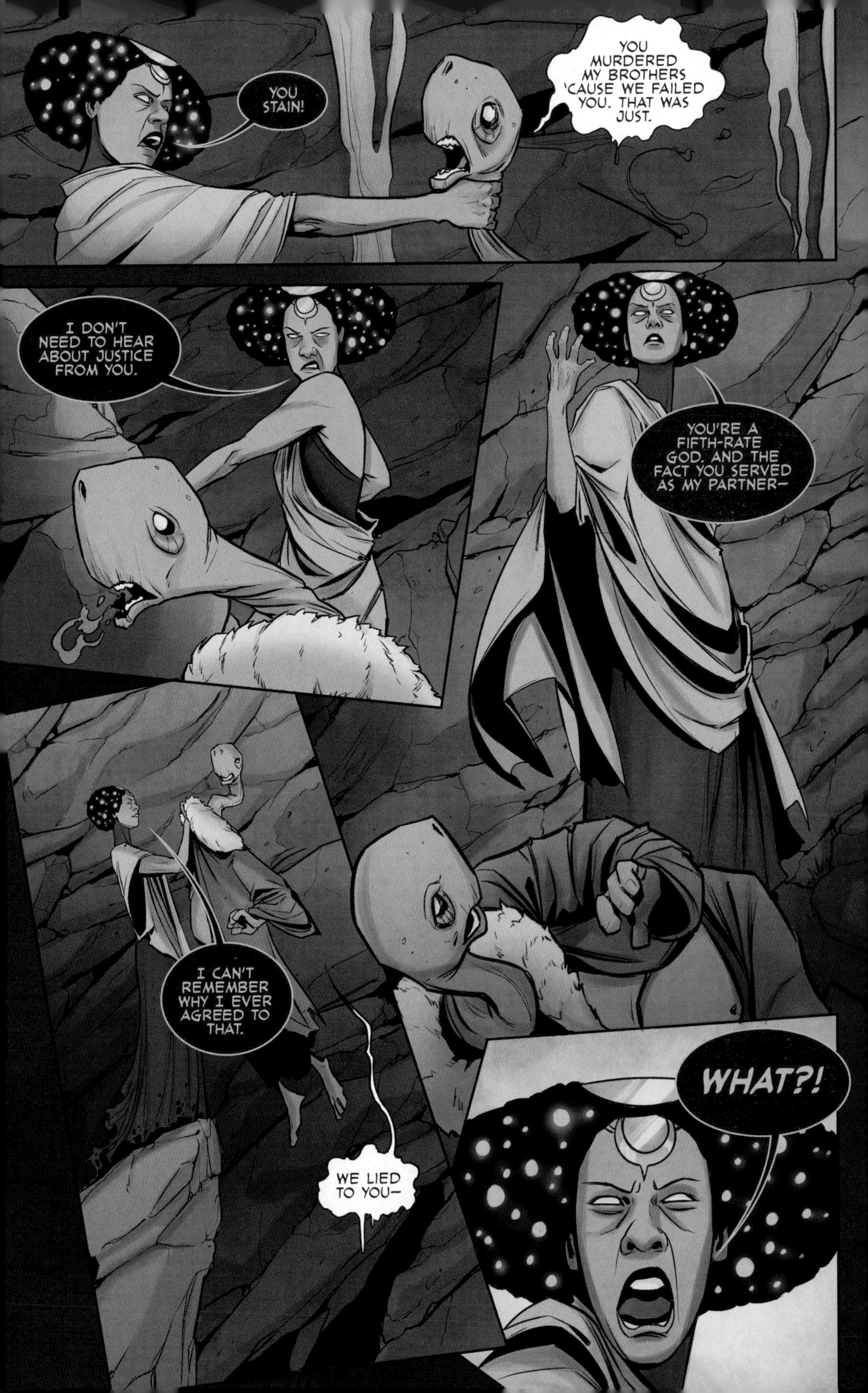
YOU STAIN!
YOU MURDERED MY BROTHERS 'CAUSE WE FAILED YOU. THAT WAS JUST.
I DON'T NEED TO HEAR ABOUT JUSTICE FROM YOU.
YOU'RE A FIFTH-RATE GOD. AND THE FACT YOU SERVED AS MY PARTNER—
I CAN'T REMEMBER WHY I EVER AGREED TO THAT.
WE LIED TO YOU—
WHAT?!

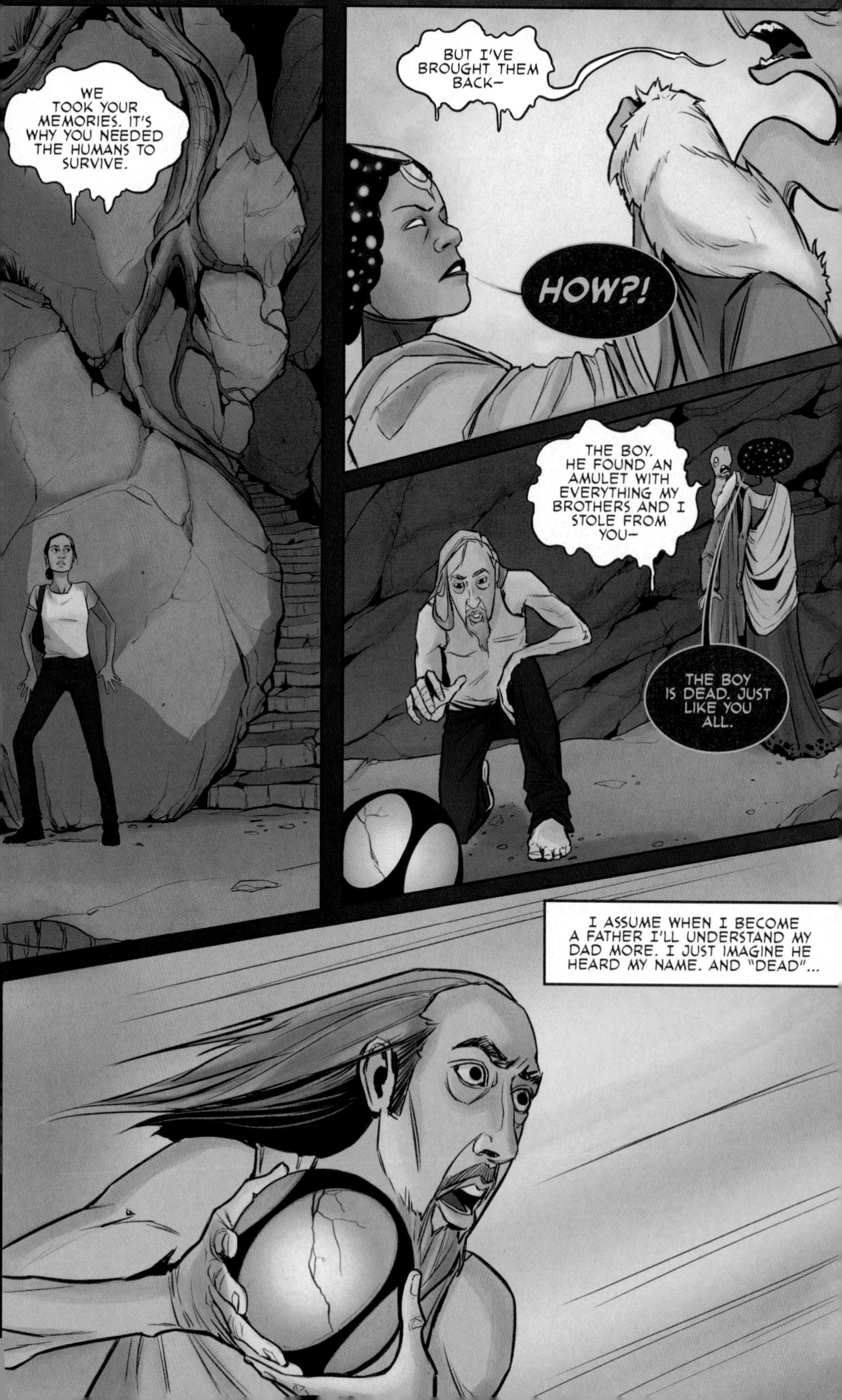
WE TOOK YOUR MEMORIES. IT'S WHY YOU NEEDED THE HUMANS TO SURVIVE.
BUT I'VE BROUGHT THEM BACK—
HOW?!
THE BOY. HE FOUND AN AMULET WITH EVERYTHING MY BROTHERS AND I STOLE FROM YOU—
THE BOY IS DEAD. JUST LIKE YOU ALL.
I ASSUME WHEN I BECOME A FATHER I'LL UNDERSTAND MY DAD MORE. I JUST IMAGINE HE HEARD MY NAME. AND "DEAD"...

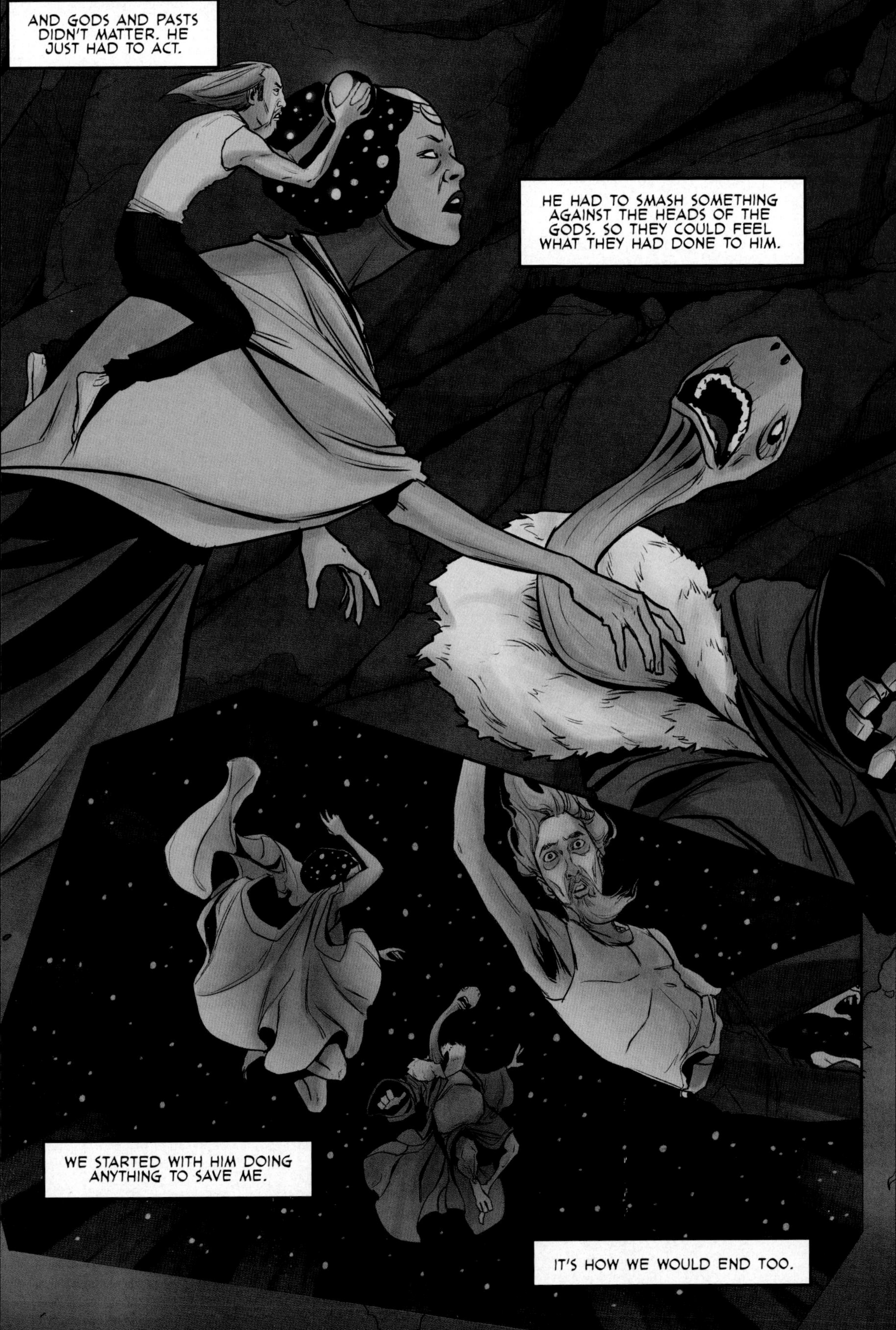
AND GODS AND PASTS DIDN'T MATTER. HE JUST HAD TO ACT.
HE HAD TO SMASH SOMETHING AGAINST THE HEADS OF THE GODS. SO THEY COULD FEEL WHAT THEY HAD DONE TO HIM.
WE STARTED WITH HIM DOING ANYTHING TO SAVE ME.
IT'S HOW WE WOULD END TOO.

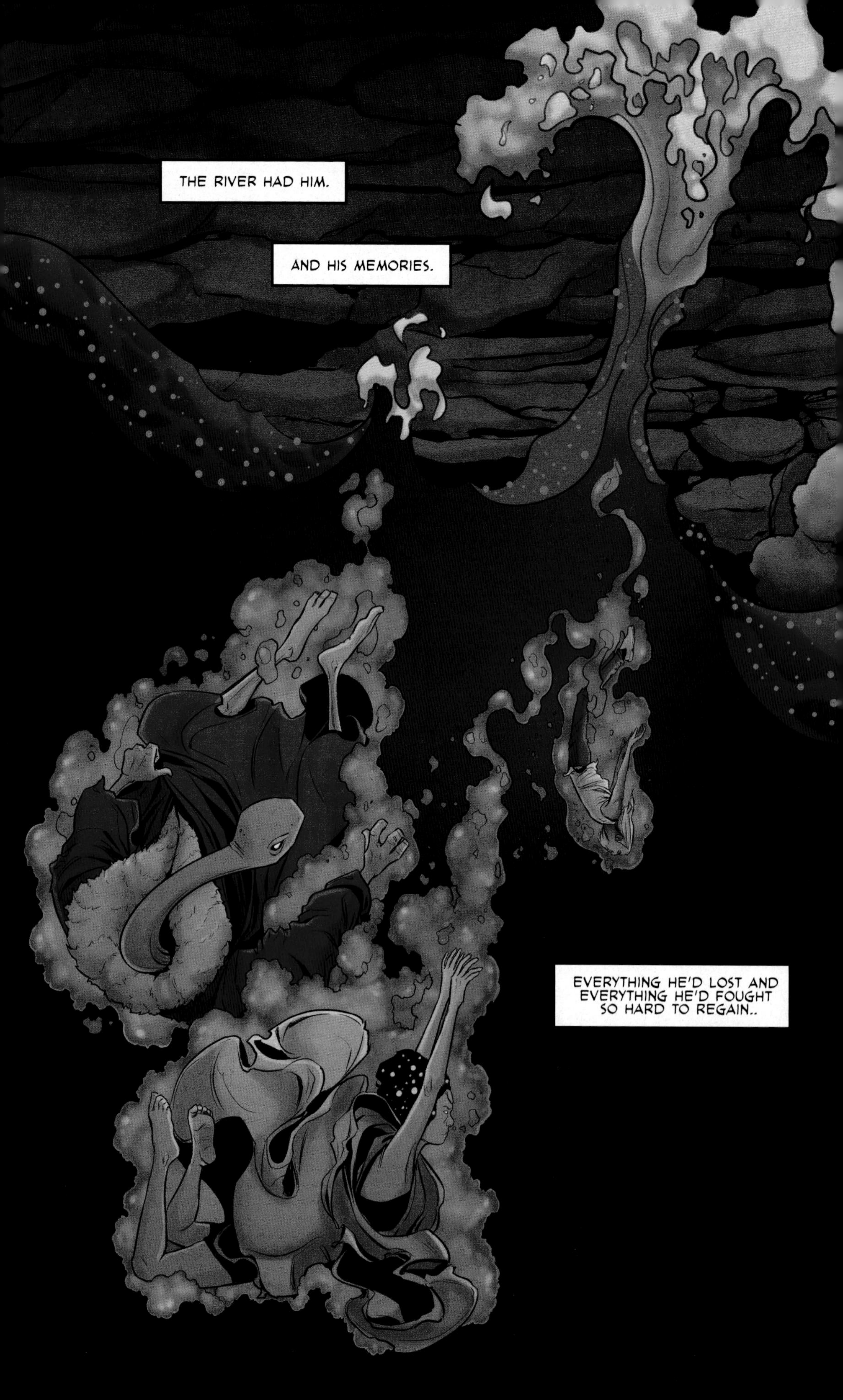
THE RIVER HAD HIM.
AND HIS MEMORIES.
EVERYTHING HE'D LOST AND EVERYTHING HE'D FOUGHT SO HARD TO REGAIN..

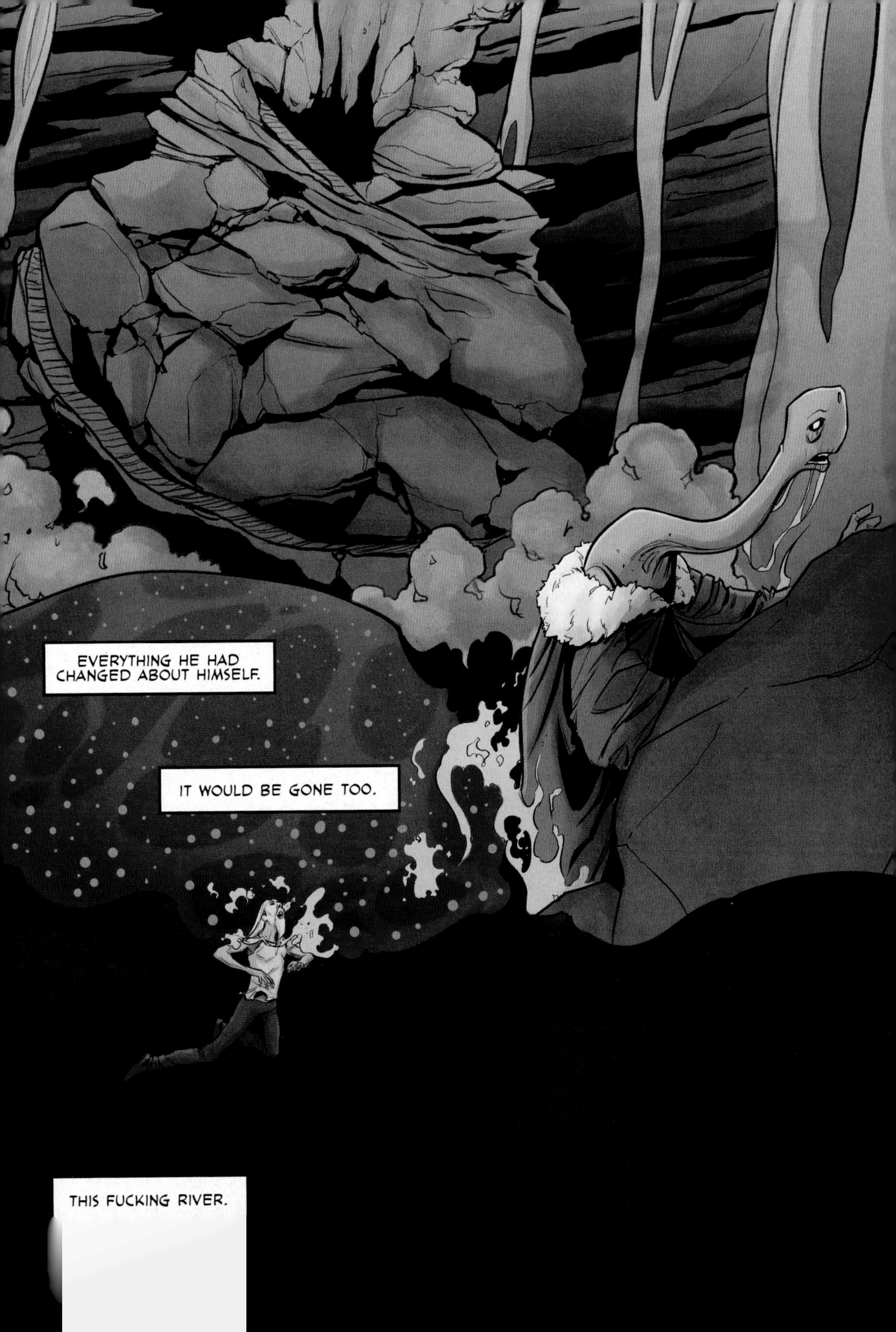
EVERYTHING HE HAD CHANGED ABOUT HIMSELF.
IT WOULD BE GONE TOO.
THIS FUCKING RIVER.

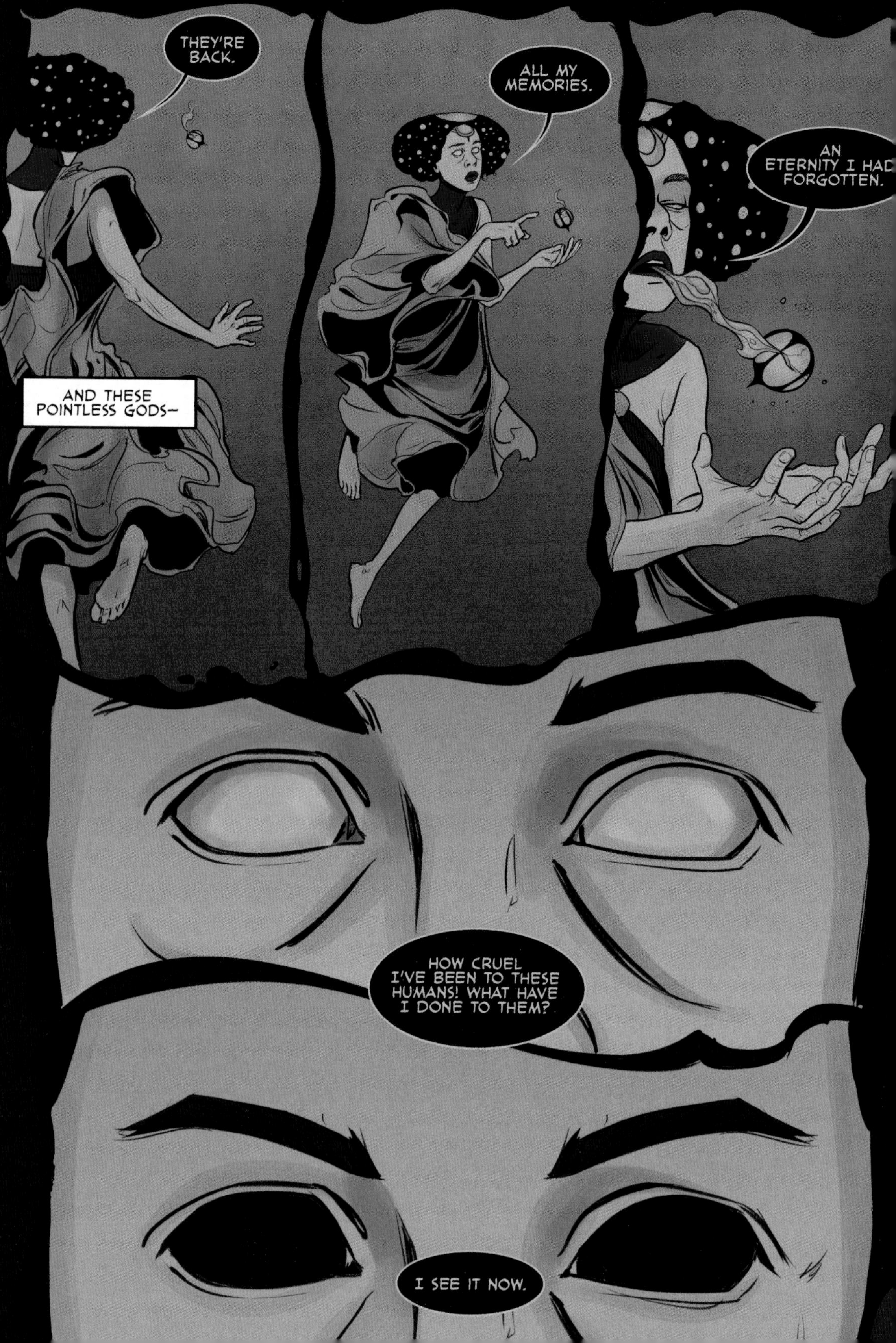
THEY'RE BACK.
AND THESE POINTLESS GODS—
ALL MY MEMORIES.
AN ETERNITY I HAD FORGOTTEN.
HOW CRUEL I'VE BEEN TO THESE HUMANS! WHAT HAVE I DONE TO THEM?
I SEE IT NOW.

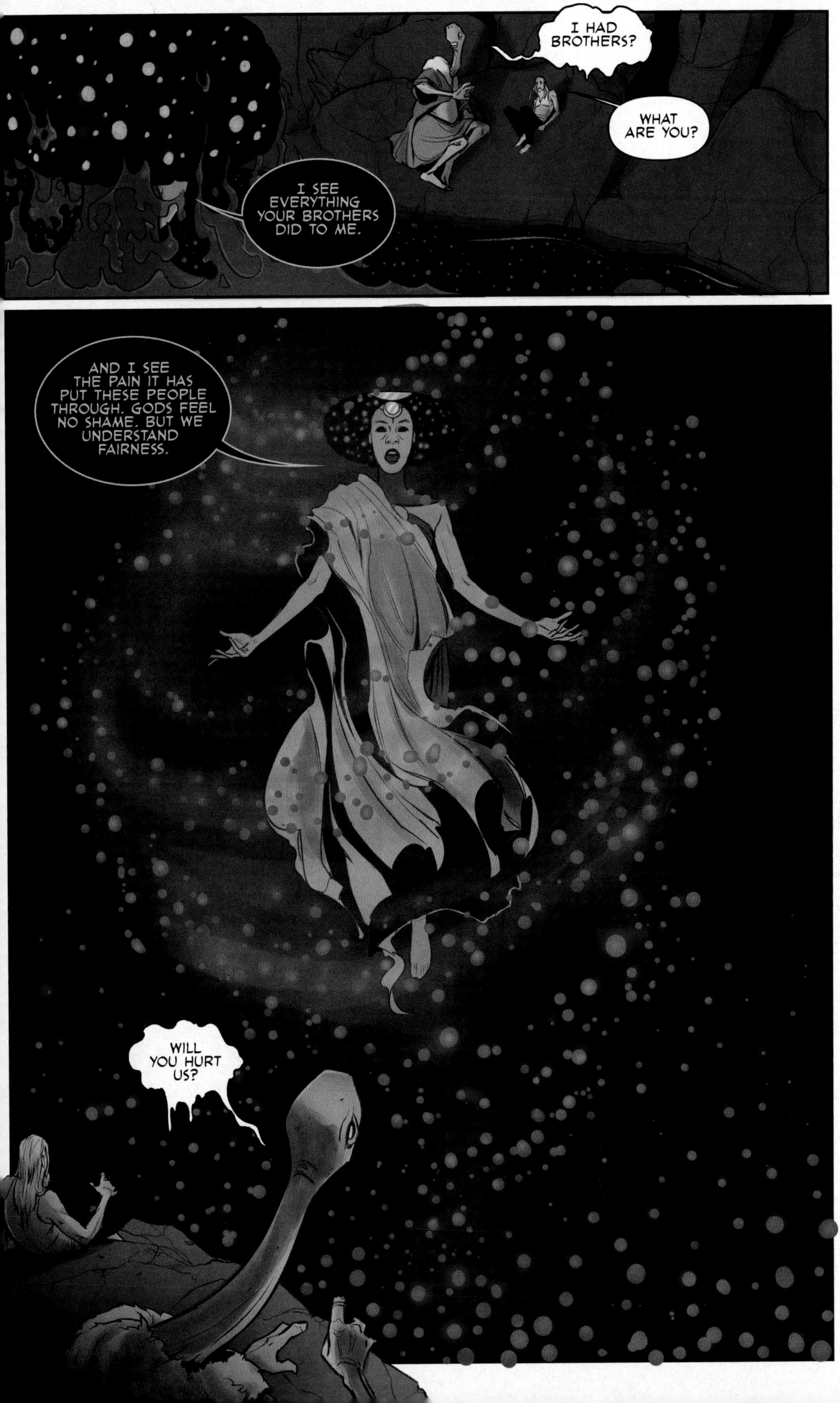
I HAD BROTHERS?
WHAT ARE YOU?
I SEE EVERYTHING YOUR BROTHERS DID TO ME.
AND I SEE THE PAIN IT HAS PUT THESE PEOPLE THROUGH. GODS FEEL NO SHAME. BUT WE UNDERSTAND FAIRNESS.
WILL YOU HURT US?

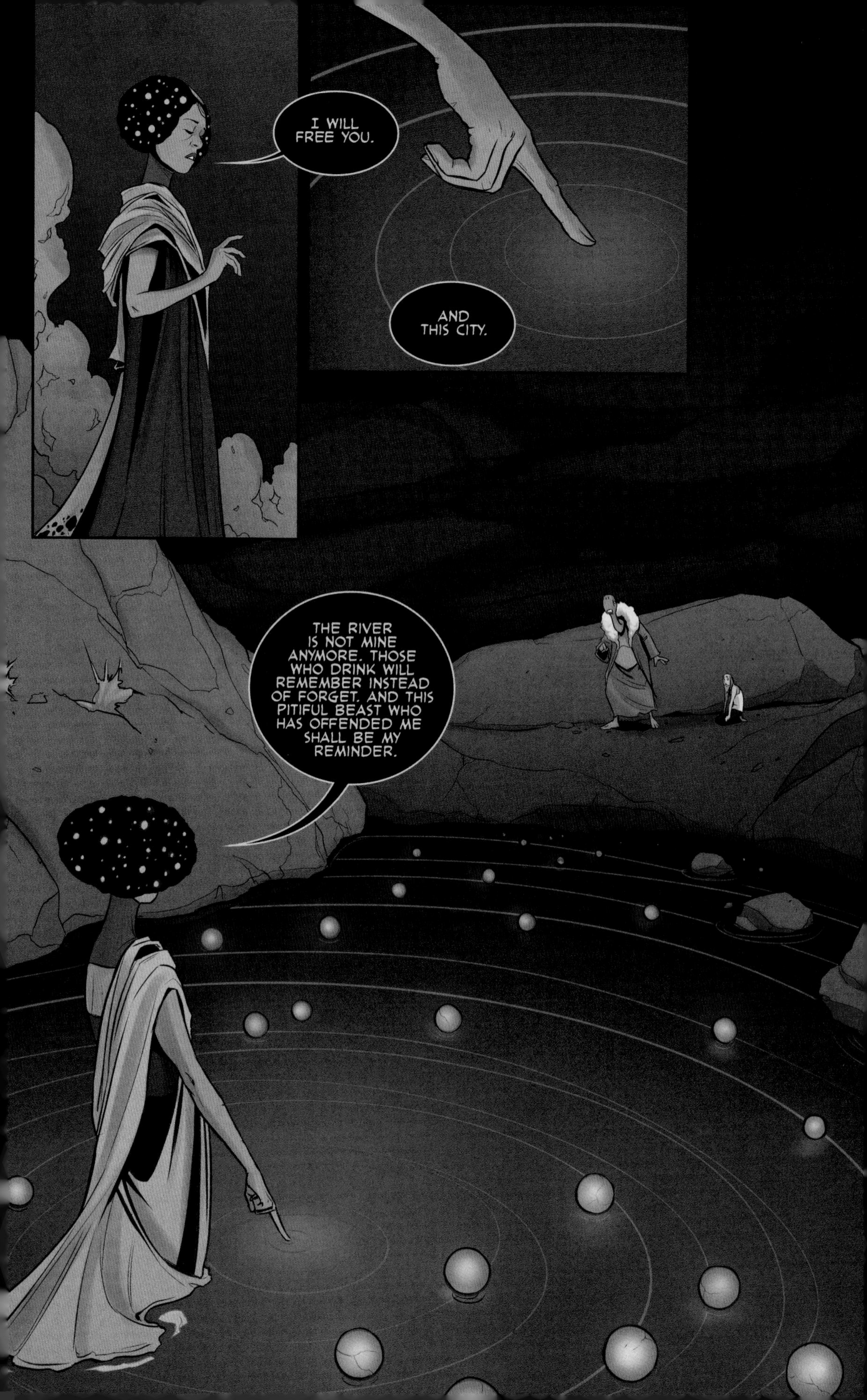
I WILL FREE YOU.
AND THIS CITY.
THE RIVER IS NOT MINE ANYMORE. THOSE WHO DRINK WILL REMEMBER INSTEAD OF FORGET. AND THIS PITIFUL BEAST WHO HAS OFFENDED ME SHALL BE MY REMINDER.

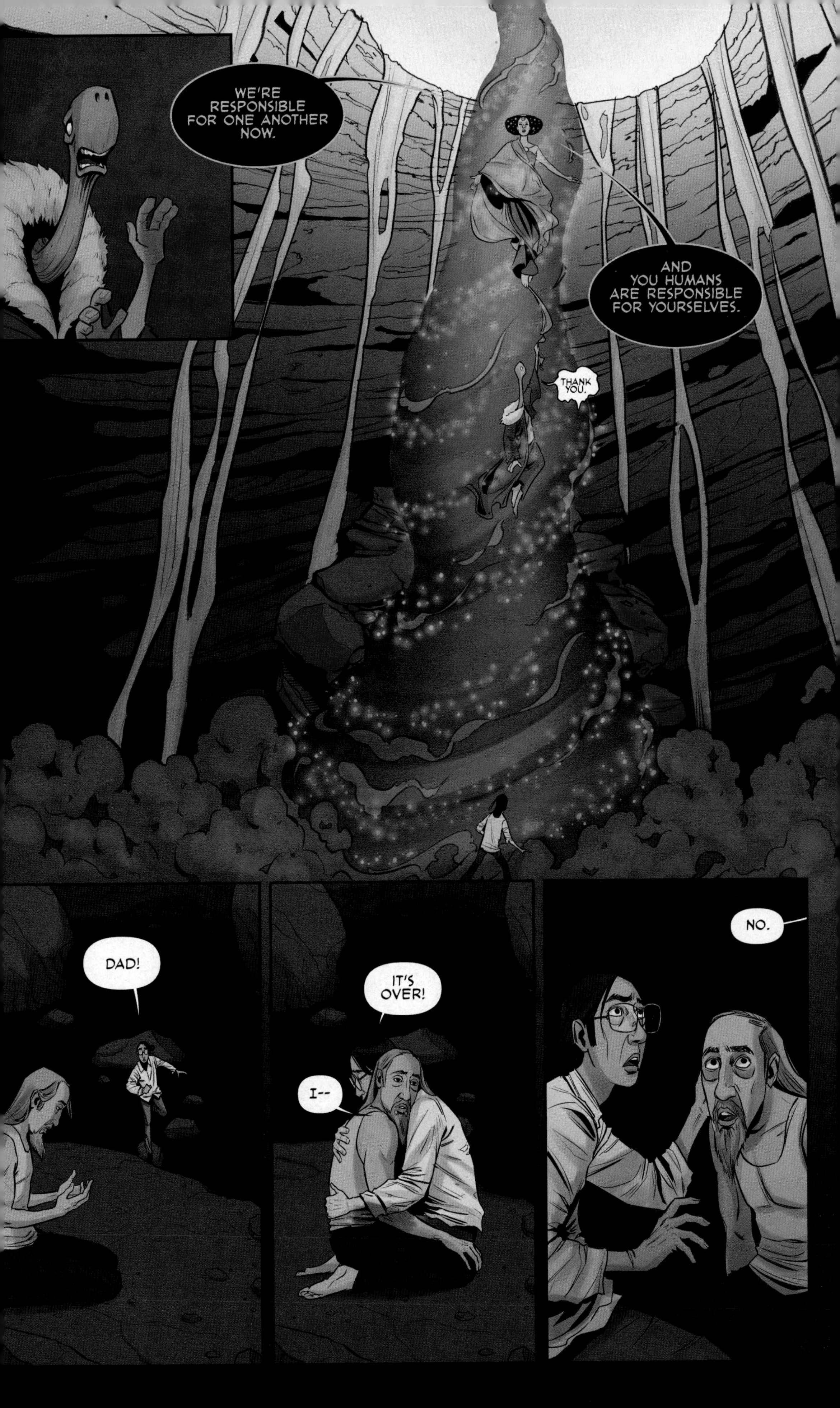
WE'RE RESPONSIBLE FOR ONE ANOTHER NOW.
AND YOU HUMANS ARE RESPONSIBLE FOR YOURSELVES.
THANK YOU.
DAD!
IT'S OVER!
I--
NO.

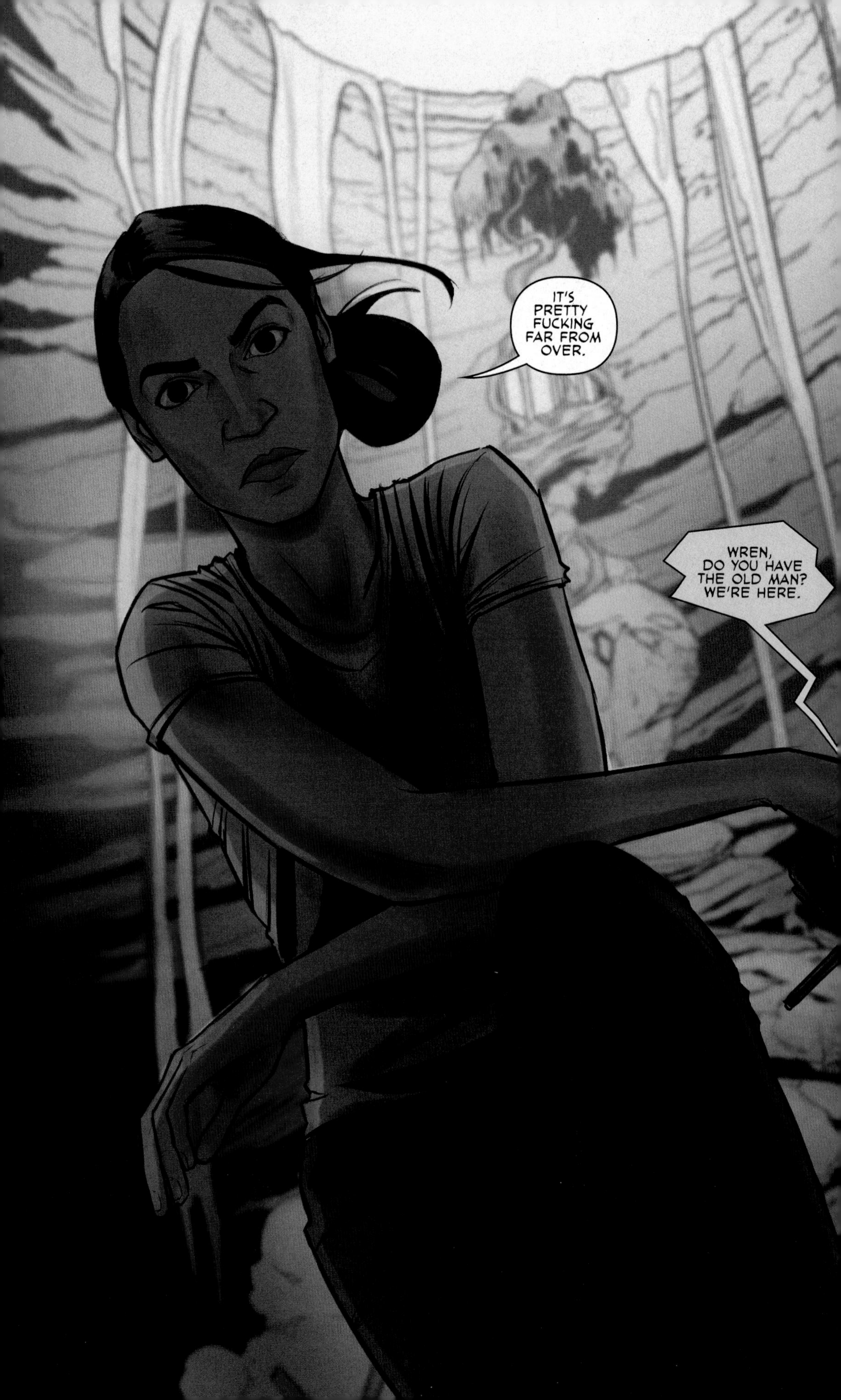
IT'S PRETTY FUCKING FAR FROM OVER.
WREN, DO YOU HAVE THE OLD MAN? WE'RE HERE.

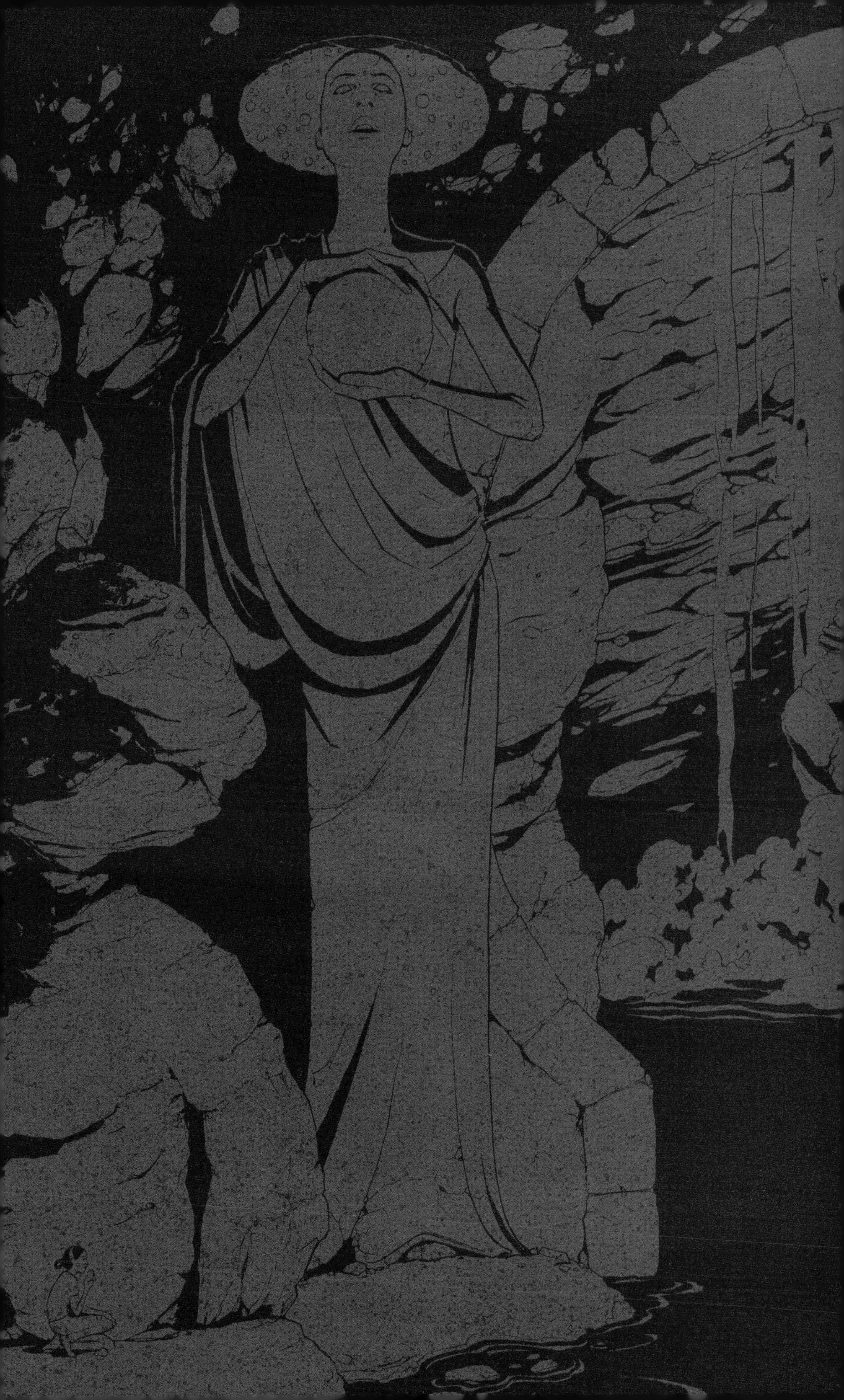

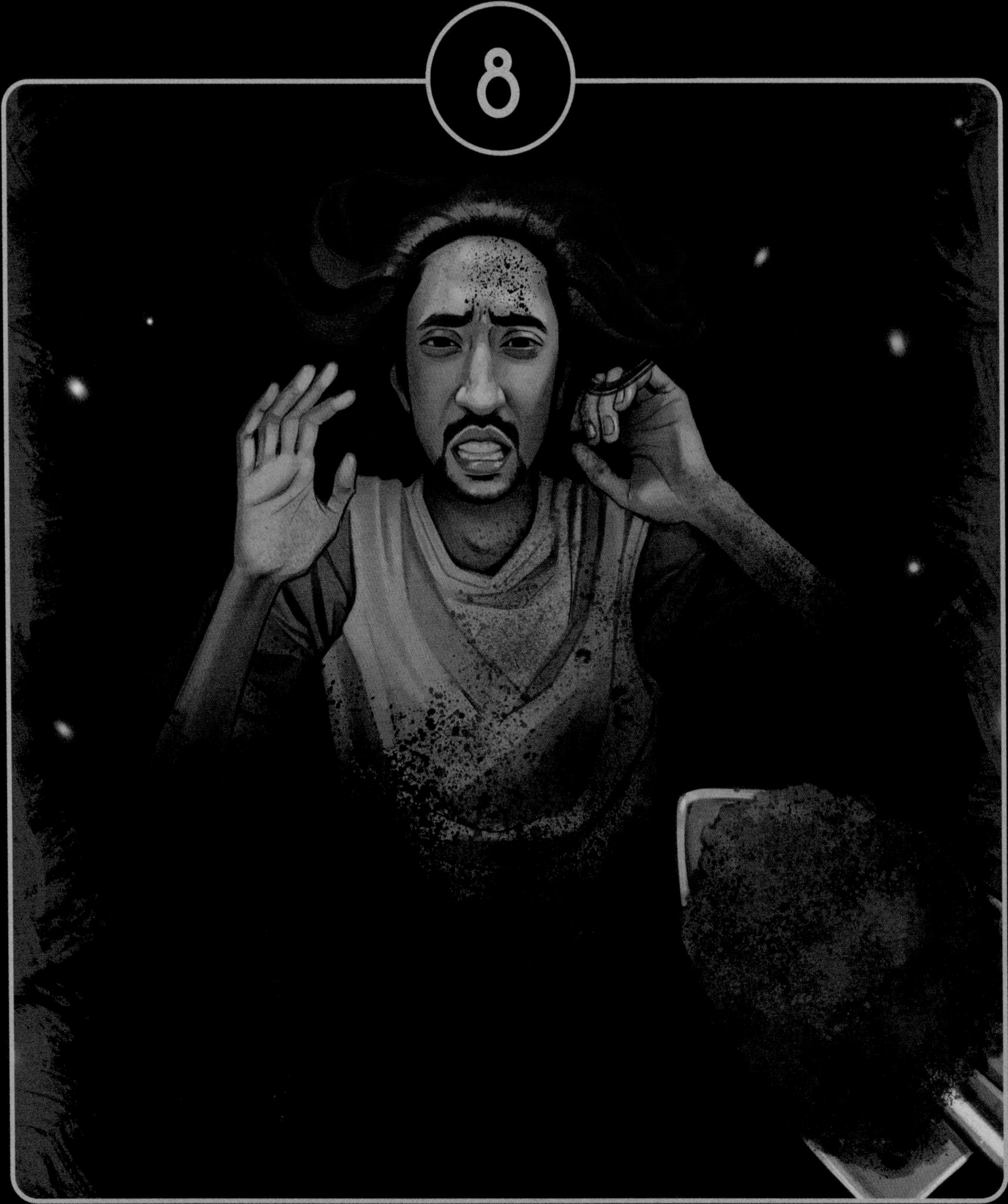
8

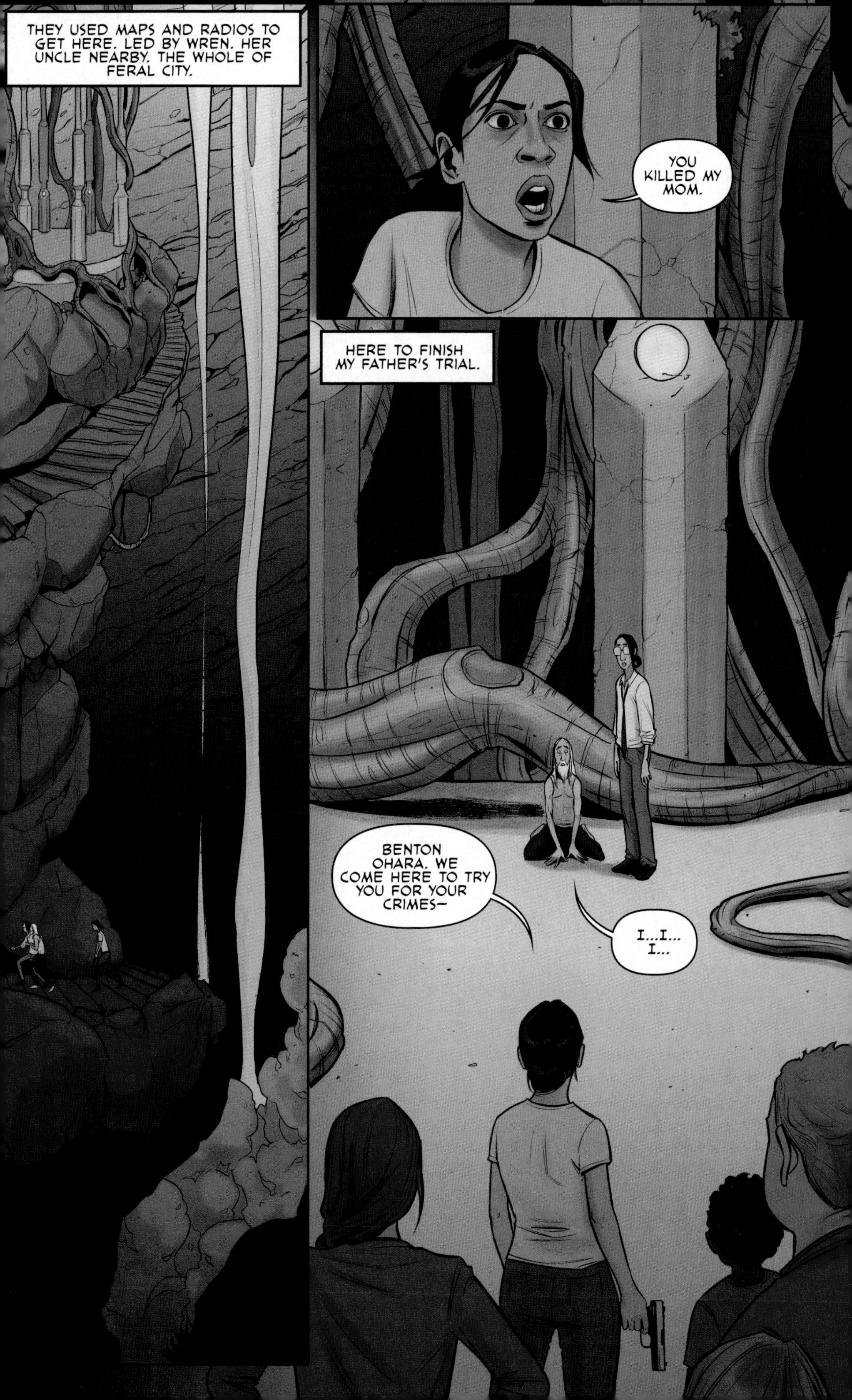
THEY USED MAPS AND RADIOS TO GET HERE. LED BY WREN. HER UNCLE NEARBY. THE WHOLE OF FERAL CITY.
YOU KILLED MY MOM.
HERE TO FINISH MY FATHER'S TRIAL.
BENTON OHARA. WE COME HERE TO TRY YOU FOR YOUR CRIMES—
I...I... I...

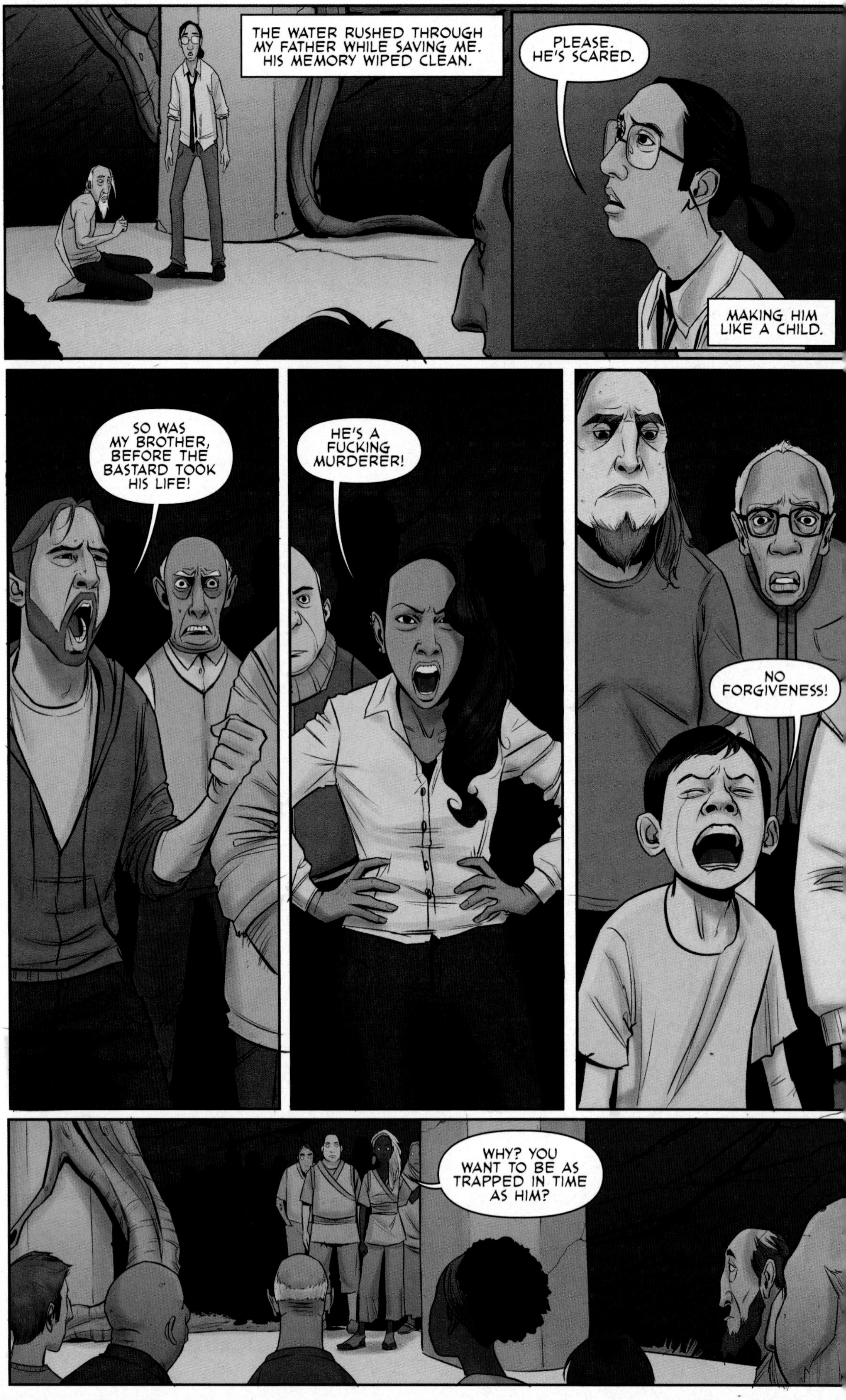

THE WATER RUSHED THROUGH MY FATHER WHILE SAVING ME. HIS MEMORY WIPED CLEAN.
PLEASE. HE'S SCARED.
MAKING HIM LIKE A CHILD.
SO WAS MY BROTHER, BEFORE THE BASTARD TOOK HIS LIFE!
HE'S A FUCKING MURDERER!
NO FORGIVENESS!
WHY? YOU WANT TO BE AS TRAPPED IN TIME AS HIM?

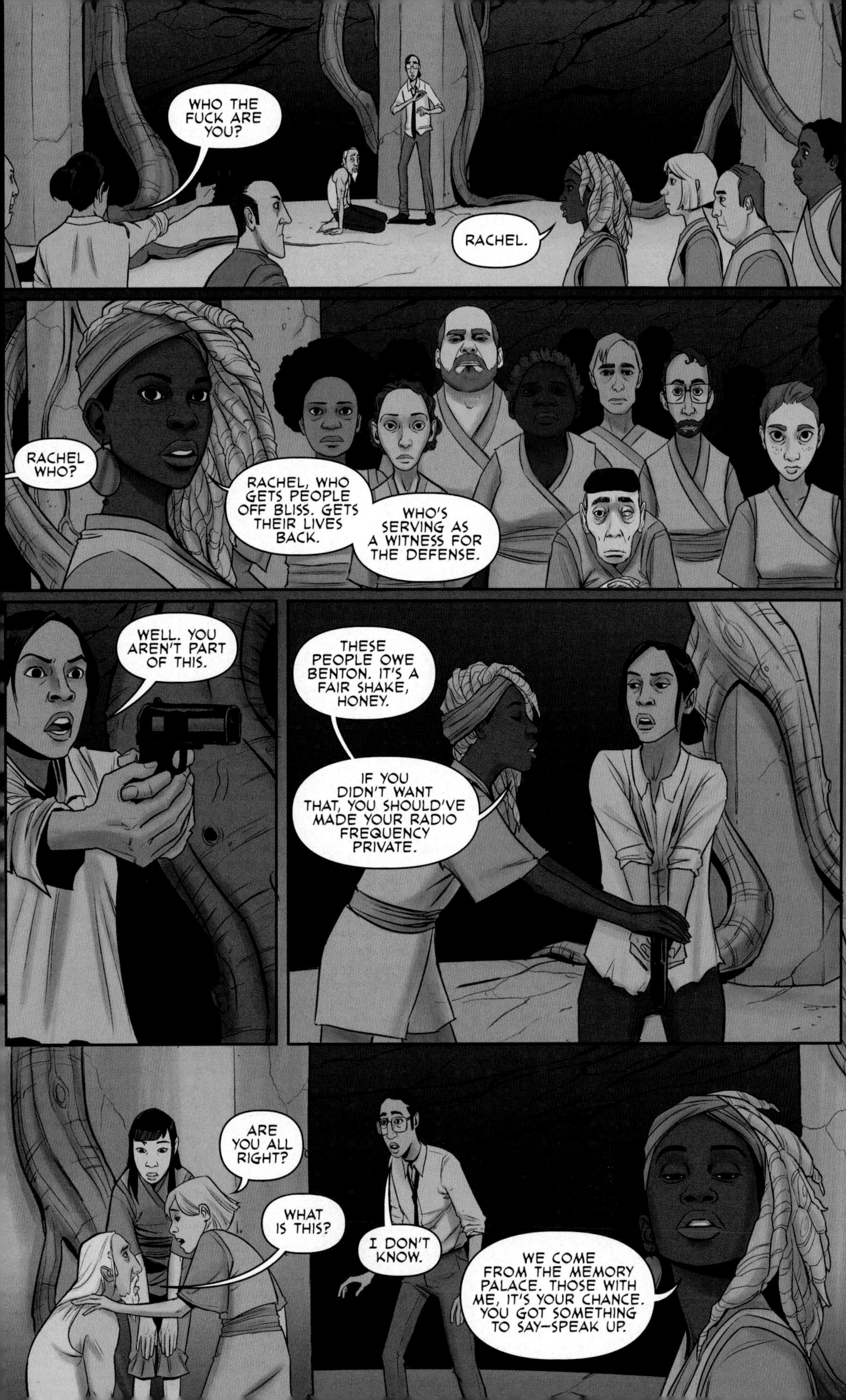
WHO THE FUCK ARE YOU?
RACHEL.
RACHEL WHO?
RACHEL, WHO GETS PEOPLE OFF BLISS. GETS THEIR LIVES BACK.
WHO'S SERVING AS A WITNESS FOR THE DEFENSE.
WELL. YOU AREN'T PART OF THIS.
THESE PEOPLE OWE BENTON. IT'S A FAIR SHAKE, HONEY.
IF YOU DIDN'T WANT THAT, YOU SHOULD'VE MADE YOUR RADIO FREQUENCY PRIVATE.
ARE YOU ALL RIGHT?
WHAT IS THIS?
I DON'T KNOW.
WE COME FROM THE MEMORY PALACE. THOSE WITH ME, IT'S YOUR CHANCE. YOU GOT SOMETHING TO SAY—SPEAK UP.

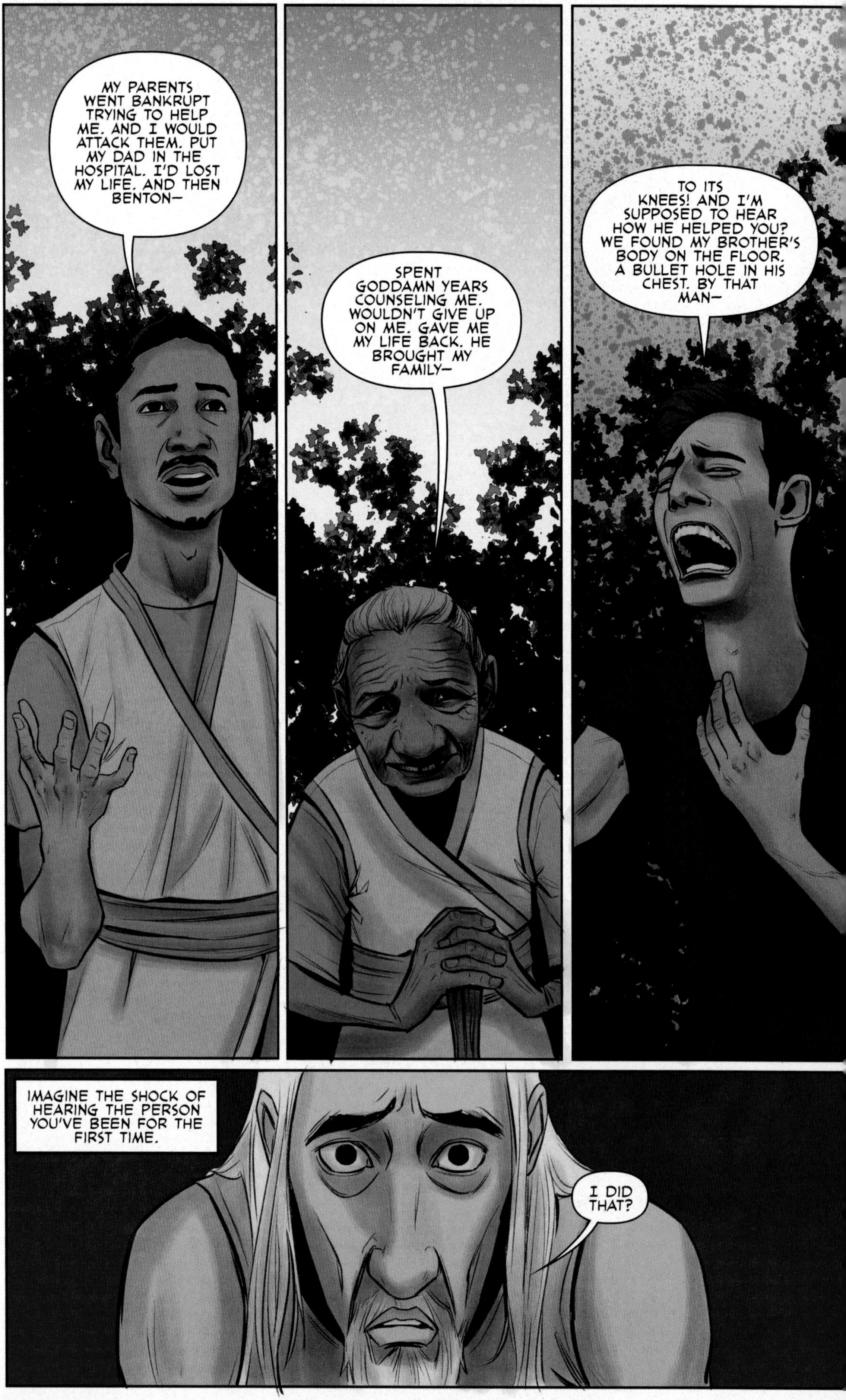
MY PARENTS WENT BANKRUPT TRYING TO HELP ME. AND I WOULD ATTACK THEM. PUT MY DAD IN THE HOSPITAL. I'D LOST MY LIFE. AND THEN BENTON–
SPENT GODDAMN YEARS COUNSELING ME. WOULDN'T GIVE UP ON ME. GAVE ME MY LIFE BACK. HE BROUGHT MY FAMILY–
TO ITS KNEES! AND I'M SUPPOSED TO HEAR HOW HE HELPED YOU? WE FOUND MY BROTHER'S BODY ON THE FLOOR. A BULLET HOLE IN HIS CHEST. BY THAT MAN–
IMAGINE THE SHOCK OF HEARING THE PERSON YOU'VE BEEN FOR THE FIRST TIME.
I DID THAT?

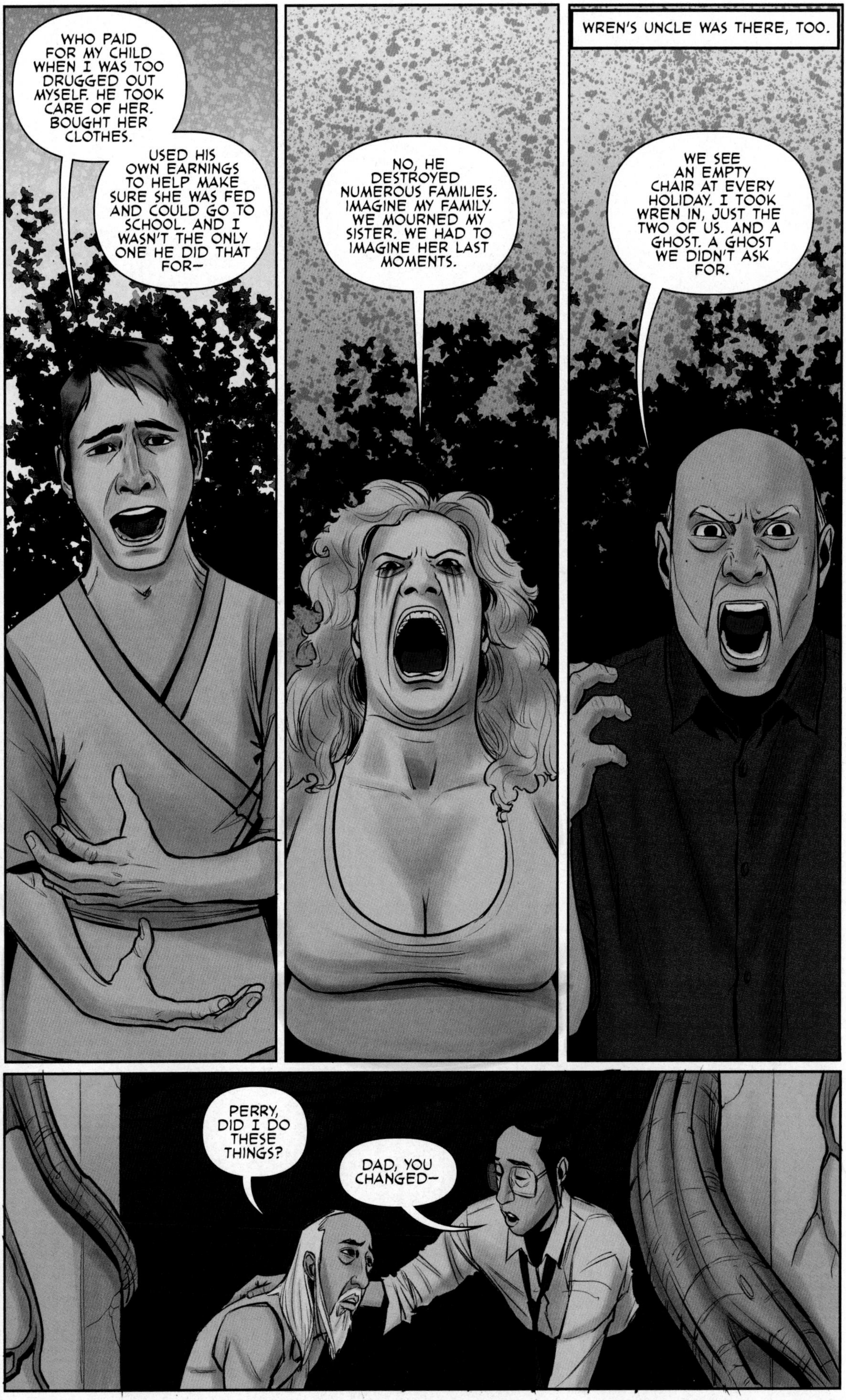
WHO PAID FOR MY CHILD WHEN I WAS TOO DRUGGED OUT MYSELF. HE TOOK CARE OF HER. BOUGHT HER CLOTHES.
USED HIS OWN EARNINGS TO HELP MAKE SURE SHE WAS FED AND COULD GO TO SCHOOL. AND I WASN'T THE ONLY ONE HE DID THAT FOR—
NO, HE DESTROYED NUMEROUS FAMILIES. IMAGINE MY FAMILY. WE MOURNED MY SISTER. WE HAD TO IMAGINE HER LAST MOMENTS.
WREN'S UNCLE WAS THERE, TOO.
WE SEE AN EMPTY CHAIR AT EVERY HOLIDAY. I TOOK WREN IN, JUST THE TWO OF US. AND A GHOST. A GHOST WE DIDN'T ASK FOR.
PERRY, DID I DO THESE THINGS?
DAD, YOU CHANGED—

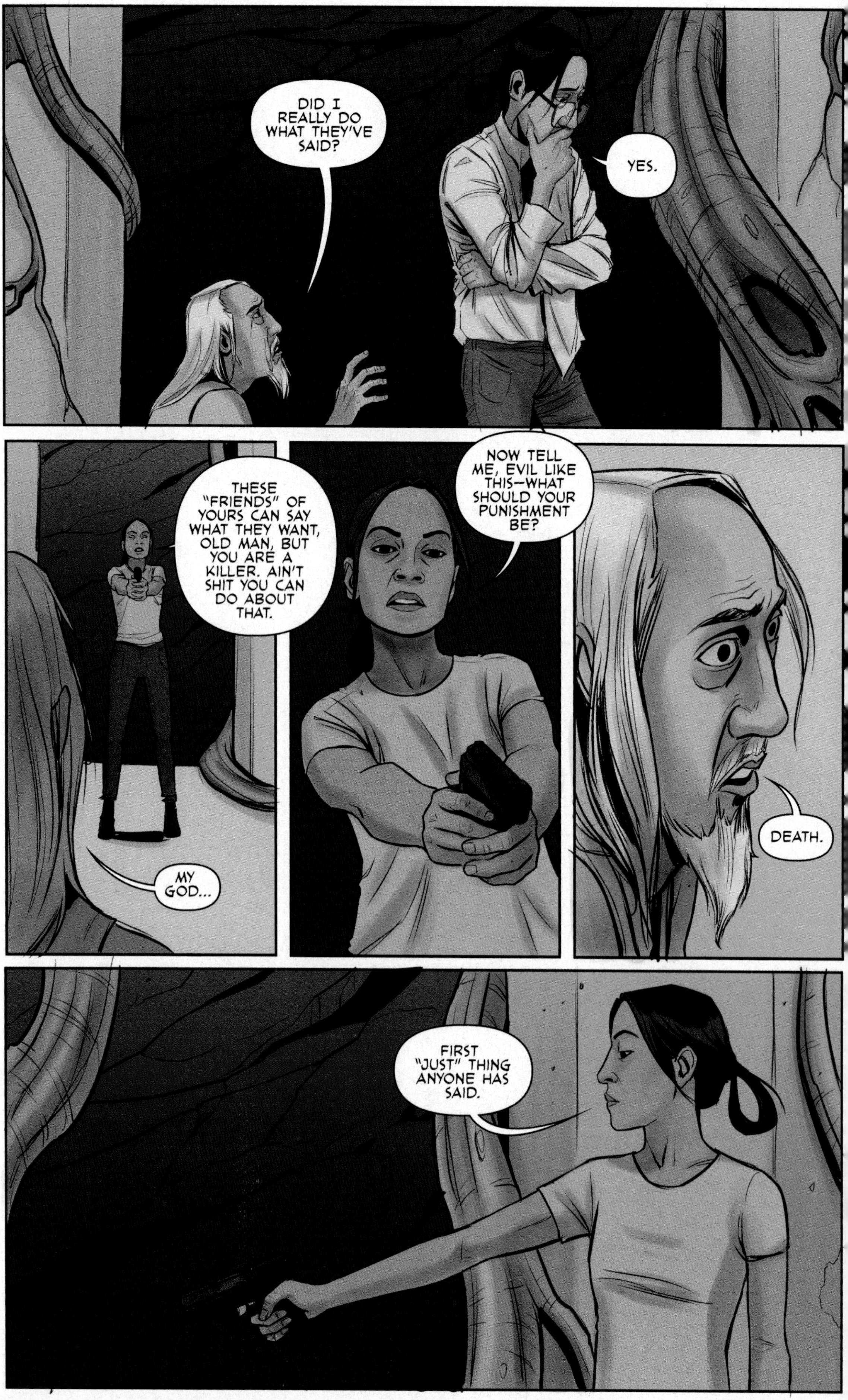
DID I REALLY DO WHAT THEY'VE SAID?
YES.
THESE "FRIENDS" OF YOURS CAN SAY WHAT THEY WANT, OLD MAN, BUT YOU ARE A KILLER. AIN'T SHIT YOU CAN DO ABOUT THAT.
MY GOD...
NOW TELL ME, EVIL LIKE THIS—WHAT SHOULD YOUR PUNISHMENT BE?
DEATH.
FIRST "JUST" THING ANYONE HAS SAID.

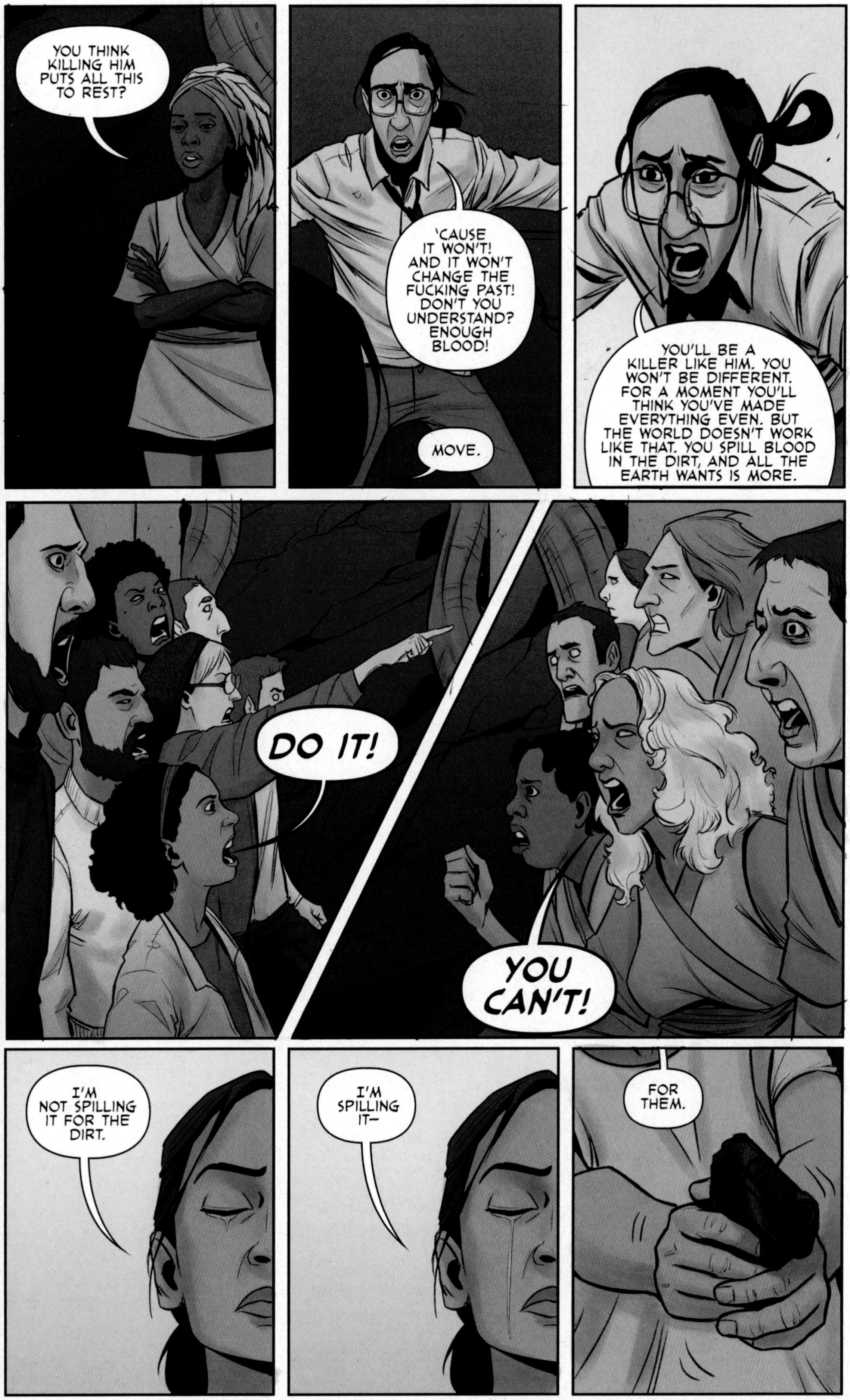
YOU THINK KILLING HIM PUTS ALL THIS TO REST?
'CAUSE IT WON'T! AND IT WON'T CHANGE THE FUCKING PAST! DON'T YOU UNDERSTAND? ENOUGH BLOOD!
MOVE.
YOU'LL BE A KILLER LIKE HIM. YOU WON'T BE DIFFERENT. FOR A MOMENT YOU'LL THINK YOU'VE MADE EVERYTHING EVEN. BUT THE WORLD DOESN'T WORK LIKE THAT. YOU SPILL BLOOD IN THE DIRT, AND ALL THE EARTH WANTS IS MORE.
DO IT!
YOU CAN'T!
I'M NOT SPILLING IT FOR THE DIRT.
I'M SPILLING IT—
FOR THEM.

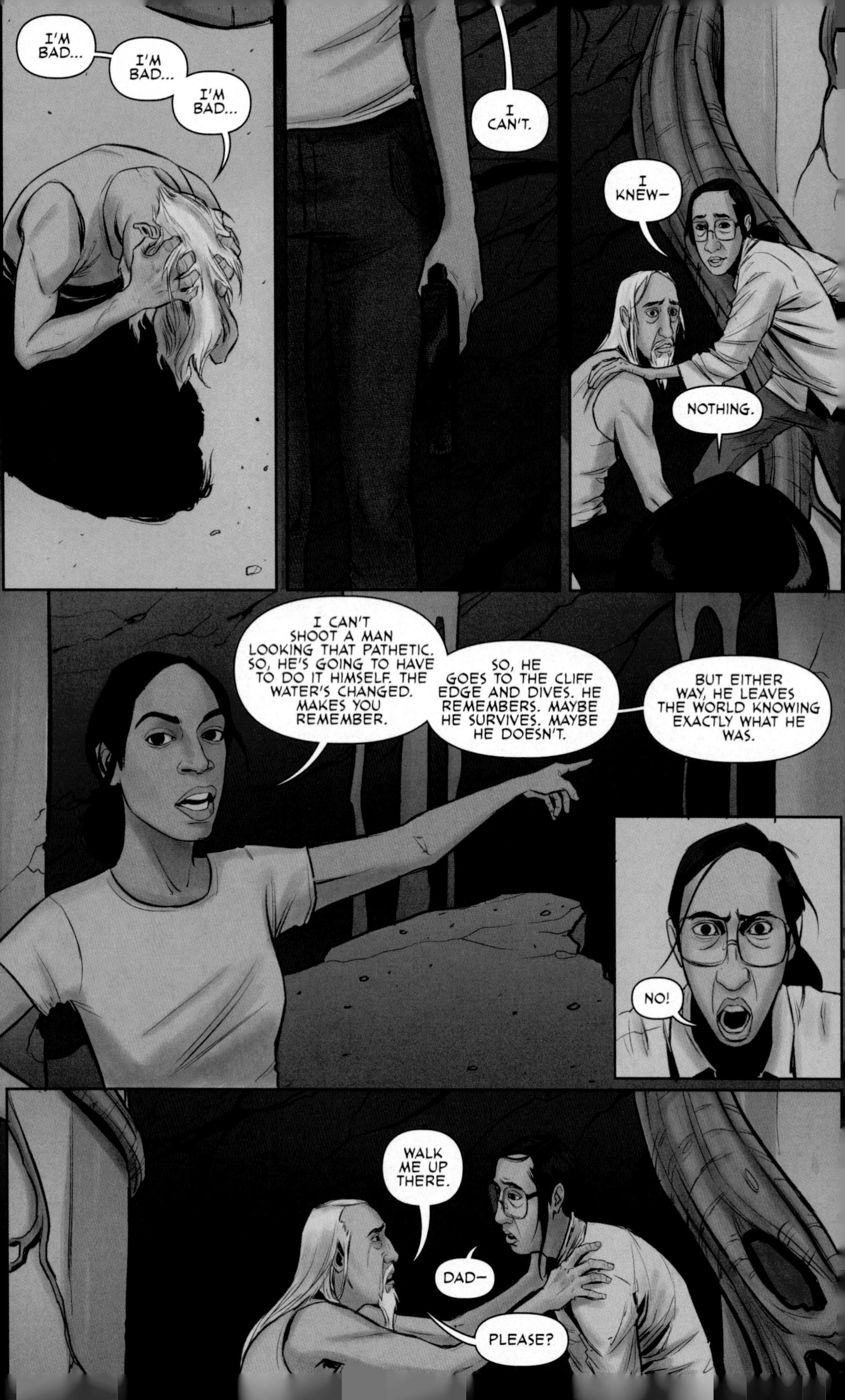
I'M BAD...
I'M BAD...
I'M BAD...
I CAN'T.
I KNEW—
NOTHING.
I CAN'T SHOOT A MAN LOOKING THAT PATHETIC. SO, HE'S GOING TO HAVE TO DO IT HIMSELF. THE WATER'S CHANGED. MAKES YOU REMEMBER.
SO, HE GOES TO THE CLIFF EDGE AND DIVES. HE REMEMBERS. MAYBE HE SURVIVES. MAYBE HE DOESN'T.
BUT EITHER WAY, HE LEAVES THE WORLD KNOWING EXACTLY WHAT HE WAS.
NO!
WALK ME UP THERE.
DAD—
PLEASE?

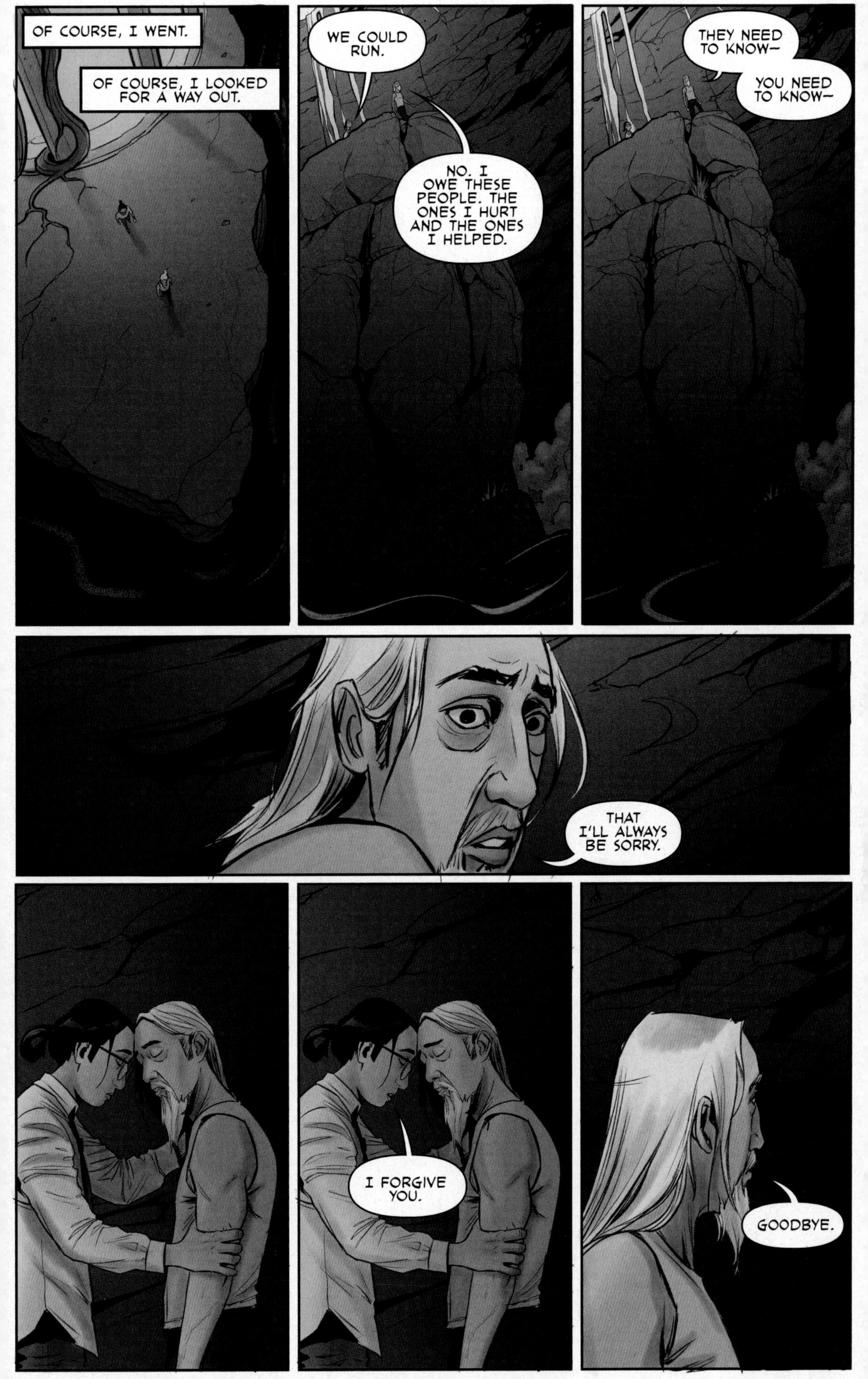
OF COURSE, I WENT.
OF COURSE, I LOOKED FOR A WAY OUT.
WE COULD RUN.
NO. I OWE THESE PEOPLE. THE ONES I HURT AND THE ONES I HELPED.
THEY NEED TO KNOW—
YOU NEED TO KNOW—
THAT I'LL ALWAYS BE SORRY.
I FORGIVE YOU.
GOODBYE.

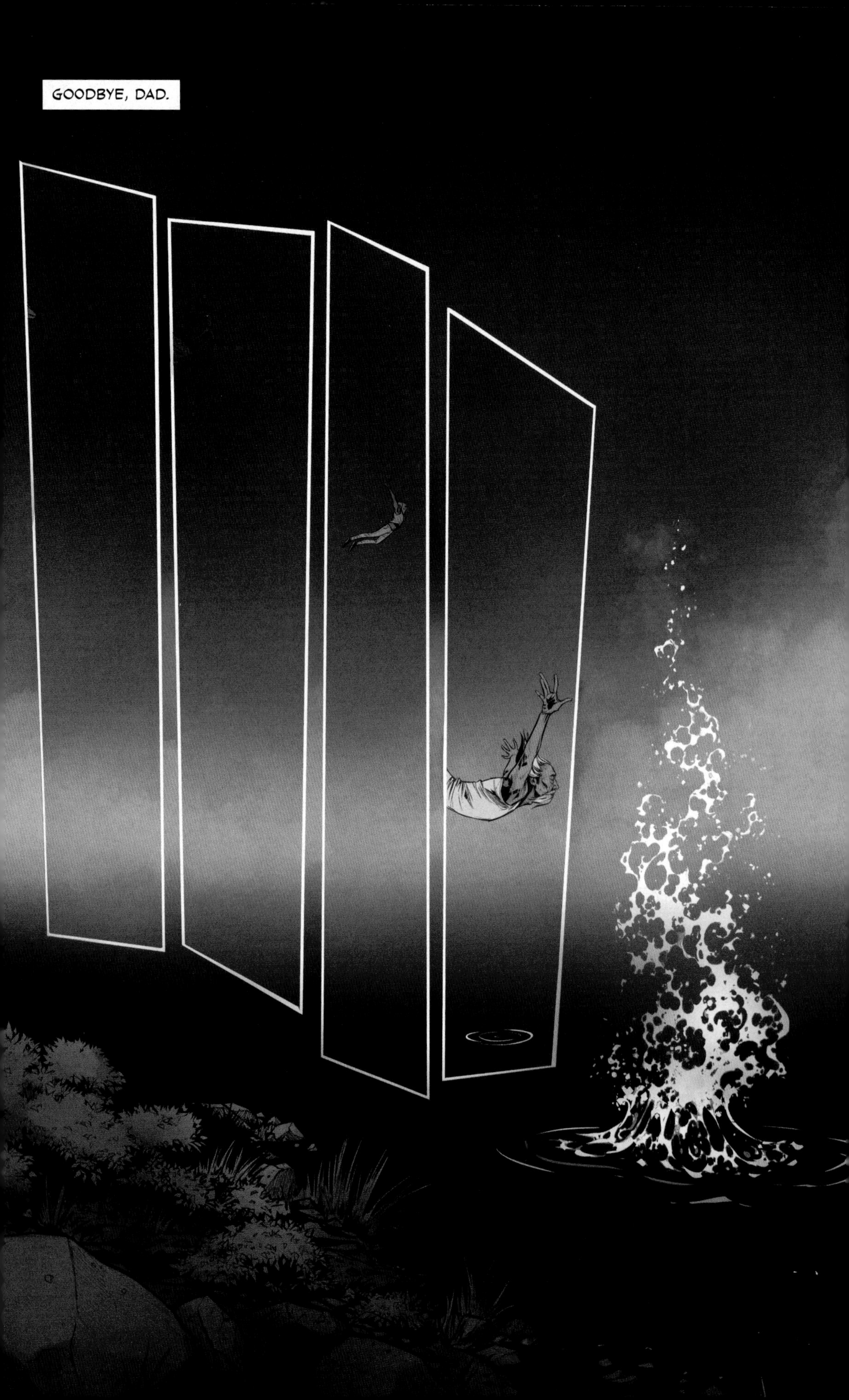
GOODBYE, DAD.

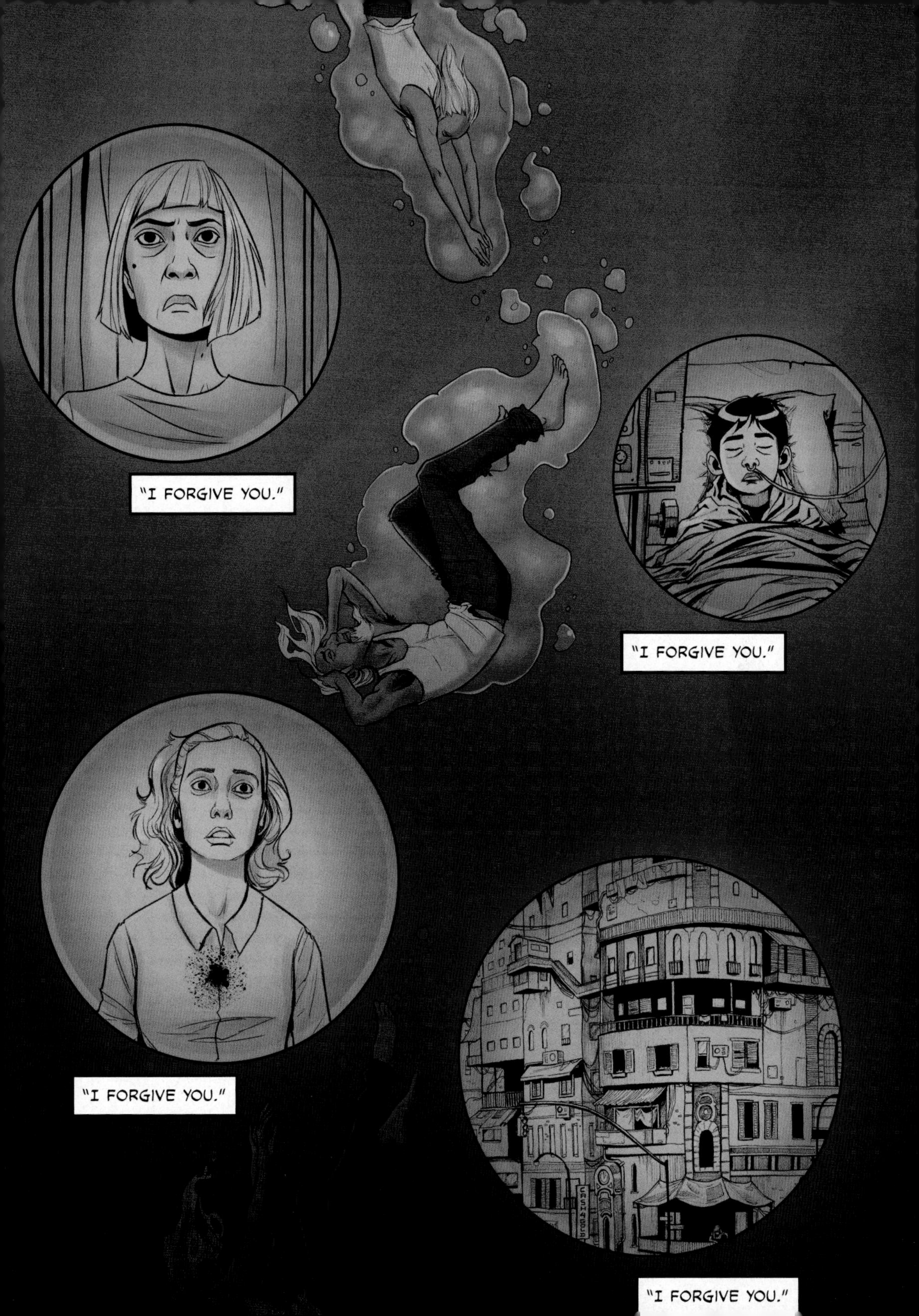
"I FORGIVE YOU."
"I FORGIVE YOU."
"I FORGIVE YOU."
"I FORGIVE YOU."

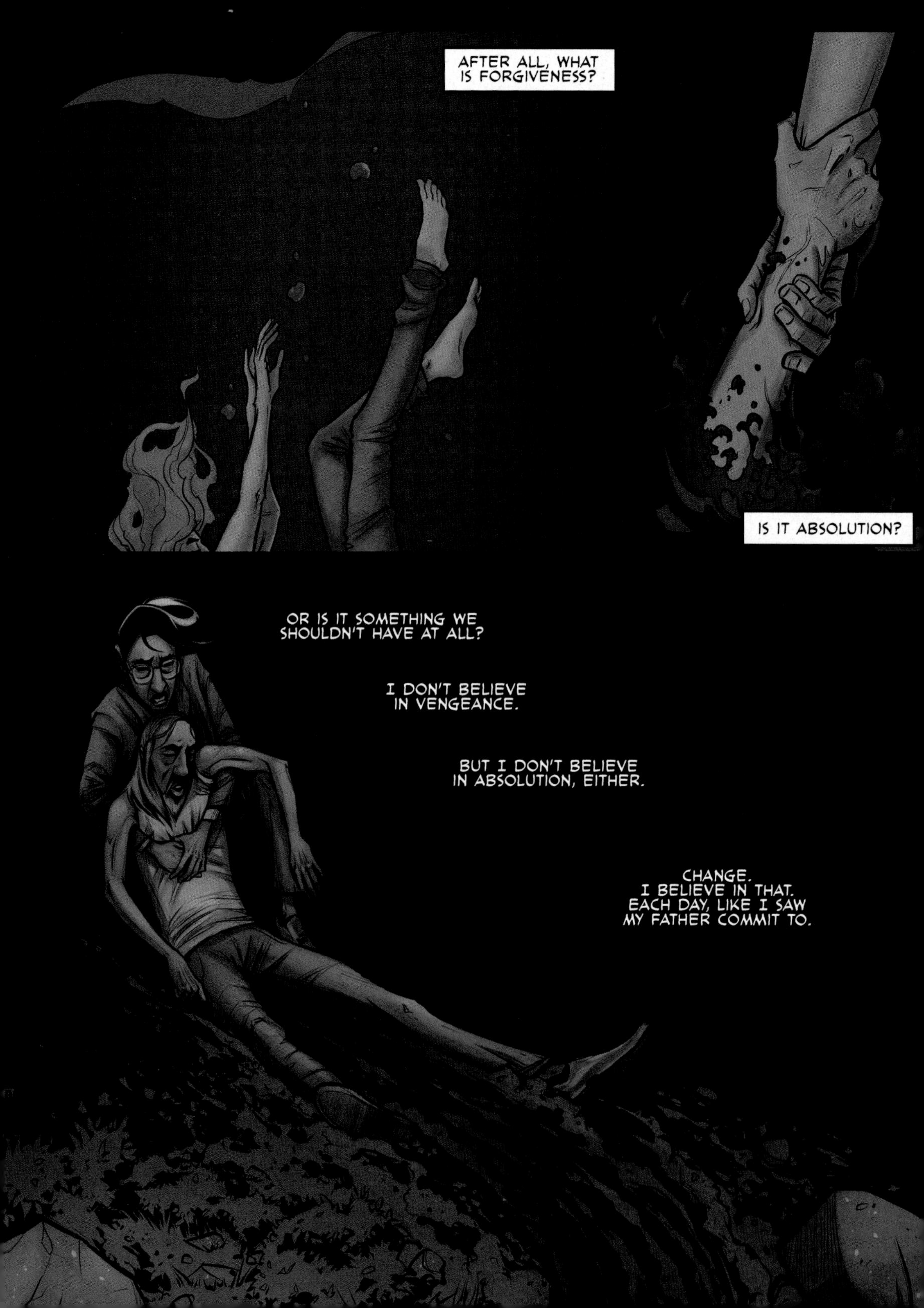
AFTER ALL, WHAT IS FORGIVENESS?
IS IT ABSOLUTION?
OR IS IT SOMETHING WE SHOULDN'T HAVE AT ALL?
I DON'T BELIEVE IN VENGEANCE.
BUT I DON'T BELIEVE IN ABSOLUTION, EITHER.
CHANGE. I BELIEVE IN THAT. EACH DAY, LIKE I SAW MY FATHER COMMIT TO.

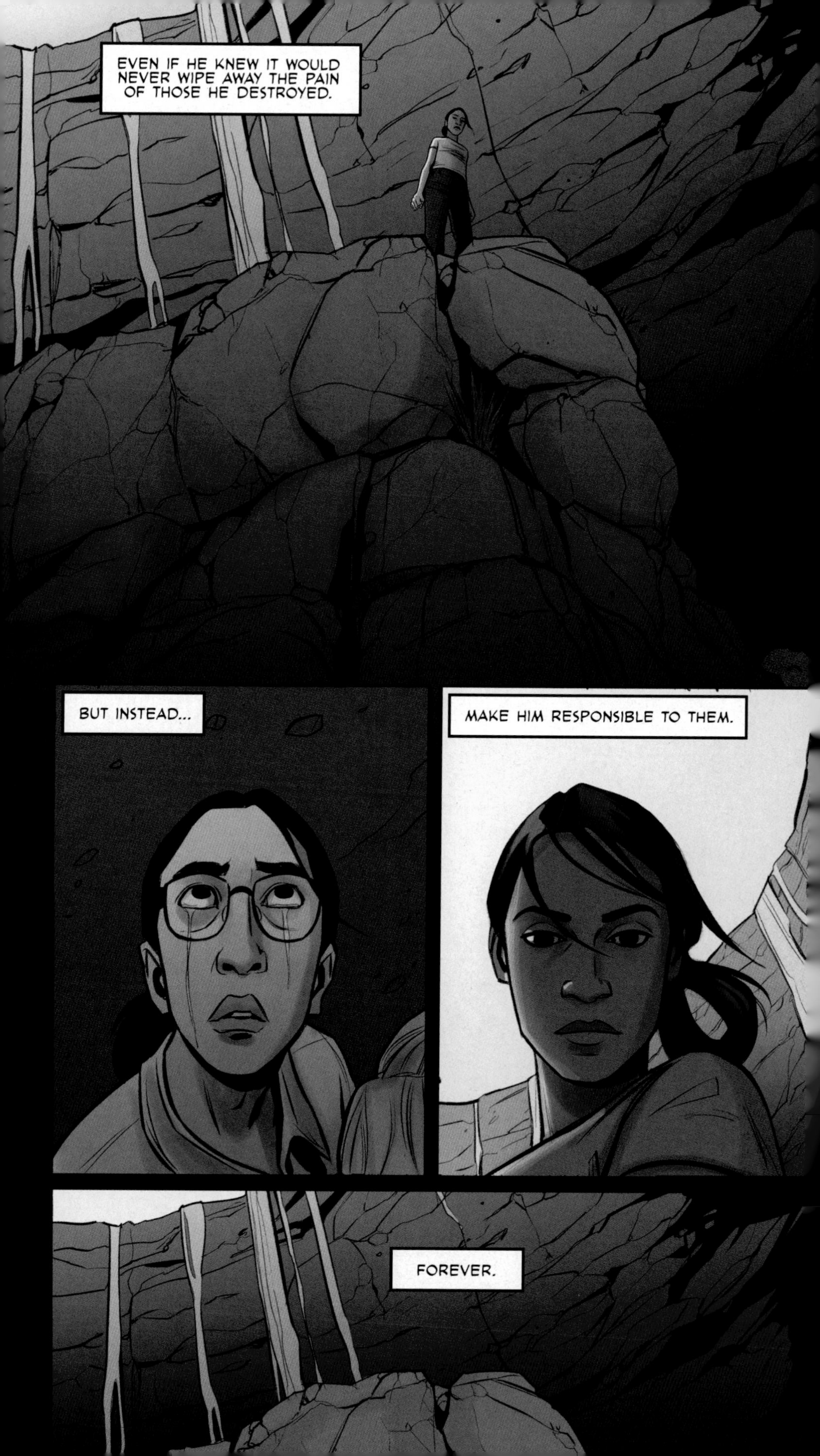
EVEN IF HE KNEW IT WOULD NEVER WIPE AWAY THE PAIN OF THOSE HE DESTROYED.
BUT INSTEAD...
MAKE HIM RESPONSIBLE TO THEM.
FOREVER.

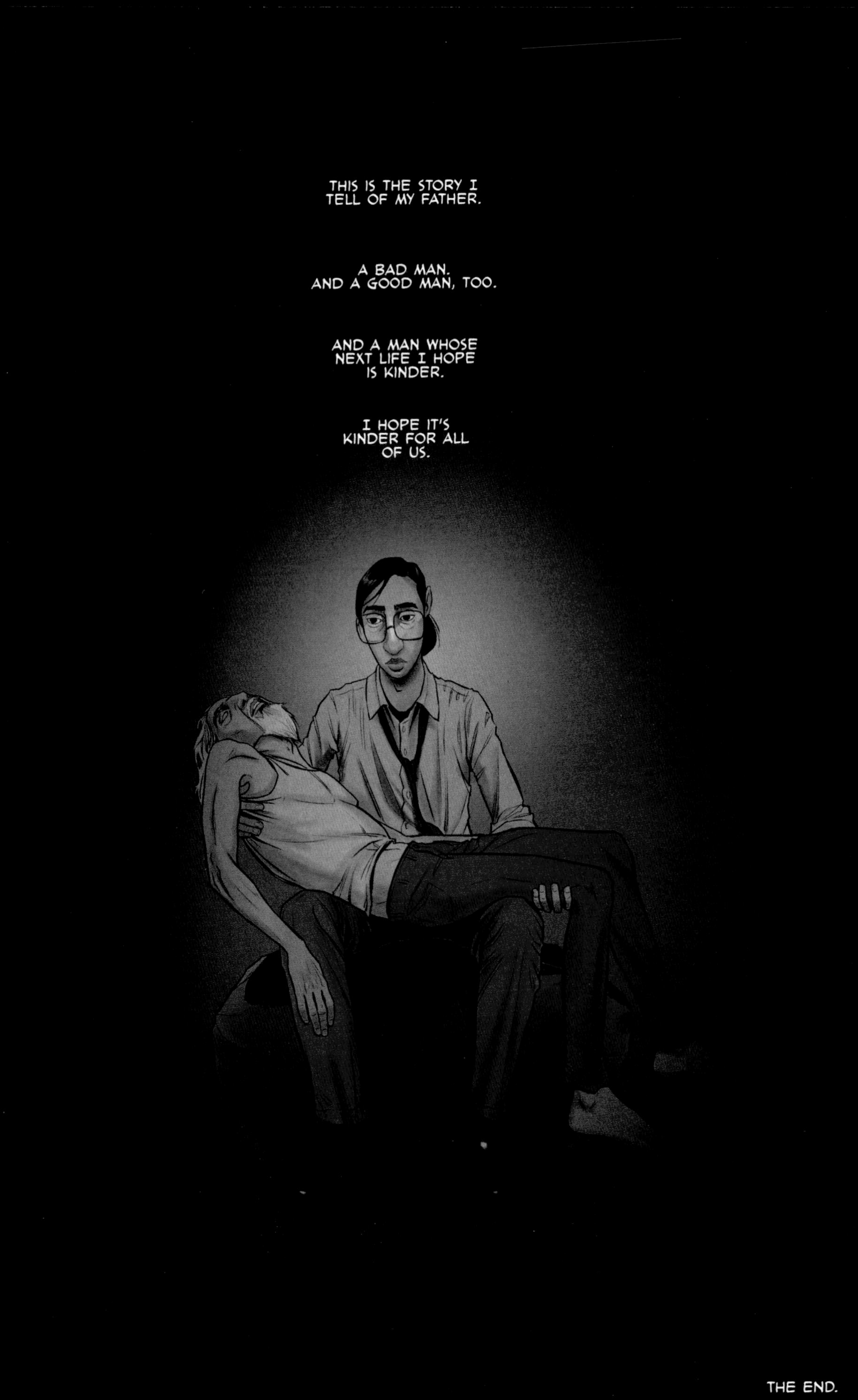
THIS IS THE STORY I TELL OF MY FATHER.
A BAD MAN. AND A GOOD MAN, TOO.
AND A MAN WHOSE NEXT LIFE I HOPE IS KINDER.
I HOPE IT'S KINDER FOR ALL OF US.
THE END.